SEEING DOUBLE

SEEING DOUBLE

Baudelaire's Modernity

FRANÇOISE MELTZER

THE UNIVERSITY OF CHICAGO PRESS

CHICAGO AND LONDON

FRANÇOISE MELTZER is the Edward Carson Waller Distinguished Service Professor in the Humanities at the University of Chicago, where she is also professor at the Divinity School and in the College, and chair of the Department of Comparative Literature. Meltzer is the author of four books, most recently *For Fear of the Fire: Joan of Arc and the Limits of Subjectivity* (2001), and coeditor of the journal *Critical Inquiry.*

The University of Chicago Press, Chicago 60637
The University of Chicago Press, Ltd., London
© 2011 by The University of Chicago
All rights reserved. Published 2011.
Printed in the United States of America

20 19 18 17 16 15 14 13 12 11   1 2 3 4 5

ISBN-13: 978-0-226-51988-3 (cloth)
ISBN-10: 0-226-51988-0 (cloth)

Meltzer, Françoise.
    Seeing double : Baudelaire's modernity / Françoise Meltzer.
        p. cm.
    Includes index.
    ISBN-13: 978-0-226-51988-3 (cloth : alk. paper)
    ISBN-10: 0-226-51988-0 (cloth : alk. paper)
    1. Baudelaire, Charles, 1821–1867—Criticism and interpretation.   I. Title.
    PQ2191.Z5M398 2011
    841'.8—dc22

                                                            2010045692

FOR MY STUDENTS

CONTENTS

ACKNOWLEDGMENTS

As always, my deepest thanks are to my first two readers: Bernard Rubin and David Tracy. Not only are they my closest intellectual companions, they are also my dearest friends. As is Raquel Scherr, who carefully read and corrected much of this book. My sadness lies in the fact that her husband, Marc Blanchard, another dear friend, did not live to read this book and critique it.

My assistants have been patient, tolerant, and long-suffering: Josh Yumibe, Doron Galili, and Ivan Ross. I am most grateful to all three. Marie-Claude Rubin, my daughter, puts up with my writing schedules and encourages me, even when she is annoyed with my various literary obsessions—in this case, with that odd and gifted man called Baudelaire.

Marie-Hélène Huet read the manuscript and gave me encouragement as well as insightful suggestions; she has always been a wonderful influence. Ross Chambers also remains an influence and a mentor in absentia. I have done my best to remain true to his example of political and textual *engagement*.

Small portions of this work were published in *Romanic Review*. I have also greatly profited from audiences who have heard versions of this book and made suggestions: at Stanford University, Columbia University, the Universities of Coimbra and Lisbon in Portugal, the Poetics Workshop at the University of Chicago, and the Porter Institute at the University of Tel-Aviv. Thanks to Sepp Gumbrecht, Helena Buescu, António Sousa Ribeiro, Marie Irene Ramalho Santos, Ziva Ben-Porat (always), Dustin Simpson, Erika Vause, Sebastien Greppo, and Elizabeth Kaminska (who has made all this doable). And to W. R. (Ralph) Johnson, who many years ago taught me the searing necessity of poetry.

    Danielle Allen, then dean of the Humanities Division at the University of Chicago, generously granted me a year's leave to make progress on this project. I am most grateful. The present dean, Martha Roth, has been supportive in every way possible. Alan Thomas, my superb editor, has been encouraging and judicious as always. Margaret Mahan is unsurpassed in her copyediting—syntactically as well as substantively; I was very lucky to have her. Finally, thanks go to my graduate students, who continue to inspire me and to whom this book is dedicated.

Every man takes the limits of his own field of vision for the limits of the world. This is an error of the intellect as inevitable as that error of the eye which lets us fancy that on the horizon heaven and earth meet.

—Arthur Schopenhauer, *Studies in Pessimism*

This is not yet another book about modernity, though that idea, with its endless definitions, runs like a badly sewn red thread throughout the study. The focus here is the poet Baudelaire and how, in the time of great transitions in which he lived, he responded as if in spite of himself with what I am here calling double vision. That is, he saw two times, or things, at once—as though his eyes, used as they were to seeing one world, could not yet assimilate, even as they focused on, a new one. He sees, in other words, both worlds simultaneously—the Paris before Haussmann, and the Paris during and after its redevelopment; France before the revolution of 1848, and France in the increasingly triumphant capitalist culture that followed; the death throes of the ancien régime with its unraveling social fabric, and the preening bourgeoisie with its nouveau riche self-satisfaction that touted social utilitarianism and "good works" to repress political guilt and crass mercantilism. Baudelaire's aesthetic strabismus is born of an inability to integrate the dying world and the burgeoning one—he sees, to repeat, both at once.

He also sees his life as doubled: before his mother married the hated stepfather Aupick, and afterward; when he inherited from his father and had money, and afterward with the establishment of the *conseil judiciaire* that was to drive him crazy until his death. Moreover, his double vision is not limited to time: he also sees two realms at once (the ideal and the

concrete), two women at once (the twinned Bénédictas, for example), one
work of art in two ways, and the optical illusions produced by various instruments of the eye. It is all a matter of seeing, and of seeing two contradictory things at the same time.

The visual is what seems constantly privileged in explaining the crisis
of modernity, and this study is obviously no exception. Benjamin speaks
of Baudelaire's poetry in terms of the gaze: "The gaze of the allegorist,
as it falls on the city, is the gaze of the alienated man. It is the gaze of
the flâneur."[1] At the same time, Benjamin describes the modern city as
the place where no one, in fact, looks at anyone else. Huge crowds jostle
one another with one tacit agreement: keeping to the right of the road to
allow for the stream of people in the other direction. In the meantime,
"it occurs to no man to honor another with so much as a glance" (182).
Overstimulation, many scholars of the period believe, is the problem of
the inhabitants of the modern, nineteenth-century city. "The psychological basis of the metropolitan type of individuality," writes Georg Simmel,
"consists in the *intensification of nervous stimulation* which results from
the swift and uninterrupted change of outer and inner stimuli."[2] Siegfried
Kracauer, the film theorist, describes a "cult of distraction" that necessarily occurs in a huge city such as Berlin. The sheer necessity of the circulation of such crowds, he writes, "transforms the life of the street into
the ineluctable street of life, giving rise to configurations which invade
even domestic space."[3] Contemplation, that earlier form of examining the
world, is impossible, as Benjamin notes, in modernity. The cinema is his
example. The cinema itself, as Tom Gunning remarks,[4] by the 1890s provides a series of visual shocks, psychic compensation for the loss of traditional modes of experience. Pascal's *divertissement*, in this view, becomes
distraction. Kracauer too uses fragmentation as a metaphor to point to the
loss of shared beliefs in modernity. Alongside the overstimulation of the
new city, then, the latter part of the nineteenth century will provide an

1. Walter Benjamin, "Paris, The Capital of the Nineteenth Century," in *The Writer of Modern Life* (Cambridge, MA: Harvard University Press, 2006), 40.

2. *The Sociology of Georg Simmel*, ed. and trans. Kurt H. Wolff (Glencoe, IL: Free Press, 1950), 409–10.

3. Siegfried Kracauer, "The Cult of Distraction: On Berlin's Picture Palaces," in *The Mass Ornament: Weimar Essays*, ed. and trans. Thomas Y. Levin (Cambridge, MA: Harvard University Press, 1988), 323–28. See also Kracauer's *The Salaried Masses*, which examines distraction in the white-collar class.

4. Tom Gunning, "An Aesthetics of Astonishment: Early Film and the (In)credulous Spectator," *Art and Text* 34 (Spring 1989): 31. See also Gunning, "The Exterior as Interior: Benjamin's Optical Detective, "*Boundary* 2, 30, no. 1 (Spring 2003), 105–30.

"aesthetics of astonishment" (as Gunning puts it, 31), as if to respond to one ocular shock with another. Parallel to the advent of cinema, it should be added, there is what Italo Calvino calls the "crisis of visibility" in the novel.[5] Perhaps Baudelaire (who lived in mid-century and thus knew no cinema) was responding similarly by insisting, according to his friends, upon being continually surprised. The constant optical shocks of modernity paradoxically use countershock as a palliative.

Following Simmel, Benjamin, and Kracauer, a "modernity thesis" has developed, arguing that a new mode of seeing begins in the nineteenth century, triggered by the change in modern life brought on by the obvious suspects: industrialization, urban life, capitalism, and technological advances.[6] This thesis holds that distraction is the main symptom of such a change—an overload of stimuli causing constant shifts in attention and thus actual physical changes in human vision. In the words of one modernity thesis advocate, "The city's bombardment of heterogeneous and ephemeral stimuli fostered an edgy, hyperactive, fragmented perceptual encounter with the world."[7] But other film theorists argue that such a notion is too simple. Haussmann himself, it should be noted, sought to change perception by altering the space of Paris: "He and his planners," writes Richard Terdiman, "foresaw that their alteration of the city would change more than its geography. They consciously sought to alter the habits and the perceptions of Parisians . . . His disposition of space was intended to communicate, was meant to determine perception."[8] There is an implied Whorfean notion here: that just as language can alter perception, the modern city space affects vision. The modernity thesis has been attacked on grounds that a change in the visual system of humans does not occur overnight.

5. Italo Calvino, "Gustave Flaubert, *Trois contes*," in *Why Read the Classics?* trans. Martin McLaughlin (New York: Pantheon, 1999), 151–52.

6. For example, David Bordwell, *History of Film Style* (New York: Columbia University Press, 2002). Also Charlie Keil, " 'Visualized Narratives,' Transitional Cinema and the Modernity Thesis," in *Le cinéma au tournant du siècle*, ed. Claire Dupré la Tour, André Gaudreault, and Roberta Pearson (Québec: Editions Nota Bene, 1999), 123–37. See also Sara Danius, who, in *The Senses of Modernism: Technology, Perception, and Aesthetics* (Ithaca: Cornell University Press, 2002), considers the aesthetics of perception in modernism in relation to modern machine culture.

7. Ben Singer, who has his own notion of the modernity thesis, in *Melodrama and Modernity: Early Sensational Cinema and its Contexts* (New York: Columbia University Press, 2001), 104. See also *American Cinema's Transitional Era: Audiences, Institutions and Practices*, ed. Charlie Keil and Shelley Stamp (Berkeley: University of California Press, 2004); in particular the articles by Keil and Singer, and by Gunning (who has a footnote concerning the politics of the "modernity thesis," 50 n. 85).

8. Richard Terdiman, *Present Past: Modernity and the Memory Crisis* (Ithaca: Cornell University Press, 1993), 123.

According to an alternate view, what has changed has to do, rather, with visual habits and the quality of how things are seen.[9] Baudelaire too responds to the city with an emphasis on vision. His admiration for the painter Constantin Guys, for example, is partly based on that artist's ability to take in the city's scenes as quickly as they are produced, and to sketch them from memory with frenzied rapidity. The painter of modern life must have an "eagle eye," and must be at home in the chaos that city streets bring to visual perception.

The idea that modernity causes a change of perception, or even of sight itself, because of ocular overstimulation was to have an analogue in nineteenth-century science. The notion of luminiferous ether was used to explain the medium by which light is propagated. Nineteenth-century scientists such as Helmholtz, Thomson, Clausius, and Maxwell, writes Gillian Beer, "were pursuing a single explanation of cosmic processes that would include light, heat, and sound and that would construe them all as motion, passing irreversibly beyond the reach of the senses and dissipating irregularly through the ether (that crucial explanatory substance that ebbed quietly out of the universe early in the twentieth century)."[10] The unfamiliar dimension added to this theory, continues Beer, "was the universalizing of wave theory (as thermodynamics continued to be called) to account for all phenomena" (ibid.). This wavelike flow of energies was seen as constantly affecting perception, particularly the visual. Gustave Le Bon, for example, that great theorist of the crowd who is regularly cited in works on the modern city and on modernity, also wrote on matter and its transformation into energy in *L'évolution de la matière* (1905) and *L'évolution des forces* (1907). The "ether" has numerous ramifications. Rosalind Krauss notes (as Beer points out) that painters in the 1870s had to come to terms with the fact that "the physiological screen through which light passes to the human brain is not transparent, like a window pane; it is like a filter, involved in a set of specific distortions."[11] The notions of filtering and distortion match the concern with how the overstimulation of the city can work to alter perception. It is not surprising that, as Jonathan Crary has shown,[12]

9. Bordwell, *History of Film Style*.

10. Gillian Beer, *Open Fields: Science in Cultural Encounter* (New York: Oxford University Press, 1996), 298.

11. Rosalind E. Krauss, *The Originality of the Avant-Garde and Other Modernist Myths* (Cambridge, MA: Harvard University Press, 1985), 15. See also Lauren Silvers, "Psychological Knowledge and the Aesthetics of Reading in the Symbolist Literary Era (1880–1905)" (PhD diss., University of Chicago, 2010), 296 ff.

12. In *Techniques of the Observer: On Vision and Modernity in the Nineteenth Century* (Cambridge, MA: MIT, 1992), 104–36.

optical apparatuses were all the rage in the nineteenth century. Indeed, the eye's ability to turn two images into one fascinates Schopenhauer in the early part of the century. "The process," he writes,

> by which children, and persons born blind who have been operated upon, learn to see, the single vision of the double sensation of two eyes, the double vision and double touch which occur when the organs of sense have been displaced from their usual position, the upright appearance of objects while the picture on the retina is upside down, the attributing of colour to the outward objects, whereas it is merely an inner function, a division through polarisation, of the activity of the eye, and lastly the stereoscope,—all these are sure and incontrovertible evidence that perception is not merely of the senses, but intellectual.[13]

In other words, Schopenhauer admires the eye for its remarkable ability to adjust to a plethora of optical stimuli (including scopic toys such as the stereoscope) and to turn them into a coherent, unified picture. What we will be considering here is how Baudelaire does the opposite: his eyes take in a coherent (or at least unitary, if chaotic) picture and turn it back into "the double sensation of two eyes"—or something close to that.

I am suggesting something else: that the period during which Baudelaire was writing corresponds to so many changes in daily life that he does not actually *understand* what he is seeing, even as he records it. It has been endlessly remarked that Baudelaire is contradiction personified: personally, psychologically, poetically, theologically, politically, socially, and every other way conceivable. Indeed, much of his poetry grows out of contradiction and antinomies—and often self-consciously. But the assumption by scholars has been that Baudelaire knew what he was seeing and recording; that he was drawing the contours of modernity (or *le moderne*) as he encountered it. T. J. Clark suggests that "modernism is the form formalism took in conditions of modernity."[14] But there is already a distance from modernity here—a type of recollection in disquiet, but recollection and digestion nonetheless. As early as Mallarmé, I will argue, there is an ability to stand back and aestheticize what Baudelaire records. With Benjamin the stance is taken, and Baudelaire has now become the icon of modernity, the poet of its city, and so on. But the poems of Baudelaire record, I want to insist, a

---

13. Arthur Schopenhauer, *The World as Will and Idea*, vol. 1 of 4, trans. R. B. Haldane and J. Kemp, The English and Foreign Philosophical Library, vol. 22 (London: Trübner, 1883), 15.
14. T. J. Clark, "Modernism, Postmodernism, and Steam," *October* 100 (Spring 2002): 163.

double vision: one of the world as it was, and one as it is. This double vision has been noted but usually laid on the altar of Baudelaire's drug use. I argue that it is a vision in which the past has not yet caught up with the present, and in which the future seems threatening. Baudelaire records his encounter with modernity as an unintelligible morass of contradictions that he cannot resolve. He records, in other words, the clashes at every level.

I say "record" not in order to diminish the astonishing power and genius of Baudelaire's poetic and critical production. I mean "record" as in graphesis: the putting in writing what surrounds the poet—lines, colors, impressions, convictions, sensation, emotion. "Record" as in chronicling and documenting the city while creating, obviously, the astonishing texts by which we know him. But "record" also because Baudelaire is so much of an honest video and acoustic artist (to force an anachronism), that he registers (at times without knowing it) the dual vision that is so often his. We could say that he *takes minutes* of the world as he encounters its lost, looming, and remembered shards. What I will show is how this double vision informs and underpins most of Baudelaire's texts (the prose poems and essays as well as the poetry). The double vision is, I am arguing, the result of a world incomprehensible to Baudelaire, a world that would later (with Baudelaire as chief spokesman after the fact) become the hallmark of modernity and the trigger for modernism. But for Baudelaire, such a double vision makes for a shattered, if at times exquisite, vision. The bourgeois notion of progress was to be resisted at all cost by Baudelaire, both because it was the *cri de guerre* of the society that had triumphed and that he loathed, and because progress meant moving toward the future, which terrified him. The writing, then, had to resist all resolution, and the contradictions had to be maintained; this aspect of double vision is willed in Baudelaire. But it is often unwilled—his writing can produce two images that do not communicate with each other, either in temporal or in conceptual ways. He does not understand in these instances, but he records.

Baudelaire hates the utilitarianism that surrounds him, and both hates and fears the future (of which death—his own as well as that of others and of things—is a large part). But Baudelaire's case is complex: he hates the capitalist oppression of the worker but loves luxury and frequently identifies with the aristocracy; he is nostalgic for the past even as he has contempt for the ancien régime (and he is a romantic only in a very limited sense); and his anxiety and tenseness are such that he is barely able to experience the present and certainly averts his eyes from it. Indeed, Baudelaire can be described, I suggest, as a mind that sees an idealized past that never was, and a shabby, nerve-wracking present that is characterized as

being continually prodded by a looming, hideous future. Hence Baudelaire's instinctive (but unconvincing) support of the workers in the revolution of 1848; and hence his admiration for many of the romantic writers who attacked the regime of Louis-Philippe, the Bourgeois King (Hugo,
Lamartine, Balzac, et al.). Baudelaire was infuriated when the bourgeoisie
turned its back on the workers after 1848. That was, for Baudelaire, the
moment when the projects of the middle class and its utilitarian agenda
materialized. Hence my initial emphasis on that revolution.

I agree with Bataille in his argument over Baudelaire with Sartre.
Baudelaire indeed manifests an "unparalleled tension," as Sartre puts it.
But, Bataille claims, the poet is not only expressing an individual necessity as Sartre would have it; Baudelaire's work is the result of (in Bataille's
words) "a material tension imposed, periodically, from without." *Les fleurs
du mal*, Bataille continues, "corresponded to two simultaneous tendencies which are forever demanding a decision: society, like the individual,
is forced to choose between care of the future and care of the present moment." Because Baudelaire's society was a capitalist one "in full swing,"
writes Bataille, the primacy of the future (and its possibility of increased
production for capitalist accumulation) counted above all. The result was
the worker's revolt on the one hand (they did not stand to profit) and "the
romantic protest among writers" on the other (because the glory of the ancien régime was replaced by utility). Thus, concludes Bataille, "in Baudelaire the denial of the Good was basically a denial of the primacy of the
future."[15]

It is useful here to recall Georg Lukács's statement that history disappears in 1848, replaced by a chaos to be ordered as one wishes.[16] It is nearly
the opposite of Bataille's notion, that history presses onto the Baudelairean
project and, like Freud's unconscious, the more it is repressed, the stronger
it becomes. This might be one way of reading the muffled voice of politics
and history itself in much of the *Fleurs du mal*. But as "explicating" a
text is frequently taming it, and just as individualizing a writer can annihilate a project (poorly applied psychoanalytic tools, for example, or a
Sainte-Beuvean approach that considers biography as destiny), seeking out
historical or biographical facts to "elucidate" a text can destroy it as well.
Baudelaire's genius is that he puts the reader into the maelstrom in which
he finds himself: history constantly interrupts the "pure" text, just as

15. Georges Bataille, "Baudelaire" in *La littérature du mal* (Paris: Gallimard, 1957),
43–44.
16. *The Historical Novel*, trans. Hannah and Stanley Mitchell (Lincoln: University of Nebraska Press, 1983), 181.

the text itself can cover over external events. Baudelaire, in other words, forces the same conceptual catachreses upon his reader as he does on himself: he puts together divergent, opposing notions; he *records* antitheses that have no obvious thesis. It is not enough to acknowledge Baudelaire's contradictions—he acknowledges them himself. My own attempt, rather, is to understand the lack of understanding in Baudelaire, to try to explicate how he does not see what he nonetheless records.

I therefore disagree with Sartre that Baudelaire wanted to be two people, "in order," he argues serenely, "to realize in this couple the final possession of the Self by the Self."[17] Baudelaire's "problem," in my opinion, is not what Poulet calls a *dédoublement*, a doubling—at least, not of the "Self." "Baudelaire," Sartre writes, rather too comfortably, "was the man who chose to look upon himself as though he were another person; his life is simply the failure of this attempt" (27–28). But Baudelaire's emphasis on contradiction and doubling should not be confused with some sort of dual personality. His frequently doubled view of the world does not betoken a doubled mind. While Sartre, too, concentrates on the gaze (mostly, one assumes, because so much of Baudelaire's poetry has to do with the eyes), he sees the emphasis on sight as some sort of grasping at identity: "And since his 'nature' escaped him," writes Sartre of our poet, "he tried to seize it in other people's eyes. His good faith abandoned him; he had to try unceasingly to convince himself, to seize himself with his own eyes" (42). Baudelaire does try to "seize" whatever life is, or means, with his eyes and through the eyes of others. But he does not look upon himself "as though he were another person"; instead, he looks at his surroundings as though they were a trigger to another world. Canonized by Benjamin as the father of modernity, Baudelaire is, rather, the one who prepares the terrain, who plants the seeds that will allow a Benjamin to come later and understand as well as perceive what in fact has been planted.

So much has been written about Baudelaire that there is much this book needn't do. Apart from the myriad of critical works cited in this study, the reader can consult André Guyaux, whose book on Baudelaire criticism from 1855 to 1905 is almost exhaustive.[18] There is also Pichois's dictionary on Baudelaire, even more comprehensive.[19] I will not be spend-

17. Jean-Paul Sartre, *Baudelaire*, trans. Martin Turnell (New York: New Directions, 1967), 26.

18. André Guyaux, *Baudelaire: Un demi-siècle de lectures des "Fleurs du mal" (1855–1905)* (Paris: Presses universitaires de Paris–Sorbonne, 2007).

19. Claude Pichois and Jean-Paul Avice, *Dictionnaire Baudelaire* (Poitiers: Editions du Lérot, 2002). For an excellent overview of the nineteenth century, see Philippe Muray, *Le 19e*

ing much time on versification or genre; nor will I be citing every important study on a given aspect of Baudelaire's work: there is just too much.
And I should add a word about my translations of the poet: they are literal
with a simple attempt at accuracy; the result is frequently less than elegant. I ask the reader's forbearance, and apologize for the harm my English
renditions inevitably visit upon the beauty of the original.[20]

I have chosen four major aspects of Baudelaire's thinking that inform
what I call his double vision: beliefs, seeing, money, and time. The first
has to do with Baudelaire's political convictions; seeing, with his notions
on art; money, with his inability to control expenditure; time, with his
inveterate absence from the present. Each of the four chapters centers on
one poem—two in verse, two in prose. Needless to say, the choice of these
texts is somewhat aleatoric: others could have produced more demon-
strations of my argument. But each poem is closely read, and shows how
Baudelaire, often in spite of himself, unwittingly, or uncomprehendingly,
is burdened with seeing double. We are all the richer for it.

---

siècle à travers les âges (Paris: Denoël, 1989). Readers interested in the overall structure of *Les
fleurs du mal* are referred to James R. Lawler's *Poetry and Moral Dialectic: Baudelaire's "Secret Architecture"* (Madison and Teaneck: Farleigh Dickinson University Press, 1997).

20. All Baudelaire references in this study, except for his correspondence (see chap. 1
n. 18), are to Charles Baudelaire, *Œuvres complètes*, 2 vols., ed. Claude Pichois (Paris: Gallimard, édition de la Pléiade, 1975), henceforth cited as *OC*. And all translations are mine, not
only from Baudelaire, but also from other writers quoted, except where otherwise indicated.

CHAPTER ONE

Beliefs (Assommons les pauvres!)

I believe that man necessarily rises against himself and that he can neither recognize himself, nor love himself to the end, unless he is the object of a condemnation.

—Georges Bataille, *La littérature et le mal*

It is merely a different view of the problem if one asks what impelled Baudelaire to give a radical theological form to his radical rejection of those in power.

—Walter Benjamin, *The Writer of Modern Life*

In his seminal study of Baudelaire, Walter Benjamin produces an extended analogy to describe the "negative essence" that suffuses the poet's vision: a photographer registers "the essence of things" as negatives on his photographic plates. But "because of the nature of earthly time and its apparatus," the photographer can do no more than register that essence; no one can read the plates, nor is there a known "elixir" that might act as a "developing agent." Baudelaire, continues Benjamin, doesn't have the elixir either. "But he, he alone, is able to read the plates, thanks to infinite mental efforts. He alone is able to extract from the negatives of essence a presentiment of its real picture. And from this presentiment speaks the negative of essence in all his poems."[1] This analogy reads a bit like a Kafka story (such as "Before the Law") but with a different ending: if the protagonist in Kafka's story dies without ever managing to get through

---

1. *The Writer of Modern Life: Essays on Charles Baudelaire*, ed. Michael W. Jennings; trans. Howard Eiland, Edmund Jephcott, Rodney Livingstone, and Harry Zohn (Cambridge, MA: Harvard University Press, 2006), 56, 27.

an open gate made for him alone, Benjamin's Baudelaire, with great effort, can succeed—he can extract the real picture from the negative. Effort becomes the elixir in Benjamin's eyes. But it is in fact Benjamin who is able to see the negatives, thanks to Baudelaire's recordings. The poet, I would argue, is himself the photographer "who photographs the essence of things" on plates that no one—including him—can yet read. And it is Benjamin—with the brilliance of his own, retrospective vision of the poet and his city—who is the elixir, the "developing agent," who turns the negatives recorded by Baudelaire into the theory of modernity.

One might say that Benjamin was so overwhelmed by the clarity of the vision he saw in Baudelaire's "photographic plates" that he thought the poet, albeit with great effort, could not help seeing "the true picture" as well. With the distance of some seven decades, Benjamin sees differently—or at least, from a certain distance—and assumes that Baudelaire sees as he does. But the poet frequently sees double, as if with superimposed images that make each discernible but the combination unreadable. Benjamin rightly points out that "underlying Baudelaire's writings is the old idea that knowledge is guilt. His soul is that of Adam" (27). The desire for the knowledge of both good and evil brings about "eternal remorse" in Baudelaire; it is his soul's "mythical prehistory." He knows, writes Benjamin, "more than others about redemption" (28). Benjamin is onto something crucial in Baudelaire that remains only partially acknowledged in the former's text but that I will be examining closely here. For there is indeed a mythical prehistory in the poet: it is his obsession with original sin. And if Baudelaire's soul is Adam, for Benjamin the poet's being-in-the-world is Eve. Such doubling, contradictory at that, is at the very heart of Baudelaire's poetry: guilt inspires his narratives even as redemption remains out of reach. Evil and debauchery are everywhere present in the city, but the concept of the good is not marshaled to provide a clear notion of sin. In this context, Georges Bataille's comment on writing itself works well with Baudelaire: "Evil and literature," declares Bataille, "are inseparable."[2] Writing, he continues, is the opposite of work and as such is equivalent to the child who disobeys his parents. Writing is guilt. Bataille's comments are as if an allegory of original sin, and we will see the extent to which writing for Baudelaire means disobeying the parent, feeling a constant but undefined guilt from a sin long ago committed and

2. From a 1958 interview on *La littérature et le mal*, accessible at the website http://parolesdesjours.free.fr/bataille.htm.

long since repressed. At the same time, sin and guilt are fundamental to Baudelaire: he would not recognize himself without them.

The work of art, notes Benjamin in a famous essay,[3] engages a new perception in modernity. The masses approach art with distraction; the art lover with concentration. Benjamin, it will be recalled, uses aura in the essay in two ways: in art objects, as the embedding of tradition; in natural objects, as the unique phenomenon of distance, no matter how close. The first withers in the age of mechanical reproduction; the second can be maintained fragilely with the naked eye.[4] The masses, in their passion for copying, try to get too close to things. The adjustment of the masses to reality and reality to the masses, adds Benjamin, is a question of thinking as much as of perception. Baudelaire resists such withering—his critical essay on photography attests to that.[5] But the poet has neither the distance nor the new perception to describe the withering of the aura. While he may not, in Benjamin's terms, be peeling away the skins of the objects he depicts, and while he certainly senses the end of what we might call a perceptual era, Baudelaire is too close to his time and its objects to gauge the development of the new way of seeing that Benjamin argues for. Baudelaire *records*; and at times he analyzes—"Le peintre de la vie moderne" is a brilliant case in point. But what he sees is double because the concatenation (and contradiction) of events (mechanical, political, mental) is such that he seems to be seeing two world pictures at the same time.

The chaos Baudelaire records in his world produces antinomies of every sort—visual, conceptual, experiential—as has been recognized by countless Baudelaire scholars, Benjamin foremost among them. One such antinomy is politics, which is constantly marked by original sin, guilt, and the impossibility of redemption. But it is not enough to talk of contradiction in Baudelaire; one needs also to recognize that his versed negatives

3. "The Work of Art in the Age of Mechanical Reproduction," in *The Correspondence of Walter Benjamin, 1910–1940*, ed. Gershom Scholem and Theodor W. Adorno; trans. Manfred R. Jacobson (Chicago: University of Chicago Press, 1994).

4. For an in-depth discussion of the various ways Benjamin uses "aura," see Miriam Bratu Hansen, "Benjamin's Aura," *Critical Inquiry* 34, no. 2 (Winter 2008): 337–75.

5. See the second section of the *Salon de 1859*, "Le public moderne et la photographie," in *OC* 2:614–19. Baudelaire blames the "multitude" for confusing real art with industry, photography being a part of the latter. Photography has, he claims, contributed to "the impoverishment of French artistic genius" (618). Poetry and progress must of necessity detest each other, he writes, and photography should recognize its duty: to remain the humble servant of the sciences and art.

were unreadable for him. He was too close, and, like all things too close to the eyes, the image is doubled. The poet's vision is thus telescoped (a term Benjamin liked to use)[6]—that is, collapsed upon itself, overlapping. And no amount of effort, mental or visual, can parse the clashing superimpositions that inevitably follow. It took a Benjamin to unravel, to decode those images. His only miscalculation was that Baudelaire, caught in the maelstrom of what was later understood to be modernity in Benjamin's sense, could see them as well.

In order to begin entering Baudelaire's double vision, and in our approach to "Assommons les pauvres," we will be considering two influences on his thinking: Joseph de Maistre and Pierre-Joseph Proudhon (in that order, the reverse of chronological). The poem in question, obviously, was not solely inspired by the two thinkers in question, and can be read (indeed, generally has been read) without taking them into consideration at all.[7] But the point here is to recognize two contradictory strands of thought that strongly resonate in the prose poem; by tracing those strands we can begin to understand the strabismus that informs Baudelaire's gaze. One eye is on the social conscience provided by Proudhon; the other follows the fulminating aphorisms of the grim Maistre. Like a faulty telescope, the two images do not merge into one: they remain simultaneous, each as if refuting the other.

In his afterword to Rancière's *The Politics of Aesthetics*, Zizek writes of a well-known visual paradox concerning a vase. "One either sees the two faces or a vase, never both of them—one has to make a choice."[8] Baudelaire, more often than not, was convinced that he had made the choice; many of his poems, however, demonstrate that he did not, or could not. He sees, and his poems image, both the two faces and the vase itself. As such, the dualities in his poems are not only the delineation of antinomies. More importantly, the poems perform the double vision that ensues, and thus present a scopic recording of modernity in combat at its inception: modernity against itself, as it puts increasing pressure on tradi-

6. Benjamin describes, for example, his own essay "The Work of Art in the Age of Mechanical Reproduction" as a "telescope" focused on a "mirage of the nineteenth century" (*The Correspondence of Walter Benjamin*, 516. In the Arcades project, Benjamin also speaks of telescoping the past through the present.

7. One of few exceptions to this tendency is Richard Burton's excellent reading of the poem in *Baudelaire and the Second Republic: Writing and Revolution* (Oxford: Clarendon Press, 1991), 276–90 and especially 324–52. His concerns, however, are entirely political.

8. "Afterword by Slavoj Zizek," in Jacques Rancière, *The Politics of Aesthetics*, trans. Gabriel Rockhill (London: Continuum, 2004), 75.

tion even as it demands an insistent present; and modernity against older modes of perception.

⟨∞⟩

Until 1852, Baudelaire was under the sway of the socialist Pierre-Joseph Proudhon (the "father of anarchy"), who on the face of it could not have been more different than the thinker who most influenced Baudelaire in his later years: the very right-wing, ultra-Catholic, and self-made theologian Joseph de Maistre. Curiously, however, Proudhon has his own "hypothesis for the existence of God," and (scandalously) announces that "God is evil,"—by which he means that a reliance on predetermination and the status quo will not solve the ills of poverty, disease, and social inequality. Whereas Baudelaire is typically thought of as having been on the left until shortly after the revolution of 1848, and then on the right upon reading Maistre soon thereafter, "Assommons les pauvres" retains a number of Proudhon's ideas about God, even as Baudelaire becomes the fairly devout disciple of Maistre. Baudelaire thus carries with him, and expresses in his texts, a double (and contradictory) vision that has gone insufficiently recognized in the numerous depictions of him (beginning with Benjamin) as the founder of modernity. Obsessed with the concept of sin and a hyper-Augustinianism by way of Maistre, Baudelaire writes the city less as a theoretician of modernity than as a producer of texts that argue the inevitability, indeed the triumph, of evil in the new urban world. Though he does (notoriously) revel in corruption and wickedness, Baudelaire's conviction that man is by definition irrevocably sinful is confirmed in his depictions of the modern, capitalist, industrial city. Baudelaire's pleasure then lies less in the escapism provided by debauchery than in the affirmation of his deepest belief: that man can never escape his sinful heritage. For this reason, Baudelaire saw his *Fleurs du mal* as deeply moral and as deeply misunderstood, a view that he was nearly alone in upholding.

But if Baudelaire was profoundly influenced by Maistre, he never left Proudhon entirely behind. The result is a clash of convictions, which, while remaining (if uncomfortably) in the poet's fermenting mind, or *exacerbatio cerebri*,[9] frequently produces a disconcerting uncertainty for

9. "Baudelairean sensuality," writes Mario Praz, "is the fermentation of the mind, *exacerbatio cerebri*." Significantly for our purposes, Praz is citing Baudelaire's analysis of the cunning Marquise de Merteuil in Laclos's *Liaisons dangereuses*. The Marquise, notes Baudelaire, writes to Valmont that she wants "not to take pleasure (*jouir*), but to KNOW." This is a desire

the reader. For one of the many symptoms of what I call double vision in Baudelaire is a sense of vertigo for the reader as well as for the poet, as if rocking back and forth at sea.[10] Indeed, such an alternating movement of rocking, even pitching, is frequent in Baudelaire's texts, as if he were performing the very dualities, and resulting vacillations, that characterize his thought.

The prose poem "Assommons les pauvres" (1865) is the concretization of such vacillation. The poem has been read variously by critics as sociopolitical—a satire of the bourgeois do-gooders of the Second Empire; as a refutation specifically of Proudhon and his theory of mutualism and equality;[11] as a mark of Baudelaire's conservatism after the debacle of 1848 (Burton); or as a demonstration of conflict between the two classes, the working class and the bourgeoisie, that emerged after the revolution of 1848. By more literarily inclined scholars, the poem has been read as a provocative doctrine of Satanism and the ensuing sadomasochistic implications (Blin); as a philosophical farce; as an allegory, much like "L'albatros," of the poet's alienation from his fellow man; as a sheer provocation born of the poet's bitterness and misanthropy; or as a product of the trauma of the failed revolution of '48 (Oehler and Chambers). Some biographers have argued that "Assommons les pauvres" shows the beginnings of the poet's apparent dementia, probably the result of tertiary syphilis. Psychoanalytic critics have argued for Baudelaire's self-loathing, his hatred of his stepfather, his masochistic and sadistic tendencies, the destruction of his *moi créateur* in favor of a cold *moi social* (Mauron), the prince-dandy narrator's exceeding narcissism (Mehlman), primary narcissism, and the

that Baudelaire shares and that Praz compares to original sin. Mario Praz, *La chair, la mort et le diable dans la littérature du XIXe siècle: Le romantisme noir*, trans. Constance Thompson Pasquali (Paris: de Nöel, 1977), 105.

10. Poulet comments on the extensive "vibrations" that inform Baudelaire's work, though he ties them, at least initially, to happier states. See Georges Poulet, *Les métamorphoses du cercle* (Paris: Plon, 1961), 397–402 ff. We will return to vibrations in chapter 4.

11. Mutualism is Proudhon's anarchic idea for getting around capitalism and state socialism—government in general—whereby each individual would possess a means of production. The word had already been used as early as 1822 by Charles Fourier, though differently. Proudhon got the term from the "mutualist" workers in Lyon. As against the dominant ideology of many other non-Marxist socialists of the day, who suggested that the state intervene as a supplier of both labor and credit for the working class, Proudhon declares that the state is not an entrepreneur. Mutualism is a labor theory of value, which would support cooperatives owned by workers and was to have included a bank. The circulation of currency was to be replaced by a newly democratized form of credit. "What is justice?" asks Proudhon, and answers: "the mutuality of guarantees that we have been calling the Social Contract for two hundred years." See Proudhon's *Idée générale de la révolution au XIXe siècle* (Paris: Garnier, 1851), 316.

death of metaphoricity (Bersani). To some extent, the poem is all of these (and then some).[12]

But "Assommons les pauvres" also, and perhaps principally, manifests a profound ambivalence on the part of the poet between egalitarianism (Proudhon) and hyper-Augustinianism (Maistre). And while in the Baudelairean text Proudhon frequently shows his hand through satire (and a bit of grudging admiration), Maistre is far darker, and more heavily weighted. For Maistre is the grim spokesman for original sin, the notion without which little of Baudelaire's work can be understood—before, but particularly after, he became an admirer of the ultramontane Maistre. The poetic confrontation of these two thinkers, diametrically opposed on most grounds, and the ambivalence of the narrator between them, produces an antinomy that is willfully left unresolved. Such a lack of resolution, such deliberate doubling, are more powerful than the poet's unconvincing (if evolving) politics. "Assommons les pauvres" is the narrative of the poet's praxis; even more importantly, it is the poet's recording, through what I call double vision, of the contradictory urban panorama surrounding him. Baudelaire's recording of that landscape has been one of the hallmarks of what was retroactively called modernity (a term Baudelaire himself was one of the first to use). The dualities, in other words, have been identified as part of the project of modernity that has famously been credited to Baudelaire. But what we will be considering here at some length, before returning to the poem, is the extent to which "Assommons" marks out more than such well-established dualities, and betrays the inability to extricate itself from two contradictory ideas, such that combat is inevitable, resolution at best artificial. The overlapping of two perspectives, their superimposition, skew the poet's visual field. Baudelaire's texts record his inability to focus on the same point with both eyes, as we have noted. In "Assommons," we are witness to a theological and political strabismus as if the poet were remembering Proudhon's social theories with one eye and reading Maistre on original sin with the other. Such recording is not an attempt to write modernity; it is rather a reeling, a pitching. We need first

12. In the order in which they are mentioned: Burton, *Baudelaire and the Second Republic*; Georges Blin, *Le sadisme de Baudelaire* (Paris: Corti, 1948); Dolf Oehler, *Le spleen contre l'oubli: Baudelaire, Flaubert, Heine, Herzen*, trans. Guy Petitdemange (Paris: Payot et Rivages, 1996); Ross Chambers, "Baudelaire's Paris," in *The Cambridge Companion to Baudelaire*, ed. Rosemary Lloyd (New York: Cambridge University Press, 2005), 101–16; Charles Mauron, *Le dernier Baudelaire* (Paris: Corti, 1966); Jeffrey Mehlman, "Baudelaire with Freud / Theory and Pain," *Diacritics*, Spring, 1974, 7–13; Leo Bersani, *Baudelaire and Freud* (Berkeley: University of California Press, 1977).

then, before returning to "Assommons," to look carefully at each of these two focal points separately, and at their embedment in the poet's thought.

HOMO DUPLEX

In 1858, Baudelaire's close friend Charles Asselineau published eleven short stories entitled *La double vie*. Baudelaire wrote the introduction and edited Asselineau's preface. In the margins of the manuscript, very much in the manner of a strict schoolmaster correcting a composition, Baudelaire asks: "Où est le verbe auquel *laquelle* sert de sujet?" (*OC* 2:95). Or he comments: "phrase mal faite" (100).[13] But he does not confine himself to correcting infelicities of grammar and style; he corrects Asselineau's opinions as well. At one point in the preface, for example, Asselineau argues that the bourgeoisie must get over the illusion that the literary reaction of 1840 was a matter of defending good sense. Baudelaire's response in the margins is unambiguous: "What difference does it make if the Bourgeoisie keeps or loses an illusion?" It is hard not to hear in this comment an allusion to Balzac's *Illusions perdues*; that novel had been published in 1837 and had to do, precisely, with the loss of a bourgeois's illusions. Baudelaire, as we know, always wants to distinguish himself from the rabble—not only the poor, but the bourgeoisie as well. His disdain for the middle class is occasionally related to confused revolutionary fervor; more often than not, however, Baudelaire hates the bourgeoisie because it has neither the taste nor the refinement of the aristocracy, with which he instinctively identifies, if only in matters of taste in clothing and furniture. But Baudelaire is above all aristocratic in his own terms with respect to art and literature. Indeed, the corrections he makes on Asselineau's manuscript show an adherence to stylistic, syntactic, and grammatical correctness that goes far beyond the schoolmaster's strict redactions. "Je n'aime pas," Baudelaire notes more than once in the margin, and adjusts the style.

It is indisputable that Baudelaire's poetry is frequently written in classical forms, with corresponding classical allusions. Proust finds "nothing as Baudelairean as *Phèdre*, nothing as worthy of Racine, even of Malherbe, as the *Fleurs du mal*. Need we even speak of the difference in times? It did not prevent Baudelaire from writing like the classics."[14] It is perhaps

---

13. All italics in citations from Baudelaire represent his own emphasis—underlined in the manuscripts.

14. "Après la guerre," in *Contre Sainte-Beuve, précédé de Pastiches et mélanges et suivi de Essais et articles*, ed. Pierre Clarac and Yves Sandre (Paris: Gallimard, 1971), 627. See also Keith Macfarlane's article on the way classical allusion changes in Baudelaire from a tradi-

Baudelaire's insistence on *le beau style* that gives him a serious classical feel, even if his subject matter is so frequently shocking, grotesque, or blasphemous to his own generation, and thus "modern" from the point of view of succeeding literary perspectives. Indeed, the juxtaposition between classical form and risqué content is in itself an aspect of modernity, as Benjamin and others have pointed out. Scandalous as he may have been in content, however, Baudelaire was conservative in his use of the French language (even in obscenity); and he was a perfectionist. He frequently took so long to correct proofs (he was known to become quite hysterical over a typo) that his editors complained bitterly. And even at the end of his life in the hated Belgium, sick as he was, Baudelaire was obsessed with going over the punctuation, particularly the dashes, in his manuscripts.

One wonders if this traditional side of Baudelaire explains why he is not included in Barthes's *Degré zéro de l'écriture* as a representative of writing after 1848.[15] There is a huge gap, Barthes argues, between a Balzac and a Flaubert, and the primary reasons for this gap are the events of the failed revolution of '48, the ensuing upheaval of class structure, and the change from a textile to a metallurgic industry in the mid-nineteenth century.[16] After 1850, in Barthes's view, it is no longer possible simply to sit down and write a novel in the *passé simple*. That tense represents, for Barthes, "the expression of an order and thus of a euphoria" (*Degré zéro*, 48). The *passé simple*, Barthes continues, implies a coherence of events; reality is neither "mysterious" nor "absurd," but "clear." The break with such a view entails a break in style—Flaubert being Barthes's prime example. "From the moment when the writer ceased being a witness of the universal to become an unhappy consciousness (around 1850)," Barthes contends, "his first gesture has been to choose his commitment to a form" (9). Baudelaire chose, for the most part and at least in his verse poetry, to remain in the classical forms. And despite the innovation of his own version of the prose poem, much of his prose is in the *passé simple*. Barthes steers

---

tional use in his earlier career to "deviant allusions" beginning around 1860. These deviant allusions, Macfarlane argues, are subverted in their internal structure, requiring the reader "to learn a new set of responses to what had been a reassuringly transparent code." The result is a kind of "double take" on the part of the reader—yet another form of doubling in, as we shall be considering, a poetics of duality. Keith H. Macfarlane, "Baudelaire's Revaluation of the Classical Allusion," *Studies in Romanticism* 15, no. 3 (Summer 1976): 442.

15. Roland Barthes, *Le degré zéro de l'écriture* (Paris: Seuil, 1953).

16. For a review of recent work on class delineation in modern France, particularly the bourgeois class, see Jan Goldstein, "Of Marksmanship and Marx: Reflections on the Linguistic Construction of Class in Some Recent Scholarship," *Modern Intellectual History* 2, no.1 (April 2005): 87–107.

clear of Baudelaire for the most part, and even considers that part of modern poetry leading to "degree zero" as stemming from Rimbaud "and not Baudelaire" (63). Obsessed with dualities and oppositions at every level, Baudelaire is also overwhelmed by his "unhappy consciousness." Indeed, we might say that Barthes's allusion to Hegel more appropriately describes Baudelaire rather than Flaubert, and that the *passé simple* is a less crucial aspect than Barthes would have us believe.

Barthes's move to put Baudelaire in parentheses for the purposes of his argument underlines, ironically, the aspect of Baudelaire we will be examining in this chapter: Baudelaire's texts create, as everyone agrees, a series of endless contradictions. Classical writing, as Barthes notes, is a question of class; and we have seen that Baudelaire is aristocratic in his tastes in literature and literary language. He admires what he calls "the Christian aristocracy" of Barbey d'Aurevilly.[17] On the other hand, he also identifies with, or at least panders to at varying times, the other two primary social classes of his time: the poor (because he felt occasional pity for them and was usually strapped for money himself) and the bourgeoisie (first, but mostly unacknowledged, because he belonged to that class; second, because he needed the bourgeois to patronize the arts and thought he could educate them).[18] Nonetheless, Baudelaire despised each of these classes at various points throughout his life.

Scholars of Baudelaire have long perceived this obsession with duality—not an impressive achievement since it is impossible to read the Baudelaire corpus without noticing the continual reference to binaries, doubles and contradiction. What everyone forgets in all this recent discussion about citizens' "rights," declares Baudelaire around 1855 and in capital letters, is "THE RIGHT TO CONTRADICT ONESELF" (OC 1:709). It is a right that he exercised flagrantly throughout his life. But through such contradiction we arrive at a less obvious result in Baudelaire—the double vision both unwanted and irrevocable for the poet, which he spent his life trying alternatively to escape and to cultivate. While the reasons for such double vision can be partially explained psychologically, that will not be the emphasis here—nor is it a sufficient explanation.

I began with Baudelaire's preface to his friend Asselineau's *La double vie* because it was written relatively late in the poet's career; by then, Baudelaire had accepted dualism as a matter of human course—at least,

17. In Charles Baudelaire, *Correspondance*, 2 vols., ed. Claude Pichois with Jean Ziegler (Paris: Gallimard, 1973). Henceforth cited as *Corr.* The above reference is to *Corr.* 2:61.
18. See "Aux bourgeois," the introduction to the *Salon* of 1846 (OC 2:415–17).

intellectually. It has been endlessly argued that the early Baudelaire is a romantic, full of admiration for that patriarch of French romantic verse, Victor Hugo. Such is undeniably the case. It has also been argued that the later, highly innovative prose poems that Baudelaire produced under the rubric "Spleen de Paris" are looser, freer, and less tied to classical style. Again, true enough. But Baudelaire is consistent in his will to contradiction, and his work resists chronological labeling. These contradictions are deployed by the poet in every aspect of existence: everyday life, politics, social class, historical events, religion, philosophy, love, psychology, textual and poetic production, style—to name just a few. These antinomies are willed, formally as well as intellectually; they are *telescoped*, to use Benjamin's term, or collide. Baudelaire himself was fully aware of dualities and doublings in his own work and in the everyday life of modernity: "Who among us," he asks in the preface to *La double vie*, "is not a *homo duplex*? I am referring to those whose mind has been *touched with pensiveness* [de Quincy, cited in English]; always double, action and intention, dream and reality; one always harming the other, one usurping the other's share" (*OC* 2:87). This is the part of telescoping, or colliding, of which Baudelaire was entirely cognizant. But it is the *un*willed aspect of the collision that reveals, I will argue, what has been called Baudelaire's modernity—one that he did not fully understand, and that was frequently unwelcome. Let us begin with the willed, and conscious, collisions; for as Baudelaire puts it, "the artist is an artist only on condition of being double, and of not being ignorant of any aspect in his double nature" (*OC* 2:543).

MORE DUPLEXITIES

"Who among us is not an *homo duplex*?" Baudelaire had asked, citing Buffon. Somewhere, writes Baudelaire, Buffon has a chapter called "homo duplex," which Asselineau's *La double vie* has "suddenly" brought back to the poet's memory.[19] The obsession with duality in Baudelaire is demonstrated by a famous comment in his journal: "There are in every man two simultaneous postulations, one toward God, the other toward Satan" (*Mon cœur mis à nu, OC* 1:682–83). These "postulations" of a simultaneous ascent and descent are further complicated by the fact that the descent

19. In fact, Buffon uses the term in his *Histoire naturelle*, in a section entitled "Discours sur la nature des animaux," in which he describes the social life of beavers (which live in villages and share all tasks in a highly successful communal life). See "Homo duplex" in "Discours sur la nature des animaux," in *Œuvres complètes de Buffon, avec les descriptions anatomiques de Daubenton*, vol. 16 (Paris: Verdière et Ladrange, 1824), 71.

is a "joy," and is connected with love for women and "intimate conversations with animals, dogs, cats, etc." We are not so far, it would seem, from Buffon's discourse on the nature of animals. But the quotation also shows that Baudelaire has no illusions about mankind; not only is man given to evil, he enjoys it. Unsurprisingly, Baudelaire will become increasingly resistant to Rousseau's "ridiculous" belief that man is by nature good.

Baudelaire remembers his Buffon correctly, and it is hardly surprising.[20] The passage can only have had great resonance for Baudelaire with respect to his own experience. In Buffon's "Discourse on the Nature of Animals," there is indeed a section entitled *homo duplex*. "The internal man is *double*," contends Buffon. "He is composed of two principles, different in their nature, and opposite in their action. The soul, that spiritual principle, principle of all knowledge, wages perpetual war with the other animal principle, which is purely material." Each of these two principles, which Buffon also calls the rational and the irrational, can produce happiness if it stands alone and is not opposed by the other; we are then "aware of no internal conflict . . . because we feel but one impulse." But when we feel both principles, when "the violence of passions makes us hate reason, we then cease to be happy." The result is an internal conflict, says Buffon in a manner that is almost proto-Hegelian: "The two persons oppose each other, and the two principles manifest themselves by producing doubts, anxiety, and remorse." We may conclude

> that the most miserable of all states takes place when these two sovereign powers of human nature exert great effort, but an equal effort which produces an equilibrium. That is the place of the deepest ennui and of that horrible self-disgust, which leaves no other desire but that of ceasing to exist, no other power but that of self-destruction, by coldly turning the weapons of fury against ourselves. (74)[21]

"Equilibrium" is understood here to mean the irresolution created by opposing forces of similar strength; it does not have the more usual meaning of stasis, that which is at rest or neutralized. Buffon here paints man as always prey to equally potent forces, with the ensuing equilibrium necessarily creating "confusion, irresolution, and misery." Here lies the

20. In the prose poem "Les bons chiens," Baudelaire writes breezily: "I have never blushed, even in front of the young writers of my century, over my admiration for Buffon" (OC 1:360).

21. True, in the same passage Buffon says that the two opposing powers fight "with a nearly equal force." But it is not clear when one is more forceful than the other, which returns us—and Buffon—to "cet état d'équilibre" (75).

difficulty of reconciling man to himself, for he is "composed of two opposite principles." Nothing could be closer to Baudelaire's own notion of
man, of existence, than this fundamental duality that is both irresolvable
and constant; an equilibrium that is permanent since neither side, neither
of Buffon's "two persons," is any weaker than the other. It is no wonder
that when thinking of Asselineau's title *La double vie*, Buffon "suddenly"
comes to Baudelaire's mind.

But if Baudelaire instinctively agrees with Buffon's two, irreconcilable
principles in man, the poet adds another layer to the conflict: the two "postulates," one toward God and one toward Satan. As I have noted, the descent toward Satan includes the desire for women and conversations with
dogs, cats, and animals in general. And this "joy of the descent" is much
like Buffon's animal or material principle. The move toward God or ascension can also be likened to Buffon's principle of mind, which the naturalist
describes as "a pure light, accompanied by calm and serenity" (71). The
choice—God or Satan—inscribes the "equilibrium" between these forces
with one of Baudelaire's most consistent beliefs: original sin as the root of
all human experience. The equilibrium can be no better resolved in this
context, since sin will always trump any move toward the good, and the
good will frequently turn out to be enjoying its own descent toward Satan
or, indeed, turn out to *be* Satan.

The repercussions of such a view on literary judgment are distinct for
Baudelaire. George Sand, for example, is a *stupide créature*, Baudelaire
writes in *Mon cœur mis à nu* (My heart laid bare), because she thinks
"a real Christian cannot believe in hell" (*OC* 1:687). She is in fact "possessed" by the devil, who makes her believe in her "good heart and good
sense" so that she can convince others in turn of their own good hearts
and sense. Because, Baudelaire nastily explains, Sand does not understand
evil; hers is a misbegotten politics with an ensuing irrational care for the
poor. Therefore, he writes (more than once) in the same text, "she has
good reasons for wanting to abolish hell." In another passage, Baudelaire
wonders about the nature of the Fall: "If it is unity become duality, it is
God who fell. In other words, couldn't creation be the fall of God?" (*OC*
1:688–89). Is God playing his own Lucifer, or is Lucifer now God, given the
Fall? Thus Rousseau, Baudelaire frequently claims, was an idiot because
he believed in the natural goodness of man. Moreover, Rousseau was overcome by his own "moral value," and was naturally stoned, without the
need for hashish. ("Le poëme du hachisch," *OC* 1:436). We see in these
examples the flipping back and forth between the categories of good and
evil; flipping to such an extent that the two categories become entirely

destabilized—which is the point—even as they maintain a constant equilibrium in Buffon's sense. Thus Maurice Blanchot describes Baudelaire's imagination as an "equilibrium in perpetual disequilibrium" (*équilibre en perpétuel déséquilibre*).[22]

Saint Augustine, whose works Baudelaire knew fairly well,[23] maintains the categories of good and evil in discrete compartments, at least conceptually. But the opening of the *Confessions* had to have intrigued Baudelaire, for there Augustine too grapples with the conundrum of the infant's innocence versus irremediable birth into sin: "Who can tell me the sin I committed as a baby?" Augustine asks God. "For in your sight no man is free from sin, not even a child who has lived only one day on earth. . . . Was it a sin to cry when I wanted to feed at the breast?"[24] Augustine formulates these remarks as the introduction to his *Confessions*; the existential landscape from which the book unfolds. But for Baudelaire, this is the question he himself unendingly asks and can never resolve: even when man appears at his most innocent, even as a child, he is by *nature* always already sinful. Philosophy and religion, he contends in "Eloge du maquillage" (1863, and part of "Le peintre de la vie moderne") order us to feed our old and infirm relatives. But nature is nothing other than the voice of our self-interest; it is nature, moreover, that commands us to beat up on these same relatives ("La nature . . . nous commande de les assommer.") (*OC* 2:715) The verb *assommer*, to beat up, is of particular importance, since it is at the center of the poem we are approaching. For now, however, I want to highlight the extent to which the doctrine of original sin, which was increasingly to obsess Baudelaire, is appropriate to the dualisms and contradictions that buffeted him throughout his life.

To begin with, every happy moment in Baudelaire is either erased (or at least compromised) by an unhappy one, as if punished by the rearing of evil's many heads. Innocence is never genuine, even when it appears so (a child for example). In the prose poem "Le gâteau" (1862), the narrator begins with a rare sense of "lightness" (*légèreté*) and something very close to happiness: vulgar passions, he tells us, seem distant, along with hatred and "profane love." This exalted state is clearly triggered by the "grandeur and irresistible nobility of the landscape" (probably somewhere in the Alps,

22. Maurice Blanchot, "L'échec de Baudelaire," in *La part du feu* (Paris: Gallimard, 1949), 143.

23. For example, Baudelaire cites (significantly) Augustine's "remorse" in the *Confessions* concerning the "excessive pleasure of the eyes," and concurs (*OC* 2:49). See also citations from Augustine in *OC* 1:210, 475, 691.

24. *Saint Augustine, Confessions*, ed. and trans. R. S. Pine-Coffin (London: Penguin, 1961), 27.

where the young Baudelaire had spent a vacation with his stepfather years earlier). The beauty of the landscape is such that, as the narrator tells us, "something" happens in his soul. But then two poor, starving children fight viciously for a piece of bread that the narrator of the poem (in his state of peaceful contentment and consequent generosity) had given to one of them out of compassion. Neither "little savage" wants to sacrifice a bit of bread for his brother. Being of equal strength, they fight until they are both exhausted. Panting and bloody, the two little boys (who are so alike they "could be twins") realize that the object of their battle no longer exists: the bread has been scattered into crumbs "like the grains of sand with which it was mixed." This "fratricidal war"[25] ruins the beautiful landscape for the narrator, and destroys as well his sense of peace. Once again, Rousseau has been slammed; but that is only part of the story—the protagonist is original sin, which emerges here triumphant and inexorable.[26]

The poem is from 1862, by which time Baudelaire had ostensibly turned quite conservative. It is usually read as a satire of the romantic country idyll (of the sort exemplified by Thomas Gray's "Elegy Written in a Country Churchyard"). In fact, despite the happy tenor of its opening, "Le gâteau" carefully prepares the reader for its inevitable, morose conclusion. To begin with, nature is almost never a simple word in the Baudelairean lexicon, and the moods it elicits are rarely to be trusted. The poem opens with a sense of calm and happiness, but there are warnings. "My soul *seemed* to me as vast and pure as the dome of the sky" (*OC* 1:297). Things of the earth reach him only dimly, like the sound of the bells on the animals of distant herds passing "far, very far away, on the side of another mountain" (ibid.). One can never, however, escape the tragic animality of being human, even in a beautiful and isolated landscape. (It is here, one might say, that Baudelaire is clearly differentiating himself from the likes of nature-loving romantics in France such as early Hugo or Lamartine.) You can fool yourself into thinking you have escaped human sordidness, that your soul is "pure" as the vast sky, but the poem again warns: the little lake the narrator is admiring is "immobile," as if stagnant; moreover, the lake is black because of its "immense depth"—so it is not so "little" after all. And, adds

25. The fratricidal war is reminiscent of the earlier poem "Abel et Caïn" (1857), one of the three poems of "Révolte."

26. Baudelaire's use of the word "savage" is also loaded with implications from original sin and no doubt influenced by Augustine's *City of God*. Maistre, too, spills much ink over the distinction between "savage," "primitive" and "barbarian," distinctions that he says Rousseau hopelessly misunderstands. See *Les soirées de Saint-Pétersbourg* (Paris: La Colombe, 1960), 65–68.

the narrator, turning what had been a charming scene into something beginning to resemble the opening of Poe's "Fall of the House of Usher," the
shadow of an occasional cloud passes over the lake like "the reflection of
an aerial giant's coat." The charm of the little lake, the narrator's sense of
purity of soul, quickly dissipate when confronted by the reality of humankind. The boys are "little men"—like the lake, not so little that they do
not contain within them the emerging seed of evil forces.

It is an image of children Baudelaire has used before. In "De l'essence
du rire" (published in 1855), for example, Baudelaire analyzes the "dual
nature" of laughter and responds to an imagined protest on the part of the
reader that "the laughter of children is like the blooming of a flower" (*OC*
2:534). Here too, children are compared to the apparent beauty of nature,
so it behooves the reader of Baudelaire to be suspicious. And, indeed, nature returns as an idiomatic metaphor: the laughter of children does differ
from the contentment of animals, because children, unlike animals, are
already not "entirely devoid of ambition." That is, "little men" (*des bouts
d'homme*) are "unripe Satans" (*des Satans en herbe*; 535). Like the brothers fiercely battling for the bread, children are still "little men" and their
fundamental evil is unavoidable: they are unripe grain (*en herbe*), but they
will be Satan's harvest in the end. In both "Le gâteau" and the essay on
laughter, we see Baudelaire didactically demonstrating, as he will do again
and again, how one must not succumb to illusions of purity, innocence,
goodness—or even happiness.[27] There may be "two simultaneous postulations in man," but original sin is always at the bottom of it all, a sort of
Unterziehung that, unlike Hegel's *Aufhebung*, which lifts up even as it
preserves the dialectic, similarly preserves the two postulations while low-
ering them into a confrontation with man's inexorable evil. The unicity of
original sin, *unum est origine* in the words of the Council of Trent, will
always overwhelm the proliferation of dualities. Original sin then, within
the good/evil dialectic, functions *structurally* like Nietzsche's overly cited
Apollo/Dionysius dualism: Apollo steps out of the Greek chorus as the

---

27. Baudelaire is not always so harsh with children. See, for example, "Morale du joujou,"
where children are described as having more imagination than adults (thus being more poetic
and open to art). They have not yet attained the degeneracy of men. But even here—a text
two years before the essay on laughter—children are not entirely free of their adult instar.
Little girls, for example, imitate their mothers and thus "already prelude their future immortal puerility" (*OC* 1:583). Others break their toys without ever playing with them; a *"Puzzling
question"* as to why, writes Baudelaire in English (587). Sadness itself begins when children
ask "Where is the soul?" of their toys. There are also "men-children," the poet notes with contempt, who keep their toys merely for display, instructing their friends not to touch them (586).

principium individuationis, only to be reabsorbed into the chorus at the play's end. So the good can suddenly emerge, shock-like (in Benjamin's sense), only to be returned to the primal soup of evil. If Nietzsche's Dionysian is close to Schopenhauer's notion of the all-consuming will, Baudelaire partakes of such an economy with his own notion of *le mal*.

The "joy of descent" is often a kind of embrace-your-fate. If there is progress in any given struggle for Baudelaire ("progress" being another fraught word for him, as we will see), it is not the inexorable move toward Spirit in Hegel, nor that toward the communitarian ideal in Marx. For Baudelaire, "progress" is in the inevitability of descent; it is, he writes in his work on Poe, "that great heresy of decrepitude" (*OC* 2:324). To continue the analogy to Hegel, Baudelaire's *bouts d'homme* in "Le gâteau" fight no less ferociously than the future lord and his bondsman; but there is no advancement to be gained from the vicious struggle, no higher ground to which a new dialectic can be lifted up, and the conflicting forces remain of equal strength and thus afford no resolution, no matter how distant. Indeed, "Le gâteau" can be read almost as a demonstration of Buffon's notion of *équilibre*. When two principles are opposed, as Buffon believed, and when they are of equal strength, it fills a man with "self-disgust" and leaves "no other desire but that of ceasing to exist." "Le gâteau," then, performs the struggle of antinomies (dialectic) at two main levels. One is that of the two little brothers fighting over a piece of bread until they are too bloodied and exhausted to continue. That struggle might be called the concretization of another, deeper level: original sin as against man's illusion of, and desire for, happiness and goodness. Original sin, in other words, is the engine motivating conflict even between children, causing the contradiction between the thought of the good and its constant defeat in the face of man's inheritance of evil.

It is the same contradiction that motivates the passage we considered from Augustine's *Confessions*: even as a baby, man is sinful in the eyes of God: "no man is free from sin, not even a child who has lived only one day on earth." Baudelaire's frequent recourse to children who demonstrate their potential for evil is a kind of reminder to himself not to be taken in by the seductive promise of goodness: for him, it will always be a promise broken. Another of Augustine's phrases from the *Confessions* could only have been endorsed by our poet: "if babies are innocent, it is not for lack of will to do harm, but for lack of strength" (28). The passage that follows in Augustine is like an earlier version of "Le gâteau": "I have seen," he says, "jealousy in a baby and know what it means." A toddler is jealous when his baby brother nurses at their mother's breast, though there is abundant milk. Can this be innocence, asks Augustine, "to object to a rival desperately in need and depending for his life on this one form of nourishment?" Such faults are not "mere peccadilloes," since they are "intolerable" in adults. Equilibrium will always yield to, or be rooted in, evil. The dialectic in Baudelaire is most often (with some exceptions) the performance of that truth.

It follows quite logically, then, that virtue is artificial, and evil natural. A passage in "Le peintre de la vie moderne" can be fully understood only in the light of Baudelaire's notion of original sin: "Crime," he maintains, "the taste for which the human animal acquired in his mother's belly, is originally natural. Virtue, on the contrary, is *artificial*, supernatural, since in all times and in all nations, gods and prophets were necessary to teach it to animalized man, and since man *alone* would have been powerless to discover it."

The syllogism continues: "Evil is done without effort, *naturally*, by fatality" (*OC* 2:715). It follows that the good must always be the result of "an art," because that takes effort. Hence Baudelaire's belief that makeup is a woman's right: "she must thus borrow from all the arts the means to lift herself above nature." In so doing, a woman should not try to imitate nature or the natural; *le maquillage* should, on the contrary, proudly admit to its artifice (*OC* 2:717). The essay on the beautiful, which precedes the one on makeup, applies the same perspective to art. The beautiful (*le beau*) comprises two parts: the eternal on the one hand, and a more relative, circumstantial element, "a period, style, moral, passion," on the other. Without this contemporary aspect, the beautiful, which Baudelaire compares to a "divine cake," would be indigestible (*OC* 2:685). The eternal aspect of art is thus both "veiled and expressed" by this duality, either by style or by particular temperament of the author. To explain this double aspect of art, Baudelaire alludes again to the *homo duplex* in Buffon's terms: "The duality of art is the fatal consequence of the duality of man." And, continuing in the naturalist's own dialectic, Baudelaire likens the eternal aspect of art to "the soul of art," and the variable element to "its body." For him, ultimately (despite a few disclaimers), the beautiful is best described by Stendhal: *le Beau n'est que la promesse du bonheur* (2:686). Perhaps that makes it a bit clearer why Baudelaire is so obsessed with *le beau*: dual in nature, eternal as well as present, it holds the promise of happiness. If the promise of goodness must always be broken, and if happiness in the human realm must always be disappointed, then at least the beautiful—which for Baudelaire means primarily art and literature[28]—can give a fleeting hope for joy.

What Baudelaire accomplishes in his endless considerations on dualities is, on the rhetorical level, twofold. First, he frequently analogizes them, as in the discussion of the beautiful, upon which he grafts Buffon's notion of soul and animality in man: the eternal aspect of the beautiful is like the soul, the variable (or contemporary) like the body. Such analogies proliferate. The other way in which Baudelaire manipulates dualities resembles antimetabole, the repetition of words in inverse order (I hate to love and I love to hate). But Baudelaire performs a conceptual antimetabole, a type of antimetathesis. The position of the antithesis is inverted, such that evil becomes natural and virtue artificial; makeup is more virtuous when caked on obviously than when pretending to be natural, and so forth. Baudelaire's dualities, in other words, manifest themselves in stylistic as well as conceptual contradiction and antimetabole, as if original sin were counterintuitive ("I was a baby and yet . . .") and one had to be forcibly reminded by wrenching everything palpable into its opposite, lest one lapse into unacceptable—because self-deluded—contentment.

We mentioned earlier the repercussions of original sin on Baudelaire's

---

28. And sometimes, though rarely, music. See especially Baudelaire's comments on Wagner: "Richard Wagner et *Tannhäuser* à Paris (*OC* 2:779–807) and "Encore quelques mots" (808–15). These comments led Nietzsche to remark that Baudelaire was "the first *intelligent* adherent of Wagner anywhere." *Ecce Homo*, ed. Walter Kaufmann (New York: Vintage, 1967), 248. It should be added, however, that Baudelaire's remarks have more to do with the idea of the *Gesammtkunstwerk*, akin to what he calls "correspondences," than they do with the intricacies of music (about which Baudelaire knew little). Significantly for our purposes here, Baudelaire believes that *Tannhäuser* "represents the struggle of the two principles that have chosen the human heart as their major battle field; that is, of the flesh with the spirit, of hell with heaven, of Satan with God." This is the duality we have been discussing throughout. But there is an unusual aspect to the constant dialectic in Baudelaire's reading of Wagner's opera. In the Overture, he writes, the voluptuous and the vulgar pleasures of the flesh dominate; then the religious theme gradually takes over, "slowly, by gradations, and absorbs the other in a calm victory, like that of the irresistible being over the sickly and unruly being; of Saint Michael over Lucifer" (*OC* 2:794). It is rare indeed in Baudelaire for Lucifer to surrender to Saint Michael, and in this sense music too provides Baudelaire with hope (even though there are times when Lucifer is Baudelaire's hero). It was Poe who said that music moves us if only briefly to an indeterminate glimpse of "glories beyond the grave." See "The Poetic Principle," in *Edgar Allan Poe: Selected Writings*, ed. David Galloway (Middlesex: Penguin, 1974), 505. The musicality of *Les fleurs du mal* is powerful and profound, but that is not the "music" to which Poe was referring. He meant, as Baudelaire does in his work on Wagner (including an enthusiastic letter to the composer), performed music. Baudelaire's death, said Wagner (who claimed to be amazed that a Frenchman could understand his music so well), was one of the two greatest sorrows in his life.

literary judgment with respect to Rousseau and Sand. His disappointment in Hugo's *Les misérables* is also directly related to belief in the inherent sinfulness of man. Hugo, writes Baudelaire with evident surprise, "is for Man, and yet not against God. He has confidence in God, and yet he is not against Man" (*OC* 2:224). These two sentences should be read as more than an attack on Rousseauism or a demonstration of Baudelaire's talent at antimetabole. Once again, they can only be understood in the light of Baudelaire's unshakable belief in original sin. If you are for Man, then you will certainly be against God. The most obvious example of this approach is Voltaire, for whom the earthquake in Lisbon proved that the notion of a loving God is grounded in incompatibility, given that the horrors of natural disasters can only have been produced by God's hand. If, on the other hand, you are for God, then you will believe that Man must necessarily deserve the tragedies that are visited upon him regularly.

The figure of antimetabole thus describes Hugo as neither a Voltaire who has given up on God, nor a Rousseau who "loves Man"; nor is Hugo an Augustinian, for whom the sin of Adam is that of humankind forever. Hugo rejects atheism, writes Baudelaire, but does not approve of bloodbaths; Hugo believes that "Man is born good" and yet, confronted with constant disasters, does not see in these "the ferocity and malice of God." So, concludes Baudelaire somewhat disingenuously, damning with counterintuitive (and very restrained) praise: "we think, along with the author, that *books of this kind are never without usefulness*" (*OC* 2:224). In any case, egotistical Happiness needs to be dragged by the hair occasionally by a "poet or philosopher" and have her nose rubbed in the blood and odor she produces. She should be scolded like a puppy (or, more likely in Baudelaire's case, kitten): "Look at what you did, and drink what you did!" Thus does Baudelaire try to find reasons to applaud a book that he hates, as his correspondence makes amply clear.[29] Moreover, to make his point he uses antimetabole—that figure of speech most favored by Joseph de Maistre, the highly conservative Catholic thinker (and brilliant stylist) who, Baudelaire claimed, had taught him "to think."

MAISTRE

Baudelaire began reading Joseph de Maistre between 1851 and 1852. As was often the case, Baudelaire was smitten (as he was, for example, upon

29. On August 10, 1862, Baudelaire writes to his mother, "Ce livre est immonde et inepte. J'ai montré, à ce sujet, que je possédais l'art de mentir" (Corr. 2:254).

first reading Poe or hearing Wagner's music).[30] First, conceptually, Maistre provides Baudelaire with a system for his notion of evil and of its inescapability: original sin, declares Maistre, is a notion that "explains everything, and without which nothing can be explained."[31] More chilling still, original sin is afflicted with repetition compulsion, for that sin of all sins "unfortunately repeats itself at every instant," according to Maistre's spokesman, the count, in *Les soirées de Saint-Pétersbourg*.[32] The problem has to do, precisely, with doubling. You will agree, says the count to his two interlocutors, that "every being that has the faculty of propagating itself can only produce a being similar to itself." Thus a "degraded" being (such as man, for example) cannot help but produce an equally degraded being. Children are doomed, and therefore "J-J Rousseau is the most dangerous sophist of his century" (54) because he thinks man is *by nature* good. (Baudelaire, as we have seen, will use almost the same logic to attack Jean-Jacques.) The advent of Darwin being yet several decades away (though what his effect on Maistre might have been is unclear at best), the count is able to add that Rousseau is also "completely devoid of real science, of wisdom, and especially of depth, with an apparent depth that lies entirely in words."

Maistre, that "soldier animated by the Holy Spirit," as Baudelaire called him (*OC* 2:526), writes virtually in aphorisms couched in powerful, almost muscular contradiction. It is a brilliant style, capable of intriguing the likes of Roland Barthes, for whom Maistre is the counterexample of what Barthes calls *le neutre*. For Barthes "the neutral" is that which escapes or confounds the paradigm of binaries. The neutral is "every inflection that, dodging or baffling the paradigmatic, oppositional structure of meaning, aims at the suspension of the conflictual basis of discourse."[33] The neutral, then, is that which shuns affirmation, arrogance, intolerance, even adjectives, and inclines rather toward silence, retreat, nuance, weariness, and answers that are "beside the point." Maistre's style is clearly

30. Several books have been written on Baudelaire and Maistre. See in particular Daniel Vouga, *Baudelaire et Joseph de Maistre* (Paris: Corti, 1957). See also Mother Mary Alphonsus, "The Influence of Joseph de Maistre on Baudelaire" (PhD diss., Bryn Mawr College, 1943). For a good discussion of Maistre's political ideas, including his influence on the Collège de sociologie, see Owen Bradley, *A Modern Maistre: The Social and Political Thought of Joseph de Maistre* (Lincoln: University of Nebraska Press, 1999).

31. Joseph de Maistre, *Les soirées de Saint-Pétersbourg*, 53. Henceforth cited as *Soirées*.

32. Maistre, that is, conflates actual sin with original sin. See in particular the discussion in "Deuxième entretien," *Soirées*, 53–55.

33. Roland Barthes, *The Neutral*, trans. Rosalind E. Krauss and Denis Hollier; ed. Thomas Clerc (New York: Columbia University Press, 2005), 211.

far from neutral, and appears as such in Barthes's study. If *the neutral* is
a concept that seeks "to baffle the arrogance of unity," the texts of Maistre magisterially perform such arrogance for the purpose of unicity in its
strictly Roman Catholic sense; indeed, the Council of Trent is Maistre's
guide to the "hyper-Augustiniansm" that infuses *Les soirées*. One can
imagine how Baudelaire, exhausted by his constant need for money, sug-
gestible in every domain, unsure in all matters save that of his own poetics (and that not always), would have been intoxicated by Maistre's uncompromising diction, not to mention his sureness of footing in matters
theological and in the ontology of evil. For if Maistre's style is grounded in
antimetabole, contradiction, and Socratic give-and-take, the thesis never
wavers: the master speaks and shows through syllogism and antinomies
that the only truth is that of Christianity—Roman Catholic and grounded
in the most pessimistic view possible of original sin.

Maistre, argues Antoine Compagnon, is one of the founders, with Chateaubriand, Baudelaire, and Nietzsche, of the "antimodern" tradition, as
Compagnon calls it—a tradition that for him "runs throughout modernity" and illustrates a "style of vehemence."[34] It was perhaps not so much
vehemence as the unremitting pessimism of his certainty that inspired
Baudelaire, as well as the continual binaries that infuse Maistre's dark
gaze upon the world.[35] One hears Maistrean echoes everywhere in Baudelaire, and not only concerning original sin. Man is *duplex* in Maistre: there
are two men in each man, one praising virtue, the other crime. Two men
who are not of the same opinion fight within the heart of one man. Contradiction is to be found everywhere, says Maistre, "since the universe in
its entirety obeys two forces." He insists that "evil has sullied everything,
and *all of man is nothing but a sickness*" *(Soirées*, 95). He draws a direct

34. Antoine Compagnon, *Les antimodernes: De Joseph de Maistre à Roland Barthes*
(Paris: Gallimard, 2005), 137.

35. Baudelaire was also familiar with other Maistre works, such as *Considérations sur la
France* (1794), which the Count in *Soirées* recommends to his audience (of two) as good reading! *Considérations* argues that the murder of the king during the French Revolution was just
such a sacrifice of an innocent for the sake of "the guilty" (the people, in other words) who
would not otherwise have fulfilled their obligation. Because Maistre believes in the divine
right of kings, the death of the king must be seen as expiation for the crimes of his people
and, hoped Maistre, prepares the way for the counterrevolution, which he was certain would
come. As we shall see, the death of Louis XVI is also a case of "reversibility" (in its Catholic,
theological sense) for Maistre. There is a universal dogma, writes Maistre, which explains why
the innocent must perish with the guilty: *"the reversibility of the pain of the innocent to the
profit of the guilty"* (emphasis Maistre's). Louis XVI's acceptance of this "dogma" is what may
save France, he adds. *Considérations sur la France* (Paris: Potey, Librairie de S.A.R. Monsei-
gneur, duc d'Angoulême, 1821), 53–54.

correlation between physical and moral ills: if there were no moral evil, he says, there would be no disease (his usual example is venereal disease; and Baudelaire, who suffered from syphilis from around the age of twenty, clearly responds to this sinister type of *correspondance*). Maistre's theory of "redemption through blood" (in capital letters in his text: SALUT PAR LE SANG) is almost Freudian in its notions of the threat of castration to maintain civilization, of circumcision as the vestigial remains of sacrifice, which is the basis of human connection with the divine. "Anywhere you see an altar," proclaimed Maistre, "there you will find civilization" (64). Freudian too (as in *Totem and Taboo* or *Moses and Monotheism*) is Maistre's idea that the secondary crime after the Fall, the crime that led to the Flood, was so terrible that we cannot remember or even imagine it. We live in the memory only of the guilt and the knowledge that we can never regain, physically or intellectually, the "golden age" before the Flood. In this way Maistre tribalizes original sin, and doubles it as well: the Fall, and then the crime leading to the Flood. If the Fall is inscribed in Genesis, the second crime is forever lost, along with the acumen man had achieved when God's anger wreaked the Flood—lost to consciousness, but not expunged.

Maistre's alarming notion of *réversibilité* had an important effect on the poet. "*The righteous,*" argues Maistre, underscoring the words, "*in suffering voluntarily, satisfies not only for himself,*[36] but for the guilty one by way of reversibility*" (*Soirées*, 255). This formula is repeated a few pages later, and the culprit is now also one "who could not otherwise have fulfilled his obligation" (*ne pourrait s'acquitter*; 268). Reversibility is the "faith of the universe" (316); it is a system of checks and balances; its economy is hydraulic (again, the Freud of the topographical unconscious springs to mind): it seeks equilibrium (that word returns). In thermodynamics, reversibility is a process that can be inverted to attain the same outcome; the system is returned to its original state. In that sense, one might describe the arc in Freud's *Beyond the Pleasure Principle* as reversibility. In its theological context for Maistre, reversibility obviously means the process by which original sin (partially, not totally, as in Paul)[37] is re-

36. Maistre uses *satisfaire* in the less usual sense of fulfilling an obligation or paying a debt, just as "satisfy" can be used in English.

37. Maistre's entire discussion on reversibility seems to rely on Romans 5:6–24. In particular, Paul says, "For just as by the one man's disobedience the many were made sinners, so by the one man's obedience the many will be made righteous" (5:19). Reversibility is supposed to work, then, in both directions: sin and grace. Maistre, however, and his admirer Baudelaire seem concerned only with the former. Baudelaire is frequently said to have (fully)

versed; but it also has a monetary economy: you owe by heredity; you pay because even if you are innocent yourself, you have inherited sin; when you pay despite such innocence, you erase the debt of another guilty party. Thus within the Maistrean universe, it is because man is by nature evil that innocence can be no refuge from suffering—on the contrary. "Men have always known that innocence will never satisfy crime," declares Maistre, "and they have moreover believed that there is an expiating force in blood, such that *life*, which is blood, could ransom (*racheter*) another *life*" (272). Ransom (*racheter* literally means "to buy back"), the satisfying of a debt, the fulfillment of an obligation, reversibility itself—this is the lexicon of debt and payment. In Maistre, redemption can be (provisionally) bought with the spilling of innocent blood.

Pichois points out that reversibility itself is less and less used in Catholicism and "has never been at the center of Catholic theology . . . because of its 'juridical,' indeed 'mercantile' slipperiness, which can make it dangerous" (*OC* 1:915). Dangerous, perhaps, but telling in the Maistrean context. The unfinished *Soirées de Saint-Pétersbourg* were published in 1821, just after the author's death. Given the rise of industrialization, capitalism, the new urban centers (developments that Maistre loathed), it is worth noting the extent to which the lexicon of these changes in the fabric of European culture creep into Maistre's willfully ancien-régime and preindustrial perspective. Maistre hates the French Revolution but believes that God's hand is more evident there than in any other human event. If during the Revolution "the Divinity employs the vilest of instruments," it is only because it is "punishing in order to regenerate."[38] He adds that in the Revolution, "God is advancing to avenge the iniquity that the inhabitants of the world have committed against Him."[39] Maistre's is then a scorched-earth theology, one that sees punishment as necessary to set man aright; one that promises redemption through the blood of sacrifice; one that in monetary metaphors formulates original sin as a debt that can never be "satisfied." Reversibility itself partakes in the economy of exchange although, as we saw with Baudelaire's own notion of origi-

---

acknowledged sin but not redemption; Maistre seems to be the inspiration for this harsh point of view. It should be added that the dominant question in *Soirées* seems also largely taken from Romans 5, where the question of original sin, justice, and the righteous is constant. Paul, unlike Maistre, concentrates on reconciliation and exultation in God. Biblical references are to The New Revised Standard Version (Oxford, 1989).

38. *C'est qu'elle punit pour régénérer.* From *Considérations sur la France*, in Joseph de Maistre, *Du Pape et extraits d'autres œuvres*, ed. E. M. Cioran (Monaco, 1957), 196.

39. E. M. Cioran, *On the Heights of Despair*, trans. Ilinca Zaripol-Johnston (Chicago: University of Chicago Press, 1992), 18.

nal sin, the evil that begins with the Fall and is repeated by the "crime" that brings on the Flood is so great for Maistre that expiation is impossible, even if redemption through blood seems, in his text, to offer a better chance at the Last Judgment. Reversibility, then, is going in the right direction as it were, but will never really get back to the point of origin that would allow for an erasure of the Fall. The debt, to repeat, can never be fully satisfied; but the coin of that realm is blood and, it strangely follows, it "is divine" (*Entretien* 7, in *Soirées*) The adjective "divine," as the philosopher Emile Cioran points out, is Maistre's favorite, modifying everything from the Revolution, to hereditary monarchy, the constitution, and the papacy.

Needless to say, "reversibility" is how Maistre understands the crucifixion. Moreover, the murder of Louis XVI seems for Maistre to be a distant reminder of the Passion—again, a sacrifice necessary for helping to reverse the sins of man.[40] As Georges Bataille puts it (after citing Maistre admiringly), "When the executioner shows the head of the monarch to the crowd, he is attesting to the perpetration of a crime; but at the same time, by baptizing the assembly with royal blood, he is communicating to that assembly the saintly virtue of the beheaded sovereign."[41] And Klossowski at the Collège de sociologie says that the moment the king's head is cut off, "*in the eyes of Sade as in those of Joseph de Maistre* and all the ultramontanes, it is the representative of God who is dying; and it is the blood of the temporal representative of God. . . . [For Maistre and other] counterrevolutionaries, Catholic philosophers . . . Louis expiates the sins of the nation" (Hollier, *Le Collège*, 520). Cioran writes in his introduction to an anthology of Maistre's works that the more one reads him, "the more one yearns for the delights of skepticism or for the urgency of a plea for heresy" (*Joseph de Maistre*, 61). Maistre, adds Cioran, never bores us, in part because he has not been domesticated by being fully understood. He is a "monster" who "lifted the smallest problem to the level of paradox and to the dignity of scandal, handling anathema with a cruelty mixed with fervor" (9).

But such a combination—cruelty and fervor—is precisely what had to appeal to the older, no longer left-leaning, pessimistic, and increasingly sick Baudelaire. The poem "Réversibilité" (1853), directly inspired by Maistre's grim view of that term, ends with the dying biblical David try-

---

40. Maistre, however, feels strongly that Louis was insufficiently assertive once imprisoned. See *Considérations sur la France*.

41. Denis Hollier, *Le Collège de sociologie* (Paris: Gallimard, 1995), 563.

ing to sap the angel's strength. The "Ange" of the poem (Mme Sabatier, one of Baudelaire's great loves) is full of the joy of light, health, and beauty. The poem rather unkindly accuses her of indifference and an ignorance of hatred, illness, wrinkles, and despair; of an inability to know shame, remorse, ennui.[42] The angel, in other words, is guilty of too easy a happiness, and David would take her innocence and health to save himself. The narrator of the poem, by contrast, presents himself as letting the angel off easy: "But what I implore of you, angel, is merely your prayers" (OC 1:44–5). While David is ready to deploy what Pichois calls the "juridical" and "mercantile" aspect of reversibility (1:915), the narrator is more generous, as he would have it, in asking "only" for intercession. Much like "Les litanies de Satan," the poem "Réversibilité" uses catechistic concepts and incantatory repetitions reminiscent of the Mass in a context that confounds expectation. Here, the angel is the woman the narrator loves, and the intercession he seeks from her is freedom from the pain caused by vices too powerful to allow for happiness, yet helpless to erase ennui.

If Baudelaire admired Maistre, the poet Vigny vigorously attacked him, calling Maistre an *ésprit falsificateur*, a "falsifying mind." Vigny vituperatively singles out precisely "the fatal theory of *reversibility* and of *redemption through blood*,"[43] and accuses Maistre of having found this theory in Origen, who, as the Pléiade edition of Baudelaire primly notes, "did not, as we know, have the odor of sanctity" (1:914).[44] Vigny's analogy with Origen

42. Similarly, in the poem "A celle qui est trop gaie," also to Madame Sabatier, the narrator sees her as overly cheerful and healthy, and wants to come to her one night to infuse her with his venom (OC 1:156–57). The poem was among those declared obscene during the 1857 trial of Les Fleurs du mal, and banned from the collection.

43. "Dark mind, falsifying mind; I do not say false, for he [Maistre] was aware of the truth." Alfred de Vigny, Stello, la deuxième consultation du Docteur-Noir, scènes du désert, ed. M. Fernand Baldensperger (Paris: Louis Conard, 1925), 180. An entire chapter is devoted to lambasting Maistre in Stello, "Sur la substitution des souffrances expiatoires," 189–95. Another chapter (37) in Stello is entitled "Perpetual Ostracism" and is equally devoted to an attack on Maistre. Baudelaire himself, in his Études sur Poe, mentions that Vigny had written a book (Stello) "to show that the place of the poet is neither in a republic, nor in an absolute monarchy, nor in a constitutional monarchy, and nobody has answered him" (OC 2:250). One critic thinks Stello may have been Baudelaire's introduction to Maistre, along with Sainte-Beuve's review (June 2, 1851, in Lundi IV, 192–216) of Maistre's Lettres et opuscules. See Margaret Gilman, Baudelaire the Critic (New York: Octogon Books, 1971), 63.

44. Vigny points out that for Origen there are two kinds of redemption, that of Christ, which ransoms the universe, and those "diminished redemptions" which save nations through payment in blood (Stello, 190); whence, we may assume, Maistre's own notions of reversibility. Vigny himself came to believe that the scapegoats for the supporters of capital punishment were none other than the poets. See Baldensperger's notes in Stello, 423–24. Maistre, writes

is in any case rather misleading, since the latter had a notion of free will quite absent in Maistre. More to the point however, is that Maistre has, since Vigny, been adopted—or at least cited—as one of the precursors of modernity, precisely because of his excesses.

Maistre's work was read and discussed at the Collège de sociologie, and it seems more than probable that Bataille's interest in sacrifice was influenced at least as much by Maistre as by Durkheim (indeed, Bataille's *acéphale* was doubtless inspired by Maistre's view of the guillotined Louis). It is worth repeating that Cioran wrote a long introduction to an anthology he produced of Maistre's most (in)famous works; that Roland Barthes considers Maistre at length in *Le neutre*; and, more recently, that Antoine Compagnon includes Maistre as a poster child for what Compagnon calls the *anti-modernes*. In all of these cases, it is the vehemence of Maistre's style that seems to attract these theorists of the "modern," of which Maistre is Exhibit A. If, as Cioran puts it, Maistre was known as the "prophet of the past" at the end of the nineteenth century (as he was by the disgusted Vigny), such a label was a luxury of sorts which that era could well afford, steeped as it was in "liberal illusion." But today he is "ours" again, continues Cioran, writing in the middle of the twentieth century, given that "he was a 'monster' and that it is precisely because of the odious aspect of his doctrines that he is living, that he is contemporary" (*Joseph de Maistre*, 9). Maistre, then, because of his vehemence, intolerance, incomprehensibility (Is he being ironic, asks Cioran? Can he possibly mean this?), and sheer excess (Bataille was to be his descendent in this logic), is dubbed one of the forefathers of modernity by late modernity itself. It would be tempting (and has been for many readers of Maistre), to say that the modern period shares with Maistre a certain violence and a concomitant nostalgia for certainty; but such a view is not entirely accurate.

I think Cioran is right when he says we can no longer afford the luxury of seeing Maistre as the prophet of the past; even more clear-sighted, perhaps, is Isaiah Berlin's conviction that Maistre is not casting nostalgic glances to the past so much as he is looking to the future, with a "pro-

---

Vigny, was one of the most brilliant philosophical minds Europe has produced, and with his doctrine of sacrifice produces the "most immoral" of ideas, the "source of all crime." No argument, adds Vigny, is worth "a single drop of blood. This is a theory for assassins" (424).

As to the comment in the Pléiade edition, which alludes to the Origenist crises that ensued from that theologian's writings, it should be said that Origen probably had the "smell of sainthood" more than most, since he was the teacher of, and friend to, a remarkable number of scholars who were later canonized.

tofascist" gaze.[45] But like Cioran, Berlin sees another, if related, "modernity" in Maistre as well: Maistre, by bringing out "those huge, socially irrational factors," anticipates Freud and Marx and writes, says Berlin, about
things "which certainly were not suspected or dreamt of in most of the
writings of the eighteenth century." And Berlin concludes, "In this sense
he is a kind of modern thinker, because he really did rip open certain aspects of social reality which were only hinted at obscurely before" (25). No
longer the "prophet of the past," Maistre is rather the terrible hint of the
future, which, while he could never have dreamt of its horrors, did "provide the material out of which it could ultimately be constructed" (26).
Even if the twentieth century—well before the horrors to which Berlin is
alluding—does not share Maistre's hyper-Augustinian obsession with sin,
it understands Maistre's fascination with evil and his conviction that it
is irremediably pervasive in the human being. The other aspect of Maistre's thinking that appeals to the modern period is his consistently anti-
Enlightenment stance. Horkheimer and Adorno may dismiss him as "a
true son of the Church if ever there was one," but they obviously feel com-
pelled to mention him, even if mainly for the purpose of deriding his misogyny.[46] Somehow, there is something of Maistre that appeals to a later
age, and it is not pretty. It is not by chance that Berlin sees him as the
precursor of Freud, for Maistre views man as filled, Berlin contends, with
"black instincts" that nothing will "ever finally quell," and with original
sin, that "nothing can ultimately exterminate" (12).

Bataille and Caillois, in the late 1930s, are particularly influenced by
Maistre's (again, infamous) notion of the executioner. For Maistre, the executioner is an "extraordinary being" who exists by dint of a "FIAT from the
power of creation" (*Soirées*, 40). Maistre, unsurprisingly, highly approves
of the executioner (*bourreau*). The moment you remove this "incomprehensible agent," says the Count in the *Soirées de Saint-Pétersbourg*, "order
is replaced by chaos, thrones are damaged, and society disappears" (41). As
Berlin notes, Maistre's imagination "swings between two extremes—on
one side extreme punishment and terror, on the other side chaos" ("Second

45. Isaiah Berlin, "Two Enemies of the Enlightenment, 3, The Second Onslaught: Joseph
de Maistre and Open Obscurantism" (unpublished lecture; see the Isaiah Berlin Virtual Library, http://berlin.wolf.ox.ac.uk/lists/nachlass/maistre.pdf), 1–26. It was the third of four
Woodbridge Lectures delivered in 1965 at Columbia University. See also "Joseph de Maistre
and the Origins of Fascism," in Berlin's *The Crooked Timber of Humanity: Chapters in the
History of Ideas*, ed. Henry Hardy (Princeton: Princeton University Press, 1998).
46. See Max Horkheimer and Theodor W. Adorno, *Dialectic of Enlightenment*, trans. John
Cumming (New York: Continuum, 1998), 248.

Onslaught," 20). Maistre himself declares, as cited by Berlin, "God who is the author of sovereignty, is also that of punishment; he has cast our earth upon these two poles; 'for Jehovah is the master of the twin poles, and upon them he maketh turn the world'" (ibid.). Again, one senses here Baudelaire's attraction to Maistre, and not only because of the Maistrean formulation of polar opposites as the basis of this world. There is also the matter of terror and punishment.

As any biography of Baudelaire points out, and as his poetry overwhelmingly attests, he is obsessed with both terror and punishment incarnated by his military, severe, and unforgiving stepfather, General Aupick. Punishment for Baudelaire is patriarchal in origin (Aupick or God), and one senses that the "crime" of humanity to which Maistre so often refers—that crime so terrible that we have "forgotten" it—is for Baudelaire (as it would be for Freud) a form of patricide. Indeed, as many Baudelaire scholars have remarked, the revolution of '48 has the poet, by more than one account, joyously announcing "We have to shoot General Aupick!"[47] As was so often the case with Baudelaire, however, his fears immobilized him, Hamlet-like. More obviously still, what is original sin if not disobeying the father/Father? There is throughout the Baudelaire corpus a desire to escape patriarchal law, though the "revolt" is usually, as if in a parody of Swedenborg, the same system inverted. The apostrophe "O Satan!" in the poem "Les litanies de Satan" is a prayer to a patriarch of a different realm, but a potent one nonetheless: the last lines of the poem refer to Satan as the "adoptive father" as against "God the Father" (OC 1:125).[48] Rebellion, in Baudelaire, more often than not recapitulates blind obedience as a mirror image. The litanies to Satan invert the Mass, and the prayer praises the devil; but we do not need deconstruction to recognize the same hegemony of male power and sovereignty. And as the poem "Le reniement de saint Pierre" savagely puts it, God is like "a tyrant gorged on meat and

47. On the evening of February 24, 1848, "Jules Buisson encounters Baudelaire at the Buci intersection, rifle in hand, which he has just fired, screaming as if in a refrain: 'We have to go shoot General Aupick'" (Corr. 1:xxxvi). The anecdote cannot be confirmed but seems very likely and is reported as such by Pichois.

48. Walter Benjamin sees in the figure of Satan here the "dark head of Blanqui." Louis-Auguste Blanqui (1805–81) was a socialist theorist and revolutionary. Inspired by Marx, Saint-Simon, Fournier, and the revolutionary Babeuf, he was frequently imprisoned from 1831 to 1870. Blanqui was the leader of the proletarian movement in the revolution of 1848. Benjamin also reminds the reader that Satan himself is doubled in Baudelaire: citing Jules Lemaître, Benjamin notes that Satan is either the "author of all evil" or "the great vanquished, the great victim." Benjamin's note reads, "Jules Lemaître, Les contemporains, 4th series (Paris, 1895), 30." The Writer of Modern Life, 56.

wine, falling asleep to the sweet sounds of our hideous blasphemies" (*OC*
1:121).[49] There is no question, in Baudelaire, that man is a sinner; but it is
equally clear that God is a despot who considers ("no doubt") the sobs of
martyrs and condemned criminals "an intoxicating symphony" (ibid.).

The executioner can himself be doubled—doubling being a recurring
gesture in Maistre—echoed by his admirer Baudelaire, as we have been noting. Every wicked person (*méchant*) must be, "by virtue of natural laws" a
self-tormenter; he is both executioner and victim. Taking his cue no doubt
from a comedy by Terence of the same name, Maistre calls such a figure
a Heauton Timorumenos (99).[50] Maistre uses this notion in his continued
discussion about why the wicked so often fare well while the good are frequently punished. The wicked, declares Maistre, citing Berthier,[51] (and an
unacknowledged French proverb) "seem to have the privilege of HEALTH
AND A VERY LONG LIFE" (100).[52] Heauton Timorumenos, a term from Terence by way of Menander, is also found in de Quincey (from a passage
Baudelaire did not translate), as well as in a posthumously published text
by the ever-cautious (and hypocritical) Sainte-Beuve. The latter holds that
poets, in addition to life's usual sorrows, are given "a trumpet and a goad."
They take pleasure, he writes, in pricking themselves in the flank with
the goad so they can blow their trumpets more frequently; and he adds,
in parentheses, "*Héautontimorouménos, self-tormenter*," the usual English translation used by de Quincey.[53] It is unlikely that Baudelaire knew
about the de Quincey source, and the Sainte-Beuve remark was not published until 1934; but Baudelaire certainly knew about Maistre's passage
in *Les soirées de Saint-Pétersbourg*.

The poem "L'Héautontimorouménos" (1855) is explicit, embodying

49. This poem, and this line in particular, are often thought, in Baudelaire studies, to pay
homage to Proudhon. As we will have occasion to see later in this chapter, Proudhon has similar views on God. See, e.g., Lois Boe Hyslop, "Baudelaire, Proudhon, and 'Le reniement de saint
Pierre,'" *French Studies* 30, no. 3 (1976): 273–86. Such views are also to be found in Lamartine's
poem "Le désespoir," where God is an unfeeling tyrant who spawns misery. The depiction of
God is similar in Edward Young's "Night Thoughts."

50. Terence derives his idea for this play from Menander. See, e.g., Lawrence Richardson Jr.,
"The Terentian Adaptation of the *Heauton Timorumenos* of Menander," *Greek, Roman, and
Byzantine Studies* 46 (2006): 13–36.

51. Guillaume-François Berthier, an eighteenth-century Jesuit and philosophy professor,
was violently opposed to the *encyclopédistes*, thus incurring the wrath of Voltaire, among others. No wonder Maistre admires "Father Berthier," as he calls him.

52. The French proverb: "Les méchants vivent longtemps" (the wicked live a long life).

53. See the Pichois notes in *OC* 1:985. I might add that it is hard not to hear a nasty *ressen-
timent* in Sainte-Beuve's condescending comments about poets: Baudelaire, while certainly
given to goading himself, was shortly after his death increasingly recognized as a writer of
genius—a stature Sainte-Beuve knew he himself would never attain.

and thus externalizing self-torture: "I am the wound and the knife! / I am the slap and the cheek! / I am the members and the wheel! / I am the victim and the executioner!" (*OC* 1:79). The exclamation points seem to cut through the page with the poem's knife. The Heauton Timorumenos is twinned, like the fratricidal brothers in "Le gâteau," or like Cain and Abel (subjects of one of the three "revolt" poems), or like Satan himself. At the beginning of "L'Héautontimorouménos" the narrator indifferently states that he will beat the beloved woman (one assumes),[54] as a butcher pounds meat and as Moses struck the rock with his rod to get water. This jarring juxtaposition (the butcher and Moses) is concretized in the figure of the narrator who will strike at the woman's eye until her tears have quenched his thirst in his private "Sahara." Butcher and Moses are combined as the pounding of the eyelid (*la paupière*), which is in turn combined with the rod to get tears in a desert bearing no relation to that of Moses; the poem gives us a willed catachretic series. The language is sexually charged: the narrator's desire, swollen with hope, grows with the thought of doing harm, knowing it "will swim on [your] salted cries." The sadism of the first three stanzas is precise and calculated. Only the adjective *chers* (dear, beloved), modifying sobs in the third stanza, begins to unravel the cold voice of willful harm. As Georges Blin notes, "The sadism here consists, not only in taunting the other, but also in holding him in bondage, in a position of painful impotency."[55]

The next stanza is the *volta*, for the narrator turns to himself: "Am I not," he asks, "a false note in the divine symphony?" Voracious Irony, he says, "is shaking and biting me," such that the narrator (playing on the feminine of the noun *ironie*) is now the victim of that allegorical female figure. Irony (in itself a form of doubling) is a black poison in the narrator's voice and blood. The tables have been clearly turned on the narrator, who is now being submitted to torture by a woman, even if an allegorical one. The next line literalizes the two sides of the Heauton Timorumenos: "I am,"

54. And assume is the best one can do. Crépet, Pommier, and Pichois have all spilled a great deal of ink trying to uncover the woman by whose initials the poem is dedicated ("J.G.F."), but there is nothing in the poem that proves it is a woman; we have only Baudelaire's obviously heterosexual proclivities to go by.

55. Georges Blin, *Le sadisme de Baudelaire*, 28. For the use of psychoanalytic theory in approaching Baudelaire, see Charles Mauron, *Le dernier Baudelaire*, and Mehlman, "Baudelaire with Freud / Theory and Pain," 7–13. In *Baudelaire and Freud*, Bersani calls Blin's study "intelligent if limited" with respect to the connection between Sade and Baudelaire. That erotic pleasure leads to crime, says Bersani, is a notion worth pursuing in both writers (89n). See also Bersani's critique of Mauron and Mehlman (136–47). Bersani reads "L'Héautontimorouménos" in conjunction with Freud and the death instinct (99–105).

says the narrator, "the sinister mirror in which the shrew sees herself." He
sees himself, in other words, as the woman Irony, that shrew who looks
back at him in the mirror as if the very distance she provides made any
genuine passion except that of wanting to do harm impossible. There follows "I am the wound and the knife." The last stanza continues the can-
nibalizing aspect of the Heauton Timorumenos: the narrator tells us that
he is the vampire of his own heart, condemned to eternal laughter, but no
longer able to smile—a horrible irony, which takes over his body and identity in the mirror. The self-tormenter, who in Terence is a mildly comical figure, becomes here the personification of evil's (literal) double-edged
sword.

If Baudelaire delineates a fairly clear dialectic—ascent toward God
versus descent toward the devil, if he then complicates it by the apparent oxymoron of the "joy of descent" and makes everything reabsorbed by
the omnipresent evil, here evil itself splits into another dialectic: sadism
against the other becomes sadism against the self. The narrator sees himself in the mirror as the goddess of the black poison of humor, which we
know from "L'essence du rire" to be "one of the clearest of man's satanic
signs and one of the numerous seeds in the symbolic apple" (OC 2:530). He
is then Eve *and* Adam, tempting himself with his own evil and harming
himself, by his very nature, as he had cruelly planned to harm his beloved
at the poem's outset. Not only are dualities everywhere, but gender is inverted (as in a mirror image) as are love and self-preservation.[56] The Heauton Timorumenos is like a snake biting its own tail, poisoning itself with
its own being even as it prides itself on poisoning the beloved.

But let us return to Maistre: his notion of the executioner as a figure
of fear remains the passage by far the most commented upon in the Maistrean opus. Berlin's cautionary lectures aside, the Collège de sociologie
was, as we have noted, clearly fascinated with Maistre. Bataille, for example, speaks at length and admiringly of Maistre's take on the executioner:
Maistre, he says, gives an impressive portrait of the executioner, of the
terror he inspires, "and rightly signals that such a living acme of abjection
comprises, at the same time, the condition and underpinnings of all greatness, of all power, of all subordination." After citing Maistre—"'It is the
horror and the link of the human association'"—Bataille continues, "One
could not explicate by a more successful formula the extent to which the

56. The argument I am making that Baudelaire is both figures at once contrasts to Benjamin's notion that Baudelaire's "soul is that of Adam, to whom Eve (the world) once upon a
time offered the apple, from which he ate" (*The Writer of Modern Life*, 27).

executioner constitutes the integral and antithetical pair that makes for the *horror* and *link* of this same association" (Hollier, *Collège*, 562–63). Caillois produces a "sociology of the executioner" based on Maistre's vision of that figure and inspired by the death of Anatole Deibler, a state executioner.[57] Caillois's work, especially in his notion of the pure and impure and the double meaning of sacred (taboo and transgression), deploys Maistre as "a major reference" (ibid., 122). Finally, as we have seen, Klossowski discusses the decapitation of Louis XVI, which, for Maistre, marks the death of God: "Louis expiates the sins of the nation" (ibid., 520). In other words, despite Maistre's strange reactionary opinions and fantastic sense of "history" (the Flood, a primitive golden age, a superior language now dead but the fragments of which remain in our etymologies, etc.), the major figures of the Collège are clearly drawn to Maistre's visions of excess. Sacrifice, ritual, religious fervor, blood as redemption, the king as a representative of the divine—these are questions that obsess the Collège in its search for "meaning" and, more to the point, in its attempts to understand the sacred as antinomous.[58] The Collège, attempting to continue the work of Durkheim but also simply to meet together, given the sinister and increasing political tensions (these lectures, after all, take place in 1938 and 39), tries to comprehend the sacred, ritual, and the contradictory bonds that make for "human associations." For the Collège, Maistre seems to be the voice of a budding modernity, one that seeks religion in the violence of sacrifice and the sacred in incomprehensible contradiction. It is as yet too early for Berlin's vision that Maistre also displays a different kind of horror, that of protofascism; and yet as Cioran remarked, the more one reads Maistre, the more one senses the urgent need for heresy.

But that is not Baudelaire's Maistre, although certainly Maistre's take on evil can only have resonated with the poet, who—despite being one of the first (but not the first) to coin the term "modernity" and "the modern"—was not himself entirely a modern. As Cioran himself admits, Baudelaire uses Maistre to fuel his own obsessions, and overturns Mais-

---

57. Diebler (1863–1939) was "famous" for having beheaded four hundred people.

58. Freud's (questionable but interesting) etymological work on *das Unheimliche* is worth recalling here. Freud notes that the word, meaning "uncanny," can also mean its opposite. In this he is strongly influenced by the work of Karl Abel and his notion that the Egyptian hieroglyphics can be read to mean their opposite (Abel writing before the discovery of the Rosetta Stone). See Freud's essay "The Antithetical Meaning of Primal Words," in *The Standard Edition of the Complete Psychological works of Sigmund Freud*, ed. and trans. James Strachey (London: Hogarth Press, 1957), 11:153–61. Henceforth cited as *SE*. See also "The Uncanny," *SE* 17:219–52. So too, Caillois for example, is intrigued by Maistre's idea that the criminal can desacralize himself (Hollier, *Le Collège de sociologie*, 369).

trean motifs by intensifying them and by giving them the characteristic of
"lived negativity" (*Joseph de Maistre*, 57). Before he read Maistre, Baudelaire already had a kind of *satanisme* in place. I have already described
the long verse prayer to Satan, "Les litanies de Satan," as an inverted lit-
urgy, with the poet serving as priest in his recitation of invocations. The
antiphonic structure ("Ô Satan, prends pitié de ma longue misère," as in
"Lord, hear my prayer."), followed by an outright prayer, mimes even as
it overturns, the structure of the Mass. The poem may have been written
as early as 1848. Antoine Adam reads the line on Satan as the inventor of
gunpowder as evidence that the revolution of '48 was on the poet's mind
(*OC* 1:1086). But *satanisme*, as Baudelaire employs the term, increasingly
becomes (to return to my earlier phrase) an embrace-your-fate, literal, if
narrow reading of Maistre: if evil is all we can depend on, then it follows
that it is stronger than the good, and its lord is therefore the master. "Capital punishment," opines Baudelaire in *Mon cœur mis à nu*, is the result of
a mystical idea, totally misunderstood today" (*OC* 1:683). Pichois's note
states the obvious: Maistre was someone who did understand it (1494).
Baudelaire's entry continues with evident Maistrean discipleship: capital
punishment is not intended to *save* society, at least not materially; it is intended to save both society and the culprit spiritually. For the sacrifice to
be "perfect," the victim must be fully conscious: for to administer chloro-
form to the condemned "would be an impiety, since it would remove from
him the consciousness of his greatness as victim and abolish his chances
of reaching heaven" (683).

There is a certain bleak irony in Baudelaire here and in other Maistrean passages; but if the concrete thinking the later Baudelaire chooses
to perform on Maistre's text is meant to shock, it is also a cry of despair.
Given the pervasiveness of antinomies and contradiction (hence, dualities) in Baudelaire, it is hardly surprising that he was attracted, not only
to Maistre's strength of purpose (which Baudelaire generally lacked), but
also to his dialectical style and, finally, to his apparent certainty.[59] "Even
as a small child," says Baudelaire in the same journal, "I felt two contradictory emotions in my heart: the horror of life and the ecstasy of life."
The contradiction, he adds, is the result of being a "lazy man of nervous
disposition" (*un paresseux nerveux*). It is a description that adds a physical
contradiction to the mental one. And we may conclude that it is Maistre's

59. Pichois notes that Baudelaire's early attraction to Fourier similarly comes from the
latter's dogmatic style, which "is precisely the one Baudelaire loved, especially during his
youth." Claude Pichois, *Baudelaire: Études et témoignages* (Neuchatel: La Bacconnière, 1967),
102.

notion of original sin that helps give a grounding to Baudelaire's abstract notions of evil and makes Baudelaire's tormenting antinomies into a theological politics of inevitability.

PROUDHON'S SPIRITS OF CONTRADICTION

Critics generally concur that until around 1852, Baudelaire was primarily influenced by Proudhon, the socialist theoretician called the father of anarchism and the writer whom Marx briefly considered to be the brightest hope for French communism. And most critics agree that after '52, Baudelaire was under the sway of Joseph de Maistre, that sociologist of original sin, as he was dubbed by many. At first glance, as already noted, there can only be a large divide between Proudhon and de Maistre. Despite their proclivity for antinomy, the two could not be farther apart in political and philosophical temperament: Proudhon to the left, and Maistre magisterially to the extreme right. But as Pichois puts it, "Whether theology or socialism, Baudelaire appreciated as a connoisseur the great scholarly philosophical machines" (*Etudes et témoignages*, 103). If Baudelaire was throughout his life attracted to irresolvable dualities, it is unsurprising that he gravitated toward these two writers, both of whom founded their rhetoric on contradiction. "Only great and dangerous contradictions betoken a rich spiritual life," proclaims Cioran in a particularly sentimental passage (*On the Heights of Despair*, 39). But where the "spirit" may lie in Proudhon's willful contradictions is far from clear.

Indeed, Maistre and Proudhon, figures of opposite extremes in political thought, have curious similarities. Though they both use contradiction as a modus operandi, Maistre's is Socratic,[60] and Proudhon's a version (very reductive, not to say plain wrong) of Hegelian dialectics—mostly because Proudhon believed his role to be the delineation of contradiction, which his thought would then brilliantly overcome.[61] The insistence on antinomy in both writers, in any case, was no doubt a large, if unconscious,

60. Socratic, that is, as in the dialogs of the *Soirées*, the work I have emphasized because it is the one that most influenced Baudelaire. *Considérations sur la France* was probably more influential in France as a whole, given that it is the French equivalent of Burke's *French Revolution*. But Baudelaire, acquainted with the spectrum of Maistre's work, was most interested in the theological and philosophical consequences of Maistre's views expounded in the *Soirées*.

61. Croce rather amusingly describes Marx's use of the Hegelian dialectic as "glimmerings" from Germany that reached Proudhon in France. Croce adds that such glimmerings "suggested to [Proudhon] the critique of economic contradictions, with thesis, antithesis, and a synthesis that, for him as well, in its own way, was anarchic." Benetto Croce, *Histoire de l'Europe au dix-neuvième siècle*, trans. Henri Bedarida (Paris: Plon, 1959), 159.

measure of their appeal to our dualism-obsessed poet. Like Maistre, Proudhon (ultimately) hates Rousseau, Hugo, Vigny, and Lamartine. Both men
were Freemasons, though Maistre was active only in his youth and more
or less abandoned the group later, and Proudhon never "practiced."[62] Moreover, despite Proudhon's antireligious views, there is a good deal of God
talk in his work. Proudhon's tutor in German philosophy, Karl Grün, and
Marx himself both conclude, upon reading *Le système des contradictions
économiques*, that the work has the distinct odor of religion.[63]

Indeed, Proudhon begins that work by bemoaning the idea of God:
"humanity thus fatally assumes the existence of God." We need a new
religion however, in which God, as hypothesis, is recognized as the infinite aspect of man. The hypothesis of God, says Proudhon, is more piti-
less than ever. But then he adds, in a passage that must have resonated
with a younger Baudelaire, "We have arrived at one of those fateful epochs
in which society, contemptuous of the past and tormented by the future,
sometimes frenetically embraces the present . . . and at other times, crying
out to God from the abyss of its pleasures, asks for a sign of salvation, or
looks in the spectacle of its revolutions, as if in the entrails of a victim, for
the secret of its destiny."[64] It is hard to imagine a more fitting description
of Baudelaire's views in the mid-1840s.

Like Maistre, Proudhon's lexicon is heavily indebted to religion, even
if his points are diametrically opposed to Maistre's. Noah appears, though
as a "legend" (whereas Maistre, as we have seen, takes the Flood quite
literally). Proudhon has *anathemas* and threatens with "excommunication"; the economy is "apocalyptic;" property is "the religion of monop-

---

62. See Pierre Haubtmann's exhaustive and voluminous biography, *Pierre-Joseph Proudhon: Sa vie et sa pensée 1809–1849* (Paris: Beauchesne, 1982), 564. Proudhon was inducted
into the Freemasons in January of 1847.

63. Marx was later to regret Grün's work with Proudhon. First, he warned the Frenchman
of Grün's "arrogance," but things quickly got worse. In a letter to Proudhon (May 5, 1846),
Marx writes that Grün is nothing but a "knight of the literary industry," a charlatan who is
dangerous and a parasite to boot. When Marx sends Engels to Paris in August of the same year,
it is for the specific purpose of reining Proudhon in and discrediting Grün. The latter, Engels
writes to Marx a month later, "has done enormous harm." The main thing Grün had done, it
would seem, was to confuse Proudhon's thoughts and to stir them up into a kind of literary
idealism and series of vague reveries. The result, writes Engels to Marx, is that "there reigns
here a confusion beyond compare" (Haubtmann, *Proudhon*, 617–39). Haubtmann concludes
from all this that "Marx could never stand a rival" (620). Nevertheless, the "damage" was
done, and Proudhon continued his interest in "literary" abstractions. His philosophical prow-
ess, however, was clearly unconvincing, as Marx quite correctly realized. Proudhon's confusion and vague reveries, in other words, were not solely the fault of the hapless Grün.

64. P.-J. Proudhon, *Système des contradictions économiques, ou Philosophie de la misère*,
3rd ed., 2 vols. (Paris: Librairie internationale, 1867), 1:20. Henceforth cited as *SC*.

oly"; Christ is the allegory for justice; the Republic is "divine" (a word
favored by Proudhon almost as much as by Maistre); and so on. Socialism
in Proudhon's text is frequently allied with other religions (as against the
more dominant Roman Catholicism, which naturally provides the majority of the spiritual tropes). Proudhon compares, for example, socialism to
the god Vishnu, "always dying and always resuscitating" (*SC* 1:37), and
God himself to anyone from Jehovah to Jupiter. Socialism is constantly
fighting "a burlesque war" with the science of economics when they both
really want "the organization of labor" (*SC* 1:45). In the meantime, while
society suffers from routine economics, socialists have "since Pythagoras,
Orpheus and the impenetrable Hermes, worked to establish their dogma
in contradiction to that of political economy" (*SC* 1:39). Socialism seems
for Proudhon to be chthonic, either of the underworld (Orpheus, Hermes)
or of the earth *tout court* (Pythagoras) but certainly redemptive. At the
moment, writes Proudhon (returning to the dominant trope), socialists are
like John the Baptist in the desert, crying out "Organize labor!" as the
modern equivalent of "Repent!" to the economists, those sinners who do
not even understand labor, which they should know best. The socialists,
however, are also burdened with the illusion that such organization of labor is their invention (when it is as old as the earth itself); further, they are
unable to say what, "according to them, such an organization should be"
(*SC* 1:44). Proudhon, one is led to imagine, is correcting all this and taking
it upon himself to call for repentance.

But religion has a more direct role in Proudhon's text. A series of intro-
ductory sentences to the *Contradictions* postulates the need for the "hypothesis of God." One reason for this need is that the notion of God "gives
meaning to history" (*SC* 1:22). What this boils down to mean is that if
God is absolute reason, then that includes social reason and therefore man
is what was previously understood to be God. Man, then (and here one
senses an odd version of Fichte), invented God in order for man to become
conscious of himself *as* consciousness. Once man had progressed, the notion of God as an external personification lessened and (dixit Proudhon)
could gradually be reabsorbed by its creator: the mind of man. What we
notice here is the extent to which progress is at the heart of such a theory:
progress makes for man's recognition that the absolute does not exist except insofar as it is imagined by humankind; man no longer needs the
myths and biblical narratives that previously stood in for his own spirit
and intellect.

Thus if the infallible describes the pope in Maistre, in Proudhon it describes man: man "never regresses, and this perseverance in his walk is the

proof of his infallibility" (*SC* 1:8). This, we might say, is what Proudhon shares with Marx: progress itself as a religion of sorts, if "religion" here can be taken to mean a grounding faith that is not to be questioned. For both Marx and Proudhon, man is by definition he who progresses, moves forward, is increasingly enlightened even if not necessarily liberated. Progress is that which neither of the two philosophers doubts; it is a willed faith in the inevitability of man's advancement. Thus Proudhon can write that God, whom man has worshipped as an all-powerful absolute, is none other than man himself, "filtered through the blazing mirror of [man's] consciousness." The point is embedded in a fascinating context: Milton's Eve, staring at herself in the mirror and reaching out to embrace her own image (like an obverse of the mirror moment in "L'Héautontimorouménos"). This moment, writes Proudhon, is "humankind, trait for trait" (1:9). The logic is a bit tortuous, but the implications remain: it is the narcissistic aspect of man that drives him to invent a god who would make man in God's—and thus man's own—image. And it is this primitive, hypocritical myth that man—having sufficiently progressed—should now be able to set aside. Man can now recognize that the image in the mirror is none other than himself. The point is not that man is God, but rather that God was a necessary belief at an earlier point of human development but is no longer needed.

The move for Proudhon is from an original triad to a new trinity, which is humanism: "God, nature, and man are the triple aspect of the one and identical being, man. Man is god himself arriving at consciousness of self." And then, in a further flurry of confused Fichtean enthusiasm, Proudhon sings the praises of the human ego: "I [*MOI*], there is no other God than YOU [*TOI*]" (1:9). Having emerged from his state of "barbarism" and "savagery" (synonyms that would have enraged Maistre), man now must recognize that *he* is the one who of necessity invented the divine. Now that the human is more educated, more scientifically knowledgeable, "anything is possible," as Proudhon promises he will show by virtue of an "invincible dialectic" (1:13).[65] If unity alone can obtain our faith, he continues, "duality is the first condition of science." Why? Because everything is contradiction and dualism in nature (body and soul, mind and matter, the I and the Not-I, etc.), yet unified—not in an absolute,

65. In a complete misunderstanding of Fichte, Proudhon serenely continues in this passage by proclaiming that if modern philosophy agrees on one thing, it is the distinction between thought and its object, "or the I and the Not-I" (*SC* 13).

but in the mind. Perhaps Baudelaire got some of his fascination with dualisms from such passages.

In any case, it is hardly surprising that Grün and his soon to be ex-friend Marx smelled religiosity.[66] Proudhon treats the concept of God as a vestigial trait of the mind, yet insists that he needs the hypothesis of God. He needs that hypothesis for a number of rather confusing reasons, one of which, it will be recalled, is "to give meaning to history." He also needs the hypothesis to found the authority of the social sciences; to legitimize reforms; to show the unity of civilization and nature; to show his good intentions; to explain the publication of his writing; and (oddly) to justify his style. And the reason for this, argues Proudhon, is that God is such a given in our thinking that the very terms of philosophy and economics are rooted in the assumption of the divine. Hence excommunication, apocalypse, sin, and so on are the lexicon to which Proudhon must have recourse if he is to persuade, through his rhetoric, that his notion of economics is the one that can save humanity from disequilibrium and inequality. Moreover, the notion of "history" is in Proudhon's opinion incomprehensible without the category of the divine to generate notions of justice, evil, and the like. To refer to a divinity, in both tenor and vehicle, as a "hypothesis" is to acknowledge that (as Derrida was to say of logocentrism, or Lacan of the phallus) the concept is at present engrained in the human mind, culture, and lexicon. But to turn to God qua God—that is, with a belief in predetermination and thus resignation—for economic reform or the eradication of poverty can only lead to business as usual, claims Proudhon, since God has always been invoked as a pretext for the powerful at the expense of the oppressed. We must slowly disentangle ourselves.

It is here that Proudhon famously announces that "God is evil." This statement, which needless to say created an instant scandal, is to be understood in terms of Proudhon's socialist ideal of equality. God, as we have seen, is an invention of the mind and the hypostatization of the absolute. As such, the divine is of necessity unchanging and static, whereas Proudhon's entire philosophy is based on the notion of progress, change, enlightenment, and the general amelioration of the human condition through "mutualism." God, by contrast, is "nonsense and cowardice; God

66. In *The Poverty of Philosophy*, Marx complains, "The work of Mr. Proudhon is not simply a treatise on political economy, an ordinary book; it is a Bible: 'Mysteries,' 'Secrets torn from God's bosom,' 'Revelations,'—nothing is missing" (Haubtmann, *Proudhon*, 717 n. 16).

is hypocrisy and lying; God is tyranny and poverty" (Haubtmann, *Pierre-Joseph Proudhon*, 681). Does this mean then that God does not exist? "Alas, no," writes Proudhon. He returns to his thesis: the concept of God is too much a part of the human imaginary to be successfully ejected: "The reality of the divine Being has remained beyond reach, and my hypothesis thus remains" (ibid.). The point is sufficiently knotty to warrant repeating: it is not that God exists, but rather that the human mind, at the moment, is unable to imagine without God. Kant remarked that humans cannot imagine anything without space and time, but that this does not mean that space and time exist. This is essentially Proudhon's argument as well: the reality of a divinity is "beyond reach"—we cannot imagine life without it, but that does not mean that a divinity exists. But for now, Proudhon argues, his hypothesis that God is, will hold.

However, this perspective coupled with Proudhon's politics makes God the ultimate enemy of man. "If there is a being who, before us and more than us, deserves to be in hell, I am forced to name him: it is God." God for Proudhon is jealous of Adam, tyrannizes Prometheus, feeds us bread "soaked in blood and tears," lays traps for us to fall into, makes us commit the sins for which we then ask his pardon (Haubtmann, *Proudhon*, 680). God tormented Job ("the figure of our humanity"), and we humans have been nonentities (*des néants*) before God's "invisible majesty." He is the (futile) hope of the poor, but the successful power of the prince. For Proudhon, in other words, the figure of God secures an unchanging world of inequity, misery, and suppression. The Satan who holds us hostage, then, is none other than God himself. But whereas before we dared not contradict God, or question his omnipotence, now Proudhon declares, in a threatening apostrophe to the deity, "we have come to know You." The idea of a divinity (whether "Eternal Father, Jupiter, or Jehovah") may be too engrained to eradicate ("beyond reach"), but now we know God for what he is: Satan, man's greatest adversary.

Much of this is inspired by Feuerbach (and, as Marx pointed out with increasing alarm, by the fuzzy humanism of Grün);[67] Proudhon's biogra-

---

67. Engels was, as mentioned, sent to Paris by Marx in the fall of 1846 to get rid of Grün. For the details, see Hauptmann's chapter "Proudhon, Marx et Grün," *Proudhon*, 617–39. It is worth noting that Grün quite correctly accuses Proudhon of misogyny: the philosopher, writes Grün to his wife, wants to put women in "reclusion" (ibid., 467–68). Indeed, in 1858 Proudhon published *De la justice dans la Révolution et dans l'Eglise*, in three volumes; an excerpt from that work appeared in 1957 as *Influence de l'élément féminin sur les mœurs et la littérature françaises (Les femmelins)* (Paris: Les Belles lectures, no. 334). The three-volume work examines Madame de Staël, de Saussure, Roland, Charlotte Corday, and George Sand. Among the gems in the excerpted essay, I will submit only a few: "The feminine element, apart from

pher Haubtmann and other scholars have made this evident. But we are interested in how all of this affects Baudelaire, and there is much here to observe. Whereas critics have spent a great deal of time on how Baudelaire was on the left before and a few years after 1848, little has been done to reflect on how much Proudhon's theological atheology might have left its imprint not only on the young Baudelaire but also on the mature poet in spite of his admiration for Maistre and his scorn for the socialist anarchism of Proudhon.[68] First, there is the point that God, in Proudhon's account, is necessarily the enemy of man, man's opposite, he with whom man must fight to the death.[69] God is "the antipode of humanity, the ontological summit from which humanity must always separate" (Haubtmann, 680). And this because, as we have seen, humans are changeable and contradictory (and have thus invented a contradictory God). God is infallible, immutable, immediate, and eternal at once; man on the other hand is mobility and lives in time. Thus, writes Proudhon, "man and God perpetually hold each other at bay and endlessly flee from one another." Proudhon concludes:

the specific quality that results in its very inferiority and makes itself known, is in the final analysis a negative element, a diminution or weakening of the masculine element, which alone represents the integrity of the mind" (5). There follows a series of impressive remarks on Rousseau, Lamartine, Béranger, and others. The essay ends with the following pronouncement: "Woman is an educator; she has a social mission and thus has a role in literary activity, since it is through the word, through poetry and art that morality is taught and propagated. But here again, and more than ever, woman needs to be supported by the severity of virile genius" (31). If she is not with a strong man, she will feminize him and become his equal: "she will fall into a type of literary nymphomania, eroticism having subjugated her thought." She will dream of equality between the sexes, but she will be lost (31). Proudhon's obsession with equality, then, does not extend to women.

68. One exception is Burton (*Baudelaire and the Second Republic*), who devotes two chapters to Baudelaire and Proudhon. Burton's interest, however, is political, not theological. So too, T. J. Clark writes of Proudhon at some length, though again less about religion than politics. Clark believes that Baudelaire's interest in the philosopher lay in the fact that he "stood for opposition to the dreams and vagueness of February [1848], the lyric illusion of the young Republic, promising everything and offering no single concrete proposal." The *Système des contradictions*, adds Clark, was "lamentable" as a textbook on socialism and an imitation of dialectic, and Marx's attack was "accurate enough." But Baudelaire read the book differently than Marx, and "made good use of it." T. J. Clark, *The Absolute Bourgeois: Artists and Politics in France, 1848–1851* (1973; Berkeley: University of California Press, 1999), 166.

69. In his Journal, Kierkegaard says almost the same thing: "Christianity exists because there is hatred between God and man" (cited in Haubtmann, *Proudhon*, 681). There are affinities between Kierkegaard and Proudhon: the former's conviction that "against God we are always in the wrong," for example; or Kierkegaard's view of the either/or as "explosive." Proudhon, however, much less radical conceptually, and armed with a reductio ad absurdum grasp of Hegelianism, always sees synthesis as the solution (which he provides) to dangerous contradiction.

There is thus a contradiction between humanity and its ideal, an opposition between man and God. It is an opposition that Christian theology had allegorized and personified under the name of Devil or Satan,
that is to say, the contradictor, the enemy of God and of man. Such is
the fundamental antinomy that I think modern critics have insufficiently taken into account. (Ibid.)

This "fundamental antinomy" has political as well as existential consequences. Indeed, at the very end of *Contradictions*, things get even more
complicated: human reason, it turns out, is itself infallible and immutable; "truth" does not change. That is why society is "unalterable" in its
essence and "irresistible" to revolution.[70] As humans we have "mysterious presentiments" despite our contradictory state. Proudhon ends his
opus with another religious analogy that, he says, comes to him "invol-
untarily": in Christian symbolism, on the Last Day the Church Militant
will succeed the Church Triumphant. (That is, the living Christians of
the Church Militant, who are struggling against sin in order to attain the
Church Triumphant after death, will at the Last Judgment be sinless, such
that the distinction between the churches will no longer be necessary.)
Proudhon then concludes with a simile for his social theory—a simile that
is less than limpid: "and the system of social contradiction appears to me
like a magical bridge, thrown across the river of forgetting" (*SC* 2:416).

What are we to make of this comparison? Clearly, Proudhon's belief in
man's "mysterious presentiments" betrays at the very least a nostalgic feel
for religion. Are we to assume that the struggle of the living (Church Militant) to attain the Triumphant—a struggle that will at the End of Days
expunge the difference between the two churches, and that all will be unified, with no need for division—is like the struggle of the poor on earth,
which will, once Proudhon's doctrine of "mutuality" is in place, similarly
melt away? Social contradiction is a magic bridge because it allows us to
cross, safe and dry, a Lethe-like river, so that we do not forget inequity?
Anarchism, and in particular the economic (rather than governmental) organization of labor, have redemptive value for Proudhon, as we have seen.
Hence the religious vocabulary and tropes; hence the blurring of abstract
concepts (equality, the good, progress, human reason) with practical ma-
terialism; hence, finally, a style of dialectics professing to "cure" contra-

70. Again, this is the sort of position that exasperated Marx: "Why," he writes in a letter
to Annenkov in December of 1846, "does Mr. Proudhon speak of *god*, of *universal reason*, of
the impersonal reason of humanity, which never errs, which has been, at all times, consistent
with itself" (Haubtmann, *Proudhon*, 717).

diction through ascension (with vestigial religious overtones), rather than *Aufhebung*. "Why," asks an angry Marx, must Proudhon "do a weak Hegelianism in order to appear strong in mind?" (Haubtmann, 717).

It is no surprise that Baudelaire credited Maistre and Poe with teaching him how to think (*raisonner*). With all due admiration for some of Proudhon's theories, rigid deductive logic—or logic, period—is not his forte.[71] We know that Baudelaire admired Maistre's relentless (if dark) syllogisms and his uncompromising pronouncements from, as it were, the Mount. Maistre can be quite crazy. Of the Spanish Inquisition, for example, Maistre proclaims that "nothing is more just, more learned, more incorruptible than the Spanish tribunals. . . . Nothing in the universe is calmer, more circumspect, more human by nature than the Inquisition's tribunal" (cited in Cioran, *Joseph de Maistre*, 176). But Maistre writes with a clarity and energy, not to mention certainty, that, combined with his view of evil, greatly attracted Baudelaire. On the other hand, the poet cannot but have chafed at the ambiguity of Proudhon's tropes and the idealistic impracticality of his theory of mutualism, even if not as viciously as Marx was to do when he responded to Proudhon's *Système des contradictions*.[72]

There was much for Baudelaire to like in Proudhon: contradiction and duality; the usefulness of antinomy; the conflation of God and Satan; the endless battle between God and man; the notion of social progress and the insistence on equality; the inevitability and necessity of revolution; the plight of the poor. But he clearly did not admire the movement of Proudhon's thought. As mentioned, Baudelaire was well versed in the "philo-

71. Not, by the way, that Poe is himself such a rigorous thinker. But Poe seems to have impressed Baudelaire by his versification, his "genius," his imagination, and his ability to create a particularly foreboding atmosphere. He also gave Baudelaire more avenues for textually evoking the melancholy they both shared. In the introduction to his translation of Poe's "The Philosophy of Composition," Baudelaire states that it is impossible for him to convey to the French reader the extent, in Poe's verse, "of the profound and lugubrious sonority, of the forceful monotony of the lines, whose wide and tripled rhymes toll like the knell of melancholy" (*OC* 2:344).

72. Whereas Marx greatly admired Proudhon's 1840 *Qu'est-ce que la propriété?* (see Marx and Engels, *The Holy Family*, 1845, chap. 4), seeing in it "a great scientific advance," he famously attacked *Système de contradictions* with furor in *The Poverty of Philosophy* (1847). Proudhon's enraged response to that attack (in the margins of his copy) is fully documented in Haubtmann, 1055–1063 and makes for great reading of what one critic calls "a psychological document" (Picard cited in Haubtmann, *Proudhon*, 736). There are also several other hands in the margins, with equally enraged annotations; one is that of a M. Crémieux, and another by a mysterious "X," whom Haubtmann suspects of being none other than the maligned Grün. Proudhon's conclusion is that he has been plagiarized: "The real meaning of Marx's book is that he everywhere regrets that I have the same thoughts he does, and that I said it before he did. . . . He is of bad faith" (Haubtmann, *Proudhon*, 1060–61)

sophical machines." And though not familiar with the writings of Marx, Baudelaire doubtless sensed what Marx condemned in Proudhon: first, his failure to rise above the "bourgeois horizon";[73] second, his use of actual social relations as the incarnation of theoretical ones rather than vice versa, such that Proudhon for Marx is "upside down." Baudelaire would have agreed to both of these criticisms, but obviously for different reasons than Marx. With respect to the first of these criticisms, it is worth noting that after his book on property, Proudhon sought less to eradicate capitalism than to reconcile the bourgeoisie with the proletariat. Marx can only have seen this as backsliding, creeping conservatism (which is certainly what it was). Baudelaire, on the other hand, who did not want to be aligned with either of the two social classes Proudhon recognized, had to be similarly alarmed by Proudhon's idealism. The prose poem "A une heure du matin" tells of the narrator's life of hypocrisy between the bourgeoisie and the poor in the "Horrible city! Horrible city!" and begs for an end to lying and "the corrupting vapors of this world." The poem ends with a prayer: "God, grant me the grace of producing a few beautiful verses that will prove to me that I am not . . . inferior to those I despise" (OC 2:288). The poet prays to produce a poetry the soaring greatness of which may save him from the fate of belonging to either of those two classes. One might add that this is also a passage in which the notion of grace actually appears; but the tenor is ironic in its misanthropic excess. The purpose of God's grace here is to allow the poet the power to write verse that will allow him to feel at least no worse than the urban "multitude" for which, joining Maistre, he can only feel contempt.

In January of 1865, writing to Sainte-Beuve from Brussels (where Proudhon himself had been exiled from 1858 to 1863), Baudelaire gives another reason for his continued disapproval of Proudhon. The philosopher had just died, and Baudelaire writes to "uncle" Sainte-Beuve to respond to the latter's articles on Proudhon.[74] Baudelaire assures the older critic that he does not think a positive reaction to Proudhon "illegitimate." And he adds: "I read him a great deal and I knew him a little. Pen in hand, he was *not a bad guy* [*bon bougre*, emphasis Baudelaire's]. But he was not, and never could be, even on paper, *a dandy!* For that I can never forgive him" (*Corr.* 2:562–63). We need to be a bit cautious with this, given that Baudelaire was continually trying to impress Sainte-Beuve, to gain his affection and (more

73. See, e.g., the entry "Proudhon" in Tom B. Bottomore, ed., *A Dictionary of Marxist Thought*, (Oxford: Blackwell, 1991), 452.

74. Sainte-Beuve's articles were published in the October–December 1864 issues of the *Revue contemporaine*.

importantly) support, the latter of which he never received (and his reception of the former is at best debatable). This despite hypocritical protestations to the contrary from the famous critic, as Proust makes singularly and brilliantly clear. Nevertheless, the point is unmistakable: Baudelaire is faulting Proudhon for having lacked elegance—both personal and stylistic. Writing to Poulet-Malassis again after the philosopher's death, and referring to the single occasion he ever dined with Proudhon, Baudelaire reports that the latter's enormous appetite amazed him, and that he told him so: "For a man of letters, you eat a surprising amount." Proudhon supposedly responded, "It is because I have big things to do." Baudelaire could not discern whether he was serious or not. At the end of the meal, Baudelaire continues, Proudhon insisted on paying—but only for his own share. "Perhaps," concludes Baudelaire to Poulet-Malassis, "you will infer a decided taste for equality and an exaggerated love of the law" (Corr. 2:469–70).[75] The ironic use of "equality" will undergird "Assommons les pauvres."

Proudhon believes that, at least in the *Lebenswelt*, his own theory of mutualism and of the inevitability of progress and equality must inevitably bring about the resolution of antinomies. For him, contradiction is hypostasized in order to be eradicated by a "compromise position" of the philosopher's invention. Synthesis is antidote: this was Proudhon's notion of Hegelianism, as Marx was to lament. Baudelaire, however, again parts company here with Proudhon: for the poet, contradiction is realism, and alternative pictures of the same event are the fact of the experiential in modernity.

Nearing the conclusion of his *Système de contradictions*, Proudhon

75. In fact, Baudelaire was writing to Poulet-Malassis (March 11, 1865) to correct an anecdote the poet had read in *La petite revue*, in which a "citizen" is described as having an experience with Proudhon similar to Baudelaire's. "That citizen, my friend," writes Baudelaire, "was me" (Corr. 1:469). Another, more famous anecdote concerning the two stemmed from August 21, 1848. Proudhon had been protesting at the National Assembly, demanding among other things that the deportation of insurgents be delayed. His journal, *Le représentant du peuple*, had been seized by the government three times in three days. Baudelaire, sitting in a café across from the Assembly, wrote Proudhon (whom he had not yet met) two notes, which were found in Proudhon's papers after his death. The first note urges the philosopher, addressed as "Citoyen," to meet Baudelaire at the café, where, he says, "I will wait *indefinitely*." Baudelaire wanted to tell Proudhon that there was an assassination plot against him. Receiving no response from Proudhon, Baudelaire wrote a second, longer letter, the gist of which is (underlined): "*Do not be at home.*" And the poet alludes to danger from "the ferocious beasts of property," thus making his affinity with the philosopher's politics clear. He adds that the government would no doubt be pleased by Proudhon's demise at the hands of such "beasts" (Corr. 1:150–52).

declares that Providence is immune to our tears; and as we gravely discuss
the justice and injustice of Providence (the very topic that opens, we might
add, Maistre's *Soirées*), "the God who has made us as contradictory as he is
himself in our thoughts, contradictory in our discourse, contradictory in
our actions, answers us with a burst of laughter" (*SC* 2:412–13). Here again,
Proudhon's God is evil, or at least malicious in his contradictoriness. But
it is worth noting the proximity here to Baudelaire's essay mentioned
earlier, "De l'essence du rire" ("On the Essence of Laughter"), written between 1844 and 1847, before Baudelaire had encountered Maistre. At the
end of the essay, Baudelaire discusses artists who create the comical, and
concludes, it will be recalled, that the artist is an artist only on condition
of being double. Like Maturin's Melmoth,[76] says Baudelaire, the artist is
doomed by his "contradictory double nature," such that his laughter is a
sickness, a hubris that perpetually works by "tearing and burning the lips
of irremissible laughter" (*OC* 2:531). "Laughter" is one of the clearest "satanic signs" of man; moreover, it is "one of the numerous seeds contained
in the symbolic apple . . . , a monstrous phenomenon" (*OC* 2:530). We are
back to the Heauton Timorumenos, the self-tormenter—the wound is also
the knife, the seed from the apple is also the sinner who eats it.

Contradiction, in other words, is not to be resolved in Baudelaire; hence
the emphasis of words such as *irrémédiable, irrémissible, irrécouvrable,*
and *irréparable*. Freud, it will be recalled, argues that the "un-" in the uncanny markes the repression of the unconscious; and Baudelaire notes that
the pride of laughter may be unconscious. But the prefix *ir-* in Baudelaire
is the perpetual re-scarring of memory—of the Fall, of the hopelessness
of human life, of the irreversibility of evil. The words themselves contain
the contradiction of man's double bind: each word contains the positive aspect (remediable, remissible, recoverable) on which the *ir-*, palimpsest-like,
produces an a priori erasure. So the lexicon performs the contradictions,
causing the positive aspect to be debarred even as it is evoked. Freud tells
us that the uncanny can also mean its opposite, thus underlining the ultimate ubiquity of the unconscious. Evil plays the same all-encompassing
role in Baudelaire (one of his frequent metaphors is the vampire), swallowing up everything, draining it of life. But the pervasiveness and inescap-

---

76. Charles Robert Maturin's *Melmoth the Wanderer* was published in 1820 and was twice
translated into French the following year. Pichois notes that Baudelaire intended to translate it
himself in 1865, but never did so. (*OC* 2:1348 n. 2) The story, which was also to inspire the Sur-
realists and André Breton in particular, is Faust-like. The devil offers Melmoth a longer life
in exchange for his soul, unless he can find someone to share his fate. The tragic death of the
innocent, Margarete-like young woman he seduces inevitably follows.

ability of evil do not, in Baudelaire, erase contradiction. Indeed, one can read many of Baudelaire's poems as an insurance policy against lapsing into comfort or ease. Moreover, contradiction functions in tandem with itself (just as the seed in the apple is also the eater of the apple): each side is superimposed on the other, like two photographic plates (to return to Benjamin's metaphor but with a different end) that produce the flash (in Benjamin's sense) of a single image of doubled outline. The image is hard to read, hard to focus on, and the lines are tangled; that is because there are in fact two images, presented as if there were only one.

This superimposition is true conceptually, theologically, and politically in Baudelaire. In "Assommons les pauvres," Proudhon does not disappear entirely from Baudelaire's text; rather, Proudhon's socialist/anarchistic vision of equality is still in Baudelaire's gaze even as he professes to turn to the father of anarchy solely for purpose of satire. As Pichois notes, "In Belgium, Baudelaire was to be obsessed by the fate and death of Proudhon" (*Corr.* 1:783). Clark adds that in 1848 Baudelaire was clearly a disciple of the philosopher, "and the encounter with Proudhon marked his work and his attitudes for the rest of his life" (*Absolute Bourgeois*, 164).

SPLITTING THE DIFFERENCE: THE POEM

"Assommons les pauvres" was written in the year of Proudhon's death, though it was apparently partially inspired by an event the year before.[77] And there is an added feature: the poem originally ended with the line, "What do you say to that, Citizen Proudhon?" (*Qu'en dis-tu, Citoyen Proudhon?*) The line was suppressed for decades—whether by the poet's friends or by Baudelaire himself remains unknown.[78]

77. In a letter to Nadar, dated August 30, 1864, Baudelaire writes that he beat up a Belgian, and adds: "That I am capable of beating someone is absurd. And the most monstrous part still is that I was entirely in the wrong. Also, a sense of justice overtook me, and I ran after the man to apologize. But I couldn't find him" (*Corr.* 2:401).

78. For an interpretation of this line and its omission, see Burton's *Baudelaire and the Second Republic*, 326–31. Burton does a helpful review of previous criticism of the poem—those who take the line on Proudhon into account, and those who don't (principally the psychoanalytic approaches of Mauron, who mentions the line only in passing, and of Mehlman and Bersani). For Burton, the line is "utterly crucial" and shows Baudelaire's ambivalence toward the philosopher who had just died. The line was present when Baudelaire submitted the poem in July of 1865 to the *Revue nationale et étrangère*, the editor of which immediately rejected it as unpublishable. The poem was published in 1869 in the first edition of *Petits poèmes en prose*. See *OC* 1:1306 for details of the poem's publication history. Pichois wonders whether Baudelaire deleted the satirical line himself after Proudhon's death in January of 1865. He also suggests that Asselineau and Banville, who collected the poems but are not mentioned

The prose poem is frequently read in the light of Baudelaire's views on 1848. Let us go over the opening: "For two weeks I had stayed confined to my room, and I had surrounded myself with books in vogue at the time (sixteen or seventeen years ago.)" Significantly, there is no precise statement such as "That was in 1848"; the reference is indirect; even willfully nonchalant within parentheses (a common ploy in Baudelaire). You have to count backward sixteen or seventeen years from 1865 to figure out that Baudelaire is referring to the failed revolution. One might argue that anybody in 1865 France, asked whether something had happened "sixteen or seventeen years ago" would immediately think of 1848. There follows the litany of books the narrator has read on how to be happy and, in particular, how the poor should be viewed (whether as slaves or as dethroned kings). These were the self-help books and social treatises on ways to help the poor—books particularly popular in the early heady days of the events of '48. But they were popular too during the Second Empire, as if the bourgeoisie needed to purge itself of its central (if willfully repressed) role in destroying the new republic and betraying the working class.

The narrator then decides to act on a bizarre hypothesis, whispered to him by a demon: "A man is equal to another only when he can prove it; and a man is worthy of liberty only if he can conquer it" (OC 1:358). In other words, if a poor man is beaten into the ground by an upper-class gentleman and retaliates, he is worthy of respect.

The theory, a kind of milder version of that in *Crime and Punishment*, is tested on an old beggar. When the beggar, after being severely beaten by the narrator, does indeed retaliate, the equally battered narrator jubilantly shares half his purse with him, and exults, "O miracle! O delight of the philosopher who verifies the excellence of his theory!" (359). In an echo of "Au lecteur" ("hypocritical reader, my double, my brother!"), the narrator proclaims, "Sir, *you are my equal!*" The poem plays on many levels: first, a moral truth, La Fontaine-esque in its didacticism. The beggar reacts to his one black eye and two broken teeth by doubling the narrator's injuries in biblical parody: his attacker will end up with *two* black eyes and *four* broken teeth. Two eyes for an eye, and four teeth for two, is the new sequence of vengeance (and so is not real "equality" after all). The narra-

---

in the ensuing 1869 edition, may have deleted the line (OC 1:1350). Kaplan, whose book is devoted to Baudelaire's prose poems, thinks the line is a "contentious jibe," and that its presence would have compromised the jibe of the poem's conclusion. For Kaplan, moreover, the line is "too ideologically specific" and would have "restricted the fable's dialogical openness." See Edward K. Kaplan, *Baudelaire's Prose Poems: The Esthetic, the Ethical, and the Religious* (Athens: University of Georgia Press, 1990), 158.

tor's division of his purse in two continues the geometry, or augmented sequence, of egalitarian literalism, and deliberate mockery of Proudhon's idea of mutualism. The final line—the beggar swears to the narrator that he "had understood my theory, and that he would obey my counsel"—is absurd enough that the narrator himself clearly doesn't believe it.

On this first level, the poem's satire of society, the intelligentsia, and its bourgeois do-good mores of phony democratic idealism could not be more crushing. The prose poem reeks of sarcasm and willfully concrete thinking from beginning to end. The ideals of '48 are revealed to be hypocritical and naïve, and applied theory becomes a boxing match. By testing two hypotheses he has read in "books of the day," the narrator is also demonstrating that theories are armchair daydreams and cannot substitute for activism. He tests them with the street as his laboratory, the beggar as his subject. Never is the revolution of '48 (or the counterrevolution) overt; but never is its legacy more forceful. Many critics end here; our task, however, is to take into account the forces motivating the poem—doubled and contradictory forces that crystallize around the figures of Proudhon and Maistre—in order to consider what I mean by two simultaneous images colliding.

In *Mon cœur mis à nu*, written around the same time as "Assommons," Baudelaire recalls "my intoxication in 1848" (*OC* 1:679). When the narrator asks himself what form ("nature") this intoxication took, he decides that it was the taste of vengeance, and the *natural* pleasure of demolition. "Natural" is italicized,[79] again a blow to Rousseau, but also a reminder of what "natural" means for the poet, as we have been considering. In this section of *Mon cœur mis à nu*, the word "natural" appears three times and "nature" once in eight short lines. The horrors of June '48 are described as the madness of the people and of the bourgeoisie, but also the "natural love of crime." We have considered the "natural" in its relation to original sin sufficiently in this chapter to recognize the inevitable connection between the two for Baudelaire. The poem assumes a Maistrean stance a priori: man is by nature sinful; it is his ineluctable inheritance, so it is not surprising that he stoops to cruelty and physical violence against the Other. Thus the journal entry, in describing the intoxication of 1848 and the horrors of the ensuing "June Days," also reveals a sentiment that matches the joyous and simultaneously desperate acceptance of the combat daemon from "Assommons les pauvres." Unlike Socrates'

79. "Italicized" here meaning that Baudelaire underlined the word. As noted earlier, the italics in which such words appear in the printed texts of Baudelaire are to be understood here and throughout as words underlined in manuscript.

"prohibitor" demon, the narrator's is an "affirmer"—a daemon of action and of combat.[80] The poet accepts this as his "nature" and that of man (and of the crowd in '48 and the bourgeoisie). "Always," as the journal puts it, there is "a taste for destruction. A legitimate taste if all that is natural is legitimate" (OC 1:679). All that is natural is legitimate; but we are not to understand these words as Rousseau would. What is natural is here brutal, evil, and degenerate, as the narrator's little tale demonstrates. The naturally corrupt state of man is thus (paradoxically) legitimate. Moreover, the sense of egalitarianism and fairness that Proudhon preached (and assumed was possible)—for example, in his suggestion of a bank based on equitable exchange and mutualism—is thrown out from the start.

In "Assommons les pauvres," Baudelaire takes on the equally insincere pose of contemptuous distance from '48 (and from politics in general).[81] That year, he writes in Mon cœur mis à nu, was amusing only because everybody was inventing utopias, "like castles in Spain." And "1848 was charming only by dint of the very excess of its ridiculousness" (OC 1:680). Bitter disappointment is here cloaked in scorn; so too, in "Assommons," compassion for the beggar (whose unforgettable gaze would overthrow thrones if the eye of a hypnotist could ripen grapes) is stifled by the narrator's violent beating of the poor man, with the "stubborn energy of cooks attempting to tenderize beef" (359). As usual, Baudelaire borrows from disparate lexicons: beating someone up is likened to pounding on a piece of meat (which, one might argue, is literally what such a beating performs). It is, one might add, the same image that opens L'Héautontimorouménos: "I shall beat you without anger / And without hatred, like a butcher." There is also pathos for the beggar's gaze—so moving and potent that it could overthrow kingdoms. But that intense gaze is conditional upon the un-

80. The "subtle Lélut and the very perceptive Baillarger" were well-known alienists of the period who believed that Socrates was insane. Baudelaire did not adhere to this view, as he wrote in a letter to Sainte-Beuve. See Pichois, OC 1:1350.

81. Despite Baudelaire's frequent protestations that he was, after '48, done with politics, he wavered on this point as well. In March of 1852, he had written to Ancelle, "The 2nd of December has *physically depoliticized* me. . . . If I had voted, I could only have voted for myself" (*Corr.* 1:188). But to Nadar, for example, he writes in May of 1859, "I have persuaded myself twenty times that I am no longer interested in politics, and at every serious question, I am again seized by curiosity and passion" (*Corr.* 1:578). Baudelaire then engages in an in-depth discussion on the Italian question as it concerns the Second Empire. He ends by citing the *Lettres diplomatiques de Joseph de Maître* (just published, posthumously, in 1858), even though he knows that mentioning that author will inspire "horror" in Nadar. Politics, writes Baudelaire to his friend, is a "science without a heart," and every real politician is both a "Jesuit and a Revolutionary." Baudelaire thus combines Proudhon and Maistre in his very definition of the political.

likely ability of a hypnotist to ripen grapes. The beggar's gaze, in other words, would be powerful only if the hypnotist's were already so. The hypothetical potency of both gazes has thus been neutralized.

The notion of the gaze is in itself to the third power: the beggar's gaze is likened to the hypnotist's, but it is the narrator who sees into the poor man's eyes with a gaze of his own. Moreover, the narrator opens the poem by telling us that for the last two weeks he has confined himself to his room, and has been reading the books in vogue around 1848. He compares such intense reading to digestion, and then to "swallowing" all the bizarre imaginings of "those contractors of the public good." Digestion or not (and let us not forget that Baudelaire's chief personal response to Proudhon is the latter's huge appetite for actual food, not books), it is from a dictionary that the narrator gets the first inkling of the idea that will form his outrageous theory. Reading and rifling through the dictionary are activities of the eye. So much has the narrator read that he feels himself in a "state of mind close to vertigo or stupidity." He leaves his apartment in "a great thirst," because the taste for bad reading "engenders a proportional need for fresh air and refreshments" (*OC* 1:358).

The activity of the eyes, then, opens the poem; then the narrator goes out and sees the beggar, whose eyes inspire the idea of the hypnotist's pseudopowerful gaze in turn. All of these gazes are flawed: the narrator's reading has been in books of poor taste and, furthermore, leads to a stupefied condition; the beggar's gaze has powerful potential, but will never amount to anything unless (as it were) pigs start flying; the hypnotist's boast is bogus: he cannot make grapes ripen with a look. The protagonist of the poem, in other words, is the gaze.

The "plot" of the poem is in itself connected with seeing. As mentioned earlier, the poet had written in 1864 to Nadar from Brussels and told him that he had beaten up a Belgian (see note 77). Baudelaire adds, it will be recalled, that he was entirely in the wrong, and that when he recovered his "spirit of justice" he ran after the man to apologize, but was unable to find him. The poet—who spent nearly three years in voluntary exile in Belgium (1864–66) until a stroke forced him to return to Paris—hated Belgium, the Belgians, and almost everything to do with that country and its culture,[82] as his voluminous writings ("Sur la Belgique") make clear. Why he stayed so long is less clear,[83] but the incident, which

---

82. One exception is the churches, most of which he admired and went out of his way to visit.

83. Nadar, who knew him well, had a psychological explanation of his own for the constantly delayed return to Paris: "Baudelaire's running away to Belgium," he writes in his

Pichois is not convinced actually occurred (*Corr.* 2:873), is duly reported by Baudelaire scholars as being the germ of "Assommons les pauvres!" Such may well be the case. My point here, however, is that the anecdote, true or not, is based on a reaction of physical revulsion and consequent violence as the result of the mere sight of a Belgian. It is as if this prose poem were constructed as an elaborate political and intellectual explanation for an otherwise inexplicable behavior. The return of the "spirit of justice" to the poet's mind allows him to tell Nadar that the whole thing was crazy and that he knew it. But "Assommons les pauvres!" evinces no such return to sanity; indeed, the poem insists on its own inner logic. As has often been pointed out, once you accept that someone can turn into a cockroach, all the rest of Kafka's *Metamorphosis* makes perfect sense. "Assommons" offers a similar paradox: once you accept an inane idea (that equality needs to be proved, and that the dignity of liberty needs to be earned) and further accept that this theory needs to be demonstrated physically by brute force, then the narrator's behavior in "Assommons" follows quite logically.

The poem itself is a type of doubled reductio ad absurdum: the absurdity of the proposition is matched by the senselessness of its conclusion. But the poem professes to uphold the proposition precisely because the praxis confirms it. Or so the poem professes to believe, in a rather nasty *recusatio* that only the exclamation points (particularly the one in the title) belie. An atavistic response—hatred for the beggar, or hatred for the culpability that grips the narrator when he sees the poor man's eyes?—is turned into a philosophical exercise in logic; the loss of control, the physical brutality, are transmuted into a cool demonstration of the theory's correctness. The visceral and senseless response to a stranger in Brussels has been transformed into a problem of social class and conflict, as well as a satire of the well-intended social theories of 1848 and their purveyors (such as, and mostly, Proudhon).

The double, as Freud points out, elicits feelings of dislike and hostility.[84] There is something frightening about the double—"a harbinger of death," as Freud's too often cited phrase puts it. There is something of the

---

memoirs, "which was extended and then prolonged beyond expectations—three years instead of the projected two weeks—could be explained in his tormented life by a vague need to escape from himself." Nadar, *Charles Baudelaire: Intime* (Neuchâtel: Indes et Calendes, 1994), 117. Clearly, the initial reason was to get out of Paris—not only because the city was driving Baudelaire mad, but also to escape creditors. Why he stayed so long thereafter, in a place he loathed, is anybody's guess, and Nadar's is as good as any.

84. In "The Uncanny," Freud tells of a train ride during which he sees a gentleman and experiences an immediate dislike for him, only to realize that it is he himself he has seen in a mirror. *SE* 17:248 n. 1.

double in the beggar, and not only because he elicits such strong feelings of (unacknowledged) hostility in the narrator of "Assommons." Baudelaire's obsession with money, his endless debts, his constant running from creditors—all of this makes the pitiful beggar holding out a hat too close for comfort. The beggar is what Baudelaire could easily become, indeed from a certain perspective did become if we consider his pathetic pleas to his mother for money as a form of begging. Or pleas to his friends. The fratricidal war between beggar and "bourgeois gentleman" is reminiscent of "Le gâteau," with the battle between the two boys for a piece of bread. "Assommons" is in this sense a curious double of the other poem,[85] with the narrator's purse divided, as against the bread that is pulverized in the fight between the boys. But the purse too will disappear, unless one is an adherent of Zeno of Elea and believes that it can be split infinitely.

Virtue (or apparent perfection) also can educe hatred in Baudelaire's texts. In "Portraits de maîtresses," one narrator complains that his mistress was "incapable of committing an error of sentiment or of calculation." For several years, he says, he admired her, his "heart full of hate." He seems to have finally killed her, though he never says so explicitly (OC 1:348–49). And there is another aspect to violent reaction: contemplative and inactive natures, writes Baudelaire in "Le mauvais vitrier," can sometimes act with astonishing rapidity "under a mysterious and unknown impulse." There are great procrastinators, the narrator of that prose poem continues, who "sometimes abruptly feel themselves propelled to act by an irresistible force, like an arrow from a bow." Neither moralists nor medical doctors ("who claim to know everything") can fathom where such an "insane energy can come from" in otherwise lazy and sensuous souls. Nor can one explain how these lazy types, unable to accomplish the simplest of tasks, "at a given minute find an excess of courage to commit the most absurd acts, and often even the most dangerous" (OC 1:285). Certainly, such would be a good explanation for what happened to the unfortunate Belgian. "Such nervous jokes are not without peril," ends the prose poem "Le mauvais vitrier," "and the cost is often high. But what difference does the eternity of damnation make to the one who has found pleasure in a second infinity?" (287).

We have so many doublings here that it is hard to navigate. There is the "second infinity," which seems to satirize Pascal and provides an es-

---

85. A point that has been made by several critics, including, for example, John E. Jackson: "The narrator and the poor man are . . . the exact correspondents of the two children of which they are like the adult version, who also find their equality in a bloody 'fight.'" Jackson, *Baudelaire* (Paris: Livre de Poche, 2001), 168.

cape from ennui. The "fratricidal war" between the beggar and the narrator is echoed by that in "Le gâteau," in "Abel et Caïn," and in the alleged
fight between Baudelaire and the Belgian. The war is further doubled by
the Heauton Timorumenos, the self-tormentor who is victim and executioner, the knife and the wound. Or by God and Lucifer, or Satan and God
the Father. Or even by the daemon of Socrates as against that of the narrator. Equality here is like Buffon's equilibrium: the clashing of forces
equal enough (physically, politically, or psychologically) such that nobody
"wins"—the forces remain destabilized, unsynthesized, irresolvable. The
war continues, even though, as in "Assommons," a deus ex machina appears (the "triumph" of the narrator's "philosophy") that professes resolution. Here too, Proudhon is satirized—the philosopher, after all, predicates
his theory of contradiction upon the promise of a synthesis that he will
provide. But at the end of "Assommons," as in "Le mauvais vitrier," the
problem of the poor has not been solved, nor has the question of social
consciousness and its concrete responsibilities toward the underclass. The
social contradiction of poverty has not been overcome; Proudhon's notion of equality is a failure. And so "Assommons" was to end with "What
do you say to that, Citizen Proudhon?"—crucial, perhaps, as some would
have it. Yet the satire of Proudhon would have been fairly obvious to any
of Baudelaire's contemporaries, even without the apostrophe.

Another contradiction is unresolved in "Assommons": that between
the theories of Proudhon and those of Maistre. We have been focusing, as
have many scholars of Baudelaire, on the satire of Proudhon in the text—
an evident ploy. What has less often been perceived is the dark vision of
Maistre that underlies the text: man is by nature evil, violent, savage.
Original sin explains "everything;" it is the mysterious force that remains
unacknowledged though demonstrated in "Le mauvais vitrier," in which
the narrator torments a poor windowpane salesman for no ostensible reason other than the narrator's own sadistic amusement.[86] But there may
be a bit of satire directed at Maistre in "Assommons" as well. After all,

86. "Le mauvais vitrier" is based on Arsène Houssaye's "La chanson du vitrier" (1857).
Houssaye's version, however, is filled with compassion for the windowpane salesman, who
cannot earn enough to feed his wife and seven (starving) children. Both "Le mauvais virtrier"
and "Assommons les pauvres" are included in *Le spleen de Paris: Petits poèmes en prose,*
which Baudelaire dedicated to Houssaye. "Le mauvais vitrier" (who is not "mauvais" at all,
unlike the cruel narrator) may therefore be an ironic replay of the Houssaye poem (also in
prose, except for the rather sentimental and histrionic refrain, "Oh! vitrier!"). For the whole of
Houssaye's text, see *OC* 1:1309–11. "Assommons les pauvres" achieves the same cruel take on
what would, from a "normal" perspective, be a source of pity and bourgeois guilt—sentiments
that "Assommons," like "Le mauvais vitrier," takes great pains to banish.

the ultramontane preached salvation through blood and punishment—precisely what the poem enacts. Indeed, "Assommons" might be read as a satire of reversibility: the narrator (the knife) attacks the beggar (the "wound") and thus "redeems" him. The redemption is not, however, theological: it is sociopolitical. "By my energetic medication," says the narrator, "I had given him back pride and life." Thus is the beggar elevated to being the elitist narrator's "equal." But at the same time, let us recall that *Les soirées de Saint-Pétersbourg* begins with the Count arguing that it is perfectly normal for the good to be punished, since we are all paying for the sin of Adam. "Assommons" literalizes this point of view, by having the narrator punish an innocent man. Sentimentality is here trumped by theological satire, a sort of willed concrete thinking: if it doesn't matter that the innocent are frequently punished, and if punishment is the only hope for redemption, then any scandalized outcry against the poem's sadism is promptly nullified.

Moreover, as mentioned above, the biblical injunction "An eye for an eye, a tooth for a tooth" is parodied in the poem as well: the narrator gets two black eyes for the one he inflicts on the beggar, and four teeth broken in exchange for two. If nothing else, the narrator possesses a self-irony that the author of the *Soirées* certainly lacked. Maistre and Proudhon are both satirized, and both strangely lionized in this poem. Proudhon is not entirely "gone" from the poet's thought, nor is Maistre so completely "digested" (to return to the recurring metaphor here); the poem has Proudhon still making the point, as it were, that the scandal of extreme poverty remains inadmissible. And Maistre's hyper-Augustinianism is literalized in a way that serves to support, rather than demolish, Proudhon's obsession with equality. We are, in other words, equally guilty of evil.

In "Le joujou du pauvre" (1862), a prose poem based on the essay "Morale du joujou" (1853), a rich little boy stands staring over a fence, his expensive gilded toy lying unheeded in the grass next to him. On the other side of the fence, a poor boy, covered with dirt, has his own toy—a rat in a box. The poor boy's parents (says the narrator), "no doubt for reasons of economy, had drawn the toy from life itself" (*OC* 1:305). The essay dates from the time Baudelaire was beginning to read Maistre, and the prose poem from the period when Maistre was a looming influence. Significantly, the later poem adds aspects that the essay lacks. Whereas the essay simply notes the "symbolic iron bars" through which the boys stare at each other, the poem makes the class distinction even more explicit. We still have the symbolic iron bars of the fence, but the poem adds that the bars separate "two worlds—the main road and the château." Moreover, the possibility of communication between the two boys is real. They both stare at the rat, "fraternally laughing with each other, with teeth of *equal* whiteness" (ibid.) The emphasis on "equal" is Baudelaire's, and can only be read as a nod to Proudhon. Here, children are truly fraternal, their laughter is genuine (and not—at least immediately—a sign of the satanic), and their equality is indicated, despite the iron bars, by their equally white teeth.

Now, of course, there is the rat—a hideous toy if ever there was one— and the boys' teeth are reminiscent, whiteness and all, of the rodent in the box. Nevertheless, this is not a fratricidal war, though the barrier between rich and poor is literalized. One might argue, admittedly, that the rat is like the boys described as "Satans in the making" in "Le gâteau"; it suggests, ominously, a foul and dangerous potentiality—like the relations between the two urban classes after the disaster of '48, the poor and the bourgeoisie. One might equally argue that it is the poor boy who has the rat, while the rich one stands safely on the other side of the iron fence, château as a backdrop. But a rat, after all, can crawl between the bars of a fence, and is contained only so long as the poor boy keeps it in its box. The political implications are very much present: both sides have teeth, and bare them. Still, there is a flash moment in "Le joujou des pauvres" in which the boys are bonded and class difference melts with their laughter. These boys too become doubles—they are joined by their childish curiosity and the budding of a friendship that will never be allowed to materialize. Filth and the gilded, poverty and privilege, will not mix—unless, of course, there is another revolution.

We have identified the protagonist of "Assommons" as the gaze, which is multiplied everywhere in the story, and we have also noted that the gaze of the beggar could topple thrones "if" the gaze of the hypnotist could make grapes ripen. "Le joujou des pauvres," interestingly enough, contains a metaphor similar in structure to the "if" sentence in "Assommons." The metaphor in "Le joujou" concerns the poor boy, who is described as "dirty, sickly, covered in soot, one of those pariah brats" (304). Then comes the phrase like the "if" in "Assommons": "an impartial eye would be able to discover the poor boy's beauty if, just as the eye of a connoisseur can imagine an ideal painting under a carriage builder's varnish, the boy were cleaned up of the repugnant patina of poverty" (305). It is, let us say at the outset, almost as unlikely that the poor boy will be cleaned up as it is that the beggar's gaze will topple thrones. But the other side of the equation has some possibility: there are art connoisseurs, the narrator of "Le joujou" is telling us, who are able to see the beautiful painting hiding under the ordinary varnish applied like that on carriages. Such connoisseurs, we should note, see two things at once: the obvious, which is slapped on and of no interest, and the underlying, hidden image which is "ideal" and a thing of beauty.

The comparison is important for Baudelaire's praxis: the connoisseur (and Baudelaire considered himself a connoisseur of art) can see beauty beneath the banal veneer of the everyday, of the poor and filthy, of the repulsive. He sees two images in one (hence, in a way, four eyes for two). This is how, to some extent, Baudelaire would have it: like Superman with his X-ray vision (anachronistic a comparison though that is), Baudelaire understands himself as looking beneath the surface of things and seeing what underlies them; indeed, that is what the poem performs, since the beauty of the boy is attested to, and the narrator already "sees" it.

"Assommons" prepares for two other images: the beggar is finally more the scopic double of the narrator than he is his potential social equal. The proliferation of gazes in the poem produces an excess of images that are not as controlled as the gaze of the connoisseur. And the combination of Maistre and Proudhon—satirically alluded to at certain times, and a source of importance and inspiration in the poet's thought at others—destabilizes any reading of the poem as either clearly satirical of Proudhon or firmly aligned with the implications of Maistrean thought. Indeed, the poem could just as well have ended with "What do you think of that, Count?" While the Paris poor may well be guilty theologically, along with everybody else, as descendants of Adam, they are innocent in the social sphere, and no more deserve to starve than to have, as children, a rat as a plaything. The sympathy Baudelaire evinces for the poor, which has often been celebrated, is on the social, political level; theologically however, every man deserves what he gets, suffering and all. This is not just contradiction, and it is more than ambivalence; it is seeing two realities simultaneously.

As we have seen, Baudelaire more than once insists on the right to contradict oneself. In his *Etudes sur Poe*, he announces: "Among the numerous enumerations of the *rights of man* that nineteenth-century wisdom returns to so often and so smugly, two rather important ones have been forgotten, which are the right to contradict oneself and the right to *go away*" (*OC* 2:306). To "go away" is underlined because it is a euphemism for committing suicide. "Assommons" certainly performs the first of these "rights" of man, and we know that Baudelaire at times seriously considered the second. But contradiction, which the Baudelairean corpus enacts fairly constantly, is not quite what I mean by the destabilization produced by conflicting ideas, clashing systems of thought, and unclear allegiances—although it is a part of it. Unlike Proudhon and Maistre, Baudelaire not only cultivates unresolved (and irresolvable) contradiction; he also does not attempt to redact or otherwise force into unison his own textual ambivalences. André Gide pointed out in 1910 that Baudelaire cannot stand obvious locutions or ready-made metaphors; it often pleases the poet, continues Gide, "to disorient the reader by a connection the exactitude of which we do not at first recognize."[87] And it is certainly the case that Baudelaire loved to shock. Baudelaire constantly needed to surprise, Nadar tells us, a trait, he continues, that inspired a bon mot from Asselineau: "Baudelaire, getting home in the evening, lies down under his bed to astonish himself" (*Charles Baudelaire*, 122). But Baudelaire is not always in control of the ambivalence, nor does he hold sway over the doubled images. He may well disorient his readers, but the world of modernity also disorients *him*.

The acceptance (or, at least, performance) of ambivalence may in part account for the movement many critics have observed in Baudelaire's verse. Jacques Rivière, a month after Gide's article of 1910, wrote: "Every Baudelaire poem is a movement; it is never at a standstill, it is not an immobile description, exalting by repeating and exaggerating the chosen theme."[88] Georges Poulet sees in Baudelairean movement a continual vibration, and adds, "Swimming, flying, rolling, drifting—all of these Baudelairean terms, far from implying a type of instantaneous irradiation, express a continual movement that, at the same time, goes beyond and melts into the span of time [*la durée*]."[89] But such motion is perhaps less true of the prose poems than of the verse. The verse frequently does have to do with a rocking motion, a theme to which we will return. A prose poem like "Assommons," however, hardly rocks gently—it careens.

Gide argues that in Baudelaire's poetry, as in all good poetry, there is a space, "that lapse of time between the image and the idea, between the word and the thing," and that this lapse is precisely the place where poetic emotion can come to dwell ("Baudelaire et M. Faguet," 512). But there is also a scopic gap—the strabismus to which I have referred—in Baudelaire, caused by two overlapping images. In the short prose poem "La soupe et les nuages," for example (published posthumously in 1869), the narrator waits for his dinner while staring out of the window, admiring "the moving architectures that God makes with vapors, the marvelous construc-

87. André Gide, "Baudelaire et M. Faguet," *La nouvelle revue française*, November 1, 1910, 513.

88. Jacques Rivière, "Baudelaire," *La nouvelle revue française*, December 1, 1910, 726.

89. Georges Poulet, *Les métamorphoses du cercle* (Paris: Plon, 1961), 401.

tions of the impalpable" (OC 1:350). These moving "phantasmagorias" are almost as beautiful, the narrator tells us, as the eyes of his beloved. Here we already have a doubled image: the clouds are like her eyes, though less beautiful. Suddenly, however, the narrator is jerked out of his reverie by "a violent punch" in his back. His "dear little beloved," whose voice is rough and charming, hysterical and hoarse from brandy, screams at him, demanding whether he's ever going to eat his damn soup. One imagines the narrator jerking from head up in the clouds, to head down looking at his soup. The lapse in the scopic is here literalized.

Once again the eyes, so important to Baudelaire, have betrayed him—as they do, for example, in "Les yeux des pauvres." In that prose poem, the narrator pities a poor family of three who are begging in front of a café; their various gazes, staring in awe at the café, he calls "the family of eyes." The narrator then turns away from the family to look at his beloved: "I turned my stares toward yours, dear love, to read in them *my* thought. I plunged into your eyes so beautiful and so strangely tender, into your green eyes, inhabited by Caprice and inspired by the Moon" (OC 1:319). But the beloved's gaze, harsh as is her voice in "La soupe et les nuages," sees the poor family merely as a source of annoyance, and wants the waiter to send them away. The narrator ends the poem by speaking again directly to his mistress, his tender words in (willed) ironic contrast with her behavior: "So difficult it is to understand each other, my dear angel, and so incommunicable is thought, even between people who love each other!" The scopic lapse is again explicit; the eyes are certainly not windows of the soul, Plato notwithstanding. Here, in other words, what is meant to be one, the lovers' souls, remains distinct, distanced, firmly two.

"The eyes," writes Pichois in one of his annotations, "are for Baudelaire mystical mirrors, given the charge of reflecting the infinite" (OC 1:1427 n. 7). Pichois tells us to consult the poem "La Beauté" (1857), where indeed Beauty (who is a "dream of stone," who hates movement, who neither cries nor laughs, who is a sphinx that is not understood) describes herself as possessing "pure mirrors which make all things more beautiful: my eyes, my wide eyes with eternal clarities" (OC 1:21). Certainly, Beauty here is charged with reflecting the infinite; but she is emphatically inhuman and has little to do with the all too human gazes we have been considering thus far. In Baudelaire's Beauty (in this poem, at least) there is precisely no scopic lapse between her gaze and the infinite: her gaze reflects the infinite because it is a part of it, and there is no alternative infinite in which to escape. She is Beauty-the-eternal, without the second element of beauty essential to Baudelaire: the contemporary aspect, the period, style, moral passion. Without this second element, Baudelaire had argued, Beauty is indigestible, "inappropriate for human nature" (*OC* 2:685). And that is emphatically what she is in "La Beauté"—inhuman. The gazes of humans, on the other hand, are nostalgic for such unity but never, for Baudelaire, attain it.

Again, consider "Les yeux des pauvres," where communication even between two lovers is impossible, emphasizing the gap between the infinite and daily life, between the clouds and soup, between abject poverty and theological justifications for the same. The gap between, or the lapse in the scopic, is where the Baudelairean prose poem situates itself, while each image remains, fully discernible, on either side. The Baudelairean text mirrors the lapse in thought, the doubling of contrary ideas, with two images that do not go together. Neither image can be expunged from his mind or from his understanding. In "Le miroir," a horribly ugly man (*épouvantable*) looks at himself in the mirror. The narrator asks him why he does so, since the image can only cause him displeasure. The man answers that according to the principles of '89 (and as if parodying "Assommons"), "all men are equal in rights; thus I posses the right to see my reflection; with pleasure or displeasure, that is only the business of my consciousness" (*OC* 1:344). The narrator, bemused, concludes that "in the name of common sense, I was no doubt right; but, from the perspective of the law, he was not wrong." Baudelaire records optically and intellectually such conundrums, but he does not resolve them. It is not just that he does not wish to resolve them; he cannot do so.

The poems are filled with contradiction, doubles, ambivalence. In "Assommons," Proudhon remains even as Maistre is the master of thought for the poet. But these destabilizing qualities, and the strabismic perspectives that follow, are symptoms of the larger issue, which has to do with the birth of modernity. Georges Bataille argues (contra Sartre) that the unparalleled tension in Baudelaire's work, and "the fullness with which . . . [it] has invaded the modern mind," can be explained not by his personal errors but by "the historically determined expectation to which these errors corresponded" (*La littérature et le mal*, 42). It is not, for Bataille, only individual necessity that is expressed in Baudelaire; the poems are also the result of "a *material* tension imposed, periodically, from without" (43). To wit: the poems were written in a society that no longer sustained the primacy of the future in conjunction with a nominal sacred. The new society forming in Baudelaire's day is "a capitalist society in full swing," one preferring the dams of the industrial age to the lakes of Versailles (and, likewise, builds boulevards in Paris to insure against the barricades of the future).

The present for this new society has no sacred, since its only purpose is to pave the way to the future. In the words of Bataille, "the process that had been prepared some time earlier started a swift metamorphosis of the civilized world based on the primacy of the future—capitalist *accumulation*" (44). Bataille then faults Sartre in the same way Croce faults Hugo: Sartre individualizes what must be seen as a sweeping current, of which Baudelaire's jaundiced views are merely the natural extension.[90]

This, then, is the strabismus recorded in "Assommons" and some of the other poems we have considered: Baudelaire cannot give up Proudhon because the poverty of the Paris underclass is crushing, demanding alms at every turn in the city's ever wider streets, continually attesting to extreme social injustice and inequity. But he also cannot give up Maistre, because the evil that can be attributed to capitalist greed (in both rich and poor), the inequality between the classes, the guilt and subsequent rage or pity such inequality produces, overwhelm the poet who seeks (and finds) in Maistre a theological justification for such suffering and a dark system of divine retribution that accounts for human misery.

Baudelaire himself uses the term strabismus, but in a quite different context (to put it mildly) from the usual ophthalmic one. In the spring of 1859, a few years before Baudelaire was to write "Assommons," he writes a letter to Nadar from his mother's house at Honfleur, pleading with his friend to send him twenty francs (no doubt for more opium, which Baudelaire used mainly, in principle at least, as a painkiller). In the third section of the letter, Baudelaire changes topics to describe two Goya paintings—*La Maja vestida* and, more particularly, *La Maja desnuda*. Mistakenly believing these to be portraits of the duchess of Alba, he asks Nadar to get permission from the man selling the paintings to make large photographic reproductions of the *desnuda*. The first Goya painting shows a woman in "national costume." But it is the same woman as a reclining nude that delights the poet: "The very triviality of the pose increases the charm of the depiction" he writes (*Corr.* 1:574). The duchess looks unpleasant and has an abundance of hair. One breast hides her armpit, and together the breasts "are afflicted with a *sursum* and divergent strabismus." Pichois notes approvingly that here "Baudelaire is showing real knowledge in ophthalmology, agreeably applied" (*Corr.* 1:1026), adding that divergent strabismus (extropia) "can, in fact, be combined with *sursumvergens* strabismus" (hypertropia). Indeed, the woman's breasts point both upward (hypertropia) and outward (extropia). Without making too much of all this, let us simply conclude that Baudelaire is more than aware of the possibilities of double vision and its physiological manifestations. And he is writing all of this, after all, to the great photographer (as well as artist and balloonist) Nadar.

Photography was where we started in this chapter—with Benjamin's conviction that Baudelaire alone, "thanks to infinite mental efforts," could read the photographic plates he produced. I have spent most of this chapter differing with that view. Baudelaire, I have been arguing, frequently registers two images at once. In this he does not resemble the connoisseur who perceives a great painting hidden under the varnish on a carriage, which is the way Benjamin would have it: Baudelaire alone, he claims, "is able to extract from the negatives of essence a presentiment of its real picture." But Baudelaire (his ability to discern beneath the surface of things notwithstanding) often produces two pictures at once, and neither is the "real" one lying underneath the one that is evident. They are both real for him, antinomies though they may be. The social and political reality of modernity is at odds with itself; the foundations of traditional morality and theology can be marshaled to explain, but not entirely to justify, the inequities that are rampant in the city. Baudelaire records that clash, and "Assommons" is one such recording. In the next chapter, we will consider how strabismus, or scopic lapse, appears in Baudelaire's view of art. For if reading the modern city entails recording its disparate images, art and art criticism can only follow for the poet who sees double.

Appendix

ASSOMMONS LES PAUVRES!

Pendant quinze jours je m'étais confiné dans ma chambre, et je m'étais entouré des livres à la mode dans ce temps-là (il y a seize ou dix-sept ans); je veux parler des livres où il est traité de l'art de rendre les peuples heureux, sages et riches, en vingt-quatre heures. J'avais donc digéré—avalé, veux-je dire—toutes les élucubrations de tous ces entrepreneurs de bonheur public,—de ceux qui conseillent à tous les pauvres de se faire esclaves, et de ceux qui leur persuadent qu'ils sont tous des rois détrônés.—On ne trouvera pas surprenant que je fusse alors dans un état d'esprit avoisinant le vertige ou la stupidité.

Il m'avait semblé seulement que je sentais, confiné au fond de mon intellect, le germe obscur d'une idée supérieure à toutes les formules de bonne femme dont j'avais récemment parcouru le dictionnaire. Mais ce n'était que l'idée d'une idée, quelque chose d'infiniment vague.

Et je sortis avec une grande soif. Car le goût passionné des mauvaises lectures engendre un besoin proportionnel du grand air et des rafraîchissants.

Comme j'allais entrer dans un cabaret, un mendiant me tendit son chapeau, avec un de ces regards inoubliables qui culbuteraient les trônes, si l'esprit remuait la matière, et si l'œil d'un magnétiseur faisait mûrir les raisins.

En même temps, j'entendis une voix qui chuchotait à mon oreille, une voix que je reconnus bien; c'était celle d'un bon Ange, ou d'un bon Démon, qui m'accompagne partout. Puisque Socrate avait son bon Démon, pourquoi n'aurais-je pas mon bon Ange, et pourquoi n'aurais-je pas l'honneur, comme Socrate, d'obtenir mon brevet de folie, signé du subtil Lélut et du bien avisé Baillarger?

Il existe cette différence entre le Démon de Socrate et le mien, que celui de Socrate ne se manifestait à lui que pour défendre, avertir, empêcher, et que le mien daigne conseiller, suggérer, persuader. Ce pauvre Socrate n'avait qu'un Démon prohibiteur; le mien est un grand affirmateur, le mien est un Démon d'action, un Démon de combat.

Or, sa voix me chuchotait ceci: "Celui-là seul est l'égal d'un autre, qui le prouve, et celui-là seul est digne de la liberté, qui sait la conquérir."

Immédiatement, je sautai sur mon mendiant. D'un seul coup de poing, je lui bouchai un œil, qui devint, en une seconde, gros comme une balle. Je cassai un de mes ongles à lui briser deux dents, et comme je ne me sentais pas assez fort, étant né délicat et m'étant peu exercé à la boxe, pour assommer rapidement ce vieillard, je le saisis d'une main par le collet de son habit, de l'autre, je l'empoignai à la gorge, et je me mis à lui sccouer vigoureusement la tête contre un mur. Je dois avouer que j'avais préalablement inspecté les environs d'un coup d'œil, et que j'avais vérifié que dans cette banlieue déserte je me trouvais, pour un assez long temps, hors de la portée de tout agent de police.

Ayant ensuite, par un coup de pied lancé dans le dos, assez énergique pour briser les omoplates, terrassé ce sexagénaire affaibli, je me saisis d'une grosse branche d'arbre qui traînait à terre, et je le battis avec l'énergie obstinée des cuisiniers qui veulent attendrir un beefteack.

Tout à coup,—ô miracle! ô jouissance du philosophe qui vérifie l'excellence de sa théorie!—je vis cette antique carcasse se retourner, se redresser avec une énergie que je n'aurais jamais soupçonnée dans une machine si singulièrement détraquée, et, avec un regard de haine qui me parut de *bon augure*, le malandrin décrepit se jeta sur moi, me pocha les deux yeux, me cassa quatre dents, et avec la même branche d'arbre me battit dru comme plâtre.—Par mon énergique médication, je lui avais donc rendu l'orgueil et la vie.

Alors, je lui fis force signes pour lui faire comprendre que je considérais la discussion comme finie, et me relevant avec la satisfaction d'un sophiste du Portique, je lui dis: "Monsieur, *vous êtes mon égal!* veuillez me faire l'honneur de partager avec moi ma bourse; et souvenez-vous, si vous êtes réellement philanthrope, qu'il faut appliquer à tous vos confrères, quand ils vous demanderont l'aumône, la théorie que j'ai eu la *douleur* d'essayer sur votre dos."

Il m'a bien juré qu'il avait compris ma théorie, et qu'il obéirait à mes conseils.

CHAPTER TWO

Seeing (A une passante)

The daily sight of a lively crowd may once have constituted a spectacle
to which one's eyes needed to adapt. On the basis of this supposition,
one may assume that once the eyes had mastered this task, they wel-
comed opportunities to test their newly acquired ability.
—Walter Benjamin, "On Some Motifs in Baudelaire"

From childhood's hour I have not been
As others were—I have not seen
As others saw—
—Edgar Allen Poe, "Alone"

"In Baudelaire's view of modernity," says Benjamin, "the theory of modern art is the weakest point" (*The Writer of Modern Life*, 111). Bataille,
nearly two decades later, observes that Baudelaire missed seeing the an-
guished modernity of his friend Manet. The painter had broken with the
past (something that Baudelaire certainly upheld in poetry) and left "eloquent painting" behind as dead, as "unanimated by anything real."[1] While
a new form of painting was emerging with Manet, Baudelaire was busy
singing the praises of other, ultimately less important artists, particularly
Charles Meryon (1821–68), Constantin Guys (1805–92), Honoré Daumier
(1808–79), and above all Eugène Delacroix (1798–1863). With hindsight,
we might say that the poet was mostly "right" in his recognition of
Daumier—perhaps because Baudelaire greatly valued caricature, because
he had a theory about humor, and because Daumier's drawings captured
the hypocrisy of bourgeois life and its political repercussions in a sardonic

---

1 . Georges Bataille, *Manet* (Geneva: Skira, 1955), 49.

manner the poet could enjoy. Caricature is in any case a different kind of art for Baudelaire: its significance lies in metaphysics, in its engagement in the comic (we have seen how humor is tied to man's essential attraction to evil), in its historical renditions of an epoch, and in its political satire. But caricature does not bear the same kinds of artistic responsibilities, or aesthetic stakes, as high art does. Daumier is the best of his kind, writes Baudelaire; but though he dubs Daumier a "really great artist" (*OC* 2:552), what he most admires in him is his "certainty," his excellent memory, his talent of observation. Daumier has the logic of the learned (*savant*) who is "transported into an art that is light, fleeting, and who works against the very mobility of life" (556). He draws what he has seen; but even he cannot rise to the "absolute comical" because he is too fond of nature (557).[2] And Daumier knows his limits, for which Baudelaire clearly admires him. An artist of the *comique significatif* (and not of the *comique absolu*), Daumier wants to appeal to ordinary French people: "He even carefully avoids," writes Baudelaire, "all that would not be the object of a clear and immediate perception for the French public" (557).

Daumier may not have attained the high level of the "absolute comical," but for Baudelaire he nonetheless captures the moral indifference, if not downright evil tendencies, of man; an attitude that Baudelaire soundly endorses. For original sin motivates Baudelaire's art criticism even as it does his poetry. Baudelaire's entire aesthetic and metaphysics, writes Jonathan Mayne, can be reduced to a "fundamental statement, . . . a passionately-held belief in the Fall of Man, and Original Sin." Transferred to the criticism of the arts in the mid-nineteenth century, Mayne continues, "the doctrine has a corollary of the greatest importance." Baudelaire's impatience with naturalism is based on a fear of, and contempt for, the "senseless and undirected impulses of Nature."[3] The latter view is perhaps a bit reductive here, but the point is well taken: Baudelaire's art criticism shows a certain wariness toward nature (with or without a capital *N*). Daumier, as we have seen, cannot rise to full greatness because he is too fond of nature—and the natural is what is worst in humankind, let us

2. In "L'essence du rire," Baudelaire divides the comical into two types: the ordinary (which he calls "significatif"), which is easy for the ordinary man to understand and to analyze, because it is double—it is art and a moral idea. The other kind of comical, the "absolute" (or grotesque) is unitary, and takes its "joy" from the fallen state of humanity (*OC* 2:535–36). Thus even the great Daumier does not attain this high level of the comical in Baudelaire's judgment.

3. Baudelaire, *The Painter of Modern Life and Other Essays*, ed. and trans. Jonathan Mayne (Phaidon Press: London, 1964), xiv.

recall. The obsession with original sin does not abandon Baudelaire when he is looking at art, any more than it does when he considers the essence of laughter. If Wordsworth joyfully and reverentially capitalized "Ye Presences of Nature,"[4] Baudelaire's frequent use of the capital *N* for nature signals a grudging acknowledgement, but also discomfort. His views on artists are affected accordingly: he was unsettled by the presence of the natural world.[5]

Much has been written on Baudelaire's art criticism, and his views on art are taken far more seriously now than they were when he published them (or than when Benjamin voiced his negative judgment). Indeed, he is frequently considered the father of modern art criticism. He had an unerring grasp of what the artist was attempting, even if he was not always on target with respect to posterity's assessments. Moreover, if Baudelaire was right about Daumier's genius, he wasn't exactly wrong about the other artists. Meryon was a superb engraver, and his series on Paris was admired as much for its painstaking accuracy as for its nostalgic vision. Constantin Guys, the Dutch-born painter in France, produced realistic tableaux of the Crimean War and often amusing (at times caricature-like) depictions of French social classes, particularly the haute bourgeoisie. Finally, Delacroix, about whom Baudelaire was unabashedly rhapsodic, was clearly an important, generally romantic artist who masterfully painted everything from the Orient to grand allegories of the French Republic, to scenes from the Bible. Baudelaire saw him as the last great Renaissance artist and the first modern.

All of these artists were the poet's contemporaries, and all of them were in the *Salons* that Baudelaire so famously wrote about. Nevertheless, there is something slightly awry about these choices, and it is not merely the fact that Manet is largely overlooked. The four that Baudelaire so admired are mostly representational, figurative artists who, though touted by

4. "Ye Presences of Nature, in the sky / Or on the earth! Ye visions of the hills! / And souls of lonely places! can I think / A vulgar hope was yours when Ye employ'd / Such ministry, [when] Ye through many a year / Haunting me thus among my boyish sports, / and thus did make / The surface of the universal earth / With triumph, and delight, and hope, and fear / Work like a sea." William Wordsworth, *The Thirteen-Book Prelude* [1805–6], 2 vols., ed. Mark L. Reed (Ithaca, NY, 1991), I, 11, 491–502. Wordsworth is clear that nature inspires awe ("and fear"), but what has been called his imaginative animism clearly links the inspiration of nature to the imagination. See, e.g., Anthony John Harding, *The Reception of Myth in English Romanticism* (Columbia: University of Missouri Press, 1995).

5. The most probing study of Baudelaire's relation to nature remains F. W. Leakey, *Baudelaire and Nature* (Manchester: Manchester University Press, 1969). Leakey notes, it should be added, that Baudelaire's relationship to nature is not only always a hostile one.

Baudelaire as the most modern of their contemporaries, engage in the kind of "eloquent painting" that, as Bataille reminds us, Manet increasingly left behind as "dead." They are artists whose works produce narratives with plots that are mostly known; or whose depictions of contemporary life allegorize by typing as much as do their paintings of biblical scenes or of mythological episodes. It is perhaps precisely because Baudelaire brings his metaphysics to bear in his judgment on art, especially painting, that he is at once so brilliantly compelling and so perplexing as a critic of art. His descriptions of paintings are stunningly profound and precise; and yet, to repeat, there is something awry. It is as if, even as he thrills in the presence of what he thinks is a great painting, the works themselves were acting as material illustrations for his own mental architecture. It is this peculiar vision, and the odd feeling of *décallage* it can provoke, that will be the focus of the present chapter. *How*, in other words, is Baudelaire seeing what he sees? By what lights (quite literally)?

THE WILL TO KNOW

Let us consider, in approaching this question, something rather revealing that Baudelaire wrote about Balzac:

> It is said of Balzac (and who would not listen with respect to all the anecdotes, small as they might be, having to do with this great genius?), that he found himself one day in front of a beautiful painting, a winter painting, all melancholic and heavy with a wintry landscape, poor peasants scattered around. After contemplating a little house from which a thin column of smoke arose, he exclaimed, "How beautiful! But what can they be doing in that cabin? What are they thinking about, what are their misfortunes? Was the harvest a good one? *They have, no doubt, payments that are due!*"

Laugh if you like, comments Baudelaire, but the "great novelist" has here given us "an excellent lesson in criticism." He himself, the poet tells us, often happens "to appreciate a painting solely for its collection of ideas or of the reveries [*rêveries*] it brings to my mind" (*OC* 2:579). Well, there we have it: Baudelaire likes to get inside a painting, to imagine like Balzac what ideas have produced it, to let it prompt a daydream.

At first glance, the Balzac anecdote as Baudelaire tells it bears a peculiar resemblance to Heidegger's reading of Van Gogh's *Shoes*: "In the shoes," writes the philosopher in "On the Origin of the Work of Art," there vibrates "the silent call of the earth, its quiet gift of the ripening grain and its unexplained self-refusal in the fallow desolation of the wintry field. This equipment is pervaded by uncomplaining anxiety as to the certainty of bread, the wordless joy of having once more withstood want."[6] Meyer Schapiro's 1968 critique, "The Still Life as a Personal Object—a Note on Heidegger and Van Gogh," returns the discussion to the realm of art history, to the museum, and to the actual ownership of the shoes. The argument between Heidegger and Schapiro, as many have remarked, is (among other things) one between philosophy and art history; between the notion of the thing's thingness, and the "proper" manner and perspective with which to approach "art." Baudelaire too is trespassing on the property of the art cognoscenti of his day by brandishing his own, intensely postlapsarian philosophy when he examines paintings. (I focus on paintings because Baudelaire thought sculpture largely "boring").[7] Like Balzac, Baudelaire wants to imagine what people are thinking about in the cabin; but unlike both the philosopher and the novelist, Baudelaire favors the urban. The "silent call of the earth" is not one that he strains to hear.[8] Nor will Baudelaire care about who owned any given pair of shoes (pace Meyer Schapiro); rather, he will ask what in the painting is the source of pleasure, and how this pleasure can be turned into knowledge. In his essay on Wagner (1861), Baudelaire makes such a critical démarche clear.

Like the written word and like a painting, writes Baudelaire, music "always has a lacuna that is filled by the listener's imagination" (*OC* 2:782). When he first hears the overture from *Lohengrin*, Baudelaire is plunged

6. Martin Heidegger, "On the Origin of the Work of Art," in *Poetry, Language, Thought*, trans. Albert Hofstadter (New York: Harper and Row, 1971), 34.

7. See "Pourquoi la sculpture est ennuyeuse," in *OC* 2:487–89. The young Baudelaire sees sculpture as being too close to nature to be great, and as having too many aspects for the spectator to know which to contemplate: "Brutal and concrete like nature, [sculpture] is at the same time vague and ungraspable because it shows too many faces at once" (487). In the early 1850s, however, the sculptor Ernest Christophe changed Baudelaire's mind about sculpture. In the *Salon de 1859*, Baudelaire writes glowingly about Christophe's work. Two poems in the 1861 edition of the *Fleurs du mal* are dedicated to the sculptor: "Le masque" and "Danse macabre." Moreover, the 1859 *Salon* has an entire section on sculpture, which discusses statues as commanding in stature, fascinating in dimensionality (*OC* 2:669–80). Statues are now allied with ghosts, that elicit the past and the beyond: "le fantôme de pierre s'empare de vous pendant quelques minutes, et vous commande, au nom du passé, de penser aux choses qui ne sont pas de la terre" (670).

8. On the landscape painting of Théodore Rousseau, for example, Baudelaire notes, "he falls into the famous modern fault, born of a blind love for nature, nothing but nature. He takes a simple study to be a composition." All the charm in Rousseau's landscapes, concludes the poet, "does not always suffice to help in forgetting the absence of construction." *Salon de 1859*, in *OC* 2:662.

into a reverie (the word recurs here). He feels weightless, in a vast expanse of light with an immense horizon. He is a soul floating in the light, with an ecstasy made of sensual delight (*volupté*) and knowledge. And he adds, immediately (to return to our point about "Nature"), that this soul is floating "far from the natural world" (*OC* 2:785). And being far from the natural world is a good thing for the poet (let us remember, to take one example we have considered, that "Le gâteau" begins in nature, only to unravel as the place most given to the display of man's depravity). Baudelaire adds that from the time of his first Wagner concert, the poet became obsessed with returning to this sensual delight that was "so strong and so terrible." He had, he writes, experienced a "spiritual operation, a revelation," but there was also "something new," which he could not define, and this incapacity angered him. He felt "mysterious intentions and a method" that were unknown to him. The poet then moves to his critical analysis: "I resolved," he writes, "to inform myself as to the why, and to transform my sensual delight into knowledge" (*OC* 2:786).

The critic, then, is motivated by the will to know. But what he must know is *why* he feels this ecstasy, which combines sensual delight and knowledge. The insistence on "why" is what eventually makes every great poet a critic (and never vice versa, which would be a "monstrosity"): "all great poets naturally, fatally, become critics. I pity the poets guided by instinct only; I see them as incomplete" (*OC* 2:793). Instinct is not enough; indeed, "In the spiritual life of the former [poets who are not guided by instinct only], a crisis inevitably occurs." This crisis is precisely the need to understand how and why art is produced. Real artists want to "reason with their art, to discover the obscure laws by virtue of which they produce, to glean from this study a series of precepts the divine purpose of which is the inevitable in poetic production." The reader will not be surprised, says Baudelaire, "that I consider the poet the best of all critics" (ibid.). Poets are the best critics because they can feel the ecstasy fully, they can fill the lacuna with imagination, they are capable of a "spiritual operation" and revelation. It is not only that they have the superior sensibility to experience these; poets also identify with the process of creation that produced the work. But even this is not enough. The intellect appears when the poet wants to understand "mysterious intentions and a method" that escape definition; the "obscure laws" that allow for artistic production; the why and the how *volupté* is transformed into knowledge.

The great arts, moreover, can be "translated" each into the other. Music, painting, and poetry "suggest analogous ideas in different minds" (*OC* 2:784). At this point in the Wagner essay, Baudelaire declares such resonances to be articulated in his own programmatic "Correspondances" (which he then amply cites). His lead in to his own sonnet is the declaration that things are always "expressed by a reciprocal analogy, ever since the day God proffered the world as a complex and indivisible totality" (ibid.). As Fredric Jameson points out (in his critique of Clement Greenberg), this attitude results in a circular flight: "the various arts—better still, the media of the various arts—affirm their absolute quality only by borrowing representational features from the next." The result, continues Jameson, is that "the autonomy of art means some absolute spiritualization or sublimation beyond the figural."[9] This conviction is basically what Baudelaire argues with his praxis of synesthesia. He is taken by the nonreferential quality of music, its capacity, as Poe put it, to move us to glories beyond the grave. Baudelaire compares three "translations" of this music: his own, Wagner's, and Liszt's, and adds that what is important is "resemblances." All three contain the sensation of "spiritual and physical beatitude; isolation, the contemplation of *something infinitely great and infinitely beautiful; an intense light* that delights *the eyes and soul to the point of swooning;* and, finally, the sensation of *space extending to the final conceivable limits*" (OC 2:785).

There is a difference, however, among the "translations" of Wagner, Liszt, and Baudelaire: the poet's own reverie, he tells us, "is much less illustrated with material objects; it is vaguer and more abstract" (ibid.). If in music Baudelaire can go directly to the abstract, in painting he uses the figural to go beyond it to a "spiritualization"—indeed, he gravitates toward the representational in the visual arts, though he quickly uses the figural to reach the "vaguer and more abstract."[10] Swann, in Proust's *Recherche,* loves Odette because the physical sight of her reminds him of Botticelli's Venus or his Zephora. She is metamorphosed, as it were, into a work of art and thus idealized (and ultimately "loved") as the trigger for the contemplation of artistic genius. Baudelaire, however, argues that he goes immediately from the figural—in painting or in reality ("La chevelure" is a good instance of this)—to the ideational: in wanting to understand the origin of the work of art (my allusion here is intended), he uses a given representa-

9. Fredric Jameson, *A Singular Modernity: On the Ontology of the Present* (London: Verso, 2002), 173.

10. Though simple copying without imagination (the queen of the faculties, as Baudelaire calls it) is insufficient. Baudelaire quotes Delacroix as saying that nature is simply a dictionary. "Those who have no imagination," adds the poet, "copy the dictionary" (OC 2:624–25). An excessive taste for "the Real," says Baudelaire in his essay on photography, can "smother the taste for the beautiful" (616).

tion to take flight into an aesthetic, and ultimately poetic, epistemology. The movement seems to be from the concrete sights, sounds, and things of the narrow (urban) world to a place of space and light, where there is room to float.

One of the best examples of such movement between realms—the narrow and concrete versus the abstract ideal—is a prose poem we considered in the previous chapter, "La soupe et les nuages." The daydreaming narrator, it will be recalled, comes back to earth, and to his soup, when his "beloved" (*bien-aimée*) punches him in the back and calls him a "cloud salesman." In the reverie that precedes this brutal gesture however, the narrator stares through the window and contemplates "the moving architectures that God makes with vapors, the marvelous constructions of the impalpable" (*OC* 1:350). So too, the narrator of the short prose poem, "Anywhere out of the world" (the title is in English) tells us that this life is a hospital ward in which every patient wants to change beds. Following his own metaphor, the narrator then offers his soul a change of scenery (Lisbon, Holland, Batavia), but the soul, uninterested in other "beds," remains mute. Finally, the soul cries out the poem's title—anywhere, so long as it is not on this earth. The poet, in other words, finds the real world paltry, depressing, stifling, and generally sick. The realm of the ideal, on the other hand, is vast and luminous and blissfully far away. But it is the concrete real that triggers, indeed launches, the move to the ideal; and it is the poet who sees the limitations of "the world" better than others. The visual artist "sees" in the same way, though it is the critic (read: poet) who is able to articulate what makes the artist great (or not), and who can reflect on what motivates artistic genius.

Thus, follows Baudelaire's own implied syllogism, any great poet must be a critic, since "genius" must turn the experience of aesthetic ecstasy into knowledge. To return to Proust: as Odette's face triggered the vision of Botticelli's Zephora for Swann, for Baudelaire any face, scene, or other painterly representation, if "great," will trigger thinking about the origins of artistic creation. Proust's character goes from materiality to aesthetic representation; Baudelaire on Wagner goes from representation to the realm of the aesthetic ideal, and then to the search for underlying precepts, the "divine purpose" of which is poetic production.

Baudelaire's well-known definition of modernity can be partly read in this light. "Modernity," he famously declares, "is the transitory, the fugitive, the contingent half of art, the other half being the eternal and the immutable" ("The Painter of Modern Life," *OC* 2:695). The transitory is the flash point of representation, the nowness of now. The other half of art is that which suggests the eternal and immutable: thinking. The first is the ability of the poet, as poet, to *recognize* moments of the sublime within material reality; the second is his ability to extract, as critic, the obscure laws allowing for the recognition of such moments. And perhaps this is why there is something awry, as I put it earlier, with Baudelaire's art criticism: it privileges the material, representational world, even as it uses it to take flight to more ethereal considerations. In so doing, however, Baudelaire's art criticism leaves the artist behind in the representational. There is nothing particularly surprising or new about the poet establishing himself as superior in his meditations on art (reminiscent, for example, of Plato locating the philosopher at the top rung of thought). But Baudelaire's notion of the representational as the launching pad for metaphysical aesthetics, and his praise of artists who capture materiality in their work, gives the poet-critic a kind of vision that is, at the very least, more complex than that of other artists (including composers). We need to look more closely at the complexity of vision that Baudelaire bestows on the poet.

Moreover, the two halves of art are not quite as clear-cut in other Baudelaire essays as they are in "The Painter of Modern Life." There are times when for Baudelaire the "transitory, the fugitive, the contingent," that formulation so seminal for scholars of modernism, grounded as it often is in the figural (in poetry as well as art), seem to be simultaneous with "the eternal and the immutable," or, at least, confused with them. Certainly, the transitory is the acknowledgment of—even as it motivates a flight from—reality in certain poems, as in "La chevelure," mentioned earlier. Similarly, the well-known poem "A une passante," on which we will be focusing in this chapter, makes the same gesture. The face in the crowd that is glimpsed in the poem is what allows for a more abstract memory—the fantasy of eternal love. There are many such poems, especially the earlier ones. Indeed, we can argue that modernity in Baudelaire's poetic praxis achieves the transitory within the "material objects" of the modern city, and uses it to imagine the immutable.

But something else is going on, something that points to Baudelaire's modernity in art in a way that his art criticism seems often to destabilize. For the transitory, the fugitive, the contingent in Baudelaire encapsulate not so much a theory of modernity as the basis of a *visual* experience, which he folds into "the new" and the modern. Baudelaire, in other words, seems to like seeing things fly by too quickly to assimilate, too rapidly to register, too fleetingly to allow thought to repose on them, letting it rather rest on the meditation of the visual that ensues. As often as Baudelaire wants wine or hashish to forget, he just as often wants a swirl of images to ward off the stagnation of spleen and the paralysis of ennui. (Both attitudes, a psychoanalytic approach might argue, are ways of coping with depression—not an unlikely hypothesis, but not my focus here.)

For example, Baudelaire obviously admires the hero of "The Painter of Modern Life," Constantin Guys. But it is significant that one of the things he admires most in the painter is his rapidity of sight, his insatiable looking, which makes him the "lover of universal life." Guys (who remains putatively anonymous as "C.G." in the text) has an "eagle eye"; an "intense gaze" on the short-lived spectacles of the city. He is always afraid he has gotten up too late and missed things he might have seen in the morning light: "How many *lit-up* things I could have seen," Baudelaire imagines Guys lamenting when the sun has set, "and I didn't see." Guys "takes pleasure" in all forms of pageantry and admires the "eternal beauty and surprising harmony of life in the capitals"; he notices any changes in dress, style, hairdos, belts, livery; he has "already seen" and inspected military parades before they have even passed by. Even Guys's output is motivated by speed: every scene in the city "enters him pell-mell" through his eyes, and the "poem" that results is virtually composed "in a few minutes." Guys tears through the execution of his drawings, "as if he feared that the images might escape him" (*OC* 2:692–93).

At times Guys seems to be playing Mulligan to Baudelaire's Stephen Daedalus: the poet's enthusiastic prose mimes the painter's inexhaustible energy, and the poet is clearly envious. The images appear "beautiful and more than beautiful, singular and gifted with a life as enthusiastic as the soul of the author." Guys is blessed with a "*childlike* perception; that is a sharp perception, magic by dint of ingenuity" (*OC* 2:693–94). At dusk, while others are at their favorite bars, "drinking the cup of forgetfulness," Guys stays out in the light later than anyone; he is where "a passion can *pose* for his eye" (693). The profusion of verbs and nouns of sight are matched only by a breathless series of catalogs describing the teeming (*fourmiller*) of life that surrounds the painter, Guys's own race to view everything around him, and his frenzied attempt to make sure his eyes take it all in so that he can draw it. The "transitory, the fugitive, and the contingent" are on several levels then: the city itself; the fleeting moments everywhere that catch the painter's ubiquitous eye; the speed with which he produces drawings; and Baudelaire's prose, as breathless as the man it describes, as crowded as the streets of the city, as fleeting as the images that for him are the modern half of art.

IMAGES AND AFTERIMAGES: THE POEM

One of the major manifestations of rapid and fugitive images is of course the crowd. "He who loves universal life," writes Baudelaire, "enters the crowd as if it were an immense reservoir of electricity" (OC 2:692). The poet speaks for Guys: "Any man," he approvingly quotes the painter as saying, "who is not overcome by one of those moments of sadness of too definite a nature not to absorb all his faculties, is an idiot! An idiot! And I despise him" (ibid.). "A une passante" (1860), a poem in which Baudelaire is clearly thinking of Guys's watercolors, begins with precisely such a sadness, glimpsed in all its instantaneity within the noise of the crowd:

> The deafening street around me was howling.
> Tall, thin, in heavy mourning, majestic pain,
> A woman passed by, and with a fastidious hand,
> Lifting, balancing the festoon and the hem. (OC 1:92–93)

Notice that Baudelaire initially evokes the visual confusion of the urban crowd through the audial.[11] When the woman passes by, the poem somehow grows silent. It does this by contrast. The howling crowd underlines its jostling chaos by way of its vulgar, deafening screams. The sentence describing the crowd is straightforward, brutal, and oxymoronic (the clichéd notion that noise makes you deaf). The sentence is in the imperfect tense, suggesting a constancy of noise matching the continual visual tumult. The woman who suddenly appears in the midst of this noise, however, is described in visual terms—her dress of heavy mourning immediately suggests the moment of sadness to which Guys alluded, and it is confirmed by her "majestic pain." As against the continual movement of the imperfect

11. Needless to say, a great deal of work has been done on Baudelaire's sonnets, which, as François Jost puts it, experiment constantly with varying forms (including the Elizabethan), such that "la plupart des sonnets de Baudelaire . . . sont libres ou libertins, licentieux ou faux, quoique sonnant fort juste." See Jost, "Evaluation ésthéthique et généalogie: L'exemple du sonnet," *Neohelicon* 1, nos. 1–2 (March, 1973): 78. In other words, the prose poem is far from being the only venue of experimentation for Baudelaire. Most critics hold that only five of his sonnets are "regular," respecting the French abba/abba/ccd/ede rhyme scheme. Baudelaire himself saw in the sonnet, precisely because of its constraints, the ability to make the "idea burst forth more intensely." Every subject is appropriate for the sonnet, and one finds there "the beauty of well wrought metal and mineral" (*Corr.* 1:676). The letter is to the critic Armand Fraisse, on February 18, 1860. For a recent study of Baudelaire's versification, see Brigitte Buffard-Moret, "Baudelaire, héritier du baroque et poète moderne: Essai de versification," in *Styles, genres, auteurs 2: Montaigne, Bossuet, Lesage, Baudelaire, Giraudoux*, ed. Anne-Marie Garagnon (Paris: Université de la Sorbonne, 2002), 113–29.

tense describing the faceless crowd, she appears in the *passé simple*, or preterit—the tense of a specific occurrence, of a singular moment that has been completed. Her movement is a rocking one, like the one we considered in the previous chapter that describes moored ships or flower stalks in the wind: "lifting, balancing":

> Agile and noble, with the leg of a statue.
> As for me, I drank, tense as an extravagant,
> From her eye, livid sky in which a storm brews,
> The sweetness that fascinates and the pleasure that kills.

The description of her is scattered with commas, creating pauses in the reading (suggesting the woman's swaying and her careful steps), at variance with the maelstrom (to use Poe's word) of the clamoring crowd (and with the jerky movements of the pedestrian trying to avoid being run over by the bedlam of traffic on streets with no sidewalks). Her distinction from the surrounding crassness is immediate: her hand is fastidious, and she is carefully protecting her long skirt from the "mud" (*boue*, the euphemism for the sewage in the Paris streets at this time).[12] The first line of the next stanza will emphasize her stately demeanor: she is agile and noble, with her leg like a statue's. Thus the contrasts: noise as against vision; screaming as against silent pain; the naked declarative syntax of mayhem as against the gentle pauses produced by commas and short clauses, mirroring her careful gait; vulgarity as against nobility; the continuum as against the sudden image of beauty that is frozen in the poet's eye for an instant of time; the imperfect tense of habituation and continuation as against the preterit in which an action has long since occurred. The crowd may have been overwhelming in its deafening noise, but the woman who passes by herself deafens the poet to the noise of the crowd: he sees only her, and no longer hears anything.

The sensation of spontaneous silence produced in this poem is a bit like the scene from the movie "Gigi," if I can briefly compare a great poem to a mediocre film.[13] But the movie does literalize such a moment of sudden quiet. The setting is the noisy Maxime's de Paris at the turn of the century. *Le tout Paris*—everyone—is there (and here of course the crowd is wealthy, and in theory much more sophisticated than the street crowd,

---

12. The more explicit term, of course, is *la fange*.

13. The original story, by Colette, does not have such a scene. Colette herself was annoyed at always being known as the author of the *Claudines* and *Gigi*, feeling that these works were too facile and less important than her others.

though equally deafening). As soon as someone walks through the doors of Maxime's, all talking stops, and all eyes are on the new arrival. The silence, in contrast to the previous din, is shocking. Once the newcomer has been briefly appraised, all talking resumes and the din is again deafening. In achieving such an instantaneous, surgical excision of sound, and such a celebration of a flash point, Baudelaire's poem is a tour de force.[14]

But bear in mind that the vision of the woman flashes by just as quickly as the visual melee that is the crowd. The poem makes the woman's disappearance as sudden as her singular emergence:

A flash of lightening . . . then night!—Fugitive beauty
Whose gaze has left me suddenly reborn
Will I never see you again save in eternity?

Poe's "Nevermore" with respect to his beloved is tactile. (Lenore will never again press the velvet lining of the cushion, nor will the poet again "clasp a rare and radiant maiden whom the angels named Lenore.") Baudelaire, however, attaches his own "nevermore" to sight: his anguish is that he will never see her again. "Elsewhere," continues the poem, "very far from here! Too late! *Never* perhaps!" The echoes to Poe here are explicit, but the loss is placed on the visual. The narrator of the poem had earlier said that he stood frozen and "drank . . . from her eye," which he compares to a "livid sky in which a storm brews / The sweetness that fascinates and the pleasure that kills." But the sweet draught is gone, because "I do not know where you are fleeing, you don't know where I am going." The use of the familiar *tu* (in *tu fuis*, "you are fleeing") emphasizes the fantasized intimacy in the instant of the glance that quenches the narrator's inner thirst. The immediate, imagined intimacy also underlines the equally sudden loss, as do the suspension dots and the dash. The abrupt loss of the visual "then night!" mirrors the loss of the audial with the woman's apparition; it also suggests the return of the noise with the disappearance of the image.

14. See also "Crépuscule du soir," where the evening ushers in a new series of noises: slamming shutters, hissing stoves, the yapping of theaters, the snorings of orchestras. The lexicon here is clearly disdainful. On noise in Baudelaire, see Ross Chambers, "Baudelaire's Paris," in *Baudelaire,* ed. Rosemary Lloyd (Cambridge: Cambridge University Press, 2005), 109 ff. For a reading of the poem in question, and more on noise, see two other articles by Ross Chambers: "The Storm in the Eye of the Poem: Baudelaire's 'A une passante,'" in *Textual Analysis: Some Readers Reading,* ed. Mary Ann Caws (New York: MLA, 1986), 156–66; and "Heightening the Lowly (Baudelaire: 'Je n'ai pas oublié . . .' and 'A une passante')," *Nineteeth-Century French Studies* 37, nos. 1–2 (Fall–Winter, 2008–9): 44–51.

The woman and the crowd are, as I have suggested, on two completely different registers: audial versus visual, everyday versus fantasy. And yet both partake of the transitory: the city crowd because its raucous confusion can barely allow for a single image (unless you have the rapidity of Guys's "eagle eye"); the woman because she is a "fugitive beauty," seen in the instant of a flash of lighting (from the sky or from her eyes—or both), and fleeing into the night and the crowd. The transitory, fugitive, and contingent moment, then, even if auratic in Benjamin's sense, and even if evidence of Baudelaire's modernity, is here initially *not* wished for by the poet. The *passante* disappears from his visual field, and the narrator is left only with his daydream:

> Elsewhere, very far from here! Too late! *Never* perhaps!
> For I do not know where you are fleeing, you don't know where I am
>   going,
> O you whom I could have loved, O you who knew it!

Present, past, and future are all here. The present tense in the first two lines of the stanza underscores the immediacy and intensity of the experience, as do the proliferation of exclamation marks and again the use of the familiar *tu* and *toi* (see full text at the end of this chapter). The doubt engendered by the pluperfect subjunctive in the first part of the last line (*Ô toi que j'eusse aimée*) emphasizes the unlikelihood of their union, even as it stresses the strength of its evocation as a thought. Finally, the imperfect tense of the second half of the clause underlines a continuity of confirmation—it is not in the conditional. Apart from this last word, *savais* ("knew"), and the first line of the poem describing the crowd (*hurlait*, "was howling"), there is only one other instance of the imperfect: when the narrator drinks (*buvais*) from her eye, again a respite of willed continuum within the flash of an instant. The imperfect tense *savais* returns us temporally to the poem's beginning. The woman has been engulfed, not only into the night, but into the maelstrom as well, which has once again taken over. The whole is the representation of the fleeting—of time, of image, of the city's masses, of thought itself. It was, in other words, all too rapid.

This woman, then, is an afterimage; a scopic phantom whose vivid emergence from the crowd remains in the mind after the ocular stimulus has occurred.[15] All the necessary elements for retinal retention that make

---

15. Benjamin, in his essay on Baudelaire, mentions afterimage in Bergson as the attempt to avoid "the alienating, blinding experience of large-scale industrialism." In shutting out this

for the afterimage are there: a bright flash of light and a lingering vision—
a kind of daguerreotype of which the iodine-sensitive silvered plate is the
mind. Baudelaire translates the retinal image into an anticipated memory; indeed, one might say that at the level of the poem the experience is
mourned as having been too rapid; but for the purposes of its metaphysics,
the poem needs such fleetingness. The poet's question—"Will I never see
you again save in eternity?"—projects the immediate past event onto the
future, and forges a visual memory onto the fragile anticipation of eternity. They will see each other again, in other words, in death. The present
has been instantly (as instantly as the flash of lightening that provides
the image) elided into a future memory, and the mutually exclusive poles
of the anachronism (the present seen both as past and as future memory)
are willed. The visual repetition (an afterimage is in fact seeing again) is
mirrored by the conceptual one: they will see each other again in death, as
I noted, when the "seeing again" will be the penumbra of the afterimage:
less clear, emerging out of the darkness, and faded, one can assume, even
in eternity.

Poe's "nevermore" (as in never again) becomes in Baudelaire an "again"
that will give memory a place to produce the apparition as re-imaged.
This is a double vision of a different sort from the one we have previously
considered—an afterimage as ocular repetition in memory. Hence, the pluperfect subjunctive near the close of the poem—*j'eusse aimée* (mentioned
above)—provides a tense that recapitulates the poem's concluding fantasy.
The recent past is combined with subjunctival doubt that looks to an uncertain future. The temporal oxymoron, then, or anachronism, is forced
upon the present (the contemplation of the event) such that memory can
preserve an afterimage. The afterimage allows for the illusion of a future
that is, in turn, always too late. Nevertheless, the image is retained; first
in the poet's retina, then in his memory, finally in the icon the poem itself
displays. The image of loss (and the loss of the image) may be the poem's
central icon, but it is imaged nonetheless.

Many critics, including of course Benjamin, have gone farther and

---

experience, writes Benjamin, "the eye perceives a complementary experience—in the form
of a spontaneous afterimage." Bergson's philosophy, for Benjamin, represents the "attempt to
specify this afterimage and fix it as a permanent record." Thus Bergson's philosophy, continues
Benjamin, gives us a clue to the experience that "presented itself undistorted to Baudelaire's
eyes, in the figure of his reader." Or in the figure of the poet: the experience of the *passante* is
arguably such a repression of the industrial experience, with the resulting afterimage. It is not
clear to me, however, that for Baudelaire the repression of the industrial city is all that can allow for the afterimage. "On Some Motifs in Baudelaire," in *The Writer of Modern Life*, 172.

called this poem an image that represents the loss of images themselves
in modernity. And yet there is a way in which the poem, for reasons I have
been arguing, is overtly cloaked in the logic of loss even as it works to
preserve the image that it articulates as already gone. It is a bit like Guys
as Baudelaire describes him: rushing to sketch, and thus to record and preserve, the image that is already escaping him. "A une passante" is consistently discussed in Baudelaire scholarship as a poem based on Guys's art,
and there is no question that the poet had Guys's drawings very much in
mind.[16] One critic sees "A une passante" as Baudelaire's demonstration
of Guys's "new aesthetic of modernity." The poem, writes Hiddleston,
like Guy's aesthetic, takes the outside world as its point of departure, uses
the fleeting and the evanescent to "make the most urgent and compelling appeal to memory and to the projective and creative powers of the
imagination."[17] But that is not all, I am arguing: despite the passages from
Baudelaire cited earlier, in which he wants to *know* how art works on the
spectator, and how the artist comes to an idea, "A une passante," because
it is initially motivated by a visual impulse that triggers the afterimage,
allows an instinctive knowledge to traverse the poem like a raw nerve. It
is a knowledge that, despite the poet's theory, is grounded not in the imagination but rather in the flash point that allows for witnessing the image
in the first place. So it is knowledge grounded in sight: *Toi qui le savais.*
The woman passing by "knows" that the narrator "would have" loved her,
had he been given world enough and time. She "knows" by the meeting of
their eyes. Vision is again the Baudelairean protagonist here; but it is the
certainty of knowledge to which the poem aspires.

CERTAINTY

Certainty is a fraught issue in our poet. Baudelaire as art critic does not
have the same voice as Baudelaire the poet. Even the *Salon* of 1845, the
poet's first and youthful venture as art critic, is sure-footed and confident.
The twenty-four-year-old Baudelaire announces, for example, that Delacroix is a genius; he clearly feels no need either to prove or to justify his
assertion: "Mr. Delacroix is decidedly the painter who is the most original

16. Pichois, for example, notes that the fourteen-line sonnet of "Passante" is "created according to the system (as Baudelaire would have put it) and the aesthetic outline of the instantaneous, which the poet explicates upon coming across Constantin Guys's watercolors" (*OC*
1:1022).

17. J. A. Hiddleston, *Baudelaire and the Art of Memory* (Oxford: Oxford University Press,
1999), 218.

of ancient and modern times" (*OC* 2:353). Baudelaire the art critic is also possessed of a rather sardonic sense of humor, something we will agree is largely lacking in the poems. He describes the painting of an insane asylum by Lécurieux as having "the uniform aspect of café au lait" (383). Or: "In any case, everyone today paints far too well" (384). On the artist Joyant, Baudelaire complains that nothing is so burdensome as having to talk about paintings that "are dragged in every year with the same depressing perfections" (394). He makes easy and self-assured judgments: "In Paris, we have the right to defy foreign reputations" (402). And so on. It is this confident voice, so different from the frequently self-doubting (and self-pitying) voice of the letters and essays, and the often cruel melancholy of the poetry, that gives a curiously different valence to the notion of certainty. I began this chapter by suggesting that there is something awry about Baudelaire's judgments on art, and that part of this oddness has to do with his privileging of the figural in art. An equally odd aspect is the poet's notion of certainty and doubt for the visual artist.

Doubt, Baudelaire announces in the *Salon* of 1846, is the absence of naïveté and "a vice particular to this century" (*OC* 2:491). Moreover, doubt leads to eclecticism, concerning which the poet concludes, "people who grant themselves so much time for reflection are incomplete men; they are lacking in passion" (473). We begin to see, then, why Guys is to be praised for his frenzied pace, and why Baudelaire similarly admires Delacroix for "executing [his works] rather quickly and with enough certitude to let nothing evaporate from the intensity of action or of idea" (764). Rapidity, it turns out, is connected with certitude. Baudelaire cites Delacroix's exaggerated story about a man throwing himself from a fifth-story window. The painter is reputed to have said that the artist needs to be capable of completing a sketch of that man by the time he hits the ground (763–64). Rapidity is thus integral to Delacroix's genius. In the *Salon* of 1846, Baudelaire explains that Delacroix's conceptions are those of a great artist and hence slow, serious, and conscientious, but his execution remains rapid (*preste*; 433).

It will be remembered that the young Baudelaire does not like sculpture. Why? Not only because it is too close to nature, but also because "it shows too many faces at the same time." Painting, on the other hand, is "despotic: and further, the expression of the painter is much stronger" (487). Goya is modern because of his "love of the ineffable" and his "certitude" of artistic means (568). Once again, the great visual artist is blessed with certainty and has no doubt in his vision. Baudelaire, as if caught in a wishful thinking of sorts, imitates in his own voice the certainty he imagines in a great painter. "The observer," he declares in "The Painter of Modern Life," "is a *prince* who enjoys his incognito everywhere" (692). Such an observer is imagined by Baudelaire as knowing exactly what he sees. This "certainty" does not, as we have been arguing throughout, characterize Baudelaire's own vision—quite the contrary.

Let us pause to note here that, as Crary puts it, for Benjamin modernity subverts contemplation; there is never pure access to a single object. "Vision is always multiple, adjacent to and overlapping with other objects, desires and vectors."[18] Yes, but in art Baudelaire insists on a single impression, a clear perspective. For the younger Baudelaire, sculpture always gives you too many perspectives: "In vain does the sculptor try to put himself in a unique point of view. The spectator, who circles around the figure, can choose from a hundred different perspectives, except the right one. . . . A painting is only what it wants to be" (487). Although Baudelaire's own writing has multiple, and certainly doubled, vision as I have been arguing, art is meant for him to have certainty, to be executed with rapidity born of such certainty, and to grant the viewer a single, clear perspective, which can allow him to dream. In the 1840s, the poet's apparently self-assured declarations on the need for an apodictic in the visual arts on the part of their producers are mirrored by a critical voice, which, mimetic of such a view, rarely permits doubt or a profusion of possible perspectives. Such a confident voice will continue in the art criticism, even if Baudelaire's views (on sculpture, for example) gradually change.

In "A une passante," certainty comes ostensibly from the meeting of the eyes, a poetic commonplace. But Baudelaire puts the image and its time so much out of joint that the certainty the poem claims is at best undermined by the *jamais peut-être!* that spreads, like sepsis, throughout the narrative. The image of the *passante* becomes afterimage first physically, then mnemonically. The loss, as I have noted, is recorded even as the image is preserved in the visual memory.[19] The result is a series of literal as well as conceptual double visions, variously repeated. First, the image of the noisy crowd and the woman who (like many figures in Guys's paintings) surges up suddenly from within it. Then, the flash that allows

18. Jonathan Crary, *Techniques of the Observer: On Vision and Modernity in the Nineteenth Century* (Cambridge, MA: MIT Press, 1992), 20.

19. Richard Terdiman argues convincingly that there was a massive disruption of traditional forms of memory in the nineteenth century, and that memory itself (and thus history) became critical preoccupations in the effort to think through "what intellectuals were coming to call the 'modern.'" Baudelaire is clearly responding to such a disruption. Terdiman, *Present Past: Modernity and the Memory Crisis* (Ithaca: Cornell University Press, 1993).

for seeing her face, eyes, clothing, and statuesque leg is recapitulated by the afterimage in the retina. The afterimage in turn becomes a mnemonic icon retained mentally in a gesture that mimes the eye's retinal retention. But then there is a move in the opposite direction: from the inside (the mind of the artist) to the outside (reality). "All those who can draw well and truly," claims Baudelaire, "draw according to the image written in their brains, and not according to nature" (OC 2:698). This decidedly graphocentric move is what Baudelaire calls a "translation"; the spectator of the painting (or of the poem) is the translator of that translation. Thus we have two more aspects of double vision: the vision of the artist and that of the spectator; and the image in the brain of the artist translated onto the paper. Moreover, we also have the artist's vision that anticipates (and indeed guides) what and how the spectator (or reader) will see, what image will finally remain. Baudelaire's description of Guys's artistic praxis, then, is also a precise formulation of "A une passante." He identifies two things as evident in "M.G.'s" artistic execution: on the one hand, a memory that demands resurrection of everything it contains ("Lazarus, arise!"); on the other, a furor or fire, which is "the fear of not going fast enough, of letting the phantom escape before the synthesis of it has been extracted and grasped" (699).

But "A une passante," more complicated even than that, is about the paradoxical retention of the image that iconicizes the phantom's escape from memory. The phantom is in itself a conceptual repetition. In French, besides *fantôme* (the usual word for "ghost"), there is a synonym that literalizes such recurrence, *revenant*, which means returning or coming back.[20] The double vision of which I am speaking here is not merely the repetition of images in differing or conflicting contexts, however. There are, we have seen, two moves toward the image itself. The first is from the flash experience to the memory; the second, for those who "can draw well and truly" goes in the opposite direction, from "the image written in their brain" to the paper on which they draw. Drawing (or writing a poem) may be a "Lazarus, arise!" in the first instance, bringing back to life an image stored in the memory (thus inscribing the repetition of the specter or Lazarus as *revenant*). But, at the same time, drawing and writing bring

---

20. On the ghost as *revenant* and its connection to Freud's "uncanny," see (among many others) Hélène Cixous, "Fiction and its Phantoms: A Reading of Freud's 'Das Unheimliche' ('The Uncanny')," trans. Robert Denomme, *New Literary History* 7 (1976): 525–48. See also "Notes on the Phantom: A Complement to Freud's Metapsychology," trans. Nicholas Rand, in *The Trial(s) of Psychoanalysis*, ed. Françoise Meltzer (Chicago: University of Chicago Press, 1988), 75–80.

images to memory that are stored even as they are proclaimed lost. Hence the bi-mnemonic "Will I never see you again save in eternity?" The image paradoxically records itself as that which cannot be seen again except after death. The image is thus a phantom to the second power: first, because it manifests itself as being that which will be "seen" again only in the after-life; second, because its evocation haunts the mind by returning (*revenant*) as an icon meaning loss. The image is thus both written in the brain by virtue of the experience (the flash) and the execution of the poem; and it is extracted from the mind, where it was already "written," as a loss that demands imaging. Afterlife as afterimage; retinal retention as preparation for memory; loss concretized by the same image that has disappeared.[21]

"A une passante" enacts the work of the image in much of Baudelaire's poetry. The swan poem ("Le Cygne") similarly represents that which is already extinct and simultaneously resurrected from the memory. Andromaque is long since dead when the narrator of that poem evokes her memory; she is resurrected, however ("Lazarus, arise!") as she who remembers what is lost, and is exiled in a place, or present, where she has no context.[22] She embodies, in other words, the two movements I have been tracing: that which is already written in the memory and externalized on paper (the poem), and that which is as if seen as an icon remembering loss, even as it emblemizes it. So too the swan in the same poem is exiled from its natural environment, which has become a memory, to the Paris streets, where it is already an anachronism in the growing city. The double vision here is again complex.

What is perceived as lost and can never be seen again manifests itself iconically as forever absent from sight. These are coeval, though rigorously contradictory, moves. It is not a contradiction that Baudelaire necessarily would have been able to articulate. It is rather a praxis that deploys itself in what we might call a confusion over certainty; a refusal to forget one position even after a new, contrasting one has taken over. It is a refusal as well to believe in the retention of the faded icon even as its loss is recorded, first by the eye and then by the mind. Contradiction here functions as a record-

---

21. Baudelaire has many ghosts in his poems, including the one in the poem titled, precisely, "Le revenant" (*Spleen et Idéal* LXIII, in *OC* 1:64). Other poems (like "Laquelle est la vraie?" and "Le mort joyeux") revel, Poe-like, in being buried alive—willfully, however, in Baudelaire's case, and including the digging of graves, frequently the narrator's own. See, for example, "La cloche fêlée" (1:71) or "Spleen" LXXVII (1:74).

22. On a different level, Andromaque is also an allusion to Mme. Aupick—widow of the "superb" M. Baudelaire, and wife (alas!) of General Aupick.

ing of the experiential at odds with memory; or, conversely, as the emergence of memory at odds with the experiential. It might seem convenient
to put such contradiction squarely into the semiotic square, that way of
picturing, as Rosalind Krauss puts it, "the whole of a cultural universe in
the grip of two opposing choices, two incompatible possibilities." Cultural
production, for Krauss reading this structuralist graph, is the imaginative
space in which "those two things can be related." It is a production, she
continues, that is finally an impossible attempt to construct such a space
for working out "unbearable contradictions produced within the real field
of history."[23] It would seem logical, then (though Krauss is talking about a
later modernism) to see Baudelaire's poetry, for example, as such cultural
production, such an imaginary space for the working out of unbearable
contradictions. But Baudelaire does not strive for such a space—imaginary
or otherwise. His contradictions are, on the contrary, two opposing spaces,
lying side by side ineluctably. Baudelaire neither seeks nor attempts
sublation, let alone synthesis; rather, he forces the clash of two incompatible spaces, which neither seek nor perform any resolution whatever. "La
chambre double," which we will consider later in this study, is perhaps the
most obvious example.

Such contradiction is not limited to the poetic image in Baudelaire.
As we have noted, Baudelaire's (unacknowledged) political connection to
Proudhon and his overt discipleship to (aspects of) Maistre exist side by
side—coterminous but not combinable. The afterimage becomes, in such
a scenario, a possible ocular model for mutually exclusive perspectives
that insist on coexistence. While strabismus allows for simultaneously
differing perspectives, the afterimage is another solution to contiguous
antinomies. The afterimage, however, posits a time lapse between the first
term and the second. Moreover, the afterimage similarly works in two directions: from the event to its retinal retention, and from the memory to
the triggering event.

We have seen that for Baudelaire there are two "evident" aspects of
Guys's artistic praxis: a memory that demands the resurrection of everything it contains (Lazarus), and the fear of not going fast enough such that
the phantom escapes "before the synthesis of it has been extracted and
grasped." The role of the image in Baudelaire goes yet another step: the
memory imprints images so as to resurrect them; but the phantom has already escaped, is already lost, and its loss is what is imaged. So the woman

23. Rosalind E. Krauss, *The Optical Unconscious* (Cambridge, MA: MIT Press, 1994), 21.

in "A une passante" is inscribed as a phantom. Will I see you again? is a question in this poem to which the answer is Yes, after death. Thus the narrator projects himself as a phantom as well in the afterlife, there to meet the phantom of the *passante* whose image he already retains as the woman who signifies remembering the loss that is always to come and that has always been. Poe's "nevermore," which Baudelaire translates as "jamais plus" becomes, in his own poem, "*jamais* peut-être!"—emphasis, by the poet, on "never," with "perhaps" serving as the possibility of the memory's ghosts.

The dual economy of the image here is close to Nietzsche's notion of what he describes as "a phenomenon which is the exact opposite of a familiar optical one." The passage strongly resonates with the dual aspect and movement of the Baudelairean image. When we look at the sun, explains Nietzsche, we turn away blinded, with "dark spots" (*dunkle farbige Flecken*) that serve "by way of a remedy." The brightness of the sun is compensated for by the eye with such dark spots acting to protect vision. Conversely, the heroes of Sophocles are at first glance penumbral, "no more than a luminous shape projected onto a dark wall, that is to say, *appearance* through and through." But when we look away from the Sophoclean actor on the stage, the picture of the hero is suddenly made up of clarity and brightness, luminous images that are the "necessary productions of a deep look into the horror of nature; luminous spots, as it were, designed to cure an eye hurt by the ghastly night."[24] The image in Baudelaire consists, as I am arguing, in two instances: outer and inner, in the simplest formulation. In the first instant, a flash of lightening highlights the *passante*, and creates, as I have been arguing, a retinal afterimage from the experiential encounter. Here we might say that the afterimage is the result of looking at the sun (the flash of lightening) and then turning away to see "dark spots": the image is retained as the eye is protected. In the second instance, the poet, reborn by the *passante*'s gaze, is plunged into darkness (*puis la nuit!*), and resurrects an image of "perhaps" seeing her again in eternity. This instant comes from being dropped inside the "ghastly night," and produces a "luminous spot" as a healing for the glimpse into the abyss. The image thus produces both ocular retention and poetic resurrection; both, if we follow Nietzsche, for the purpose of protecting the observer.

24. Friedrich Nietzsche, *The Birth of Tragedy and the Genealogy of Morals*, trans. Francis Golffing (New York: Doubleday, 1956), 59–60. Nietzsche is also thinking of Plato's man, after being released from the cave, who is initially blinded by sudden exposure to the sun (*Republic* 7.515d-516b).

SCOPIC SYLLEPSIS

"... et, bien qu'il ne soit pas rare de voir la même cause engendrer deux
effets contraires, j'en suis toujours comme intrigué et alarmé."
—Baudelaire, "Le crépuscule du soir"

We have wandered here into a syllepsis of sorts—that rhetorical term that
describes a predicate that is meant to belong to one subject but is attributed to two (or more): "Fix the problem and not the blame," for example,
where the verb "fix" is used in two senses, the second following incongru-
ously upon the first. Something similar happens visually in Baudelaire:
his doubled image is mimetic of his double vision. It is a process I will
call a scopic syllepsis—that is, the single notion of "image" functions in
two different, often incongruous contexts within the same glance. The
first image is retained as an afterimage protecting the eye; the second, already in the mind, is immediately resurrected from the memory, where it
may have been stored for a long time, or an instant before the encounter
occurs, or anything in between. The scopic syllepsis is the poetics of the
image working in two different economies under the same mental rubric;
it yields, however, two different images. It is, one might say, the poetics of
strabismus. The image itself functions to protect the eye from an overly
intense visual experience, caused by "a deep look into the horror of nature." Visual and mnemonic afterimages in Baudelaire are, in a sense, the
result of the wound that the city's intensity bestows both physically and
mentally on its observer's gaze. That wound is a direct consequence of
the times: the abolition of the past (the destruction of the old Paris, archi-
tecturally as well as socially and culturally) and the ubiquity of a present
shaped by a bourgeois world of triumphant commerce. Baudelaire wants
neither.

Around the same time Baudelaire was writing "A une passante," he
was also translating (and adapting—that is, summarizing large portions
in his own words) de Quincey's "Confessions of an Opium Eater." The
text tells the story of a young university student who flees his tutors and,
starving on the streets of London, begins a platonic relationship with a
sixteen-year-old girl named "Ann," who is likewise starving. De Quincey,
Baudelaire's narrator tells us, is "a kind of peripatetic" in the streets of
London; a "philosopher of the street, constantly meditating through the
whirlwind of the city" (OC 1:456). The student leaves London for a few
days, to try to get some money to pay his creditors. When he returns, he

cannot find Ann. He does not know her last name, and she is not at their appointed meeting place.[25] He finally gives up trying to find her, realizing that he fears seeing her again, but he does "see her" again in his dreams: "I no longer desire to see her," Baudelaire translates, "but I dream of her, and not without pleasure, as of a person long since lying in the grave" (*OC* 1:462). Here too, seeing is emphasized: "If I saw her for one second, I would recognize her among a thousand . . . ; she had a sweet expression, with a particularly graceful way of holding her head."[26]

De Quincey's story of Ann is like a prolonged and hypotactic narration of "A une passante." If we had any doubts, Baudelaire's own summary makes the connection clear: "Has Ann completely disappeared?" he asks. "Oh, no!" he answers. We will see her again (*nous la reverrons*) in opium dens. And then he adds: "strange and transfigured phantom, she will slowly emerge in the smoke of memory, like the genie in *A Thousand and One Nights* in the vapors from the bottle" (or, we might say, like Lazarus arising). Once again, Baudelaire has distilled hypotaxis into parataxis. Poe's stories, for example, develop atmosphere with lengthy description—the opening of "The House of Usher," to cite a famous instance. That opening goes on for two pages and begins, it will no doubt be recalled, with the impression caused by the sight of the "melancholy House of Usher":

> During the whole of a dull, dark, and soundless day in the autumn of the year, when the clouds hung oppressively low in the heavens, I had been passing alone, on horseback, through a singularly dreary tract of country. . . . I know not how it was—. . . an insufferable gloom pervaded my spirit.[27]

25. In what may seem a counterintuitive move, I am retranslating into English Baudelaire's translation of de Quincey into French. The Baudelaire texts, however, take sufficient liberties with the original that I am translating his own summaries and renderings. Baudelaire himself writes, in notes for his lectures in Brussels, that he has altered this "excessively curious English book" by adding "here and there, my personal reflections. But to what extent I infused the original author with my own personality, that is what I would now be unable to say." Charles Baudelaire, *Œuvres complètes*, ed. Y.-G. Dantec and Claude Pichois (Paris: Gallimard, 1961), 463.

26. Proust too will play on the doubled notions of seeing again in a similar vein. Swann, we are told by the narrator, after he is no longer in love with Odette, will never see *that* Odette again. But, says the narrator, Swann is wrong—he will see the Odette he loved one last time, in a dream: "il eût voulu, en pensée au moins, avoir pu faire ses adieux, pendant qu'elle existait encore, à cette Odette lui inspirant de l'amour, de la jalousie, à cette Odette lui causant des souffrances et que maintenant il ne reverrait jamais. Il se trompait. Il devait la revoir une fois encore, quelques semaines plus tard. Ce fut en dormant, dans le crépuscule d'un rêve." *A la recherche du temps perdu* (Paris: Robert Lafont, 1987), 1:313.

27. Edgar Allen Poe, *Selected Writings*, 138.

Poe too compares a certain desperation to an opium den, as does de Quincey in describing Ann's fate. Poe's narrator feels "an utter depression of soul which I can compare to no earthly sensation more properly than to the after-dream of the reveller upon opium—the bitter lapse into every day life—the hideous dropping off of the veil" (ibid.). Here we have the dream and the after-dream, a conceptual parallel to the image and the afterimage. But Baudelaire can achieve in one line the same setting produced by the two-page exposition to Poe's tale. The first line of the fourth "Spleen" poem reads: "Quand le ciel bas et lourd pèse comme un couvercle" ("Spleen" LXXVIII, in *Spleen et Idéal, OC* 1:74). The line is like a précis of the entry into Poe's tale. What I am saying here is not quite fair, of course, since Poe is writing prose and Baudelaire poetry, and Baudelaire, having translated Poe, has clearly taken from him central images (the sky likened, for example, to a heavy lid). Poe's narrator decides that he cannot know what gives rise to this feeling of intense gloom ("this power lies among considerations beyond our depth"; *Selected Writings*, 139), and that perhaps a reorganization of the "details of the picture" could "annihilate its capacity for sorrowful impression."

All of this denial is vintage Poe, rendering the House of Usher all the more threatening by virtue of having its gloomy surroundings half-heartedly discounted by the apprehensive narrator (what a rhetorician would call *recusatio*). Nevertheless, the movement in Poe is from the outside (the picture, the scene, the impression, the "first glimpse," and then the inverted image of the House in the "black and lurid tarn") into the narrator's mind. He is unnerved by the very act of looking at the scene: "What was it—I paused to think—what was it that so unnerved me in the contemplation of the House of Usher?" (138). The narrator has "shadowy fancies" that crowd upon him, as he puts it. External reality (for lack of a better term) has provided the gloom that has imprinted itself on the narrator's thought.

But what Baudelaire does in the "Spleen" poem in question is to combine the external scene with incursions of pictures in the mind. The sky is low and heavy on the spirit, as in Poe; but in Baudelaire, hope is a bat whose timid wings bump into rotted ceilings. On the outside, there are (for example), bells shrieking at the sky: "Suddenly bells leap with fury / And throw a frightful howling toward the sky" (*Des cloches tout à coup sautent avec furie / Et lancent vers le ciel un affreux hurlement* ; *OC* 1:75). The bells seem to allude to Poe's familiar poem of the same name, but in Baudelaire the bells are again extrapolated into the conceptual through simile: they are likened to wandering spirits without a homeland—ghosts of a sort, yet again. At the end of the poem, a funeral procession takes place (with neither drums nor music) within the poet's mind, and dread (*angoisse*) plants its black flag on the poet's bowed head. The image of the bat—three stanzas before the end—as the metaphor for hope is indirectly evoked, or remembered, in the poem's last line. Flying helplessly into rotted ceilings, the bat that is hope cries out, vanquished by the black flag planted on the poet's skull. It is as if not only hope but thought itself had tried in vain to escape the confines of ennui. The poem plays with an alternating inside/outside throughout: a population mute with hideous spiders "spins its webs in the depths of our brains" (*Vient tendre ses filets au fond de nos cerveaux;* 75) The population, not the spiders, traps thought, filling the brain with its webs. Throughout the poem, the inescapability of ennui is inscribed on the mind; but the mind itself conjures up images which, in turn, are projected onto the world even as they are stimulated by it.

My point here is not to rehearse all the extant readings of a rightfully famous poem; rather, it is to point out how the acute melancholy described by Poe and triggered in his narrator by the scenery, is transmuted by Baudelaire into an internal scenario that echoes and oscillates with the external one, thus heightening the anguish and spleen. It is this back-and-forth movement between the mind's image and the experiential vision triggering it that creates the geometry of the visual in Baudelaire's poetics; what I am calling scopic syllepsis. The poet takes his metaphors from the city and transforms them into abstractions (the bat that is hope, the leaden-lidded sky that is spleen); but he also works from the inside out, cathecting his gloom (in the Spleen poems) onto things: "I have more memories than if I were a thousand years old," he writes in "Spleen" LXXVI, and adds that an old piece of furniture, its drawers filled with notes, verse, hair binding old receipts, hides "fewer secrets than my sad brain" (*OC* 1:73).

De Quincey's lengthy story of Ann (which clearly resonated with Baudelaire) is also achieved with brevity in the sonnet "A une passante." The search for Ann in de Quincey goes on for pages (even though Baudelaire abridges many passages); and when she is "found," it is for the reader to imagine a future Ann, ghostlike, haunting the opium den. The search for her, by this peripatetic philosopher of the street, is like an earlier version of what was to become Baudelaire's flâneur (indeed, what better definition of the flâneur than de Quincey's phrase?). But as with Poe, de Quincey's search for Ann engages external reality, whereas Baudelaire's search for the *passante* takes place in the dialectic he described in Guys but which is his praxis as well: the dialectic between images already in the memory and the attempt to grasp an image in reality before it becomes a phantom, which of course it already is. De Quincey (via Baudelaire) transports Ann from within the real world and converts her into a phantomlike creature barely discernible in the smoke of the opium den. Her ghostly appearance is a trope of sorts—the fate of those who are impoverished and living in the streets of London. Baudelaire's poem, on the other hand, transfigures differently: it removes the conjunctions of narrative into a lightening of recognition, and creates a series of paratactic images triggered by his own city. The only conjunctions in his poem are flash points (as against narrative)—the woman in Baudelaire appears in the confusion of the crowd only to be swallowed up in the same instant. There is no trope here; it is rather a shock, in Benjamin's sense; but it is also a resurrection of memory and a stimulus that is imprinted, as we have seen, on the eye and the mind.

Baudelaire asks the same question of the *passante* that his summary has de Quincey ask of Ann: has she disappeared entirely? In "A une passante," the answer is yes; the caveat that he may "see" her again after death is a way of ensuring the afterimage as fleeting and transitory on both the physical and mnemonic levels, and yet (paradoxically) as retained. De Quincey relates pathos within the experiential: Ann is lost to him except in dreams, though she may be somewhere in the teeming city and its drug dives. So too, Poe's poem "The Raven" slowly relates a story in which a bird's croaking is gradually metamorphosed into a tragic fact: the poet will nevermore see the woman he loves; she has died. Baudelaire, on the other hand, goes farther than a ghost economy; he presents a chthonic notion of memory triggered by an instant and carried to the mind by an afterimage. The process—from the experience to the afterimage, to the memory of the loss, to the promise of seeing again within death—is as immediate as the loss itself. The instant also moves, as we have noted, from the image already inscribed in the mind (which in Baudelaire's case we might call the a priori belief in irrevocable loss) toward the visual event as if to classify it. The two images, the two movements, are recorded simultaneously. Or, given the constraints of writing, and the gap between the event and its afterimage, we might say that the images are produced through *accumulatio*, as Longinus would have put it. Such dual movement, a syllepsis of sight, is the other kind of double vision that the reader of Baudelaire continually comes up against.

So the afterimage awakens a déjà vu that closes off the possibility of seeing again, even though it has just done so, and by force. This action might explain the *peut-être* that follows the *jamais*. The poem, in suggesting the image of the *passante* as a possible ghost (*revenante*) is not only hoping for the return of the woman; more deeply, it is asking to hold

on to the image in the visual chaos of the city—the image in the mind as
well as the image of the woman who instantly stands out from the crowd.
It is imaging itself, in other words, that Baudelaire fears losing, just as he
describes Guys frantically sketching so as not to lose the image in front
of him. Baudelaire thus writes a "perhaps nevermore" more complex than
Poe's, and more motivated by a historical crisis than de Quincey.

In a long commentary on *Le Spleen de Paris, petits poèmes en prose*,
Pichois points out that those poems were written when Paris (thanks
largely to Haussmann) was no longer the Paris of Baudelaire's youth.
Spleen de Paris describes a city of construction, ruins, frequent horror,
melancholy—an everyday life of urban misery. Pichois explains the result
in scopic terms: "Déjà vu calls the poet to the recognition of the never
seen [*jamais vu*]" (*OC* 1:1296). The new, industrial city certainly offers
scenes and panoramas that had never been seen before. But "A une passante" erects the déjà vu as a never-to-be-seen-again, even as it registers
the shock of the never-seen-before as afterimage. So too, the narrator of
"Le Cygne" notes that he "sees only" the ruins of the old Paris among the
rubble of the soon to be new: "I see in my mind alone this whole camp of
shanties, / This pile of rough-hewn columns and shafts" (*Je ne vois qu'en
esprit tout ce camp de baraques, / Ces tas de chapiteaux ébauchés et de
fûts; OC* 1:86). It is this contradictory visioning, this culture of transition,
that lies at the foundation of much of the poet's imaging.

WHICH IS THE REAL ONE?

A prose poem of Baudelaire's, also in *Spleen de Paris*, literalizes this doubling of images, confusion of déjà vus, and repetition that is somehow
nonidentical.[28] It also concretizes the fear of losing the image. The poem is
hypotactic in that, like de Quincey and Poe, Baudelaire fully narrativizes
the event in graphic continuity; and it is literal in that he concretizes the
phantom (the vanished woman) that appears to return. It is the prose poem
"Laquelle est la vraie?"—one that is particularly Poe-like in tone and style.
The narrator meets a beautiful young woman. Her name, significantly, is
"Bénédicta." She is "miraculous," a blessing "too beautiful to live long."
She dies, and the narrator buries her himself. As he is standing by her
grave, "in which my treasure lay buried" (*où était enfoui mon trésor*), he
sees "a little person who singularly resembled the deceased." This person

---

28. "Laquelle est la vraie?" is consistently compared by critics to another, "La chambre
double," a text to which we will return in chapter 3.

tramples on the fresh grave "with a hysterical and bizarre violence." Between bursts of laughter, she says to the narrator, "It's me! I am the real Bénédicta! And as punishment for your madness and your blindness, you will love me as I am!" But the narrator, furious, shouts "No!" three times, and stamps (thus imitating the little person) so hard on the "recent sepulcher" that his leg sinks up to his knee in the ground, such that he will remain "bound, perhaps for ever, to the pit of the ideal" (*OC* 1:342).

There is much to unpack here. Is the "little person" the ghost of Bénédicta? She is certainly her double of sorts. Her name, moreover, primarily means "blessing," but also means "well said," which may give a certain validity to the second Bénédicta's hysterical claim. Further, the second Bénédicta functions as a kind of witch, who is not only the opposite in temperament to the first (apart from her bizarre behavior, the second woman uses the vulgar *fameuse canaille* to describe herself as being of the "rabble"), but also condemns the narrator to a punishment for his madness (in seeing the wrong Bénédicta) and at the same time for his blindness. The second Bénédicta is a literal afterimage, a concrete déjà vu, perhaps a ghost who has returned. She is, moreover, the antinomy of the first Bénédicta, and the poem performs this contradiction (as critics all note) symmetrically: two paragraphs on the first woman, and two on the second. The first Bénédicta is full of the "atmosphere of the ideal," and her eyes elicit "all that makes one believe in immortality." The second Bénédicta, perhaps the fake one, makes such a belief horrifying at best. There are shades, as well, of "A une passante" in the prose poem's images and lexicon. Once again, the eyes of Bénédicta (the first one) are what suggest "the ideal, grandeur, beauty, glory." Similarly, the eyes of the *passante* are what capture the poet's heart: "Fugitive beauty," that poem reads, "whose gaze has left me suddenly reborn." The first Bénédicta is lost to the narrator presumably forever. "A une passante" asks whether the narrator will ever see the woman in mourning again, answering with its own version of "nevermore": "*jamais* peut-être!" "Laquelle est la vraie?" formulates its own "perhaps" with eternity: the narrator will remain attached, he tells us, "perhaps forever."

As with "A une passante," "Laquelle est la vraie?" ("Which Is the Real One?"; an alternate title, published a week after Baudelaire's death, was "The Ideal and the Real") struggles between the image of the experiential realm and that of dream or contemplation, personified by the two women—or is there only one? Both poems put the emphasis on flight. "A une passante" gives us *fugitive beauté* and *j'ignore où tu fuis*. "Laquelle est la vraie" gives us a treasure that is *enfoui*—a slightly differing etymology,

but certainly assonant with *fuir*. [29] The narrator, moreover, has known the
first Bénédicta for only a few days before she dies. It is as if modernity's
"the transitory, the fugitive, the contingent"—those traits of flight which,
it will be recalled, make for one-half of art, according to Baudelaire, with
"the eternal and the immutable" as the other half—were actualized in the
two poems. "Laquelle est la vraie?" sets up, in literal fashion, the question
of the poet caught between two imaged realms, neither of which can be
eradicated though each contradicts the existence of the other. The narrator
of the prose poem may have his foot sunk into the ideal, but it is the tomb
of his beloved, such that the ideal and death are united. At the same time,
he remains above ground, forced to contemplate the real world in a manner that insults what he loves most. Vision is again the protagonist: blind
to the real Bénédicta, as the second one would have it, he has eyes only for
the ideal, which is a grave: "my eyes remained fixed onto the place where
my treasure lay buried" (*mes yeux restaient fichés sur le lieu où était enfoui mon trésor*).

If "Laquelle est la vraie" does nothing else, it performs the quandary
of uncertainty—that very quality that Baudelaire professes to hate in the
artist. The title itself announces doubt as its crisis. The poem's symmetry
(two stanzas for each Bénédicta), adds to the uncertainty, since it gives
equal weight to each possibility. Moreover, the poem questions not only
which of the two women is the real Bénédicta; it also asks whether it is
ultimately the ideal that is *la vraie* or whether it is everyday life, the material world. The ideal, after all, may be a treasure, but it is dead; the world
may be a horror, but it is alive. How much clearer an image for such contradiction can there be, if not the man with his foot caught in a grave
he wants to bring back to the light, but who is forced to contemplate an
image that itself refuses to be buried? One is reminded of Tiresias's comment to Creon, in Sophocles' *Antigone*: "For you've confused the upper
and the lower worlds" (lines 1068–71). The uncertainty between visions
goes against the confident voice of the young art critic who hates too many
choices and perspectives (sculpture), and who admires the artist who simply *knows* with certainty (e.g., Daumier, whose artistry is marked by his
certitude). "A une passante" ends, as we have seen, with the word "knew"
(*savais*), but the double vision of the poem's imaging undercuts that word,

29. For students of Mallarmé, it is worth noting here that this Baudelaire prose poem
might be called a fuller, more traditional rendering of the crisis articulated in Mallarmé's famous swan poem, "Le vierge, le vivace, et le bel aujourd'hui." The swan, which cranes its neck
toward the sky, has its feet trapped in ice because of the *vols qui n'ont pas fui* (flights that did
not flee)—again, the foregrounding of *fuir*.

so that it remains as the cruel memory of certainty that is perhaps (*peut-être*) to be realized again in death. Indeed, the next-to-last line uses the notion of knowing in a negative way, and that twice: "For I do not know where you are fleeing, you don't know where I am going" (*Car j'ignore où tu fuis, tu ne sais où je vais*). The present tense here intensifies the sense of *not* knowing. With *savais* in the following (and last) line, knowing is destabilized by the imperfect tense—there was a moment when you knew it; you do not know it any longer.

Marshall Berman has argued that our vision of modern life tends to split into material and spiritual planes, with some critics concentrating on the first and others on the second. Such dualism (political, economic and social on the one hand, and "pure spirit"—autonomous artistic and intellectual imperatives—on the other) removes us, in Berman's view, from "the interfusion of [modernism's] material and spiritual forces, the intimate unity of the modern self and the modern environment." But the first wave of those who wrote and thought about modernity, continues Berman, "had an instinctive feeling for this unity," which gave their visions "a richness and depth that contemporary writing about modernity sadly lacks."[30] I am largely in agreement with Berman's notion of the richness provided by such unity, though Baudelaire (as Berman himself believes, oddly) is not. In the first part of "Exposition universelle, beaux-arts" (1855), Baudelaire rants against notions of progress. It is, he complains, "that modern lantern that throws shadows on all known objects." Progress is like an optical instrument that obstructs, rather than facilitates, the object of its gaze. The average Frenchman with his newspaper has a brain similarly confused by shadows, such that "things of the material order and of the spiritual order are so strangely confused!" Indeed, the man has been so "Americanized" by his zoocratic and industrial philosophies that "he has lost the notion of the differences that characterize phenomena of the physical world and the moral world, from the natural and supernatural" (*OC* 2:580). Berman reads this as "reactionary bombast" on Baudelaire's part, and adds that the poet is "perfectly reasonable in fighting the confusion of material progress with spiritual progress." Baudelaire is, however, "as silly as the straw man in the café" when, says Berman, the poet defines art in a way that has no connection with the material world at all (*All That Is Solid*, 138–39). For Berman, Baudelaire has made such a "leap"

30. Marshall Berman, *All That Is Solid Melts into Air: The Experience of Modernity* (London: Verso, 1983), 131–32. The early modern thinkers Berman has in mind are, along with Baudelaire (to whom Berman devotes a chapter), Goethe, Hegel, Marx, Stendhal, Carlyle, Dickens, Herzen, and Dostoevsky.

into the transcendent that he leaves Kant "far behind" and turns the artist into a "walking *Ding an sich*" (ibid.). The poet, then, floats "untouched" above the material world. But this is clearly wrong: despite the scornful tone that often accompanies the certainty in Baudelaire's art criticism, despite the ensuing generalizations that seem to come too easily from his pen, Baudelaire is himself confused about the place of the spiritual in relation to the physical. Indeed, the prose poem "Laquelle est la vraie?" actually performs such confusion, starting with its title.

Progress, "that obscure beacon" (*fanal obscur*), is particularly wrong-headed for Baudelaire because it assumes that material advances (steam power, electricity, gas lights, "chemical matches," etc.) were miracles unknown to the Romans and thus "fully bear witness to our superiority over the Ancients" (*OC* 2:580). This is the positivist philosophy that is "an error very much in vogue" for Baudelaire, and one that he thoroughly rejects—which is not to say that he understands all that he is seeing. As I have been arguing throughout, he records—and judges—from different standpoints for different contexts (as Berman himself observes). Whatever Baudelaire may have thought at varying points about material conditions, his poetry consistently questions those conditions and their place with respect to the artist, visual and textual. Contradiction, both willed and unintentional, proliferates in his texts. But the material world in Baudelaire's poems is consistently either the trigger (whether good or not) for the verses, the backdrop from which protagonists can emerge, or that which must at all costs be escaped. In all cases, the "physical" is paramount and its visual stimuli fundamental. So too, the social is implied constantly, even if the perspective is neither politically consistent nor philosophically uniform.

Though the material conditions of "A une passante" have not been foregrounded in this chapter, I am assuming them and weaving them in with what Berman calls "spiritual" considerations (which I would call aesthetic and poetic). Baudelaire cannot be "done" otherwise. For example, lest the reader think that all of the present discussion on the poem remains on the level of the purely conceptual (poetic, abstract, and so on), it should be borne in mind that the irresolvable dialectic hypostasized in "Laquelle est la vraie?" uses class structure to show the hierarchization of the struggle: the first Bénédicta, the ideal, has eyes that spark the desire for grandeur, beauty, and the glories of the immortal; the second one calls herself *fameuse canaille*, a notorious woman of the rabble, as mentioned above. But it is the second Bénédicta who insists on being *seen* precisely because of the narrator's "blindness." His resulting punishment, she cackles, is that he "will love me as I am." No amount of glazing, in other words, can be put on everyday reality to make it beautiful, to transform it into that which it is not; it insists on being seen as is. Its vulgarity and horror are signaled in a class-conscious manner by the aesthetically obsessed and frequently snobbish Baudelaire: reality is the lower class in the big city. At the same time, as we saw in chapter 1, the poet seems to have a grudging admiration for the "rabble": the underclass reflects the evil (mal) that is man's wont; it is less hypocritical, more real. Evil is the symptom of the sickness called original sin, and it will not allow itself to be ignored or repressed.[31]

More often than not, the ideal in Baudelaire is (rather unsurprisingly) garbed as aristocratic; inaccessible perhaps, fleeting, and (even) dead, but the poet insists on remaining faithful to it even as he describes, as in "Laquelle est la vraie?" a position that is literally untenable. As in his famous poem about the albatross, Baudelaire's poet here cannot walk because his "wings"—his vision of an ideal—prevent him from elegant movement on the ground.[32] For Baudelaire there is what we might call an aristocracy of sensibility, frequently depicted by women whose eyes suggest great and noble things, even if their class is not of similar "heights." Baudelaire's hatred of (and obsession with) the material world, however, is depicted as the underclass even as it is closer to the truth concerning what he sees as the natural qualities of human beings. "A une passante" moves quickly to the "less concrete," as Baudelaire said of his reverie on Wagner. "Several days" are not available, as they were with Bénédicta, for the narrator to get to know the beautiful woman he encounters in the crowd. More fleeting still, the passante's gaze initially makes the narrator feel "reborn"—she performs a resurrection of sorts for him; no doubt the renewed belief in the possibility of the ideal, and the sense of being alive

31. A great deal of work has been done in the last two decades on the political, social and historical aspects of Baudelaire's work—after, of course, the seminal work of Benjamin much earlier. See, in particular, the following scholars, of whose work I continually make use in this study: Richard Terdiman; Ross Chambers; T. J. Clark; Richard Burton; Dolf Oehler; and Jonathan Monroe, A Poverty of Objects: The Prose Poem and the Politics of Genre (Ithaca: Cornell University Press, 1987). My own approach is emphatically not meant to ignore such considerations, as I hope my first chapter makes clear. Indeed, their work has largely undergirded my own.

32. Another example of the albatross dilemma is, weirdly, Baudelaire's discussion of Poe on various fantasies (or hoaxes) concerning animals on the moon, and the extent to which (interestingly enough) these strange forms of life can be seen with a telescope: "the wings of the man-bat cannot support him in an atmosphere as thin as the moon's." But, adds Baudelaire, summarizing Poe, it is not enough to have a telescope; the celestial body being observed needs to be sufficiently illuminated (OC 2:294–95).

again in what had been the deadening noise and movement of the crowd. But she is swallowed into the night, and the narrator is literally blinded by the dark, not merely by his illusions as in "Laquelle est la vraie?" And though many critics assume that the *passante* is upper class because of her statuesque leg, her regal gait, the mourning clothes that she tries to protect from the filth of the city street—there is in fact no reason to support this claim. She is the representation of a nobility of thought for the poet. The *passante* herself, however, may be as poor as the rest of the crowd that engulfs her. She may symbolize the dignity of poverty in her sorrow—much like the narrator in that poem, well aware of his own loss, and his inescapable mourning. Baudelaire uses the stereotypes of class to underline an aristocracy of mind and taste, such that the dignity ascribed by the poet to a working-class woman, for example, emerges all the more distinctly from the squalor that is her material world. This is one way of reading the *passante*.

OPTICAL GAPS

The memory of any event engages repetition—even if "only" the repetition of representation. Deleuze argues that repetition is a form of pure difference, since the former entails a displacement. I cannot know that something is repeated unless I recognize it as having occurred before. A gap, or lapse, is thus at the heart of repetition. Deleuze cites the famous remark by Hume to underline his point: "*Repetition changes nothing in the object repeated, but does change something in the mind which contemplates it.*"[33] What is significant about Baudelaire's praxis in such an economy is that he forces the gap, both in scopic and temporal terms. In other words, when he sees the *passante*, he inscribes the event as a priori lost in the memory, even as it is inscribed therein as scopic repetition—already in place (written in the brain of the artist, we remember) and to be called forth (Lazarus, arise!). Relevant here is Timothy Reiss's observation: with Galileo's *Sidereus nuncios* (1610) on the telescope, "modern technological thinking was provided with its most eloquent metaphor, as Galileo interposed the distance of the telescope between the human mind and the material world before it, the object of its attentive gaze."[34] The telescope as metaphor posits not only a space between the eye and the object of its gaze; it also

33. Gilles Deleuze, *Difference and Repetition*, trans. Paul Patton (New York: Columbia University Press, 1994), 70. Italics Deleuze's.

34. Timothy J. Reiss, *The Discourse of Modernism* (Ithaca: Cornell University Press, 1982), 24.

questions whether what we see is really what we get (a scopic question
that ultimately leads, I would argue, to its conceptual analog in Kant's
first *Kritik*). Is what we see through the telescope a repetition of what we
see with the naked eye, what really is "out there"? These subjective instruments (which need the human eye in order for the object of their focus to be
seen) question what is "out there" but not how the seeing itself functions.

The very interposition of the "gap" questions the ocular repetition
(if enlarged) of what is thus seen again. So too with the microscope, eyeglasses, and the magnifying glass, which also place a distance between
the eye and what is observed. It is a difference that specifically intrigued
Baudelaire. In "De la couleur," the third part of the *Salon* of 1846, the poet
muses on how nature is always harmonious in its use of color. The example Baudelaire gives is a woman's hand: the pink skin, blue and green
veins, and so on. But, adds the poet, "The examination of the same object with a magnifying glass will provide . . . a perfect harmony of grays,
blues, browns, greens, oranges, and whites, warmed with a little yellow."
The harmony of colors is present both in what is seen by the naked eye
and in what is seen with the magnifying glass; but the colors are not the
same. The ability to see the deeper, magnified colors is the natural gaze of
the artist: "The magnifying glass" (*la loupe*), concludes Baudelaire, "is the
eye of the colorist" (*OC* 2:424).[35] The two available perspectives—those
provided by the naked eye and by the scopic instrument—are like scientific analogues for seeing double, or for expecting an a priori double vision
of sorts. In one of his fragments, Baudelaire actually personifies the gap
between the eye and the object of its scrutiny, in this case the moon. A
spectator sees a large black cat "between him and the moon." The cat,
back arched, is meowing, making a noise like a water mill. "Soon he [the
spectator] saw it swell up to the sky . . . and pirouette until it fell to the
ground, from which it arose in the form of a salmon, with a tie around its
neck and a pair of boots on backwards" (*OC* 2:979).[36]

---

35. As against Benjamin, who writes in his own essay on photography that the aura is "the
unique appearance or semblance of distance, no matter how close it may be." To bring things
closer is as much a passion of the day, he adds, as the overcoming of the unique by means of its
reproduction. He later complains that every day "the need to possess the object in close-up in
the form of a picture, or rather a copy, becomes more imperative." The aura, he famously concludes, is thus destroyed. "Little History of Photography," in Walter Benjamin, *Selected Writings*, vol.2: *1927–34*, trans. Rodney Livingstone and others; ed. Michael W. Jennings, Howard
Eiland, and Gary Smith (Cambridge, MA: Harvard University Press, 1999), 518–18. See Pichois,
OC 2:1030–31, for the history of this fragment.

36. There is for Baudelaire an image having to do with killing unbearable perfection. It is
clearly inspired by Poe's tale "The Black Cat" (1843), which Baudelaire translated. In the Poe

There is ample reason to believe that Baudelaire was aware of the scientific interest in the afterimage, that process which in his work becomes an *après-coup* of memory or (conversely) the recording on the page of an image triggered by the one already in the artist's brain. In the first few decades of the nineteenth century, Jonathan Crary writes, there was a shift from the geometrical optics of the seventeenth and eighteenth centuries to physiological optics, "which dominated both scientific and philosophical discussion of vision in the nineteenth century." One result, Crary continues, was the study of retinal afterimages, along with "peripheral vision, binocular vision, and thresholds of attention." The preoccupation with the defects of the human eye defined the normal, and "generated new technologies for imposing a normative vision on the observer."[37]

Nineteenth-century culture was fascinated in various optical devices, and Baudelaire was no exception. He frequently mentions dioramas, kaleidoscopes, and magic lanterns. Also popular in his day were the stereoscope, phenakistiscope, stroboscope, zootrope, and any number of other optical instruments and toys. The young Baudelaire writes to his brother Alphonse about receiving a phenakistiscope. The word, says "Charles" (as the young Baudelaire is generally called by scholars), is as odd as the invention itself:

> It's a piece of cardboard in which there is a little mirror that is put on a table between two candles. It also has a handle on which you put a round cardboard pierced all over with little holes. On top you put an-

---

story, the owner of a cat cements it into a wall along with his wife (whom he has murdered). His crime is discovered by the police when the cat lets out "a wailing shriek, half of horror and half of triumph." The cat had been too cloying, too constantly present, just as his wife had been uncomplaining and "the most patient of sufferers." Poe, *Selected Writings*, 329. Similarly, Baudelaire's "Le vin de l'assassin" is a poem about a man who murders his wife by throwing her into a well, adding stones on top of the body for good measure. He loved her, but couldn't stand her reproaches concerning his drinking (*OC* 1:108–9). Again, in a similar vein, one of the narrators in "Portraits de maîtresses," kills his lover because she is too perfect, too good. Life with her had become, as with Poe's narrator of the black cat, an overwhelming nightmare (*OC* 1:348–49). In each of these cases, love becomes intolerable and is destroyed only to come back haunting. On Baudelaire and cats, see the poet's own two poems "Le chat" (*OC* 1:35, 50–51) and "Les chats" (66). See also Michael Riffaterre's wonderful reading of the second: "Describing Poetic Structures: Two Approaches to Baudelaire's 'Les chats,'" *Yale French Studies* 36–37 (1966): 200–242.

37. Jonathan Crary, *Techniques of the Observer: On Vision and Modernity in the Nineteenth Century* (Cambridge, MA: MIT Press, 1992), 16. "The retinal image," writes Crary, "is perhaps the most important optical phenomenon discussed by Goethe in his chapter on physiological colors in the *Theory of Colors*" (97).

other piece of cardboard with a drawing on it. The drawing faces the mirror. You make it turn, and you look in the mirror through the little holes and see very pretty pictures. (*Corr.* 1:22; November 23, 1833)

The phenakistiscope was given to Charles by his stepfather, with whom Charles initially had good relations (calling him "Papa"), but whom the poet came to see as his nemesis.[38] The gift of this optical gadget occurred in the period when General Aupick had great hopes for his young stepson—that he would do well in school and grow up to rise in military or social ranks. The phenakistiscope was the gift of upper-class parents to their spoiled children, an expensive toy.[39] The cost of such an object was symptomatic of Aupick's acceptance of Charles as a member of his own class—an acceptance that was, of course, to change drastically. Aupick's message seems to be that you can skew and distort your perspective on the world for fun when you are a child; but, once an adult, playing around with vision must end, for the world is a serious and organized place, which offers success to those who merit it. Baudelaire, however, will spend his adult years trying to recapture the gaze of a child, willfully distorting the very conformity of the world that Aupick respected and his stepson loathed.

In "Morale du joujou," the adult Baudelaire speaks directly to these fancy playthings, and to the phenakistiscope in particular: "There is a kind of toy (*joujou*) that tends to proliferate of late, and about which I have nothing good or bad to say. I am speaking of the scientific toy. The main fault of these toys is that they are expensive. But they can be amusing for a long time, and develop in the child's brain a taste for the marvelous and surprising" (*OC* 1:585). He mentions the stereoscope and the phenakistiscope; he then gives a fairly lengthy (and adult) description of the latter. When you put your eye in front of the "little windows," the figures reflected in the mirror dance in fantastic ways. On the other hand, Baudelaire has nothing but contempt for the highly popular stereoscope, in part because that instrument is based on the viewing of photographic images, which Baudelaire feared would replace art. [40] But toys that allow the play

38. Pichois's note says that in the margins of this letter there are three drawings, intended to clarify the instrument, "worthy of interesting a psychoanalyst" (*Corr.* 1:701).

39. See, in this regard, the prose poem "Le joujou du pauvre" (*OC* 1:304–5), to which "Morale du joujou" is related.

40. And because it allows for pornography. In the essay on photography, Baudelaire complains about the "love of obscenity" manifest in the stereoscope as peep show: "millions of

of images in the eye are worthy of fascination for the poet and are not, as
he points out, without pedagogic use.

The year Baudelaire died, Hermann von Helmholtz gave a lecture
called "The Recent Progress of the Theory of Vision," in which he discussed the way in which the stereoscope can reproduce the depth perception of human binocular vision. The Wheatstone Stereoscope, the one
Helmholtz described, uses two flat images, which combine to give the illusion of depth. What is thus demonstrated, explains Helmholtz, is that
"two distinct sensations are transmitted from the two eyes and reach the
consciousness at the same time and without coalescing." The two sensations become a single picture, "of which we are conscious in ordinary vision." That single picture, however, is not produced by "any anatomical
mechanism of sensation, but by a mental act" (cited in Krauss, *Optical
Unconscious*, 133). We are back to Zizek's point, mentioned in the previous chapter, about the paradox of the two faces of a vase—you see either
the faces or the vase, never both. The mind does not like, in other words,
two images at once; it performs the "mental act" of producing a single
picture so quickly that we are not even conscious of the act itself. Unless,
of course, you are willfully strabismic like Baudelaire—burdened with a
double image that extends to the function of the image itself, as I have
been arguing. Baudelaire's double vision is present in his unconscious, we
might say, and reveals itself in the (conscious) images of the poems. Perhaps it is not entirely surprising, then, that he feels a certain hostility
toward an instrument that conflates disparate, two-dimensional images
with the instantaneous reflex of visual unity.

The stereoscope, writes Crary, was inherently *"obscene"* in that it
"shattered the *scenic* relationship between viewer and object that was
intrinsic to the fundamentally theatrical setup of the camera obscura"
(*Techniques*, 127). It creates a disturbance of the usual functioning of optical cues, producing flat images, which the mind forces into greater dimensionality. The experience of the observer is not one of *adequaetio*, then,
but of disjunct images, which the mind forces into visual common sense.
The stereoscope, in Crary's words, marks "a radical repositioning of the
observer's relation to visual representation" (128). In other words, the original stereoscope is a referential illusion that prepares the way for photography, a technology that the more modern version of the stereoscope was
to use as its basis. The binocular vision that the stereoscope mimes is per-

avid eyes," he writes, "bend over the holes of the stereoscope as if on the skylights of infinity"
(*OC* 2:617).

haps, as Lacan would put it, a little *too* evident for Baudelaire. This is, in any case, a possibility, an unconscious reflex of hostility. The stereoscope does not provide the poet with the fresh gaze of a child; it reenacts the body's nonidentity with itself, and widens the chasm between the image of what is seen and the thing itself. It is an instance of what Krauss calls "redoubled vision"—seeing yourself seeing, "a kind of *cogito* of vision," as she puts it (*Optical Unconscious*, 19). We are back to Kant's First Critique, which somebody once described as being in a dark room with the projection on a screen of an image of that same room. How do you know if what is on the screen is really what the room looks like? You don't. Or, as Kleist so famously put it after reading the same Critique, how do you know, if you are wearing green glasses, whether things are green because of the glasses or because they really are green? You don't.

But this is not Baudelaire's major source of torment; his, rather, is trying to depict a world of contradictory, disjunct events without giving in to the normalized unity and depth of a stereoscope, or the retroactive logic of a photograph, or the collaboration between the eyes that makes for normal human sight. Baudelaire's crisis is a search for an apodictic, one that does not sacrifice antinomy on the altar of logic. He keeps the two visual options at once—*laquelle est la vraie?* The stereoscope's power to elide two disparate images into a single one (with depth) is exactly what Baudelaire does *not* want to do—and this, I believe, he senses without fully understanding it. Moreover, there is no theatricality in the stereoscope, as Crary notes; it is the recapitulation of the human eye's ability to synthesize disparity. And Baudelaire, as we have seen, prefers theatricality and the artificial to the natural. Better to look at the optical illusions produced by a phenakistiscope or the shards of color produced by the kaleidoscope—both less obvious in their blending of two images into one—than to be confronted with the anatomical properties of the eye and the more obviously betrayed mental automatism toward visual unity. (In this, by the way, he is very much unlike his autopsy-obsessed mentor, Poe.)

In any case, all of these optical toys and gadgets—many (like the phenakistiscope) invented in the eighteenth century—were somewhat the rage in the early to mid-nineteenth century for those who could afford them. Whereas the microscope, the telescope, eyeglasses, and the magnifying glass were scientific attempts to heighten the visual and to make it more accurate for the eye, the ocular gadgets were meant to show how optical illusions and distortions can produce a myriad of fantastical images, and thus put into play the subjective view of the spectator. Again, Crary: "While the phenakistiscope was of course a mode of popular entertainment, a leisure-time commodity purchasable by an expanding urban middle class, it also paralleled the format of the scientific devices . . . for the empirical study of subjective vision" (*Techniques*, 112). In fact, notes Crary, these devices taught as much about the observer as they did about illusion. The physical position required of someone using a phenakisti-scope "bespeaks a confounding of three modes: an individual body that is at once a spectator, a subject of empirical research and observation, and an element of machine production." It is a question, he adds, "of a body aligned with and operating an assemblage of turning and regularly moving wheeled parts." Baudelaire's description to his brother (along with three drawings) attempts to describe such a triangulation. What was in question, writes Crary, was "a need for knowledge of the capacities of the eye and its regimentation dominated many of them" (ibid.).

The diorama too involved wheels moving, and was a source of interest for Baudelaire. In the *Salon* of 1859, the poet bemoans the lack of real talent among the landscape artists. "I wish I could be brought back to the dioramas," he writes, "whose brutal and immense magic could impose a useful illusion on me." Why? Because such things are false, writes the poet, and thus "are infinitely closer to the real." Landscape artists are liars, he adds, "precisely because they forget to lie" (*OC* 2:668). We are back to the logic of makeup: women should be made up in an obvious manner because makeup is unnatural and therefore all to the good. A successful panorama must be theatrical, colored more vividly than life, so that the spectator can be enchanted rather than bored. (Again, so much for the stereoscope, which duplicates the eye's behavior). So too Guys—the "lover of life" for Baudelaire—is like a mirror in a huge crowd; "a kaleidoscope endowed with consciousness that, "with each of its movements, represents multiple life and the moving grace of all the elements of life." It is no surprise, given the multiplicity of perspective and consciousness in vision, that Baudelaire's next sentence in this passage underlines the fragmentation of the self: the lover of life, the living kaleidoscope, "is an *I* (*moi*) insatiable for the *not-I*, which, at each instant, renders and expresses it in images more animated than life itself, always unstable and fugitive" (*OC* 2:692).[41] Multiple life means multiple images for the poet, proliferating like multiple *I*'s.[42]

41. Baudelaire no doubt got his *I/not I* vocabulary from Proudhon, who imported it, as we noted in chapter 1, from his very superficial knowledge of Johann Gottlieb Fichte's philosophy.

42. Ross Chambers writes that "the 'lyric I' had always been a privileged figure. Suddenly, in late Baudelaire, the 'I' who speaks (in) a poem becomes a dubious and even problematic

The bombardment of images in modern urban life is honed into a praxis that serves, not only as a symptom of modernity (as Benjamin has it), but, as noted earlier, as a defense system for the eye as well as the mind, transformed into a type of poetics to manage the confusion that Baudelaire's own poetry records and simultaneously experiences—what I have called scopic syllepsis.

"Every epoch has its manner of dress, its gaze, and its smile," writes Baudelaire (OC 2:695). The multiple images of the city, and the nineteenth-century study of the subjectivity of vision, combine to give the poet the notion of varying visual fields for different periods and a human gaze that changes correspondingly over time. This notion of an essentialized epoch, it should be noted, is not limited to Baudelaire. In a large encyclopedia on the French, Les français peints par eux-mêmes, produced between 1841 and 1843, a certain Frédéric Soulié makes a similar assumption: "Nature has its types, society has its types, every nation has its types, and finally each epoch has its types." [43] The type is not without importance in Baudelaire's poetry; it is a belief in the symptoms of an era that allows someone like Daumier, for example, to be understood as capturing that era through the type. All the more reason for Baudelaire to have admired the caricaturist, then: he drew the various instars of an age.

But while there is a monolithic notion of notre époque in Baudelaire, and of other epochs as well (the ancients, for example, are frequently described as "thinking this," or "doing that"), there is also a notion of seeing differently from a subjective standpoint. Everyone sees the same object under the microscope, presumably—at least in theory; but the kaleidoscope allows for fantasies and distortions of the individual gaze. Inner vision is of equal importance to outer. A great painter, says Baudelaire in reference

authority . . . whose aloofness and melancholia, which enable him to *see* the problem that escapes others, also make him *part* of the problem he sees: an observant 'eye' indistinguishable from a socially embattled 'I.'" I agree that this is the case with the late Baudelaire; but the earlier one does not question his subjectivity, and Baudelaire overall rarely *"sees"* the problem that escapes others. Rather, as I have been arguing throughout, he records the problem he sees without necessarily understanding its full implications. Ross Chambers, "Baudelaire's Paris," in *The Cambridge Companion to Baudelaire*, 102. See also, in the same article, Chambers's insightful comments on missed encounters in Baudelaire and lines of intersection, including references to "A une passante" (105 ff.).

43. Frédéric Soulié, "Le second mari," in Léon Curmer, ed., *Les Français peints par eux-mêmes: encyclopédie morale du dix-neuvième siècle*, 8 vols. (Paris: Schneider et Langrand, 1841–43), 4:193. In the essay "Comment on paie ses dettes quand on a du génie," Baudelaire himself alludes to the publisher and editor Curmer, without naming him, as "a rich and prosperous merchant" (commerçant) to whom *Les Français peints par eux-mêmes* is offered as a series of newspaper articles (OC 2:7).

to Delacroix, must have an "eye illuminated by an interior light." The artist's greatest battles come from within, he continues; "the most curious revolutions and events occur under the sky of the skull, in the narrow and mysterious laboratory of the mind" (OC 2:429). Clear and confident as this may sound for Baudelaire's painter and his "certitude," the reader will remember in the poem "Spleen" the bat that is hope, bereft of its night vision, flying helplessly against the decaying rafters of the mind until, resigned, it gives up on its own allegorical significance. The dramas of the mind are not as triumphant (to say the least) in Baudelaire the poet as in the poet as critic. Subjective vision from within carries a Poe-like raven of sorts—it is not merely sitting on the pallid bust of Pallas just above the chamber door; it is perched inside the mind as well. Baudelaire, in other words, idealizes the certitude of the painter's vision—in both the external and internal gaze—but this does not help him to apply such lack of doubt to his own artistic productions. A confident voice dominates his art criticism, mimetic of a judgment that suffers neither doubt nor eclecticism in the visual artist. But the writing of Baudelaire the poet is driven by aporia—a doubt that is visual as well as conceptual. "Which Is the Real One?" is a clear symptom of such aporia.

Modernity may undercut contemplation, as Benjamin contended, but it also insists on spectatorship. And the result of concentrating on the latter is politically a fallacy, Hannah Arendt believes, one that "consists in describing and understanding the whole realm of human action, not in the terms of the actor and the agent, but from the standpoint of the spectator who watches a spectacle." But such a fallacy, she continues, also contains an inherent truth, which is that all stories "unfold their true meaning only when they have come to their end," so that it appears as though "only the spectator, and not the agent, can hope to understand what actually happened in any given chain of events."[44] In the confusing epoch that is Baudelaire's, spectatorship is not only the superior and ironic perspective of the dandy, or the ambling gait and nonchalance of the flâneur; spectatorship is a stance (or *Haltung*, to use Friedrich Schlegel's term) that allows enough distance to delude oneself into putting things seen into some kind of historical order, sense, or sequence—as if they were done and could thus be assessed. Doubt, in other words, is repressed through the imposition of a distance posing as control. But like the distance Baudelaire describes between the cat's eye and the object of its scrutiny, the distance between the spectator and the scene is haunted by a lurking chasm

---

44. Hannah Arendt, *On Revolution* (London: Penguin Books, 1965), 52.

of sorts—the fear that seeing is perhaps not only inaccurate but blocked by incomprehension.

Optical illusions are not cultivated by Baudelaire the poet merely as a form of relief from the dangers of seeing; in his day they were widely regarded as phenomena that turn the spectator's eye onto him- or herself, providing the individual with fantasy and thus helping to repress the fragmentation that seems everywhere evident—turning such fragmentation into visual play. Spectatorship, in other words, also turns inward. Indeed, the kaleidoscope literalizes fragmentation, as Baudelaire makes clear (the lover of life, it will be recalled, is himself a kaleidoscope endowed with consciousness, whose every movement echoes the multiplicity of city life). For Baudelaire, contemplation is so confused by the city, so disturbed by its splintered noise and sights, that confusion becomes a necessary gloss on life itself, and inner fragmentation the subject's promise of hidden intellectual and poetic riches. This is a desperate point of view.

Schopenhauer comments angrily on the "torture which thinkers have to endure from noise." Even a great mind becomes like an ordinary one "the moment it is interrupted, disturbed, distracted, and diverted." But the philosopher, writing in 1851 from the then relatively small town of Frankfurt, could still be self-righteously outraged by the street noise that prevented him from concentrating. Is the thinking mind, he complains, "to be the only thing that never experiences the slightest consideration or protection, to say nothing of respect?" The remarks are heavily class-conscious. Whip-cracking, writes Schopenhauer, drives him crazy, "for it robs life of all peace and pensiveness." Hammering, dogs barking, children screaming are nothing compared to the crack of a whip. "That such an infamy is tolerated in towns is a crude barbarity and an iniquity. . . . There can be no harm in drawing the attention of the proletarians to the mental work of the classes above them, for they have a mortal dread of all such work."[45] Schopenhauer recommends to the reader a "poetical epistle" on the subject "by the famous painter Bronzino," who gives a description of "the torment that one has to endure from the many different noises of an Italian town" (645). The Bronzino text in question was published in 1771, and should put us on the alert. The mere fact that Schopenhauer can still distinguish hammering from dogs barking, and children screaming from

45. Arthur Schopenhauer, "On Din and Noise," in *Parerga and Paralipomena: Short Philosophical Essays*, Trans. E. F. J. Payne (Oxford: Clarendon Press, 1974), 2:642–44. With respect to vision and subjective images of the eye, see a good recent edition in French of Schopenhauer's color theory: Arthur Schopenhauer, *Textes sur la vue et sur les couleurs*, ed. and trans. Maurice Elie (Paris: J. Vrin, 1986).

the crack of a whip; the fact that he is infuriated on unselfconsciously, even self-righteously, class-conscious grounds (the need of peace and quiet for the superior mind and the thoughtless noise of the hoi polloi); and, finally, that he cites as support a text from the eighteenth century—all of this demonstrates how different Paris is from Frankfurt in 1851. "The deafening street around me was howling," begins Baudelaire's "A une passante" some ten years later. The noise of the modern city is constant, and all its sounds are fused into what Ross Chambers translates as "screeching" (*hurlait*). "The universal toleration of unnecessary noise," fumes Schopenhauer, "for example the extremely vulgar and ill-mannered slamming of doors, is simply a sign of mental bluntness and a general want of thought" (645).

The inhabitant of mid-nineteenth-century Paris has long since given up fuming, has long since been unable to hear doors slam as a distinct noise, has long since abandoned all hope for curing a city gone mad with din. A text from 1771 would be as useless as would be indignation about the clamor. Schopenhauer still lives in the old world; Baudelaire is trying to adapt to the audial and visual chaos of the new. Both, however, typify the noise as vulgar and low class. Schopenhauer rhetorically asks if there can be protection from the din for the thinking mind; Baudelaire knows there can be no such protection, and conversely turns more and more to the melancholic confines of the mind to ward off the noise and confusion. Similarly, Freud later formulates the "envelope" around consciousness— the perception-consciousness system that, among other things, protects the mind from too many stimuli (especially audial) and stores up experience in the memory.[46] The mind itself, however, is for Baudelaire increasingly at risk from the mob. But it does have recourse to inscribing pictures in the brain. Somewhat like a museum, the brain stores images for future use.

The splintering of the ego that follows the bedlam of the modern city is based not only on the study of subjective vision, though the latter follows nicely from the former. The nineteenth century produced the "uprooting of vision," as Crary puts it, and much has been written about how

46. The perception-consciousness system changes in Freud when he abandons the topographic model of the mind and shifts to the tripartite model. It is curious to note, however, the extent to which Baudelaire's notion of the mind and its images, and his need for protection from the noise of the crowd, in a sense prefigure Freud's formulation of the perception-consciousness system in the "Project for a Scientific Psychology" (1895), in *SE* (London: Hogarth, 1966), 1:295–387.

the human eye had to adapt to the ensuing visual and audial maelstrom, to use Poe's word yet again.[47] And, indeed, the subject is splintered in its spectatorship as well. But Baudelaire's notion of the artist in itself provides a kind of self-protection: he formulates a gaze for the art critic that turns the madness of the city and the contradiction of his own poetics, convictions, and observations into a means of protection through a belief in the artist's perception and correlative certainty.

For one thing, Baudelaire celebrates rapidity in the artist.[48] Indeed, apart from his conviction that photography threatens art, he may also have scorned the daguerreotype because of the slowness with which that technology records the image, and the fact that the gaze, once the scene to be recorded has been chosen, is somehow extrapolated from the scene and absorbed into the process.[49] But let us recall that the artist who can sketch fast enough to record the ever changing city scenes (here, Constantin Guys) is in fact miming the city's fast pace—even if he can never quite catch up with it. At night, the artist (Guys) draws while the rest of the urban population sleeps. And it is at night that the artist recaptures what he saw on the streets. He uses his pen as a sword and presses hard, "violent, active," hurrying as if "fearing that the images might escape him." The artist then performs a "Lazarus, arise!"—"And things are reborn on the paper," writes Baudelaire; "the phantasmagoria has been extracted from nature" (OC 2:693–94). There is here no recollection in tranquillity, à la Wordsworth; rather, we have collection in rapidity (sketching *in situ*), and then drawing from sketch and memory as quickly as possible. Memory has been "cluttered" (*encombrée*) with what the sketch tried to distill, and memory unburdens itself with the force and rapid strokes of a fencing match (*s'éscrimant*) to create the work.[50] But it is the artist's superior perception—to be understood above all as his gaze—that allows for the

47. For example, among a myriad of others, Benjamin, in a footnote: "The daily sight of a lively crowd may once have constituted a spectacle to which one's eye needed to adapt" (*The Writer of Modern Life*, 383 n. 41). See too, concerning fin-de-siècle spectatorship, Vanessa R. Schwartz, *Spectacular Realities: Early Mass Culture in Fin-de-Siècle Paris* (Berkeley: University of California Press, 1998).

48. Including the writer. "To write fast," notes our poet, "you must have thought a lot—have carried a subject with you, during walks, in your bath, at the restaurant, and almost at your mistress's" (OC 2:17).

49. And the photograph does not return our gaze. See, on this aspect, Marc Fumaroli, *Paris, New York et retour: Voyage dans les arts et les images* (Paris: Fayard, 2009).

50. The fencing metaphor particularly interested Benjamin. See, e.g., *The Writer of Modern Life*, 97.

retention of images (phantasmagoria) between the event, its sketched and nearly instantaneous inscription, and its nocturnal rerendition. Rapidity is essential, but the expert perception of the eye is the driving force of the work of art.[51] Moreover, the work of the artist's eye is itself described in a violent battle metaphor. During the nocturnal work, the artist, bent over his desk, is shooting (*dardant*) at the blank paper with his gaze, "the same gaze he had earlier riveted on things" (693).

The image that emerges is "the result of a *childish* perception, that is, an acute perception, magical by dint of its ingenuity!" (694). The eye of the child is open and unfettered by cliché or social demands. Perhaps the closest an adult may come to it is in optical toys and instruments, which reclaim for the eye a certain childlike wonder, or fresh vision. The lover of life, to return yet again to that figure, is like a kaleidoscope endowed with consciousness that, "with each of his movements, represents multiple life and the moving grace of all the elements of life" (692). So the furious pace of the city must be matched by furious rapidity in the artist; but it must also be met with the freshness of a child's vision. The kaleidoscope here is a metaphor for the rediscovery of the child's sight, of wonder at the colorful movements and scopic proliferations of the city. The kaleidoscope also, as we have noted, imposes symmetry on shapes and colors. So too, the artist's material that clutters the memory is "arranged, harmonized, and submitted to this forced idealization" (694).

Both the gaze that Baudelaire praises in Guys and its rapidity in recording are also performed in "A une passante." Indeed, the poet's own deployment of the gaze is forcefully displayed in the poem. The flash of lightening that allows the poet to see the *passante*, or that he sees in her eyes, shows his own rapid perception; he too stores the image in memory so that it can be "reborn" in the poem; he too creates, like a kaleidoscope, an arrangement out of the chaotic colors, noises, and scenes of the city. "A une passante" is more, then, than the poetic interpretation of a Guys painting—although the poem is, as I have noted, certainly that. It is even more than the shock Benjamin so persuasively demonstrates as being at

---

51. For a more recent privileging of rapidity in the artist, see Rosalind Krauss's rendition of her conversation with Michael Fried concerning the artist Frank Stella. According to Fried (writes Krauss), Stella thought that the "greatest living American" was the baseball player Ted Williams, because Williams "sees faster than any other living human." Williams's eye was so fast, is the claim, that he could see the stitching on the ball. "In that speed," continues Krauss, "was gathered the idea of an abstracted and heightened visuality. . . . Vision had, as it were, been pared away into a dazzle of pure instantaneity." Rosalind E. Krauss, "The Story of the Eye," *New Literary History* 21, no. 2 (Winter 1990): 283–84.

the poem's core. For Benjamin, the poem is both "an eternal farewell," and the "sexual shock that can beset a lonely man." It affects the nature of the poet's emotions, revealing "the stigmata which life in a metropolis inflicts upon love" (*The Writer of Modern Life*, 185). The poem is, as Benjamin puts it, happiness drawn from "the misery of the times"—the combination of antinomies: happiness and yet again, misery (ibid., 161).

Indisputably. But the poem also performs the artistic gaze that Baudelaire so admires in Guys and Delacroix. "À une passante," in other words, mimes (and aspires to) the possibility of the artist's rapid and confident gaze in poetry, and, in addition, serves as an affirmation of the poet's ability to marshal that gaze. The poem may be about loss, but it is also about the power of the image in poetry, and the demonstration of such power in the poem's production. The poetics of "À une passante" (how to deploy the image in poetry) are at odds with the poem's narrative (the loss of an image "perhaps" forever). It is this scopic syllepsis (the poet's manipulation of an "image" is not the same as the experiential "image" of the *passante*) that makes for the poem's complexity and rich texture. Moreover, the certainty of the artist/poet's gaze is undercut by the poem's doubt with respect to the experiential (Will the narrator see her again?) and by its chthonic memory (perhaps he will see her in eternity). This contradictory notion of the image makes for yet another kind of double vision—a scopic syllepsis—in Baudelaire's corpus and, at the same time, for the staging of the poetics of imagery.

ENERGY: THE BAROQUE

The intensity of a child's gaze, as mentioned earlier, is a source of admiration and nostalgia for the poet. Such a vision can be recaptured with various optical toys, but also by putting oneself in the position of seeing everything with renewed admiration—like a rekindled awareness. For example, Baudelaire describes Guys's vision as similar to another *tableau* (Baudelaire's word)—Poe's short story, "The Man of the Crowd." A convalescent sees a man in the crowded city whose physiognomy intrigues him. The convalescent, his curiosity becoming "a fatal, irresistible passion," rushes through the mass of humanity to find the man. Guys, writes Baudelaire, is similar to the story's narrator—the painter is in a perpetual state of convalescence. Like a child, and like a man recovering from a serious illness, Guys has the faculty "to be vividly interested in things, even those most trivial in appearance" (*OC* 2:690). "À une passante" shares much of this, except that in the text on Guys we might discern a nostalgia for the fresh

gaze of the child ("The child sees everything as *newness*; he is always intoxicated"; ibid.), combined with a determination to share what Baudelaire
sees as the energy and certitude of the great visual artist. Moreover, the
convalescent and the child take nothing for granted; they are not prey to
the crushing melancholy produced by the infamous Baudelairean ennui.

And there is something about the energy of the crowd that not only
bludgeons with its noise and chaos, but exhilarates the poet as well: "The
pleasure of being in the crowds," he writes in *Fusées*, "is a mysterious
expression of the joy in the multiplication of the number" (*OC* 1:649).
Fundamental to "A une passante," and to the discussion on Guys and Delacroix's immense energy of vision and production, is the poet's desire not
only for certainty but also for renewed vigor, rebirth, exuberance. These he
rarely possessed himself, just as he rarely experienced in his poetic praxis
the certitude he demanded of "artists." It is as if the visual for him could
grant a certainty that the written could never attain, and produce an energy peculiar to the visual artists he celebrates. This despite the fact that
the visual for him sets off a duality of images, as we have seen, that too
frequently produce—and outright celebrate—doubt. Indeed, Baudelaire's
notion of rebirth is in fact resurrection from the dead. "Lazarus, arise!" is
not an "Open Sesame" that allows for entry into a realm of hidden trea-
sures, nor is it a mandrake root that, once pulled, similarly opens up a
hitherto invisible parallel world (as for example, in Ludwig Tieck's "Der
Runenberg").[52] Baudelaire's metaphor for rebirth, for feeling the intensity
of life—as Delacroix did for him, or Guys—is the miracle of raising the
dead. Already as if dead, in other words, he looks to artistic vision and the
rapidity of its ability to capture the image for some means of redemption,
some way of feeling alive, if only as a return from the dead. Many of his
poems concern not only ghosts but graveyards.

We are once again inside a ghost economy. To return to Benjamin, with
a different perspective, Baudelaire is eternally saying farewell to the world
("Anywhere out of the world!") even as he clutches at it to return. Poetry, like the *passante*, sometimes seems to promise a return to a present
that—despite the city, the confusion, the noise the same poetry suggests
(and never directly depicts, as Benjamin points out)—can be felt, and even

52. Ludwig Tieck, "Der Runenberg," in *Tiecks Werke*, ed. Eduard Berend (Berlin and
Leipzig: Bong & Co., 1908), 1:117. In an analogous (though humorous, as opposed to Tieck's
sinister) vein, E. T. A. Hoffmann's *Der goldene Topf: Ein Märchen aus der neuen Zeit* (Stuttgart: Reklam, 1969) opens with the student Anselmus upsetting an applecart belonging to an
ugly old woman. The woman shrieks a rhymed curse at him, "ins Kristall bald dein Fall—ins
Kristall!" (5). Everything starts from there, and Anselmus will indeed end up in a bottle.

felt with happiness. Double vision in Baudelaire is also this antinomy: the desire to die in order to escape the world and to find eternity, versus the desire to return from the dead in order to escape death and to find, finally, life.

The gaze in "A une passante" presents things largely as black and white—the dark confusion of the crowd, the bright burst of lightening, the plunge into darkness, the poet's rebirth and then despair, his turn to anticipated memory. Similarly, what Baudelaire wants generally in art is clarity—but in color—and the figural. He admires the painter Louis David, for example, likening his painting (and in particular his *Marat*) to Balzac: "All of these details are historical and real," writes Baudelaire of that painting, "like a Balzac novel: the drama is there, alive in all of its lamentable horror; and, by a strange tour de force that makes this painting David's masterpiece and one of the great curiosities of modern art, [the painting] has nothing of the trivial or the ignoble" (*OC* 2:409–10). The painting (from 1793, though Baudelaire saw it at the Musée Classique du Bazar Bonne-Nouvelle in 1846) is thus praised for its figural exactitude and its precision of detail (the artist Meryon will be similarly praised). But it is hard to see "modern art" in this David. We do find one attribute in Baudelaire's description of the David painting that we know ignites his admiration for painters closer to his heart (Delacroix and Guys, of course): David's *Marat* (which Baudelaire significantly calls an "unaccustomed poem") was done with "extreme rapidity," the poet tells us. "Cruel like nature," he continues, "the painting has all the scent of the ideal" (410). And in an ironic tone, Baudelaire asks the politicians "of all parties," and even "the fierce liberals of 1845" permission to be moved by *Marat*. "This painting was a gift to the weeping nation," he writes, "and our tears are not dangerous" (ibid.).

He also mentions another of David's works, *La mort de Lepelletier de Saint-Fargeau*, a painting that had been paired with *Marat* at the Convention and has since "mysteriously disappeared."[53] Lepelletier, a member of the Convention, had cast the deciding vote for the death of the king. On

---

53. The painting was later bought and destroyed by Suzanne (along with any copies), the royalist daughter of Lepelletier—an irony, since after her father's assassination, the eleven-year-old girl had been formally "adopted" by the French nation. On this and other details, including Lepelletier's funeral, see Amable-Guillaume de Barante, *Histoire de la convention nationale* (Paris: Furne et Cie and Langlois & Leclercq, 1851), esp. 2:329–31. The baron of Barante is quite a royalist himself—appalled by the execution of Louis. Working from the verbatim minutes of the Convention's meetings, Barante produces a gripping, detailed account of the Convention and the Terror.

the evening before the king was executed (January 21, 1893), Lepelletier was assassinated, in a restaurant at the Palais Royal, by an enraged royalist named Pâris. Baudelaire, who never saw the painting, suggests that the spectator could have discerned the writing on a sword that hovered near the ceiling, over the prostrate body of Lepelletier—much as one can read, in the *Marat*, the Girondin names that Marat had been writing (dictated to him by Corday) just before his murder. In the lost painting, the sword, an allusion to that of Damocles, reads "Pâris, garde du corps" (ibid., Baudelaire's note). Lepelletier was considered the first martyr of the Revolution, and received a hero's funeral. His body, displayed in the Place Vendôme, lay on a bed covered in blood; the body was naked to the waist so that the wound was fully visible. David, who had helped to organize the funeral and had placed the body in that pose, painted *Lepelletier de Saint-Fargeau sur son lit de mort* while the body lay in state. Barante tells us that the painter set up his easel next to the body, working on his painting such that "he gave the people the spectacle of the painter copying that bloody model" (*Histoire*, 330). Baudelaire may have known this anecdote—Pichois tells us that the poet is "pretty well informed" on the matter[54]—but even if he didn't, it casts an odd light on the notion of painting quickly so as to capture the moment. The painter, in this case, turns his work into theater: he artificially creates the "moment" that he then publicly demonstrates himself to be capturing. He publicly records a violent death as if it had only just occurred (much like Manet's *Execution of the Emperor Maximilian* and Goya's *The Third of May*, on which the former is based, fascinate Bataille; both depict the instant of death). It is a curious beginning for a painting that was later to be suppressed. The spectator, to return to Arendt on modernity, is indeed witnessing a spectacle.

Baudelaire's critical voice, in any case, not only is confident itself, and not only demands certainty from the artist; it also inclines his eye toward paintings that are themselves clear in form and line, that are representational and loyal to detail, and that depict a moment in history in a manner emphatically representational. The neoclassicism of David may seem a curious choice for Baudelaire's admiration, but Baudelaire's essay here focuses on two main figures of the Revolution, Marat and Lepelletier. In 1846, Baudelaire specifically approves of David's revolutionary politics. History and politics are never far from the poet's thoughts, even though he

---

54. *OC* 2:1290. Lepelletier's daughter apparently removed another sentence from the painting: "Je vote la mort du tyran," the statement that the members of the Convention used to vote "yes" for the death of the king.

will try to repress them after the debacle of 1848; and in 1846 the Revolution is still simmering (and is about to explode again). He may have admired a painter whose art could so openly serve to manifest his politics; Baudelaire's remained far more oblique (and frequently, as we have seen, contradictory).[55]

It should also be remembered that David did no still lifes and only one landscape that we know of; and Baudelaire, who liked neither genre, can only have been pleased by such avoidance on the part of the painter. But let us keep in mind that David's neoclassicism, with its larger-than-life mythological figures and its unambiguous renditions, must also have appealed to the poet as a form of certainty, a visual apodictic of sorts, which Baudelaire openly held in high regard. Pichois admires the "independence" of Baudelaire's judgment of art here (OC 2:1289), and there can be no doubt, as I have been emphasizing, that the young Baudelaire's criticisms are surprisingly well versed in art history, and that he possesses a natural sense of aesthetics in the visual arts. And he is writing about art at a time of transition—one of those shifts in the tectonic plates of culture that so obsesses Foucault, for example. At the time of Baudelaire's art criticism, the fault line between romantic and neoclassical art is fairly evident; more ambiguous in the late '40s and '50s, however, is the increasing divergence between romantic and almost-impressionist painting. Baudelaire's views on art are symptomatic of such a time of transition, and of the nonfigural direction painting was to take.

Hobsbawm, in his famous book on revolution, contends that the subject of David's *Madame Récamier* "faces the world with sharp precision in toilette and setting inspired by classical antiquity, as interpreted by the French Revolution."[56] Her gaze, then, is straightforward and clear—unlike the blank gaze that was famously and increasingly to inhabit impressionist portraits. Romanticism, on the other hand, as Hobsbawm would have it, is symbolized by "the undefined swirl of the ballerina Fanny Essler" (ibid.). In both cases, he remarks, there is an interest, if divergence, in luxury goods and in style.[57]

55. As Albert Boime puts it. See his *A Social History of Modern Art*, vol. 1: *Art in an Age of Revolution, 1750–1800* (Chicago: University of Chicago Press, 1987), 454.

56. E. J. Hobsbawm, *The Age of Revolution, 1798–1848* (New York: New American Library, 1962), fig. 68.

57. For Giorgio Agamben, Baudelaire is especially aware of "the novelties and importance of the challenge offered to the work of art by the commodity." Such awareness produces poetic texts that, for Agamben, absorb the fetishistic aspect of commodities, which nevertheless "withdraw them from the tyranny of the economic and the ideology of progress." This is a less than convincing point concerning Baudelaire himself, though it is an intriguing claim.

Hobsbawm may have been no art historian, but what his easy generalities betray is that there is (generally speaking, once again) a visual crispness in neoclassical art, and a fuzziness or soft blurriness in romantic art. It is the difference between a David and a Delacroix. Much as Baudelaire admired the latter, he was decidedly attracted to the visual certainty of the former. Baudelaire's understanding of modern art derives not only from Delacroix and his use of colors, but also from the great mythological, highly realistic David paintings. Both artists, it should be noted, are emphatically representational, and both paint stories—mythical, biblical, historical.

Despite his love of optical clarity, many of Baudelaire's poems partake of romantic blurriness and are bathed in various forms of twilight, the *Zwielicht* of which the German *Frühromantiker*, among others, were so fond. These poems occur in an in-between light; a dim visual field that fosters ambiguity, ambivalence, and doubt. The prose poem "Le crépuscule du soir," for example, praises indistinction in light and mind: "Day ends. A great relief is felt in poor minds tired by the day's labor; and their thoughts now take on the tender and indecisive colors of twilight" (*OC* 1:311). Or the mental confusion caused by hashish, with its accompanying unfocused vision. Or the hazy sky at dusk in "Paysage": "It is sweet, through the haze, to see / The star born in the azure, the lamp at the window / The rivers of coal rising to the firmament / And the moon pouring its pale enchantment" (*Il est doux, à travers les brumes, de voir naître / L'étoile dans l'azur, la lampe à la fenêtre, / Les fleuves de charbon monter au firmament / Et la lune verser son pâle enchantement*). This in-between time is as if the temporal equivalent of double vision. In the poem just cited, the blue of the sky is the legacy of the day, while the star promises the night. Perhaps it is because Baudelaire experiences a double vision that he is intrigued by twilight, which often in his work, as here, is depicted as two times existing at once, rather than as a blurred amalgam of both. Indeed, twilight "excites the insane" precisely because it is neither here nor there. (We will have occasion to consider two times existing at once in chapter 4.)

Baudelaire likes twilight because (as with Novalis), it is the promise of night—and night, which darkens the minds of the insane, illuminates (*fait la lumière dans*) the poet's mind (*OC* 1:313). Baudelaire may claim that he is insatiably avid for "the obscure and the uncertain" ("Horreur

---

Stanzas: Word and Phantasm in Western Culture, trans. Ronald L. Martinez (Minneapolis: University of Minnesota Press, 1977), 41–42.

sympathique," *OC* 1:77), but the uncertain frequently consists of two con-tradictory options, each visually crisp and figuratively concise. The uncer-tain, in other words, is located not in the blurred contours of romanticism (Hobsbawm) or in the hazy visions of what was to become impressionism. In the prose version of "Le crépuscule du soir," sunset traces, in its soft pinks, the "complicated sentiments that do battle in the heart of man." Twilight resembles the dark, transparent gauze that dancers wear, the gauze permitting occasional glimpses of "the muted splendors of a bril-liant skirt, as when the delicious past pierces through the blackness of the present" (*OC* 1:312). Night may be coming, but it allows for "the fires of fantasy, which are bright only under the deep mourning of the night." This statement might serve as a road map for the claim in "A une passante": the *passante's* actual mourning clothes allow for the poet's glimpse into the light of her eyes, transporting him in "fires of fantasy" despite the night that descends on him and into which he loses her. The "delicious past" pierces through the night as memory, despite the blackness of the pres-ent. The usual claim is that Baudelaire is romantic—in his early works, at least—and that "Le crépuscule du soir" shows us a kind of undefined swirl, like that of the ballerina Fanny Essler, to return to Hobsbawm. But Baudelaire's dancer is about seeing back into the past through the night of the present; the vision is clear, and the poet's gaze is steady. As usual, however, there are overlapping dimensions. The dancer wears two skirts, and it is the dark, transparent outer one that bears visual traces of the un-derlying, shimmering past.

Far more often, the uncertain in Baudelaire is intellectual—even theological—as in "Laquelle est la vraie?" Both Bénédictas seem com-pletely plausible and, visually, entirely in focus. The twilight, in other words, and even the fog, smoke, and haze that so frequently inhabit Baude-laire's poems do not meld into a single image of mistiness but, rather, mask worlds very much in focus, even if they are mutual antinomies, or if one seems to cover the other only to let it shine through all the more.

No doubt this is why Baudelaire so admires Delacroix. That painter, as Bataille notes, signifies nothing more (along with Ingres) than "survival at the breast of 'decrepitude,' a prolongation of the past. Nothing in their work is revealed to be new. Their painting is, in this, similar to that of the past, charged with holding its part in the eloquence of the system" (*Manet*, 44–45). Baudelaire loves Delacroix, of course, and loves above all his use of colors. But the poet does not ask himself about Delacroix's vi-sual field. Eloquent painting, Bataille had written, was dead or dying, and Baudelaire didn't see it. The blank stare that so famously informs the personages in Manet's paintings occurred with increasing frequency, as all art historians have noted. But it appeared mostly in works painted after Baudelaire's death. It is the blank stare that leads Bataille to write (about Manet's "Le balcon," 1868–69) that the profound "secret" in the work is that the "beauty and the density of life are perceived without disturbing the waiting of the one with open eyes" (*Manet*, 85).[58] The one with open eyes (found again and again in Manet's *œuvre*) is at the center of the line of vision in the paintings but not at the center of our attention. For Bataille, Manet is the founder of modern art because his paintings celebrate the silent autonomy of vision." It is not a quality that appeals to our poet.

The blank stare, witness perhaps to the debilitating aspects of modernity, is not Baudelaire's. The gaze that does not see what the spectator notices in a Manet painting is not in Baudelaire's conceptual vocabulary. His gaze on the gaze of others is precise; the place where his gaze falls is the center of the poem, even when the vision is doubled or overlaps another. When he looks in the eyes of the poor in the poem "Les yeux des pauvres," those eyes are precisely described; we know what they are thinking. And while the poet discovers that his lover is having different thoughts from his own (she wants, it will be recalled, the poor to be removed from her sight), and while he realizes that he really doesn't know what she is thinking at all, her gaze is not a blank. Mysterious at times, yes; cruel, malicious, bored/boring—but not blank. "Le ciel brouillé," for example, compares the lover's eyes to a hazy sky: "Your gaze is as if covered by a vapor," he writes. "Your mysterious eye (is it blue, gray or green?)" His mistress's eyes may "reflect the indolence and pallor of the sky," but they are "alternatively tender, dreamy, cruel" (*OC* 2:49). They are certainly not blank. Even the *passante*—if we put aside the fantasy of endless love that is destroyed by the city at night—has a gaze that is depicted as in focus, as connected with thought, with melancholy. With respect to the blank gaze as depicted by Manet, Baudelaire is not there (yet); the subject, we might say, has been seriously eroded in Baudelaire, and its predilection (indeed, eternal appetite) for evil is clear. But its sovereignty is not yet in question; its wholeness not yet at risk, even though it is beginning to fragment. When the poet addresses his soul, it answers that it wants to go "anywhere out of the world." But the poet is going with his soul; he is not quite split off from his own subjectivity.

58. Philippe Muray also argues that there is a secret in Baudelaire, to do with the poet's hatred of the Belgians, "a secret that has been hidden for a century: Baudelaire calumniates the Belgians only because he finds them rife with all the French obsessions, beginning with that nightmarish free thought." *Le 19e siècle à travers les âges* (Paris: Denoël, 1984), 666.

And so Manet, as critics constantly remind us, receives little attention from the poet—this despite the fact that Manet had included Baudelaire in *La musique aux Tuileries*, that large painting of a well-heeled crowd in which the poet in a tall hat is just discernible.[59] He also did two etchings of Baudelaire. After the poet's death, he wrote to Asselineau, who was editing Baudelaire's work, and asked if he could contribute them to the editions. Manet suggested that one—the now constantly reproduced sketch of Baudelaire alone, also in a tall hat—be for *Spleen de Paris*; and that the other (the poet bare-headed) "would go well in a book of poetry."[60] Manet recognized Baudelaire as a kindred spirit of modernity, even if the feeling was not really mutual. And although the painter was at that same time writing with increasing impatience to Ancelle for reimbursement after Baudelaire's death (Manet had lent the poet a total of 1,500 francs near the end of his life), his generosity toward Baudelaire was greater than Baudelaire's had been to Manet—at least, in terms of professional recognition.

Every discussion of Baudelaire and Manet includes the poet's famous letter to his friend when Manet's *Olympia* was exhibited to cries of horror, titillation, and real anger at the *Salon* of 1865. Manet had written to Baudelaire, who was in Belgium, to complain, and the poet is less than sympathetic. "So I have to talk to you about you again," the poet writes, as if groaning in boredom. And he adds:

> I have to apply myself to showing you what you are worth. What you are demanding is really stupid. *They are making fun of you*. The *jokes* annoy you. They are not doing you justice, etc., etc. Do you think you are the first man put in this situation? Do you have more genius than Chateaubriand and Wagner? And yet they were the brunt of great mockery. It didn't kill them. (*Corr.* 2:496–97)

This is hardly what might call a friendly shoulder to cry on. Clearly, Baudelaire is responding thus because he too has been the brunt of jokes and the source of great scandal; and he too has survived. More to the (not

59. Where, it should be added, the well-heeled crowd appears "dans nos cravates et nos bottes vernies" (our ties and our patent leather shoes), just as Baudelaire had demanded of "the real painter" (*Salon de 1845*, in *OC* 2:407). All the stranger, then, that he did not see in Manet the praxis of the poet's theory. See, on this subject, Sima Godfrey, "Strangers in the Park: Manet, Baudelaire, and *La Musique aux Tuileries*," in *Baudelaire and the Poetics of Modernity*, ed. Patricia A. Ward (Nashville: Vanderbilt University Press, 2001), 45–60.

60. Françoise Cachin, Charles S. Moffett, and Juliet Wilson Bareau, *Manet, 1832–1883* (New York: Metropolitan Museum of Art and Harry N. Abrams, 1983), 158.

entirely avowed) point, Baudelaire does see himself as on a par with Wagner and Chateaubriand. That is not, however, where he sees Manet, as he proceeds to make very clear:

> And in order not to make you too arrogant, I would like to say that these men are models, each in his genre, and in a very opulent world. And you, *you are nothing more than the first in the decrepitude of your art*. I hope you will not resent me for the off-handed [*sans façon*] way in which I am treating you. You know my friendship for you. (*Corr.* 2:497)

Pichois's note immediately points out that the sentence in italics "is often forgotten by those who are determined to have Baudelaire understanding and praising Manet" (*Corr.* 2:914). Baudelaire did neither. Indeed, this is clearly the passage Bataille has in mind in his comments on Manet when he puts "decrepitude" in quotation marks. For Baudelaire, Manet's strange perspective on the visual is further proof that painting is going down a new road, which he, the poet, sees as further proof of the descent of mankind. Muray calls the decline of Baudelaire at the end of his life "katabasis"—a rhetorical term for descending. But it was Baudelaire who saw most contemporary art as so much more decrepitude. Art was changing, and though he did not like most of it, he diagnosed the change as the wrong kind of decadence.

And art was certainly changing. In 1867, a young Zola, who was to write increasingly about art, published an article in *La revue du XIXe siècle* called "A New Manner in Painting." By then, Baudelaire had already been stricken with paralysis and was to die the following year. Manet, writes Zola, has been completely misunderstood by the public. He has found a way to paint that puts aside previous styles and schools; he paints in an "original language," which is his own way of seeing. The public, adds Zola, will not stay blind to Manet's talents long: the future is his.[61] But Zola became increasingly perplexed with Manet's impressionistic paintings—the writer thought he had found a painterly naturalist, but was totally disillusioned. By 1879, Zola did not include Manet in his Salon of important painters. Manet's troubles with the public, Zola now writes, stem from a difficulty in execution—"I mean that his hand does not equal his eye." He is the most subjective of painters, continues Zola,

---

61. Émile Zola, "Une nouvelle manière en peinture: Édouard Manet," in *Le bon combat: De Courbet aux Impressionnistes, anthologie d'écrits sur l'art*, ed. Gaëtan Picon and Jean-Paul Bouillons (Paris: Hermann, 1974), 77–93.

and if he were as good technically as he is perceptually, Manet "would be the great painter of the second half of the nineteenth century." As it is, however, his paintings are "imperfect and uneven" (*Le bon combat*, 205). Zola, strangely enough, is coming around to what was Baudelaire's own assessment of Manet's work twelve or so years before. Has Zola become more conservative? Probably. But he continues to admire that painter's eye, while he raises doubts about his technical abilities. Baudelaire had seen Manet as one of the best within an art of total decrepitude.

Where Zola and Baudelaire would no doubt have agreed was on the question of art's social purpose. Two years before Baudelaire's death, Zola published an article attacking Proudhon's notion of art. For the utopian anarchist had also written a book on art—as he saw it. The painter Courbet (for whom Baudelaire had had rapidly decreasing admiration) had asked Proudhon for a catalog text on the social role of art in society. Proudhon had complied, and *Du principe de l'art et de sa destination sociale* was published posthumously in 1865, a few months after Proudhon's death. Art should be at the service of humanitarian utopias, Proudhon had argued. Art exists to serve the social amelioration of man. An indignant Flaubert wrote to Edmond de Goncourt (August 12, 1865) that such a thesis was "socialist belly-aching" at its worst. In "Proudhon et Courbet," a twenty-five-year-old Zola confidently declares that putting art in the service of ideology is a terrible idea and leads to "social realism." Art for Proudhon is "an idealistic representation of nature and of ourselves, aiming for the physical and moral perfection of our species."[62] Zola is diametrically opposed to Proudhon's views: "In a word," he declaims, Proudhon "wants art to be the product of the nation, while I insist it be the product of the individual" (*Le bon combat*, 41). Proudhon's rationalism, his realism, "are in truth nothing but the negation of art" (46). The man is incompetent, sneers Zola, concluding his diatribe with the remark that Proudhon should have called his book *On the Death of Art and its social Uselessness* (47).

Baudelaire, meanwhile, said nothing about Proudhon's views on art—views that, on the face of it, could not possibly have been more antithetical to Baudelaire's own. Perhaps Baudelaire remained silent out of respect, since his old political mentor had just died. In the poet's general and confused collection of newspaper clippings and notations, comments, essays, and so on—later to be called *Pauvre Belgique!*—he had cut out the article

---

62. Émile Zola, "Mes haines: Causeries littéraires et artistiques," *Le salut public*, August 26 and 31, 1865. The text appears as "Proudhon et Courbet" in *Le bon combat*, 36–47 (see p. 38).

from *L'indépendance*, which, in announcing the philosopher's death, had rather nastily reviewed Proudhon's shifting beliefs. *"Remarkable tact,"* Baudelaire jots down with his old irony (*OC* 2:881–82). He had retained respect for the philosopher, and did not approve of the obituary's supercilious tone.

Or perhaps Baudelaire didn't respond to Proudhon on art because he himself was already suffering minor strokes. He was having difficulty expressing himself at times, and was ever more obsessed with his hatred for Belgium, the country to which he had fled in order to escape his creditors—but also to escape Paris, which, he maintained, was killing him.[63] His beliefs were channeled into loathing the Belgians; he no longer wrote with the confident tone he had once had and that a young Zola was now taking up. Baudelaire became fixated on the Belgian use of the verb *savoir*. In their spoken French, he scoffs in *Pauvre Belgique!* the Belgians use the verb to *know* (*savoir*) when they should use to *be able* (*pouvoir*). He offers examples, the first of which is a fragmented dialogue with an imagined interlocutor:

> "When are you leaving?"—"I do not know to leave"—"Why?"—"I don't have any money."
>> I did not know to sleep.
>> I do not know to eat any longer.

While Baudelaire is here demonstrating his disdain for the Belgian misuse of the French language, we might also see here a decreasing confidence in his own locutions and, more abstractly, in his own connection of not-being-able with not-knowing. Not being able to know, not to know how to write, or how to produce more poems, or how to find money to eat. Every locution he gives, let us note, is in the negative. And Baudelaire does not, at this time in his life, "know" how to sleep, how to eat, how to get money, or how to leave Belgium (despite friends like Nadar, who ask him why—in precisely the same way as in the little dialog just cited—he would not leave Brussels). It is as if language itself were increasingly suspect, and once again the Belgians seem to perform what leads to a sort of linguis-

63. Most critics note that by the early 1860s, Baudelaire was having trouble getting published and was suffering from writer's block. Pichois thinks Baudelaire might have believed a change of air and habits could return him to creativity (*OC* 2:1470). Certainly the frenetic notations on Belgium can be read as a desperate attempt to overcome such blockage, though, as some scholars have come to realize, the Belgian papers are not without merit.

tic paranoia in Baudelaire: "The Belgians pretend that they do not know Flemish, but the proof that they know it is that they yell at their servants in Flemish" (OC 2:879). The Belgians pretend not to know, but they know. They have a secret language; Baudelaire fears that he is losing his own.

Critics have too easily dismissed the Belgian writings as the confused work of a man who was getting sicker by the day, who could no longer think straight.[64] *Pauvre Belgique!* may be obsessive, but it is lucid. It bears the lucidity of a writer who uses hatred and scorn for one country to displace his equally negative feelings for his own. But if the writings on Belgium form a clear displacement of anger from the French and France to the Belgians and Belgium, there is also a displacement from self-loathing to Belgian-bashing. *Noli me tangere*, writes Baudelaire, is a nice motto for Belgium, "for who would want to touch that stick covered in shit?— Belgium is a monster. Who would want to adopt it? And yet it contains several elements of dissolution" (OC 2:953). Later, in a line that seems to prefigure Bataille, Baudelaire repeats himself with a different conclusion: "*Noli me tangere*—nice motto for her [Belgium]. She is sacred" (954). Baudelaire's contempt for the Belgians' ambiguity of language (bad locution, an underlying, unacknowledged foreign language) may be displacement as well: the loathing of that country also permits a hatred of the self, which remains unabated by the hatred of others. So *Pauvre Belgique!* betrays a falling off of the control of language, a fading of the belief in the capacity to find the word. The endless ranting on "Belgian locutions" thus performs another displacement, again from himself. Belgium is a sacred monster, and Baudelaire had often seen himself in the same terms. Like prostitutes, criminals, murderers—all of the cast that populates Baudelaire's stage—Belgium manifests the fallen condition of man and is, as such, sacred (as in connected with God) in its spectacle of evil and folly.

There is, however, a brighter side to all of this: where language fails for Baudelaire, vision (again) serves as a kind of savior. At this late time in his life, it is with architecture that Baudelaire feels at home—particularly churches. He goes, for example, to the church of Saint-Loup at Namur several times. (The last time he visits that church he suffers the stroke from which he never recovers.) Belgium is the place where Baudelaire discovers the baroque. He begins to connect his beloved Delacroix not to romantic art but to baroque effusion and ornateness. He remembers his own enthusiasm for Rubens. In his notes for what was to have been a book on the

---

64. Muray is a fairly rare exception to this point of view.

philosophy of the history of architecture, Baudelaire writes that the Saint-Loup church at Namur "is the masterpiece of all Jesuit masterpieces" (*OC* 2:950). Belgium may be a country of fog and "black greens" (*verdure noire*; 2:951), but it has luminosity in its Jesuit churches and in the architecture and décor of the vaults, those triumphs of Counterreformation Catholicism. For what is the Counterreformation in terms of aesthetics, if not (among other things, of course) an emphatic celebration of representation, of delight in the visual?[65] Baudelaire thrills at the endless carved fruit that decorates the vaults of Saint-Loup; he loves its figural exuberances; he revels in the ornate. Had he finally found in the baroque a way of recognizing what it was he loved in art, in the visual? Was he beginning to overcome his contradictions—even his double vision? More to the point, did he need to overcome them?

Benjamin explains Baudelaire's endless contradictions as the result of liking nothing about the age in which he lived: "He did not have the humanitarian idealism of a Lamartine or a Hugo, and it was not given to him, as it was to Verlaine, to take refuge in religious devotion." The result, concludes Benjamin, was a lack of convictions, and because Baudelaire had none, "he assumed ever new forms himself. Flâneur, apache, dandy and ragpicker were so many roles to him" (*The Writer of Modern Life*, 125). Baudelaire was certainly theatrical, and constantly needed to be surprised (his friends, we mentioned earlier, used to joke that Baudelaire would sleep under his bed to surprise himself). But he venerated energy, particularly in art—the energy in a Delacroix or a Rubens, whom he late in life identified as baroque. Whereas Baudelaire had tried to define artistic energy by its rapidity (Guys, then Delacroix) of visual intake and of execution, in his last years in the hated Belgium he saw energy in the exuberant décor of the vaults of Saint-Loup and other baroque structures. He came to identify that energy, not only with Rubens and Delacroix, but also with his new

---

65. This, ironically enough, in spite of the last session of the Council of Trent, which in 1563 produced a decree on art with notably puritanical guidelines regarding religious depictions (a decree that Emile Mâle was to claim marked the death of medieval art). The guidelines included no nudity (not even the infant Jesus), no pagans, no inciting of lust, and (fascinatingly) nothing "confusedly arranged." Representation itself, however, was not at issue, though the church did make clear that one was to worship the person imaged, and not the image itself. The proliferation of fruit and other carved still lifes in the church of Saint-Loup is one common baroque response to the limits on religious art: paint nature, and arrange it as "confusedly" as you like. While Protestants in northern Europe were scrubbing their churches of statues for fear of idolatry, baroque churches in seventeenth-century Catholic Europe justified their rich ornamentation and lavish interiors by claiming to convert people with an emotional, awe-inspiring art.

friend, the artist Félicien Rops (the only Belgian who could speak Latin, and whose French was unflawed, claimed our poet). We can thus better understand Baudelaire's acceptance of Delacroix's varying styles and approaches to figural art. What these artists all have in common is vibrant color, figural sharpness, larger-than-lifeness, and endless energy.

With Baudelaire, it is not only a question of too little conviction among the artists of his day; it is equally one of too much nervous energy in search of over-the-top artistic démarches. In the baroque, Baudelaire found much of what he was looking for. This is not a discovery, however, that the writers of modernity—and of Baudelaire—can fully accept (Bataille first among them). How can Baudelaire, the father of modernity as so many proclaim him to have been, be entranced by the baroque when there was Manet, right under his nose, inventing modern art? How can he have been so taken by the visually distinct, not to mention ornate, when modernity was beginning to see that less is more? For Baudelaire, more is more, if we mean the image, the visual, and their energy.

And if the city was noisy, dirty, full of the pathetic poor and the self-satisfied bourgeois, the great breeding ground of hypocrisy, what it could provide was visual stimulus—color, movement, and eyes that might capture your gaze and your fantasies and allow you to remember the past. Art could do the same. And for a hypertense, frequently overwrought, and generally splenetic Baudelaire, what better way to look for solace than in visual abundance—proof that vitality subsists, that life can be, that you can *know* life in its profusions, including its squanderings or satanic manifestations. Such abundance was triumphantly provided by the baroque churches that Baudelaire saw in Belgium. Was part of the attraction the fact that they were Jesuit in conception and frequently in creation, as Muray argues? It is possible. Baudelaire's sentences often refer to Jesuit architecture (*le style jésuite*). Moreover, Baudelaire was (even more) fixated on hell when he was in Belgium. The poet writes that it has frequently occurred to him that Belgians were "formerly criminal and abject spirits, imprisoned in their deformed bodies. One becomes Belgian for having sinned. A Belgian is his own hell." Or again, "a Belgian is a hell living on earth" (*OC* 2:954). Belgium is what France would have become had the reign of Louis-Philippe, "a nice example of constitutional mindlessness," continued (955). But France (by Baudelaire's own admission) is no better off with Napoleon III, so that this distinction between the French and the Belgians is less and less convincing. We may suppose, however, that the energy that goes into hating the Belgians is better than no energy at all. It is an energy that is continually abated by visiting a baroque church. The delight of the eyes can calm the feverish mind. The triumph of baroque art is in its explosion of vitality.

⋘∞⋙

Baudelaire's father was a painter—a very mediocre one, but an artist none-theless. The poet tells us that when he was little, his father would take him to art galleries and museums (quite a contrast to the rigid General Aupick). His father taught him about art. Baudelaire had very fond memo-ries of this father (who died when the poet was six), and most biographers attribute his love of art (and of literature, for which his mother had almost no interest) to his father. The love of art is thus tied to admiration for a father whom the poet idealized, and all the more so given his growing aversion to his stepfather. "A une passante" not only engages the scopic syllepsis of Baudelaire's doubled image-machine; it also performs the way in which the visual, and the eyes, can produce a hope for happiness even within an economy of melancholia. The visual provides a brief respite from unhappiness, but a respite nonetheless.

Where no relief was ever to be found, however, was in the literal econ-omy of money. Here Baudelaire could never succeed, never feel secure. Al-most every one of the innumerable letters he wrote to his mother—until he was incapacitated by his final stroke—concern money. Money, too, functioned for him as a doubled system. It existed as a kind of failed al-legory for living. So it is to money that we now turn.

Appendix

A UNE PASSANTE

La rue assourdissante autour de moi hurlait.
Longue, mince, en grand deuil, douleur majestueuse,
Une femme passa, d'une main fastueuse
Soulevant, balançant le feston et l'ourlet;

Agile et noble, avec sa jambe de statue.
Moi, je buvais, crispé comme un extravagant,
Dans son œil, ciel livide où germe l'ouragan,
La douceur qui fascine et le plaisir qui tue.

Un éclair . . . puis la nuit!—Fugitive beauté
Dont le regard m'a fait soudainement renaître,
Ne te verrai-je plus que dans l'éternité?

Ailleurs, bien loin d'ici! trop tard! *jamais* peut-être!
Car j'ignore où tu fuis, tu ne sais où je vais,
Ô toi que j'eusse aimée, ô toi qui le savais!

CHAPTER THREE

Money (La chambre double)

Faith is to believe what you do not yet see; the reward of this faith is to
see what you believe.
—Saint Augustine

The human gaze has the power of conferring value on things;
but it makes them cost more too.
—Ludwig Wittgenstein, *Culture and Value*

"**M**oney," wrote Max Weber, "is the most abstract and 'impersonal'
element that exists in human life."[1] Not, however, for Baudelaire.
Abstract, no doubt—he never understood how money worked; but impersonal, never—almost every one of Baudelaire's relationships, indeed his
entire life, was tainted with the problem of money. At eighteen, Baudelaire
inherited his father's fortune; within a year and a half, as is well known,
he had spent nearly half of it. In 1844, a *conseil judiciaire* was chosen in
the person of Narcisse Désiré Ancelle, notary public. As many critics have
noted, Baudelaire thus returned to a virtually childhood status: he had to
ask Ancelle for anything he needed in funds, apart from the small amount
that he received monthly, drawn from what was left of his inheritance. It
was to be a relationship fraught with frustration, anger, and resentment
for Baudelaire, and certainly not an easy one for the slow, meticulous, and
generally rigid Ancelle.[2]

1. "Religious Rejections of the World and Their Directions," in *From Max Weber: Essays in
Sociology*, trans. H. H. Gerth and C. Wright Mills (London: Paul, Trench and Trubner, 1947), 331.
2. At the end of his life, Baudelaire entrusted monetary relations with his editors, including the list of all his publications and their unfinished transactions, to Ancelle. Baudelaire had
long since recognized that the notary public who had given him so much difficulty and was

Mauron, in his renowned psycho-critical study of Baudelaire, claims that the poet feared bankruptcy because of what it would do to his *moi social*.[3] This social *moi* is not to be overlooked in Baudelaire; in his younger years, his image is carefully constructed with beautiful clothes and expensive things. The young poet clearly wants the social status and distinction that money can provide. But Mauron's easy distinction between Baudelaire's *moi social* and his *moi créateur* does not work, or at least suffice: the social *moi* in Baudelaire, especially given his notion of the dandy, does not distinguish so neatly between the creativity and aesthetics of his life, on the one hand, and of his textual productions on the other. While such a blurring of the aesthetic in both realms was possible only so long as Baudelaire had money, it does not follow that his views changed even as his circumstances were necessarily to alter for the worse.

When Nadar first meets the young Baudelaire (around 1841—Baudelaire is twenty) in the Jardin du Luxembourg, the poet cuts a "bizarre, *phantomatic* [sic]" figure, but he is fashionably and carefully dressed. He is "elegant, dressed all in black except for his beef-blood tie."[4] His shoes are "irreproachably polished," and his shirtsleeves are very white and of the finest linen. And our poet is wearing pale pink gloves! ("I said 'pink,'" writes Nadar, as if readers might think they had misheard). Baudelaire is wearing a large hat, under which an abundance of very black, curly hair can be seen, falling thick around his shoulders.[5]

---

so unmovable, was also honest and had always had entirely good intentions (and incredible patience) with respect to his extremely difficult client. Indeed, near the end of Baudelaire's life, Ancelle writes to Poulet-Malassis that Baudelaire "has bad moments occasionally with respect to me. I forgive him most willingly" (*Corr.* 2:633).

3. *Le dernier Baudelaire*, 24. More accurately, Mauron believes that the poet's 1861 bankruptcy is in fact social. Mauron also takes issue with Jacques Crépet, arguing that the young Baudelaire probably spent only a third of his inheritance before he was stopped by the Tribunal's choice of a *conseil judiciaire* (23, n.4).

4. Nadar, *Charles Baudelaire intime: le poète vierge* (Paris: Ides et Calendes, 1911), 36–37. Baudelaire's very manner of dress is willed contradiction: the black suit is the uniform of the romantics in France, and then of the bourgeoisie; the blood-red tie is the symbol of republicanism (and even Jacobinism). For Baudelaire's own definition of romanticism, see *OC* 2:421. For his view on the clothing of his epoch see "De l'héroïsme de la vie moderne," in *Salon de 1846*, *OC* 2:494. There he asks, "Is this not the necessary dress of our epoch, suffering and wearing even unto its black and thin shoulders the symbol of perpetual mourning?" He adds that the black suit and the redingote not only have their "political beauty, which is the expression of universal equality, but also their poetic beauty, which is the expression of the public soul." He concludes that such dress forms "—an immense parade of undertakers, political undertakers, undertakers in love, bourgeois undertakers. We are all celebrating some funeral or other" (ibid.). Interesting with respect to the *passante*, who is in mourning.

5. Nadar, *Charles Baudelaire*, 36–37. Two years later (1843), Gautier describes Baudelaire as having "jet black hair" that is cropped close "and coming to regular points on his daz-

Baudelaire invites Nadar and a few other friends (including Théodore de Banville) to his lodgings. Baudelaire is still at the Hôtel Pimodan, in rooms that Nadar describes as "vast and comfortably furnished." There is a large rug ("a luxury for us," writes Nadar), excellent art, and "a large, very modern and welcoming armchair" (39). The walls of the study/living room are covered in black and red paper, and though there are no bookcases, beautiful editions lie strewn about the large antique table on which Baudelaire works. There are crystal wine glasses of exquisite green. Gautier, Banville, Asselineau, Prarond, and other friends (as well as some who were less than friends) were also to write about these rooms after Baudelaire's death, with equal admiration for their taste, elegance, and comfort. Baudelaire's small apartment, writes Banville, "in its bizarre and personal elegance, was exactly like him." It was exactly like him in other ways too. The Hôtel Pimodan, an *hôtel particulier* built in the seventeenth century on the Ile Saint-Louis, had once been quite grand. By the time Baudelaire moved in, however, it had become a bohemian apartment building, full of artists and writers, with dyers working out of the ground floor. Baudelaire lived on the top floor and had a good view of the river.

The beautifully appointed apartment inside a bohemian center (where the infamous Club des Haschichins met for a while) allowed for a built-in contradiction of everyday life for Baudelaire, and clearly such a contradiction suited him perfectly. His friends write that he fluctuated between being a great dandy (say Asselineau and Charles Cousin, for instance) and being as outrageous as possible—a wild bohemian. His appearance, in other words, matched the Pimodan. Champfleury recalls that Baudelaire was given to extravagant mood swings: one day he would be at the height of sartorial elegance and general cheer, carrying a bouquet of flowers; the following day he was just as likely to appear head bowed, "like a Carthusian monk about to dig his own grave."[6] "That was one of Baudelaire's pretensions," writes another friend, Louis Ménard; "we knew he was rich and a dandy, but he very much liked to pass for a poor bohemian."[7] Even Baudelaire's face changed so much that a few years later, when he sat for

---

zling white forehead." His eyes, adds Gautier, were "the color of Spanish tobacco." Théophile Gautier, *Souvenirs romantiques* (Paris: Garnier, 1929), 268.

6. Champfleury [Jules Husson-Fleury], *Souvenirs et portraits de jeunesse* (Paris: Dentu, 1872), 135.

7. In *Baudelaire devant ses contemporains*, ed. W. T. Bandy and Claude Pichois (Paris: Klincksieck, 1995), 43. This collection provides numerous testimonies and recollections, from throughout the poet's life, by Baudelaire's friends, enemies, and acquaintances.

a portrait by Courbet (*L'homme à la pipe*), the painter complained that he didn't know how to portray him.[8] Baudelaire could change his physiognomy, Courbet continued, "like a convict on the run" (ibid., 137).

Baudelaire could never decide whether he wanted to appear poor or rich, bohemian or conventional, a *clochard* or an aristocrat, a shabbily dressed writer or a dandy. In the early 1840s, when he had money, his affectation (or careful cultivation) of beautiful clothes was a combination of extreme elegance (he did not want his suit to appear too new, too shiny, for example) and forced indifference. In the 1868 "definitive edition" of the *Fleurs du mal*, Gautier describes Baudelaire as adhering to "that sober dandyism that rubs its clothes with sandpaper to remove their Sunday-best shine and brand-new quality—so dear to the philistine and so disagreeable to the real *gentleman*" (*Baudelaire devant ses contemporains*, 21; English in the original). Even when impoverished, he still bought fine clothes and was incessantly indebted to various tailors.

But clothes, as our poet writes in his famous essay on the dandy, are not the dandy's main interest—that is only what people of "little thought" believe. For the "perfect dandy," clothes are merely "a symbol of the aristocratic superiority of his mind" (*OC* 2:710). Nor does the dandy "aspire to money as if to an essential thing; an indefinite credit could suffice for him." The dandy is above monetary concerns: "If I have spoken of money," explains Baudelaire, "it is because money is indispensable to people who make a cult of their passions." But the dandy does not desire money for its own sake, and "abandons such coarse passion to vulgar mortals." What is dandyism, then? "It is above all the ardent need to make oneself into an original, contained within the external limits of propriety. It is a kind of a cult of the self." And, adds Baudelaire, the dandy is always blasé; too arrogant to be surprised himself, he enjoys surprising others. If he is sick, he will be stoic (ibid.). Somewhat bizarrely, the military man as depicted by Guys is also a type of dandy for Baudelaire, precisely because of the soldier's nonchalance. Like the dandy and the woman of the world, the military man is "rarely surprised." Moreover, he possesses a "martial insouciance, a strange mixture of placidity and audacity," and Spartan (Lacedaemonian) courage (*OC* 2:708–10).

Such nonchalance was unattainable for Baudelaire, though he never ceased admiring those who possessed it. His dress, Nadar tells us, was clearly "meditated," not effortless (*Charles Baudelaire*, 36). His gait, his

8. Champfleury, *Souvenirs et portraits de jeunesse* , 135.

friends tell us, was always jerky and odd—hardly the indifferent elegance he so desired.[9] And Baudelaire's relation to money was the same: while he wished to be above financial concerns and to live serenely on "indefinite credit," such worries were in fact at the center of his life, and creditors were mercilessly to pursue him until his death (indeed, even afterward).

In any case, Baudelaire was never to live again as he did in the Hôtel Pimodan. That apartment was to be replaced by ever smaller, uglier, and more cramped quarters. Once he left the Pimodan (where he stayed longer than anywhere else), Baudelaire was to move constantly, each time with fewer of his belongings, less of his furniture, and decreasing comfort.[10] We can, of course, depersonalize such a situation, and join Jameson in claiming that "the only satisfactory semantic meaning of modernity lies in its association with capitalism" (*A Singular Modernity*, 13)—clearly an unassailable point. Yet Baudelaire's life-long struggle with making ends meet, robbing Peter to pay Paul, begging his mother, his half-brother (early on), Ancelle, friends, editors, and publishers for money—these activities are so consistently intense and even hysterical that they warrant serious scrutiny. As the letters to his mother in particular demonstrate, even if we take into account their often histrionic tone and guilt-inducing intent, there were times when the poet had no winter coat, no place to live, and nothing to eat. Usually, it was his "fault"—if we take fault to mean, within the economy of capitalist morals, lavish expenditure and an inability (or refusal) to recognize the correspondence between spending money and its material consequence. It was one type of correspondence—unlike synesthesia, admiration for Wagner's *Gesamtkunstwerk* and Swedenborg's doctrines, and experiments in hashish—that the poet neither comprehended nor wished to endorse. "Let us not forget," writes Nadar, "that as if born under the motto of the Ravenswoods, 'The Hand Open!' Baudelaire had begun by more than liberally dissipating a fortune and, given that, did not avoid pressuring his friends—of which I was one" (*Charles Baudelaire*, 45).

An interesting allusion on Nadar's part, since it refers to Walter Scott's *Bride of Lammermoor*, a novel of 1819, quickly available in French translation. Delacroix was to do a highly romantic self-portrait in which he de-

9. It has even been suggested, by a number of critics, that Baudelaire showed symptoms of Tourette's syndrome, complete with mild coprolalia.

10. The narrator of the prose poem "Les projets," *Le Spleen de Paris* XXIV, imagines living in three different places: a palace, a tropical country, or a simple Parisian inn. He concludes (like Huysmans's des Esseintes in *A rebours*) that his imagination is fertile enough to obviate the need to "constrain my body to changing places." This is the opposite of what Baudelaire experienced, and he was always to dream (in vain) of a permanent home (*OC* 1:315).

picts himself as, most likely, the novel's doomed and romantic protagonist, Edgar Ravenswood. Most likely because there are those who think
Delacroix paints himself as Hamlet, an opinion that Baudelaire himself
seemed to hold (*OC* 2:593). The portrait, from 1821, is dark and morose and
more or less follows the Spanish style of Ravenswood's clothing as Scott
describes it. Moreover, "Raveswood" [*sic*] is written in the painter's hand
on the frame. More relevant for our purposes, however, is the fact that
Nadar gives the motto of the Ravenswood family as "The Hand Open,"
whereas the novel itself gives it as "I Bide my Time."[11] The first motto
works better for Nadar's point: Baudelaire was generous to a fault when he
had money, but asked for handouts (another kind of open hand) when he
was in financial trouble.

In *La fanfarlo*, that fairly autobiographical short story of Baudelaire's,
the protagonist, a writer called Samuel Cramer, delivers an incensed dis-
quisition upon discovering his ladylove reading Walter Scott. All those
novels are ridiculously full of characters with daggers, swords, and horses,
he tells her. Armor, dishes, furniture, gothic inns, and châteaux filled
with melodrama proliferate everywhere. "What a difference from our good
French novelists," says Cramer, "where passion and morals always take pre-
cedence over the description of material objects!" (*OC* 1:557). The narrator
then notes that Cramer has become insufferable, the type whose "profes-
sion ruins the conversation" and who will speak as intently to a rag picker
as to anyone else on a street corner "to develop his opinionated views"
(1:559). It is a description, as Pichois points out, in which Baudelaire's contemporaries would have recognized the poet himself. Further, the passage
seems to reject the description of objects as literarily unsound, whereas
Baudelaire at this time was obsessed with "material objects," and, furthermore, his great hero at that time, Balzac, was famous precisely for describing objects in order to set the scene. The narrator of *La fanfarlo* takes the
moral high ground; but Baudelaire himself, in 1847, was much more like
his protagonist. Material objects, in other words, make for a problem. He
wanted to be like the dandy who scorns objects though he possesses the
most expensive and tasteful of them; but in order to scorn such things,
Baudelaire had first to acquire them. And that is what brought about his
financial and, to a large extent, psychological ruin.

We have, once again, a contradiction; and, once again, a binary opposi-

---

11. There are several instances of the open hand in Scott, and I will give but two here.
The novel *Waverly* mentions a Gaelic proverb, "May the open hand be filled the fullest." And
Canto I, stanza X, of "Marmion" reads, "stout heart, open hand." Did Nadar get confused? Or
did he know Scott so well that he was conflating texts?

tion will not suffice to explain it, though it is certainly symptomatic, as always, of a profound ambivalence in Baudelaire. Money lends itself (as it were) to such a duality: it is meant to represent, or symbolize, material value in the bank (which historically it has done in less than convincing ways), and at the same time, its expenditure is linked to a decrease in assets—an abstract consequence at the time of expenditure. It is a consequence which, I will argue, Baudelaire could not or would not make. For example, in February of 1854, Baudelaire writes to his mother asking (as usual) for money. "I'll explain to you in a few words what has often created my problem with respect to the rent," he writes. "It is that, for several months now, I didn't owe 40 francs but 100. I had another apartment in the building, which remained empty, and which I had taken on with the expectation of a sudden improvement in my affairs. Finally, I gave it up and now I am even" (*Corr.* 1:268).

Baudelaire's belief in a "sudden improvement" in his finances is on the level of fantasy, but he puts it into place concretely on the level of financial obligation. Moreover, to the extent that he does "calculate," it is with respect to his mother's affections. He blackmails her by demanding money as proof of love. "I can never see you," he complains in the same letter, "I cannot go to your house and you *do not want* to come. This is a very bad calculation on your part, because you will never know what good I sometimes feel that I would experience in seeing you. You don't believe it, you mock a tenderness which you believe feigned." He ends by telling her to refuse him money, but at least to come see him: "do not refuse me both at the same time." The connection between money and love is clear to him: if his mother loves him, she will help to pay his debts. But the material connection between expenditure and its effect remains completely abstract and a fantasy, despite Baudelaire's recognition of "calculation" and its principles.

EXPENDITURE

Baudelaire's disinterest in money, his hatred of the greed and profiteering that were the hallmarks of mid-nineteenth-century Paris, are complicated by his love of beautiful things. After the mid 1850s, Baudelaire often wrote to his mother to say that he was paying dearly (literally) for his love of things and his earlier extravagant expenditures.

The consequences of financial expenditure are concretized in Balzac's *La peau de chagrin,* a novel that Baudelaire mentions more than once. In that tale, a young man finds a magic shagreen that grants wishes. But every wish makes the skin shrink. It is not much of a leap to assume that the novel is (among other things) an allegory of spending money: each wish "costs" the diminution of the "asset," the skin. Balzac, of course, had his own financial problems, which a twenty-four-year-old Baudelaire writes about at some length, and with some disdain, in "Comment on paie ses dettes quand on a du génie"—an article published anonymously in 1845. The article is fairly smug, except that it admits that the "great man" was in "that mortifying situation that we all know, in which each minute that flies by takes with it, on its wings, the chance of salvation." Eyes fixed on the clock, the "genius of invention feels the necessity to double, triple, increase tenfold his own strength in proportion to the time that diminishes, and to the rapid approach of the fatal hour" (OC 2:7). Time is always linked to money in Baudelaire—but here it is a quite literal connection, since the "fatal hour" is when the creditors appear, demanding to be paid Moreover, contrainte par corps (imprisonment for debts) was still common in France when Baudelaire wrote the article. The law was not abolished until the year of the poet's death.[12]

Note, however, that Baudelaire can fathom the frightening and very real consequences of not paying a creditor, but he does not make the connection within the money economy at the time of the expenditure. He is, in other words, concerned with distraint of goods (as in, famously, Madame Bovary and indeed at various points in Baudelaire's own life) and possible imprisonment; but these fears occur after the fact of excess expenditure. Balzac, who seemed to have had the same problem, was able to find devious and successful means to avoid bankruptcy. Baudelaire professes to scorn the novelist's flirtation with dishonesty. In a scenario very similar to the one sketched out in Balzac's Illusions perdues, Baudelaire tells us that the "great man" had a bill of 1200 francs due the next day. "Balzac" offers to write a series of articles for a newspaper editor (as long as he is paid 1500 francs up front), promising publication for the following day. The editor agrees and pays. The "great man" then offers an unknown young writer 150 francs to write most of the articles by the next morning, and another writer to complete the rest (presumably for the same amount of money, but with time less pressing). The first articles appear, on time,

12. Contrainte par corps was briefly outlawed in France in 1793 and again in 1848. It was permanently abolished on July 22, 1867. On the history of contrainte par corps in nineteenth-century France, see Erika Vause, "In the Red and in the Black: The Culture of Commercial Debt and Credit in Post-Revolutionary France," (PhD diss., University of Chicago, 2011).

under a third name.[13] Baudelaire concludes that this is not some joke for a minor newspaper but "that the great writer could work out a bill of exchange as easily as the most mysterious novel with the greatest intrigue" (*OC* 2:8). We might add that if both ghostwriters were given 150 francs, "Balzac" had "earned" exactly the amount due. This is the kind of "calculating spirit" that Baudelaire professes to scorn, and a balancing act (in both the tactical and financial sense) of which he was incapable.[14]

Zola, in a curious piece entitled "The Influence of Money in Literature," praises Balzac for the very reasons that the young Baudelaire mocked him. It is worth taking a close look at aspects of Zola's essay, since it demonstrates the extent to which he felt at home in a world for which Baudelaire could only feel contempt. "We must study the amazing case of Balzac," writes Zola, "if we want fully to examine this question of money in literature." He continues with conviction and optimism:

Balzac was a genuine industrialist, who produced books to bring honor to his signature. Overwhelmed with debt, ruined by unfortunate ventures, he took up his pen again as the only tool that he knew how to use and that could save him. Here the question of money is posed decisively. It is not only his daily bread that Balzac asks of his books; he asks them to make up for the losses he incurs in industry. This battle lasted a long time; Balzac did not make a fortune, but he paid his debts, which was already pretty good.[15]

This attitude—that writing is labor like any other industry, that writers should work and not wait around for subsidies, that the state is not responsible for "subsidizing the profligate writers whose constantly open hands had squandered millions" (184), but rather that debts are the shame and

13. The young man was Edouard Ouliac, who, Pichois tells us, did not deserve Baudelaire's attack. The second, "lazier" writer was Théophile Gautier. The first article appeared signed "G. de N." (no doubt Gérard de Nerval). For this and information on the various publications of this Baudelaire essay, see Pichois's notes, *OC* 2:1080–83. The articles themselves, which "Balzac" proposed to the editor, formed *Les français peints par eux-mêmes*, a book that did in fact appear between 1841 and 1843, as noted in the previous chapter of the present work. It is a work mentioned by Benjamin as well, who calls it "socially panoramic" literature (*The Writer of Modern Life*, 34).

14. The narrator in "Portraits de maîtresses" who claims (or insinuates) that he has killed his wife uses the word in the same way: his wife was "a person incapable of committing an error of sentiment or of calculation" (*calcul*; *OC* 1:348).

15. Émile Zola, *Le roman expérimental* (Paris: Faquelle, 1923), 183. Originally published in *Le Messager de l'Europe*, Saint Petersburg, March, 1880. Zola was also to write the novel *L'argent*, the eighteenth in the *Rougon-Macquart* series (1891).

responsibility of the writer, that great men "need flatter no one" and owe their talents and glory solely to their "own efforts" at their country's service, without any expectations of return—this attitude is the bourgeois work ethic of nineteenth-century capitalism. "Money has emancipated the writer," proclaims Zola, "money has created modern letters" (190). No doubt such a view goes far to explain Lukács's general dislike for Zola: the writer is pleased with a work ethic that recognizes labor and glorifies genius once it has proved itself through hard work and long effort. There is an implication in Zola's diatribe that those who work hard will be rewarded and that, it follows, the poor are those who malinger or sink into the paralysis of depression. This is precisely, of course, the attitude toward poverty that Dickens used a good deal of ink rejecting. Moreover, Zola likes the economy of money a lot: "It is stupid to rant against money, which is a considerable social force," writes the father of naturalism (189). All work is worthy of payment. Why is there this great indignation against money? asks Zola, when "Business is on one side, literature on the other" (192). The question of money "is simply one result in the transformation that the literary spirit has undergone in our time." For young writers, Zola says, the solution is simple: "Work; it all lies in that." He concludes with a ringing endorsement of the epoch, of hard work, and of the joys of being liberated from the old patronage system:

> Count only on yourself. Tell yourself that if you have talent, your talent will open all firmly closed doors, and will place you as high as you deserve to rise. Above all, refuse handouts from the administration. Never ask for the protection of the state; you will lose your virility in so doing. The great law of life is battle; no one owes you anything. . . . Respect money. Do not fall into that infantile railing against it, like the poets. Money is our courage and our dignity, we the writers, who need to be free to say everything. Money makes us into the leaders of the century, the only possible nobility. Accept your times as one of humanity's greatest; believe firmly in the future without pausing to consider fatal consequences, the excesses of journalism, the mercantilism of low literature. . . . You who are born today, do not fight against social and literary evolution, for the geniuses of the twentieth century are among you. (201–2)

All is right with the world, it would seem, and if God is not necessarily in his heaven, the money system is there to reward the deserving and to ignore the idle and ungifted. Handouts from the government render the (male) writer effeminate; life is a struggle, so get on with it and stop complaining. The future is yours. One has the distinct feeling that Zola is talking about Baudelaire (who is never named in the essay) when he tells young writers to stop crying out against money "like the poets," since money is "our courage and our liberty." Nothing here could be farther from Baudelaire's views—on money, work, writing, the writer, the future, journalism, life. For in Baudelaire, money outs a kind of schizophrenia—which, let us remember, etymologically means "split mind." It is as if the dual (or symbolic) aspects of money clashed with the contradictions Baudelaire generally sought and cultivated.[16] Clashed, however, on many levels.

First, it clashed on the level of the new culture of modernity brought in with a capitalist economy. Money, within such an economy, alludes to an extant, if abstract order that not everyone was ready to join. Simmel's magisterial book on money explains the complexities of such an order—complexities, however, that are writ large and in a rational manner. "By and large," notes Simmel some thirty years after the poet's death, "one may characterize the intellectual functions that are used at present in coping with the world and in regulating both individual and social relations as *calculative* functions." Their ideal, he continues, is to conceive of the world as "a huge arithmetical problem."[17] The determination of abstract value by money is analogous, for Simmel, to the determination of abstract time by clocks. They both provide a system of "definite arrangements and measurements that imparts an otherwise unattainable transparency and calculability to the contents of life, at least as regards their practical management" (*The Philosophy of Money*, 445–46; one is somewhat consoled by the last part of that sentence). Calculation (the reader will have noted the importance of the word) and intellectuality are joined, for Simmel, in modernity: "The calculating intellectuality embodied in these forms [time and money] may in its turn derive from them some of the energy through which intellectuality controls modern life." So here we have a sort of symbiotically generated motor of modernity: the calculating aspects of modern money and the pocket watch produce a kind of intellectuality that in turn

16. I am not using "schizophrenia" for the same ends as Deuleuze and Guattari, though their connection of that mental state with capitalism is well taken in this context. See Gilles Deleuze and Félix Guattari, *Capitalisme et schizophrénie*, vol. 1 of *L'anti-Oedipe* (Paris: Editions de Minuit, 1972–73).

17. Georg Simmel, *The Philosophy of Money*, ed. David Frisby, trans. Tom Bottomore and David Frisby (London: Routledge, 2004), 444. It should also be noted that Bataille sees calculation as the opposite of excess. See Georges Bataille, "The Notion of Expenditure," in *Visions of Excess: Selected Writings 1927–1939*, ed. and trans. Allan Stoekl (Minneapolis: University of Minnesota Press, 1985), 127.

takes its energy from such technologies and is thus able to "control modern life." One can hardly imagine a less congenial culture for Baudelaire or, indeed, for most other thinkers grounded in the human sciences. And, sure enough, Simmel tells us that such relationships of technology, calculation, and intellectuality "are brought into focus by the negative example of those types of thinkers who are most strongly and fiercely opposed to the economic interpretation of human affairs: Goethe, Carlyle and Nietzsche" (clearly, Baudelaire should be added to this list.) These writers are, Simmel tells us, "on the one hand fundamentally anti-intellectual and on the other completely reject that mathematically exact interpretation of nature which we recognized as the theoretical counterpart to the institution of money" (ibid.). Nietzsche "anti-intellectual"? Goethe?

But "intellectual" means something very specific to Simmel. The money economy, on Simmel's balance sheet, creates the preponderance of intellectual over emotional functions. Indeed, "intellectual energy is the psychic energy which the specific phenomena of the money economy produces"—in contrast to "energies generally denoted as emotions or sentiments which prevail in periods and spheres of interest not permeated by the money economy."[18] Since money is a means, "the conditions and concatenations of reality are incorporated . . . because we possess an objective image of actual causal relationships." Once we understand the purpose of money, we can intellectually move to "a perfect view of the total situation." And this purpose is established by the will (*das Wollen*), which is "not blind" but, rather, colors the contents of the world. "The intellect (*der Intellekt*) is the mediator through which volition adjusts itself to independent being" (430). Money for Simmel is pure energy and absolute symbol. It is abstracted from its material support; its dynamics invade theory and praxis. Money is, in other words, a near-ubiquitous economy that produces an intellect of calculation. It is part of *Lebensanschauung*—it establishes sociability, culture, and value. (One might reemphasize here that Baudelaire, in writing to his mother about her "bad calculation" with respect to her visits, has himself fallen into the money economy even as he derides it. Shows of tenderness are to be paid for, or exchanged for the effort of a visit or that of lending money, or both.) Keep in mind that Simmel's work was published in 1900 (the same year as Freud's dream book, and four years before Weber's work on the Protestant ethic); so it was just able

---

18. *The Philosophy of Money*, 429. In the sentence just cited in translation, Simmel uses *seelische Energie* (mental energy) as against *Gefühl* or *Gemüt* (feeling or disposition). But the entry to the chapter posits *intellektuellen* over *Gefühlsfunktionen*, which the English translation follows.

to look back on the economic upheaval that the nineteenth century had brought to western Europe.

Weber complains that Simmel identifies capitalism too closely with money economy, though he also praises the last chapter of the money book as a brilliant analysis.[19] Indeed, even from the brief quotations I have given from Simmel's lengthy and complex work, it is clear that he sees "money economy" as the new capitalism that has washed over everything with the advent of the industrial revolution. And while Weber insists that "unlimited greed for gain" is not the purview of capitalism alone, that system is identical with "the pursuit of profit, and ever *renewed* profit" (*Protestant Ethic*, 17). For Simmel, money, as the last section of his final chapter puts it, is the historical symbol of the relative character of existence. Nothing, of course, could be farther from the nonchalant, superbly elegant, but indifferent, jobless dandy. Part of Baudelaire's fascination with the dandy is that as the acedia-suffused descendant of Rameau's nephew, the dandy has no useful métier; he is not trying to make a profit; greed is not in his vocabulary—he leaves that to the vulgar. And while Simmel notes that the marginalized are those who handle money, that is, the usurers, Baudelaire's dandy is a different kind of marginalized figure. Marginalized of his own volition, the dandy for Baudelaire is a snob who has no interest in the adulation of high society (unlike, of course, the basic bourgeois nouveau riche). Whereas Proust, for example, narrates the decline of the aristocracy in France and the concomitant bourgeois social climbers (even Swann is not immune to social success), Baudelaire's dandy is a loner, above the vulgarity of trying to make it either financially or socially. He is "an institution above the law." The dandy is a member of a dying breed ("a setting sun"), unfazed by the bourgeoisie's attempts to create "a new sort of aristocracy" based on those "celestial gifts," as our sarcastic poet puts it, "that work and money can confer" (*OC* 2:711–12).

But the dandy has time and money "in vast measure" (710)—and therein lies the rub for Baudelaire. The dandy may be willing to settle for indefinite credit, as we noted, but he can pay his creditors. He surrounds himself with beautiful objects with no thought of *épater le bourgeois*, but he can afford to buy them. During his brief period of wealth, the young Baudelaire, as we have seen, lived with things both exquisite and expensive. If money is a symbol of real value elsewhere (as in a bank vault), it is by definition dual: the bills or coins in your pocket as against what they

19. Max Weber, *The Protestant Ethic and the Spirit of Capitalism*, trans. Talcott Parsons (New York: Scribner, 1976), 185 and 193.

represent in the bank. But Baudelaire is never able or willing to understand that expenditure reduces your assets or, to use Balzac's concretization of this aspect of money, shrinks the surface of the shagreen. Baudelaire always separates expenditure from its consequences. He can lament at self-pitying length the poverty that crushes him, he can make endless lists of how much he owes and to whom, but he does not—or will not—make the connection *at the moment of expenditure* between the act of spending and its results. One among innumerable examples: in the *Carnet*, Baudelaire makes lists of debts to the hat maker, the tailor, the launderer, taverns, restaurants, and so on. The lists meticulously note how much is owed, but they rarely take into account how much Baudelaire has to draw from. His notion of "assets" is first his mother and then his friends. If all else fails, he (very reluctantly) turns to Ancelle, who controls his modest trust fund. It is not only a question of living beyond your means; rather, with Baudelaire, it is a question of living as you see fit, regardless of your bank account. He was frequently (and increasingly) famished, cold, avoiding creditors. What he kept banking on, literally in a sense, was what editors owed him, and what he assumed would be the triumph of one of his texts. His lists of debts continually appear side by side with texts to be published, how much he will be paid, what he hopes a given text will bring.[20] And more than once he publishes the same text with different editors in order to be paid twice.

The symbolic aspect of money, in other words, is a symbol we can only assume Baudelaire refuses to recognize. Simmel would explain this incapacity as the distance of the modern urbanite from the production of objects: "Since the emergence of a money economy we are no longer directly confronted with the objects of economic transactions. Our interest in them is disrupted through the medium of money" (*The Philosophy of Money*, 478). The particular abstract existence that is urban life, as Simmel puts it, has increased our distance from nature. Nature actually "rejects us," and is "something internally unattainable, a promise that is never fully kept and an entity that responds to our most passionate devotion with a faint resistance and strangeness." And that is why, continues Simmel, landscape painting has developed in modern times—it is an art that "depends upon distance from the object and upon a break in our natural unity with it." But this is not Baudelaire, except in one respect: he does not understand money as exchange or even as transaction. He desires fine things and sees money as some sort of necessary abstraction needed

20. E.g., *OC* 1:744 and *passim*, and most of *Carnet*, 713–80.

to attain an object. The mode of production for that object interests him not in the least. And while Baudelaire may be a typical "urbanite" who is distanced from nature, he is far from having a romantic response or "passionate devotion" to natural beauty (the exception being the sea, because it suggests immensity and movement—precisely what Baudelaire likes in good art, it will be recalled; *OC* 1:696).

Indeed, Baudelaire as urbanite does not even feel nostalgic for nature, nor does he bemoan its distance from the city. In the midst of the city—which he sometimes hates—he does not see nature as the antidote to urban life; nor does he admire landscapes in reality or in art. At best, nature can be a metaphor to evoke nostalgia for a lost past, as in parts of "Le Cygne." During the romantic revolution, writes Baudelaire in the *Salon de 1846*, landscape painters followed the Flemish school and "gave themselves over exclusively to the study of nature." But their talent consists mainly "in an eternal adoration of the visible work, in all of its aspects and in all of its details." Such painters are not sufficiently philosophical or reasoning; they are not concerned, as are greater artists, with "the harmony of principal lines, or in the architecture of nature" (*OC* 2:479–80). These painters do not understand that the natural, in man, is his penchant for evil; his ineluctable move to the corrupt. They are, rather, concerned with an "adoration of the visible," whereas Baudelaire is obsessed with "another world," as he puts it in "La chambre double," the poem we will be considering. No doubt the poet's hatred of photography is an extension of this point of view; or, more accurately, photography for him is nothing more than the continuation, in a different medium, of landscape painting: photography records the visible work. "Definite art, positive art, is a form of blasphemy," he writes in "La chambre double."

The visible work that Baudelaire admires is that of the true artist, of the dandy's bearing and attire, of artifice, of the carefully artful and artificial (as noted in the essay on makeup). When he has money, he buys books with fine bindings, expensive pieces of furniture, and important works of art. He buys costly fabric for his clothes and decorates his apartment with exquisite taste. Does our poet really not understand that his assets are shrinking, or is the young Baudelaire also flying in the face of nineteenth-century bourgeois morality—namely, that you only spend what you earn? In a sense, he is thumbing his nose at bourgeois notions of equilibrium—you spend to the extent that your income allows, you keep your assets and expenditures balanced. But since he ignores the connection between expenditure and capital, he extends his larger notion of expenditure—which includes energy, anguish, debauchery, unhappiness, writing—to money.

There was anxiety, in Baudelaire's day, about the government's printing of money; an (understandable) anxiety that the money was not backed by a gold standard.[21] Baudelaire, on the other hand, spends without any such concern; his concerns come later, with the bills. The materiality of money (its engraved figures, its different periods) is memory; it is, as Rebecca Spang notes, the reproduction of social knowledge.[22] But the young Baudelaire chooses amnesia. He spends an alarming amount of his inheritance in record time, and feigns surprise—or is perhaps genuinely surprised—when told how much his trust has shrunken in the space of a few months. After the establishment of the *conseil judiciaire*, he will spend the rest of his life looking for money without admitting that he understands, or agreeing to understand, the effect of expenditure on his holdings. To his death, he will see money as an annoying, outrageous, and ultimately terrifying necessity to get what he wants. His attitude is something like that of people today who continually lose their passwords and are thus unable to access their computers and the texts locked therein. Baudelaire, to continue my analogy, is not interested in the password; he has eyes only for what is in the computer. He will never see money as an exchange, a code, a system of signs. He sees only what he wants and, increasingly, what he needs. From beautiful objects that money can get him, he moves more and more to bare necessity: he needs money to eat, to stay warm, to buy a winter coat. His early, histrionic letters to his mother, filled (as all critics have noted) with emotional blackmail, end up fulfilling their own prophecies: at the end of his life, he really *is* freezing, starving, desperate for a coat.

It is as if Baudelaire preferred to remain indifferent to the vulgarity of a money economy, regardless of the consequences. The irony, of course, is that as a result of such willed indifference, Baudelaire was to spend most of his life thinking about nothing *but* money: how to get it in order to get something else, including peace of mind. Money becomes the only antidote for Baudelaire to the mental poison of constantly think-

21. See, e.g., Michael Tratner, "Derrida's Debt to Milton Friedman," *New Literary History* 34 (2004): 791–806, esp. 794.

22. Rebecca Spang, "Taking the Old Regime out of Circulation: Money and Memory in Nineteenth-Century France," paper presented at the Modern France Workshop at the University of Chicago, January 30, 2009. See her *Stuff and Money in the Time of the French Revolution* (forthcoming). My discussion at the end of this chapter is indebted to Spang's research.

ing about money. Nevertheless, there remains for him a continued lack
of contiguity between expenditure and its monetary consequences. It is
as if money's connection to a gold standard to which it putatively refers
were a foreign language that Baudelaire chooses not to believe in, even
as all those around him are speaking it and the entire culture is determined by it.

Once divested of the control of his money, Baudelaire falls into debt
through endless credit transactions. He rarely keeps his side of the bargain
until the creditor becomes so threatening that Baudelaire resorts to begging for small amounts of cash from his mother, or from Ancelle. In his
letters to his mother, he begs not only through emotional extortion (he is
sick, has no coat, no heat, nowhere to live). He also uses social shame to
prod General Aupick's highly bourgeois wife, and later proud widow, when
maternal guilt is insufficient to motivate her. Baudelaire may hate the
bourgeoisie, but he fully understands its perspectives. Indeed, that may be
the very reason why, like his contemporary Flaubert, he hates that class: he
understands it all too well, even (and perhaps especially) if the bourgeoise
is his mother. "I was forgetting," he writes to his mother on February 8,
1857, "something quite vulgar and very important. I am without linens
and have a cold. Could you find me three or four large handkerchiefs,
which I will return to you, laundered?" (*Corr.* 1:371). This is both a passive/
aggressive posture of martyrdom (all I ask for are a few handkerchiefs, but
do not worry—I will send them back to you clean), which follows a list of
his writings that will render very little revenue. "I must pay 2,000 francs
right away. I will have only 400 francs to pay the expenses of two months.
It is atrocious." There are scores of such letters, always with the same de-
fensiveness about having to ask for money, explanations about being un-
paid by publishers, lists of the works that will, surely very soon, bring in
the amount of cash needed for the creditors, ever hovering. The concern
about money is, moreover, described as so burdensome that it risks destroying his creative powers. "What divinity will smile upon me?" he laments. "Let us hope that then my imagination, wearied by such concerns,
will not be extinguished!" (ibid.).

Baudelaire's delight in beautiful things is not grounded in the bourgeois desire to surround oneself with expensive objects in order to display
economic stability and financial success (or to attempt erasing the guilt
of '48 with the soothing accumulation of art objects). His is an aristocracy
of taste, unmatched by his pocketbook. When neither his mother nor Ancelle (who was always unbending) agrees to lend him money, Baudelaire

turns to his friends and his editors. As I have noted, he even resorts to dishonesty at times, selling the same piece to two different publishers. If his article on Balzac's manipulative manner of extracting money is riddled with disdain, Baudelaire himself was to fall into much more desperate straits, and less ingenious solutions for rustling up money.

What does it mean not to understand—or to choose not to understand—the code that is money, the sign system upon which it circulates? One can argue that it is merely a childish response to responsibility, an inability to run one's life in a mature fashion. To remain in a childlike state will presumably give the poet the care and nurturing he desires from his rather unreliable mother. One can also say that such a refusal to understand is a response to the transitional time that is Baudelaire's—the dandy, after all, disappears with consumerism, and Baudelaire is witnessing the "setting sun," as he himself puts it, of the ancien régime economy. Capitalist consumerism, in Baudelaire's time, is about to take over. Thirdly, one can see in Baudelaire's willed ignorance an incapacity to grasp the allegorical aspect of a money economy. Money refers to a gold standard; it is a code grounded in representation. Expenditure exhausts resources, though this consequence cannot be foreseen if one relies solely on credit. So Baudelaire relies on credit. Credit is not only Baudelaire's way of getting what he wants when he can't pay for it; it is also a way of occluding the effects of expenditure; of delaying their results.

"WORDS PAY NO DEBTS"[23]

All of this would be mainly biographical, were it not for the fact that Baudelaire's debts gradually invade his texts; indeed, debt and text become almost inextricable. His journals are filled with lists of works to be published, or promised to editors. Alongside such lists are other lists of debts owed or payments promised to creditors. Business is on one side, literature on the other, Zola was to claim serenely. No such clean distinction exists in Baudelaire between money and literature. His lists of what he owes to the tailor, the laundress, the landlord, and the restaurants he frequents become echoes of the texts he still needs to finish and what the editors owe him or he them. Indeed, his publications grow alongside and in tandem with his debts, and the list extends to sketches for works to be written, arguments to be made (such as *Pauvre Belgique!* which remained unfin-

23. *Troilus and Cressida*, act 3, sc. 2.

ished). In the *Carnet*, he makes lists of how much he should get for a text, how much he owes, how much he wants to borrow, what he still has to write. For example, one page lists the many people to whom Baudelaire needs to write. Alongside this list is another of things to be "resolved" (*OC* 1:741), part of which reads:

RESOUDRE
La vente de *cinq volumes*
L'affaire GAUTIER
L'affaire EUREKA
L'emprunt de 2400 *2900*
Villemain 300
Poèmes 900

Under this list are two more, side by side: "To Pay" and "To Do" (works to be written or finished). Again, I reproduce here only part of each:

A PAYER		A FAIRE
Ravisé	500	*Poe*
Jousset	500	*Villemain*
Moi	500	*Duranty*
	1500	*Eaux-fortes mardi*
		Musées

Finally, just before these lists (740) we find a catalogue on how long each work will take:

Poe	3 jours
Musées	1 jour
Duranty	1 jour
Eaux-fortes	1 jour
Poèmes	10 jours
Eureka	4 jours
Villemain	6
Dandies	6
Peintres	5
	40

Within the series of Baudelaire's journals (*Fusées, Hygiène, Mon cœur mis à nu*), observes Pichois, the *Carnet* "is at once the least literary and the most intimate."[24] And he adds: "Literature appears here in its most day-to-day aspect. Rather than a journal, in the literary sense, it is an agenda, in the etymological sense" (1516). Let us follow Pichois here: the etymological sense of agenda is from the Latin *agendum*, gerundive form of *agere*, to do or act. Certainly the *Carnet* lists what needs to be done or acted upon—but this gets us nowhere. It is as if by making the lists, Baudelaire were trying to force himself to accomplish what needed to be done. The *Carnet* functions more, in my opinion, as a series dicta from the poet to himself—much as in the journal *Mon cœur mis à nu* he writes (and underlines) sentences such as: *To want every day to be the greatest of men* (*OC* 1:702). Or the list of plans and projects in *Fusées*, including phrases such as "bring cop[ies] to Michel" (his editor; *OC* 1:655). Or, in *Hygiène* (670), he tells himself what to do at his mother's house in Honfleur:

Review and organize all my *letters* (two days).
And all my debts (two days). (Four categories: bills, big debts, small
    debts, friends)
Organization of etchings (two days)
Organization of notes (two days).

Again in *Hygiène:* "If you worked every day, life would be more bearable" (ibid.). Or, in a passage from the same text that combines the list of debts with dicta to himself, we read:

Jeanne 300, my mother 200, me 300. 800 fr. a month. Work from 6
in the morning till noon, fasting. Work blindly, without a goal, like
a madman. We shall see the result. . . . Glory, payment of my debts.
Jeanne and my mother *rich.* (671)

So it would seem that there is a way in which Baudelaire does see effort—work—as producing money. And yet by the 1850s and '60s, the poet is less interested in acquiring fine things for himself, and not only because he can no longer afford them. Rather, he wants to attain "glory" so that his genius is recognized, so that he can pay his debts, and so that the two women in his life (Jeanne and his mother) can live well (and thus, one imagines, recognize his talent). Moreover, he wants to work to make life

24. The *Carnet* originally comprised seven notebooks of twenty-four pages each; five are left, and some are missing pages (*OC* 1:1516). The asterisks indicate entries that were crossed out by Baudelaire (ibid.). The *Carnet*, a title given to the documents by editors, is dated July 1861–November 1863. See Pichois's entire discussion on this text, 1515–17.

more bearable, as we have seen: even bad work, he writes, "is better than reverie" (672). And he becomes obsessed with not dying poor: "I want to spend my life working," he writes to his mother in 1864, and he adds, underlining, "I do not want to die in poverty" (*Je ne veux pas mourir dans la misère; Corr.* 2:377). Work, then, for the purpose of warding off ennui, for avoiding impoverishment, for attaining recognition: "Work inevitably engenders good mores, sobriety and chastity; consequently health, wealth, successive and progressive genius, and charity," he preaches, sounding like Benjamin Franklin. Do what you are doing, he continues in Latin (*Age quod agis*). And work, finally, to shake off the constant awareness of original sin: "The taste of productive concentration must replace, in the mature man, the taste of weakening [*déperdition*]" (*OC* 1:649).

The journals, then, are often more socially conservative than what Mauron calls the social *moi*. There are the usual remarks that "the man who prays every night is a captain who puts sentinels in place. He can sleep." Prayer becomes a sort of Pascalian wager to find peace of mind. There follows a recipe for preventing *crises* (of what? Tertiary syphilis? Anxiety? Lassitude? The onset of the stroke that would kill him?). The "unliterary" *Carnet*, as Pichois would have it, seeps into the more "literary" journals because the former is like a distilled version of the latter. The aphorisms of *Fusées* are echoed by the imperatives and lists of the *Carnet*, which in turn reappear in *Mon cœur mis à nu* and *Hygiène*. (The combination of lists of debts and texts were to reach a paroxysm in the unfinished *Pauvre Belgique!* and in the letters during 1864 and 1865, the last two years of the poet's active life before the stroke that incapacitated and ultimately killed him.)

With numbers proliferating everywhere—from how many days a given task will take, the number of editions to be given to whom, to the number of grams of lichens and sugar in the recipe for "health"—numbers themselves attain a kind of *correspondance*: "*Everything* is a number," declares Baudelaire; "Numbers are in *everything*. Numbers are in the individual. Intoxication is a number" (649). It is true, as Pichois points out in a note to this passage, that Maistre himself was interested in the symbolic value of numbers, and thus may have inspired Baudelaire's numerical enthusiasm (*OC* 1:1474). And in "Le poème du hachisch," Baudelaire waxes dreamy on how musical notes become numbers: "if your mind is gifted with some mathematical aptitude, melody, the harmony heard . . . [all] transformed into a vast arithmetic operation, wherein numbers engender numbers" (*OC* 1:419). Such mystical abstractions may well be the only way Baudelaire knows how to tolerate the endless list of money owed, of counting francs and *sous*. The antidote is the world beyond the here and now, providing escape from the very nonabstract numbers. "With every letter to a creditor," suggests Baudelaire in *Fusées*, "write fifty lines on an extraterrestrial subject and you will be saved" (*OC* 1:656). Saved from the soul crushing burden of bills, lists, and numbers; saved from the horrors of everyday life. Numbers here below, in their concrete sense, are nothing but wagers born of despair. "When Jesus Christ says 'Blessed are those that hunger, for they shall be filled,'" writes the poet, "Jesus Christ is making a calculation of probabilities" (*Mon cœur mis à nu*, 704). And there is that word again, calculation; it is a word that belongs to the numbers of the here and now in this context, not to mathematical abstractions. We will return to this passage from the beatitudes.

On the one hand, Baudelaire lives in parallel worlds with respect to money: the world of expenditure and the world of debt.[25] These are noncontiguous dimensions, as I have shown, and if the second (debt) is a constant reminder of the first (expenditure), the reverse does not follow: expenditure is not affected by the memory, advent, or reality of debt. Moreover, expenditure can have a certain sensual timelessness about it; while debt is crushingly attached to time. And time, as we saw in the essay on Balzac, signals the arrival of the debt collector: "the rapid approach of the fatal hour." So numbers are in two different worlds: the abstraction of harmony and its infinite geometries, and the hideous necessity of counting to make ends meet—or to keep the *huissier* at bay. The *huissier* is not just a bailiff; he is also someone who comes to evict you, to repossess property for which you have not paid, to handle your possessions once you have declared bankruptcy, to bear witness to the signature of documents. He is the specter that haunts Baudelaire's life, and the bad joke that keeps reminding the poet that everyday life exists, and extracts consequences. The *huissier* is, then, the proof that the other world (of dreams, fantasy, images, abstractions, calm) is always vulnerable to interruption by the concrete world of the everyday.

The prose poem "La chambre double" evokes a beautiful room in

25. These parallel worlds are not the same as those Jameson writes about. "In this transitional era," he notes, "people . . . still live in two distinct worlds simultaneously." Jameson is here referring to the fact that most people in nineteenth-century France belong to a local village or region, "while pursuing their life work in the very different world of the big city." *A Singular Modernity*, 142. This does not really hold true for Baudelaire, who was actually born in Paris. His constant promises to visit his mother in the small town of Honfleur in Normandy, and his idealization (to some extent) of this town by the sea, is another matter. He spent a great deal of time and ink imagining visits there; in fact, he rarely visited.

which the calm and aromas are so intoxicating that it is as if time itself had disappeared.[26] But the room dissolves with the "terrible, loud knock reverberating on the door." The narrator hears it like a blow to the stomach. It is a specter who enters, and he is one of three possible figures: a *huissier* "come to torture me in the name of the law"; a concubine "come to cry poverty and add the trivialities of her life to the pain of mine"; or a messenger (*sauté-ruisseau*) from "a newspaper publisher demanding the rest of a manuscript" (*OC* 1:281). All three of these figures have to do with money. The first is the bailiff who could be coming to repossess the items in the room, or to take the narrator to prison for debt. It is worth repeating that this is a fear with which Baudelaire lived constantly. In December of 1855, he writes to Ancelle: "Last evening I had the courage to go home and to my usual restaurant, despite my terrors" (*Corr.* 1:330). Hiding from the *huissier* becomes a trope for isolation, contempt for the "establishment," misanthropy, and despair.

The second figure, the concubine, resonates with Jeanne Duval, who continued to demand money from Baudelaire until his death. A year after her son's death, Mme Aupick writes to Ancelle, telling him that she has an enormous pile of letters from Jeanne to Baudelaire. In all of Jeanne's letters "I see incessant demands for money. Never a word of affection, or even of thanks. It is always money that she wants, and wants immediately." Even in April of 1866, when Baudelaire was on his sickbed, paralyzed, continues Mme. Aupick, "she plagued him, tormented him for money, which had to be sent to her without delay."[27] The third figure too, as mentioned, has come with a demand for a manuscript.

All of these figures—the *huissier*, the concubine, the messenger—want money or textual output (for which presumably Baudelaire has already been paid but has not yet produced). They are all collectors, in other words, and once again demands for money are equated with demands for texts. It is the plague of such daily concerns that the *chambre* in the beginning of the poem erases, abolishing time as well: "No! There are no more minutes, no more seconds! Time has disappeared; Eternity reigns, an eternity of delights!" But it is this "paradisal room" that disappears with the "Specter's brutal knocking." The return to daily life is violently introduced with the resurgence of memory. Right after the brutal knocks, we read: "Horror! I

26. The fifth prose poem of *Le spleen de Paris*, "La chambre double" was first published in 1862.
27. In Eugène et Jacques Crépet, *Charles Baudelaire*, Étude biographique d'Eugène Crépet, revue et complétée en 1907 par Jacques Crépet (Messein, n.d.), 59 . Cited by Joanna Richardson, *Baudelaire* (New York: St. Martin, 1994), 496.

remember! I remember!" And now there is a different eternity—that of en-nui. Time has returned, the narrator tells us: "Time reigns sovereign now. And with that hideous old man has returned as well all of his demonic cortege of Memories, Regrets, Spasms, Fears, Anguishes, Nightmares, An-gers, and Neuroses" (*OC* 1:281). Time reigns and "has taken up its brutal dictatorship again." The beautiful room has been replaced by a tawdry one; the furniture is "stupid, dusty, chipped" Everything is soiled, the windows are dirty. Again, texts are part of the economy of daily life: manuscripts lie around "crossed out or incomplete." The *saute-ruisseau*, one infers, will not be able to collect a completed work for the newspaper—a textual debt in arrears.

The elision of texts and money is crucial. Of course, producing texts generates money for Baudelaire and other writers of the period who resort to journalism; but that is not the only point. Writing is a source of income, but that very function makes it alien to art for Baudelaire (though not for Zola, as we have seen). Like the dandy, too elegant to concern himself with financial matters, the artist is too caught up in the lofty aspirations of po-etry to lower himself into the money economy. And yet the subsistence of both the dandy and the poet depends upon the commodification of the aes-thetic. The value of the text as income potential, as commodity, both for editors and for authors, is analogous to the dandy's fetishization of appear-ance, gestures, and tastes. Both the dandy and the artist in this period are in transition—the artist adjusting, as Zola forcefully argues, to the end of the patronage system; the dandy, to the capitalism and a commodities cul-ture that will ultimately destroy him (he is thus a setting sun). Aesthetics are paid for, like any other commodity; texts are valued as generating po-tential readers and therefore income. Texts become contaminated by the capitalist culture in the early part of the nineteenth century in France, and this is part of what Baudelaire rails against. He writes, and is para-doxically paid, to attack the very monetary culture by which he lives, as if in spite of himself. He may not live well, but like it or not, he is trapped in the bourgeois economy that he detests.

Money and writing are part of the same system of exchange; texts are an available resource that money rewards. Zola finds this distinction be-tween business and literature normal; Baudelaire, on the other hand, can-not tolerate it. Well aware that the two are one, or that most literature can-not be created without a subvention, Baudelaire lives in poverty as if by principle, even though he complains ceaselessly. Credit, after all, is what does him in financially, so one cannot argue that the poet is somehow above all fiduciary engagement. At the same time, our poet wants not only peace of mind but stable living quarters—which takes money. In a letter of 1855 to his mother, in which he asks for enough money to get his own apartment, Baudelaire tells her that the building he has chosen "is elegant and above all calm. I will thus be housed like an honest man, finally!—It will be, as I was telling you, a real rejuvenation. I need a life absolutely secret, and complete chastity and sobriety" (*Corr.* 1:328). He was to have neither, and the monastic life he imagined would follow was never to be. "La chambre double" imagines a first room that responds to Baudelaire's fantasy of calm and secrecy; the second room is a return to reality—to the seedy furnished apartments he loathed and to which his debts condemned him.

The elision of text and money is parallel to that between biography and poetry. The journals, we have noted, produce analogs between the lists of debts and the texts to be produced. Time itself is measured in money: "two days" is a way of measuring not only time but the income that can be produced within that time. When money is the issue, distinctions between "literature" and "diary" or "journal" become almost superfluous. Within the money economy that underscores Baudelaire's texts, the category of genre—correspondence, poem, diary, or journalistic article—becomes at best putative. The point here is not to render the poems autobiographical or vice versa; rather, it is to show the extent to which capitalism imbues all of Baudelaire's textual production and the relational arrangements of their properties. Baudelaire's natural tendency is expenditure, not economy, and this at all levels (daily life and writing). The etymological basis of economy, *oikos*, has to do with the management of the home and the goods needed to run it. But these are foreign to Baudelaire. His wishful thinking that he will finally be "housed like an honest man" is not only a longing for peace and quiet; it is also, as his subsequent reference to "chastity and sobriety" makes clear, a wish to be domestically organized, to be economical. It is the desire to count on the presence of objects and goods in a home, rather than constantly to fear their seizure.

But it is a desire that is not, in fact, his own. There is an extent to which Baudelaire wants to be parasitic of the society he loathes—not only in order to avoid the tedious thrift of the bourgeois class, and not only to refuse gainful employment and thus avoid falling into the self-righteous and economic morality of that class. In his identification with the underclass on the one hand, and with an aristocracy of the mind (and the dandy) on the other, Baudelaire falls into expenditure as the mark of the poetic and aesthetic. Expenditure is the coinage of art, its energy. But we are speaking here of physical and mental expenditure that lead to illness. Such a view is not, of course, Baudelaire's alone. Early German romantics write of what they call *Kunstkrankheit*—the sickness which is art. The composer Joseph Berlinger, in Wackenroder's *Outpourings of an Art-Loving Monk* (1797), for example, is destroyed by the intensity of his own art: it drains the life out of him.[28] Tieck and Novalis write similarly of the exhaustion and illness that come from artistic production. In these early romantic texts, the illness of art is twofold: art is like a drug or obsession that saps the artist's strength and overrides all else in life; and the production of art in itself demands a hypersensitive temperament and endless energy that eventually weaken and destroy the artist. Art, in this perspective, is an expenditure whose coin yields abstract satisfaction in exchange, but rarely tangible goods for life. Baudelaire buys into this romantic notion; his letters to his mother speak endlessly of his fatigue, ill health, depletion. He is constantly drained by his writing, but equally by the pressure to find money to support himself. What he calls "false infinity" or the "artificial ideal" may originate in medicines and drugs, but "all guilty excesses," including the solitary and concentrated intoxication of the literary writer, result in depletion. ("Le poème du hachisch," *OC* 1:403).

For Baudelaire, the expenditure of energy yields texts, but these do not in turn provide a sufficient income. His hyperexpenditure is thus a combination of a certain romantic notion of art and the continual demands of daily life; both are exhausting for him. Yet daily life is for Baudelaire the enemy of his poetic production, and the obstacle between him and writing. He is worn down both by writing and by his attempts to avoid the *huissier*. The word "work" (*travail*) appears increasingly in the journals and letters. There are only two ways to forget the crushing weight of time, he writes in *Hygiène*: "Pleasure and Work. Pleasure uses us up. Work fortifies us. Let us choose" (*OC* 1:669). A few entries later, he scolds himself: "If you worked every day, your life would be more tolerable" (670). Or: "I suppose that I attach my fate to several hours of uninterrupted work" (671). And "The only way to earn money is to work in a disinterested (*désintéressée*) manner." This last statement betrays an almost superstitious notion in Baudelaire: the strategy for making money is not to think about it: the word *désintéressée* in French meaning (as in English, though less frequently) without concern for financial benefit.

Such an attitude of disinterest is, of course, part of the problem for

28. "Das merkwürdige musikalische Leben des Tonkünstlers Joseph Berlinger," in Wilhelm Wackenroder, *Herzensergiessungen eines kunstliebenden Klosterbruders*, published with the help of Tieck (Stuttgart: Reclam, 1964), 104–26.

Baudelaire with respect to money. Here he tries to turn such disinterest into a virtue. If you have talent, you will rise "as high as you deserve to," as Zola will later preach. Baudelaire at times (as we have seen) tries to believe in this work ethic of merit, but nothing in his life lends itself to trusting such a creed. The descriptions of constant mental and physical erosion in Baudelaire are many. It is here that one can say that the poet is caught between the romantic (*Kunstkrankheit*) and the modern (capitalism as permeating his daily life). To his mother, he incessantly complains about how much work there is to do, how hard he is trying to do it. It is a skewed work ethic, but one nonetheless. The race against time gradually shifts onto his life: "Too late perhaps!" he writes, echoing the last line in his own poem, "L'horloge": "Sleep, old coward! It is too late!"

Although his logic is willfully anticommercial, Baudelaire is obsessed with money and commerce even as he professes to revile them. To the young literati, a barely older Baudelaire writes in 1846, "Never have creditors; pretend, if you like, to have them, that is all I allow you" (*OC* 2:19). It is as if pretending to be in debt were the mark of a true poet. Goethe, that scion of respectability, probably had no creditors, our poet remarks, but E. T. A. Hoffmann certainly did. Baudelaire clearly identifies with the latter, who "died at a time when a broader life was allowing his genius a more radiant expansion." Baudelaire's "Conseils aux jeunes littérateurs" also include a section on salary. Here he admits that "beautiful sentiments do not bring riches." At the same time, however, he comments that those young writers who do not exert themselves to improve a work, knowing they will earn little money for it under any circumstances, have been robbed by none other than their own indolence. They will in any case be poorly paid, but "they could have found honor in that"; having made little effort, "they have dishonored themselves" (*OC* 2:15). These are the writers, he adds, who see no point in making an effort. They want to sell a work for 200 francs, "and, when rejected, they come back the following day to offer it at a 100 franc loss." The reasonable man, he concludes, says to himself, "I think it is worth this much, because I have genius; but if concessions must be made, I will make them, to have the honor of being among you." In other words, the capitalist economy of payment for goods does not necessarily work in art; art holds itself to another standard, Baudelaire argues here, one that does not measure its value by the money for which it is exchanged.

Yet none of these lofty sentiments describe Baudelaire's own life or his attitude toward fiscal matters. He haggled with editors, hid from his creditors, and complained about the energy he expended on his writing. Benjamin, in *The Writer of Modern Life*, remarked that Baudelaire frequently equated writing with fencing (97).[29] Indeed, in "Conseils" the poet tells us that when he was interrupted by a creditor during a fencing lesson, he chased him down the stairs, shouting insults. His fencing master, "who could have blown me to the ground," was appalled. How could a poet and a philosopher behave in such a way? Baudelaire, out of breath and ashamed, realized that he had wasted time that should have been used for his lesson, was rebuked by a man he admired, and had not even injured the creditor! "Hatred," he concludes, "is a precious liquid," and an expensive one at that, "for it is made with our blood, our health, our sleep, and two-thirds of our love! We must be stingy with it!" (*OC* 2:16). Even in 1846, Baudelaire is conscious of saving his energy and of conserving his hatred for appropriate targets. He wants to be like the fencing master, who, though capable of doing great harm, husbands his strength—which is, after all, the essence of fencing artistry. But an artist cannot save energy if he is to be true to his art.

Writing is erosive; it is an expenditure that does not allow for conservation or hoarding. A critic's poorly aimed attack (*éreintage manqué*) is expended energy that returns to destroy: "it is an arrow turned against you . . . , a bullet that can ricochet and kill you" (*OC* 2:17). The obvious working metaphor is grounded in the martial arts and weaponry; the danger is clear. One might argue that not much is new here—considerations on the expenditure of energy with respect to writing and self-defense abound in literature. One thinks of everything, from the anecdote of Samuel Johnson carrying a stick lest he meet the hated MacPherson, to Nietzche's use of s*tylus* for pen, of which Derrida was to make much.[30] But in the romantic notions of the artist that still suffused the atmosphere around Baudelaire, writing is like old age in Shakespeare's seventy-third sonnet: artists are consumed by that which also nourishes them. So too, Mallarmé's letters to Cazalis bemoan how much the poet is consumed by his art. In a letter describing the writing of his poem "L'azur," for example, he describes destruction as the poet's Beatrice.[31] Destruction is Baudelaire's muse as well, and writing itself wears him down as much as do

---

29. Also in "Conseils," see the section "De l'éreintage," which can be loosely translated as "On exhausting effort." Here Baudelaire compares critical (verbal) attacks with self-defense, and mentions Granier de Cassagnac, a famously vituperative critic and fencer (*OC* 2:16–17).

30. See Jacques Derrida's *Spurs: Nietzsche's Styles*, trans. Barbara Harlow (Chicago: University of Chicago Press, 1979).

31. *Mallarmé: Correspondance 1862–1871*, vol. 1, ed. Henri Mondor and Jean-Pierre Richard (Paris: Gallimard, 1959), 246.

the horrors of daily life. But if art is depleting, expending energy elsewhere can also destroy artistic production. In *La peau de chagrin*, Balzac's protagonist Raphaël expends his energy on lovemaking. "Happy every day," writes Balzac euphemistically, Raphaël has no energy for writing—he will not, in other words, amount to much of an artist. Baudelaire says something similar in *Mon cœur mis à nu*: "Fucking is to aspire to enter another, and the artist never comes out of himself" (*OC* 2:702). Like time, energy is limited and needs to be controlled. But the same does not hold true of money. Money depletes Baudelaire because the lack of it takes him away from his writing (or, at least, provides a good excuse not to write); yet the expenditure of money, to repeat, is perhaps the only depletion Baudelaire has no trouble accepting. In an era when the consumer is emerging, when advertising is driving buyers to spend, Baudelaire is frantic about being himself expended, consumed—by the need for money, for time, for energy. Thus the first, idyllic room described in "La chambre double" attempts to depict a world above daily life and its financial miseries, and a place where energy, like time, ceases to gnaw away at the poet's being.

DEPLETION: THE POEM

By the 1860s, Baudelaire is aware that he has outspent himself at every level: "I consider myself very guilty, having abused life, my faculties, my health, like having lost twenty years in reverie." But his contempt for the working class emerges once again. Such reverie, he writes, "puts me above a crowd of brutes who work every day" (*Corr.* 2:332). Determined to work in order to catch up with his debts and to write what he has in mind, the Baudelaire of the 1860s tries to rechannel his energies from daydreaming to concentration (another word that appears regularly in this period). But his self-commands to be industrious, his firm resolutions and assurances to his mother, are sabotaged by his ennui. He calls ennui by many other names as well, the most common being laziness (*paresse*); it torments him constantly (and famously). In March of 1864, he writes to his mother, "I have fallen into a hideous lethargy. Not only am I behind in books, articles of all sorts (promised and paid), but I am overwhelmed by urgent affairs" (*Corr.* 2:350). On New Year's Eve of 1863, he had written to her:

> All that I will do, or all that I hope to do this year [1864], I should have and could have done during the one just past. But I have been taken over by a horrible malady, which has never ravaged me as much as this year. I mean *reverie, stagnation, discouragement*, and *indecision*. . . . Is

this malady real or imaginary? Did it become real once imagined? Is it the result of a physical weakening, an incurable melancholy as a result of so many years full of shocks, spent with no consolation in solitude and ill-being?

The only thing he still wants is "a *vague* desire for celebrity, for vengeance, and for luck [*fortune*]" (*Corr.* 2:342). "Fortune," let us notice, is a nice ambiguity in French (as in English), meaning both luck and wealth. The defeat of the *guignon*, bad luck, would lead first and foremost to a life devoid of constant worries about money. But, as he puts it in a poem of the same name, one would have to have the endurance of a Sisyphus to lift such a heavy burden; "L'Art est long et le Temps est court" (*Le guignon, OC* 1:17). Baudelaire has not only spent his money; he has also spent himself and the time left to him. Lethargy is punctuated by periods of panic about dying too soon: "Will I have the time," he writes from Brussels to his mother in 1865, "(supposing that I have the strength for it) to repair all that I have to repair? If I were certain at least to have five or six years ahead of me" (*Corr.* 2:433). The physical blends with the psychological in the texts of every genre he produces.

Again, I will not engage in yet another psychoanalysis of Baudelaire (Charles Mauron, among the first of many, did that); or to examine the poet's intimacy with melancholy (Ross Chambers has accomplished that with brio).[32] Rather, I want to highlight the way in which the resources of Baudelaire's various texts struggle with the economy of expenditure, and this in both senses: waste and the production that comes of spent energy. The world of art is constantly threatened by lethargy for Baudelaire; but writing itself is equally endangered by the rapidity of time, with all of the ensuing financial and literary implications. Will he pay the creditors on time? Will he write fast enough to become famous? The world of art is outside of time, whereas the world of reality, of daily life, is tyrannized by temporality. Money does not exist for Baudelaire within art; money browbeats the poet in daily life. Do these two realms meet?

They are supposed to—one remembers Baudelaire's definition of Beauty: that which combines the timeless with the specific character of an epoch. And yet "Laquelle est la vraie," it will be recalled, with its two Bénédictas, suggests two parallel worlds that have little if any contact, even if the ideal one is occasionally violated, or even threatened, by the

---

32. See Chambers, *The Writing of Melancholy: Modes of Opposition in Early French Modernism*, trans. Mary Seidman Trouille (Chicago: University of Chicago Press, 1993).

existence of the other (the brutal knocking at the door in "La chambre double" is one such violation). As the expenditure of money in Baudelaire is unconnected to its financial consequences, so "Art," as we have seen, is frequently disconnected from clock time (*le Temps*). The realm of art is often filled with the soothing, rocking motion of boats (as in "L'invitation au voyage") or of carriages (*OC* 2:724); the realm of daily life is the ticking of time, with the jerkiness that ensues (as in the dashes and exclamations points that perforate the poem "L'horloge," or the city's pedestrians dodging carriages on the terrifyingly busy streets, or even the poet's own twitching gait and odd tics). What these parallel worlds have in common is maximal expenditure with no surplus, and it is this economy that permeates the texts. "La chambre double" concretizes these two worlds. They do not meet; rather, the loud knocking makes one recede to make room for the other. But the memory of the first persists, just as the first Bénédicta lies buried but remembered in the face of the snickering second world.

Such a dual organizational structure reveals a different kind of double vision. We are not talking about a parallactic effect here—where the same object seems to change depending on the perspective by which it is viewed. That would be a more common, or even initial, reading of "La chambre double"—a room seen first through the effects of a drug, or of a dream; and then the same room seen in the sobering morning light.[33] It is true that within the horror of the second room, the only thing that seems to smile at the poet is the vial of laudanum. But while the drug would help to muffle the reality of the real, it would not necessarily return the poet to the paradisal vision of the first room. The point here is that as with the two Bénédictas, two separate women who bear no apparent relation to one another except in name, the second room described in the poem is in fact an utterly different one, serving mainly, in its shabby horror, to make nostalgia for the first room all the stronger. Although the title "The Double Room" suggests that it is in fact the same room seen in different perspectives (thus parallactic), the two worlds in the two visions are quite distinct, just as the two dissimilar women share the same name in the other poem. The poet here is explicit: he has smelled the perfume "of another world."

33. As, for one example among many, René Galand, who reads the poem as a reverie that puts into play the opposition between reality and dream, the ideal and spleen, which "visibly reflect the two faces of time that temporality puts on for man: Eternity and Time." See his *Baudelaire poétiques et poésie* (Paris: Nizet, 1969), 469. Pichois agrees with Crépet that the poem is autobiographical, the poet bemoaning his fate of constantly living in shabby hotel rooms, and wishing for a permanent home (*OC* 1:1312). No doubt.

The second room, even as it is presented as a memory ("Horror! I remember! I remember!"), paradoxically intensifies the memory of the first. Like the second Bénédicta, who claims to be the real one, the second room also insists upon being viewed as the only reality. The poet hears the clock saying to him, "I am Life; unbearable, implacable Life!" Conversely, like the first Bénédicta, the first room is outside of time (Bénédicta is dead, after all, and thus in the realm of the eternal for the poet). But the first room is as fragile as the first Bénédicta: "all of this magic has disappeared with the brutal knocking of the Specter." Again, in an inversion, it is the ghost of reality that comes to destroy the concrete vision of the first, ideal room. As the poem about the two women asks, "Which is the real one?" so this poem asks the same question. The reality and horror of daily life do not mean that the paradisal room is not another, equal reality. At the same time, however, the poet does not succumb to hope, that cruel maker of dreams burdening the sad men in the prose poem "Chacun sa chimère" ("To Each his Dream"). "La chambre double" ends with the narrator being driven by time, like an ox. Time holds a dual stick (*double aiguillon*)— reminiscent of the twin hands (*aiguilles*) of a clock. The narrator is an ox, a donkey, a slave. He is, moreover, damned. We will consider this latter, religious point, a bit later. The emphasis here is that there is no hope: time drives the slave that is man; the beautiful first room may be forever unrecoverable, as if the magical formula "Open, Sesame!" had been irretrievably lost. But that does not mean, to continue my analogy with Ali Baba, that the cave with its jewels does not exist.

The first room provides, above all, a feeling of peace based on acedia—a peace without guilt and without the financial and personal consequences of indolence. It is a room of moist and dreamy immobility, in which everything, Swedenborg-like, resembles everything else. Similes abound: the room "resembles a reverie"; the furniture seems elongated, dreaming, and appears to have a somnolent life "like the vegetal or mineral"; the material covering the furniture speaks a mute language "like flowers, like skies, like setting suns." As the room comes into further focus, metaphors begin to take over: the soul is taking a bath of indolence; it has "something of the dawn, bluish and pinkish." It is a "dream of sensuality [*volupté*] during an eclipse." The muslin of the curtains "weeps abundantly in front of the windows and bed. It bends down in snowy cascades." The focus then shifts to a more specific personification: "l'Idole," sovereign of dreams, is sitting on the bed. The narrator asks himself how she got there, who brought her, what magical power placed her on the throne of reverie and delight. It makes no difference, he decides: he recognizes her. The camera (so to speak) moves in closer to the *Idole*'s eyes, described in a series of metaphors whose vocabulary suggests that a bit of evil has entered. The eyes are a "flame that cuts through the dawn"; her eyes are "subtle and terrible," and have a "fearful malice" that attracts, subjugates, and devours the gaze of whoever is imprudent enough to contemplate them; they are "black stars," which the poet admires with curiosity.

Art itself matches the purity of reverie. The walls have no bad art, the narrator tells us in the fourth paragraph. There is only the "sufficient clarity and a delicious obscurity of harmony." This oxymoronic description is in itself reminiscent of a modern chiaroscuro. The art is not well defined, which would be "a form of blasphemy"; there is nothing analytic about this art, adds the narrator—criticism, he seems to be saying, and the intellectual, have no place in this atmosphere, in which "the sleeping mind is rocked by hothouse sensations" (*OC* 1:280). What good daemon has granted him such mystery, silence, peace and perfume? We then reach something like the fulcrum of this first room's description: "Ô béatitude!" It is such an unusual cry of happiness from Baudelaire, such a moment of grace, that the reader is startled. But the reason for such beatitude lies in contrast to daily life, which is already boring its way into the bliss. Indeed, this "supreme life" has nothing in common with "what we generally call life," even at its happiest (281).

For as everybody from Kant to, rather recently, Jameson has noted, the autonomy of the aesthetic is not achieved by separating art from daily life; nor, indeed, is such a separation possible. There can be no "reclaiming aesthetic purity from the morass of real life, of business and money, and bourgeois daily life," observes Jameson.[34] And although Jameson is largely talking about later modernity, the point holds for Baudelaire. Kant's notion of art's purposiveness without purpose (*Zweckmässigkeit ohne Zweck*) attempts to combine the aesthetic move to production (or productivity) with the inherent purposelessness of art on the pragmatic level. But no such combination, or integration, works for Baudelaire. The first room, it will be recalled, contains "no artistic abomination"—that is, no art that is definite or positive. Pure art must remain, he wants to believe, apart from clock time, and thus ethereal and as if somnolent and indistinct as the hallmark of its aesthetic purity. The poet dreams of a world of art uncontaminated by money; especially as money is one of the primary symptoms of time. Will there be enough time to produce, so as to earn the money necessary for Jeanne, for himself, for the debts Baudelaire

---

34. *A Singular Modernity*, 176.

accumulates? Will the *huissier* find him before he can flee? Will his (ever fewer) belongings be seized? Will he ever receive sufficient recognition so that he can help to support, rather than be parasitic of, his mother? These are the ceaseless concerns that come knocking at the door. Again there is a ghost in the poem, but it bears repeating: a *huissier*, a concubine crying poor and presumably begging the narrator-poet for money, or the messenger from a journal demanding payment in the form of a manuscript. Money is the unspoken protagonist of the second room, and is blissfully absent from the first.

Let us consider, by way of contrast, Coleridge's "Kubla Khan, or A Vision in a Dream." The poem was similarly inspired by laudanum and interrupted by the infamous Person from Porlock. But what was destroyed for the English poet by that interruption was the inspiration for the poem, the élan that drove its production, the memory of the images. Coleridge did not, upon emerging from his trance, find himself confronted by shoddy and seedy surroundings; he did not equate the poem with an escape from his daily life; he did not consider himself to be in a hideous other place, far from "another world." Coleridge, to begin with, had money—at least enough to put food in his mouth and clothes on his back. But that is not, of course, enough of an explanation. Despite his bouts of depression, anxiety, and self-doubt, Coleridge is above all concerned with the poetic imagination.[35] His belief in it does not waver, nor does he think the dream lies somewhere separate from life. He may describe a vision in a dream, but we may generalize and say that it is for the purpose of conveying a sentiment, sensibility, atmosphere. Dreams, in other words, are precisely for that purpose. The real world contains dreams and their visions, and it is the poet's task to convey them. Baudelaire's two rooms, however, are as distinct and as noncontiguous as Kant's definition of noumena and phenomena.

As critics have regularly noted, there is a complete symmetry of opposites in the two rooms: the furniture, curtains, windows, to name just a few, are rigorously opposed in the two worlds. The first room is clean, full of light pastels, perfumed, expansive, warm, timeless, and visited by the "Idole"; the second is dusty, dirty, stinking fetidly of tobacco, narrow, cold, subjugated by time, and precipitated by the "specter." It is perhaps facile to make the comparison with Coleridge's production of Kubla Khan; but my point is that for the English poet, a dream is that which is neces-

35. See the recent collection of essays, *Coleridge's Imagination: Essays in Memory of Pete Laver*, ed. Richard Gravil, Lucy Newlyn, and Nicholar Roe (Cambridge: Cambridge University Press, 2007).

sarily unrelated—though integral—to the world of daily life. As such, the dream is naturally perceived as exotic, bizarre, unusual. It is determined by the standard of reality; it is not a reality unto itself with respect to the real world, but it springs from it. For Baudelaire, on the other hand, the world of the first room serves to underline the horror of the here and now and the irrevocable loss, not of a poem, but of the world of the first room. Once again, double vision: he sees, remembers, both rooms at the same time. Each negates the presence of the other (as with the two Bénédictas), but they are both there in his mind all the same. He does not awaken to normal existence; he is expelled from the paradise of the first room and awakens a stranger to the familiar. This is not a desire for the unity of opposites, the *coincidentia oppositorum*. It is rather the attempt to remove one world for the sake of holding onto the other, and the inability to do so.

Such a double vision of two worlds is also, more concretely, Baudelaire's experience of life in Haussmann's Paris—none of *Le spleen de Paris* is anterior to Haussmann's renovations of the city.[36] Haussmann is all about money: the eviction of hundreds of poor people from their homes to make room for the new boulevards, and the resulting sudden confrontation of the poor in the same space as the rich. Indeed, "Les yeux des pauvres," it will be recalled, describes a visit to one of the fancy new cafés that cropped up with Haussmannization, and being faced with a poor family that has, no doubt, been left homeless in the wake of one of Haussmann's bulldozers. The poor of Paris, left to beg, live in a city parallel to the city of the well-off. But Baudelaire is acutely aware of two worlds that are noncontiguous: the Paris he knew, which is quickly disappearing, and the new Paris, rapidly being created. Both, significantly, lie in ruins. The old, medieval Paris is being steadily demolished, leaving the dust and debris as crumbled vestiges of its existence. But the future Paris also lies in ruins, its blocks of new stone and columns yet to be built. As Baudelaire puts it in "Le Cygne," he sees "this heap of rough-hewn columns and shafts, / Grass, big blocks made green by the water of the puddles / And, gleaming in the window panes, a confused bric-a-brac" (*OC* 1:86). As with the poem about the two rooms, the old Paris and the new do not touch except in the evidence of their mutual destruction.

The swan poem marks a time and place of transition between a recollected past and an imagined future, with the wreckage of both marking

36. See Pichois on this point, *OC* 1:1296.

out a present built on a no-man's-land: "Paris is changing!" writes the poet
in the second part of the poem,

> But nothing in my melancholy
> Has moved! New palaces, scaffolding, blocks,
> Old neighborhoods, everything becomes allegory for me
> And my dear memories are heavier than boulders." (Ibid.)

Indeed, the poem is full of allegory: the exiled proliferate, starting with
the dedication to Victor Hugo, to the swan, to Andromache, to the thin
Negress searching for the coconut trees of "superb Africa," and to "whoever has lost what is never, never to be recovered." These are only a few
of the poem's lost ones (the poem ends, a bit less than successfully, with
the narrator thinking of "still many others!"). Baudelaire, then, is deter-
ritorialized in his own city; a stranger once again to the familiar—as in
a dream of being home but where nothing looks like home. At the end of
the poem, he says that his mind has exiled itself in a forest, wherein an old
memory blows the hunter's horn. We are far from the Swedenborg-esque
forest of "Correspondances," where everything resonates with everything
else. And we are not in nature either, since the forest is in the mind. Baudelaire often depicts nature by first abstracting it as a mental construct or
metaphor, like the bat beating its wings against the walls of the mind. In
the swan poem, as many have noted, the mark of modern poetry is in evidence: defamiliarization (*étrangeté*, to use Pichois's term). Baudelaire goes
from clarity to mystery; from the classical notions of imitating nature and
platonic ideals to obscurity (*OC* 1:1004).

   The future and the past lie in ruins around the narrator in the poem,
but the no-man's-land that provides the space for such a juxtaposition is
a place of paralysis, ennui, melancholy, and the heavy burden of memory.
The poem expresses that feeling of exile with a series of personifications
and allegories, each one adding to the sense of estrangement. Everything
becomes allegory, with each allusion accumulating to render the weight of
memory and despair. "Le Cygne" thus has in common with "La chambre
double" a sense of estrangement in the familiar, and of being exiled in
what is purportedly the real world. But "La chambre double" does not rely
on allegory (except perhaps for the "Idole" and the "specter," which have
allegorical aspects). Rather, it functions in a system of what we might call
negative correspondences—the oxymoronic symmetry mentioned earlier.
Such correspondences, however, do the opposite of Baudelaire's famous

poem by the same name: in "Correspondances," each thing answers the other to suggest a higher unity, a near-Platonic idea. Like Plato's Socrates arguing for ambidexterity because it more closely relates to our original oneness, "Correspondances" believes in perfumes that have the expansion of infinite things, and that "sing the transports of the mind and the senses." "La chambre double," on the other hand, begins inside a place where things are infinitely expansive, only to sink, like Plotinus's dehydrated images of the re-descent into the world, into a realm that the poet acknowledges as his own: "Yes!" he cries out, "this hovel, this sojourn in eternal ennui, is truly mine." As "Le Cygne" puts it, as "A une passante" suggests, and as Poe's raven repeats, "La chambre double" describes what has been lost and is perhaps never to be recovered. But the poet's eye remains on the lost realm even as he is in bondage, like an ox, a donkey, or a slave, to the here and now, which is the realm of the damned. Like "A une passante," "La chambre double" portrays a moment of grace that is almost immediately, and probably irretrievably, lost. Simultaneously, paradoxically, the same moment elicits an image that signals the hope for a return, for a retrieval, sometime within an unknown future that will allow for reunion.

This economy of a lost past on the one hand, and of its unlikely but nonetheless anticipated return in the future, is not limited to the notion that chronological time has taken back its power. It is also the economy of the advent of Christ and the promised Second Coming, to which the poem briefly but emphatically alludes with its emphasis (twice, the second time in italics) on "good news" (*bonne nouvelle*).[37] The first "good news" is on the level of the misery of being: there is only one second in human life that has the announcement of good news as its mission. Happiness, it would seem, is at best so fleeting that it has gone before it is grasped. The second

37. *Le salut publique*, that short-lived journal that Baudelaire was to edit with Champfleury and Toubin during the revolution of 1848, has an article entitled "Bonnes nouvelles." The article, which most scholars believe to be by Baudelaire, proclaims the "good news" that the kings of France and Belgium have both fled, and that the new Republic has already been announced in Dijon. But there is also a religious aspect: two priests were protected from the angry mob by a larger crowd, and a wooden statue of Christ in the chapel of the Tuilleries was triumphantly—and reverently—carried to the church of Saint-Roch in Paris. Hence, concludes the article, "the Revolution of 1848 will be greater than that of 1789; moreover, it begins where the other ends" (*OC* 2:1033–34). It was optimism of the sort that Baudelaire was later to deride; it is significant, however, that in 1848 he saw the union of religion and republican fervor as an indication of the success of the new revolution. Baudelaire also worried about the possible destruction of art in the 1848 revolution: "Let us not cease repeating it," he writes, "respect for objects of art and industry, and for all products of intelligence" (1032). (Industry here means manual labor.)

"good news," in italics, is more complex: there is a certain kind of good news that "causes an inexplicable fear in everyone." What is the nature of this fear, one wonders? In Christianity, the good news is that Christ has died for humanity's sins; the gospels themselves (etymologically as well as textually) are the telling of this good story. The "inexplicable fear" may have to do with the notion that Jesus removes original sin—which explains everything, as Maistre had written, thus leaving us with nothing, should it be eradicated.

Or is it the fear of eternal life? Such a reading returns us to the only "Second" that brings good news, which can now be seen as the second in time announcing death (hence the capitalization of the word), and thus a different kind of the end of time, bringing with it the good news that Jesus also preaches—the end of fear. But the only escape from time is death, and despite the promise of Jesus, the fear of death remains, as our poet would have it, ubiquitous. There is the added fact, within Christianity, that one may be left in eternal damnation; a sort of echo of the damnation that is life ("Go ahead and live, damned one!"). So the poem gives us a conundrum: the only way to escape from the crushing ennui and (contrarily) rapidity of time is to die. In death, one may be annihilated, if it turns out that Jesus is wrong; but even more terrifying, one may be left with the weight of eternity. To what is one finally a slave? The only happiness lies in that other, earlier room. "My kingdom is not of this world," says Jesus. Baudelaire makes the same claim, but with the difference that he cannot attain the kingdom that he claims as his own. Like the albatross, in the poem of the same name, the poet belongs to a realm to which he has no access, and he lives in a realm of the everyday in which he can only be awkward. The realm to which he is condemned, the most familiar one, is one in which he is a stranger. Moreover, such an estranged situation is manifest in the body: the physical jerkiness that characterizes life in reality, including the cold, hunger, filth, disease, and ugliness that surround him. Haussmann's renewal project is a concretization of this existential impasse: it destroys the past, promises an unfamiliar future, and leaves a vacant lot as the place of the present.

It is in this economy, both material and conceptual, that the future seems to become a Second Coming, Jesus's return as déjà vu, as that which returns in the sense of specter ("I remember! I remember!"). For Jesus is the unacknowledged specter that comes knocking at the poet's room of bliss. And it is no laughing matter: the Word Incarnate knows anger and tears, writes the poet in his essay on laughter. "But," he continues, "he has never laughed. In the eyes of Him who knows everything and can do

everything, the comic does not exist" (*OC* 2:527). It is not surprising that
this passage comes on the heels of an allusion to Maistre. The poet wonders whether that "animated soldier of the Holy Spirit" was the one to have
noted that "the sage only laughs while trembling" (526). Or, as Baudelaire
puts it later in the same essay, the sage trembles when he realizes he has
laughed, because laughter is "of diabolical origin" (528). So there was no
laughter in the Garden of Eden, writes Baudelaire, adding, significantly,
"In the earthly paradise (which we suppose to be past or to come, memory
or prophecy, like the theologians or the socialists) . . . joy was not in laughter." The Garden of Eden, then, is precisely that which is remembered and
still to come; that which is lost and perhaps to be regained. Jesus, too, is
remembered and still to come, as is the *passante*, as is the first Bénédicta,
and as is the first room.

It is a dual economy, with a Januslike perspective, of which Baudelaire
at times can make fun. In *L'école païenne*, Baudelaire tells of a banquet
commemorating the February revolution (of 1848), in which a toast was
offered by a young man ("educated and intelligent") to the god Pan. Pan,
announces the young man, is the god of the revolution; indeed, he *is* the
revolution. The poet asks if Pan isn't dead. "No, the god Pan is not dead!"
explains the young man. "The god Pan still lives," and he adds, lifting
his eyes tenderly to the sky, "He will come back." The narrator tells us
that the man sounds as if he's talking about "the prisoner of Saint-Helen."
The young man explains that we need to return to "the real doctrines,
obscured *for an instant* by the despicable Galilean" (*OC* 2:44). Thus Pan,
who evokes Napoleon and Jesus, is the real god, the one who really will
return.

As theologians were mixed in with socialists in the discussion on
laughter in paradise, and as priests and the statue of Jesus heralded a new
and successful revolution, so here the political and the religious are also
combined. There are those who wait for Napoleon to return from his exiled
imprisonment, those who believe that the god Pan—the Revolution!—will
reappear, and those who wait for Jesus's Second Coming. Clearly, religion
and politics are never very far apart for Baudelaire. Moreover, exile here
seems predominant. Just as the swan poem concerns a sense of estrangement, portrays a series of exiled or marginalized figures, and is dedicated
to Victor Hugo, the literary star whose long exile gripped all of France,
so too exile has theological as well as personal or political overtones for
Baudelaire. Man is in exile from his home territory, the Garden of Eden—
yes, of course. More complicated than that, however, is that Baudelaire depicts, in "La chambre double," a mind exiled from another reality, which

is unattainable. A mark of modernity no doubt—the stranger in an overly familiar but thoroughly alienating land. "Anywhere out of the world!" is the cry that his soul gives him, in English—as if a foreign language were more natural than his native one. The foreign, in other words, is less alienating than the familiar, no doubt because it makes no pretense of being "natural."

But the Januslike perspective I have been describing is not only theological, political, and personal; it is an economy that is constantly, if at times obliquely, laced with money. Let us return to the entry from *Mon cœur mis à nu* in which Baudelaire writes, "When Jesus Christ says, 'Blessed are those that hunger, for they shall be filled,' Jesus Christ is making a calculation of probabilities" (*OC* 1:704). For Baudelaire, one assumes, Jesus's calculation is that the existence of God is a given, and that there is therefore a probability that those who hunger in life will be sated by God in the afterlife. You get rewarded, in other words, for your suffering on earth—or, at least, Baudelaire's Jesus is betting that there is a real chance you will be rewarded. *Calcul* thus has an element of wager. "Calculation in favor of God," writes Baudelaire, underlining the phrase in *Mon cœur mis à nu*. The text forms a syllogism resting on the notion that since nothing exists without a purpose, and I do not know what that purpose is, someone "wiser than I" does know. "I must then pray to this someone to enlighten me," concludes Baudelaire; "it is the wiser course" (*le parti le plus sage*; *OC* 1:678). This is a wager less pragmatic than Pascal's famous one, and more tortuous. While Pascal argues that if there is no God, and I believe in him, I have lost nothing, Baudelaire wants to *know*. He prays for intellectual enlightenment from whoever is wiser than he. If he were to believe in a being that did not exist, he would be the first to say that a great deal is lost. The difference between the two wagers is that of covering your bases on the one hand (Pascal), and insisting on knowing the truth (Baudelaire) on the other. One might argue that Pascal, given his intense faith, is simply trying to convince others to believe in God. Baudelaire, however, wants to know whether he should believe, precisely what or whom he should believe in, and on what grounds. He wants to know what the wiser one knows; that is not Pascal's concern.

The beatitude on hunger expresses a calculation that has a monetary aspect, as Baudelaire would have it: you toil and suffer, you get paid later (a system that caused Nietzsche to loathe Christianity, let us remember). Indeed, every dictionary definition of the word *calcul* includes numbers and aspects of economy: estimates, evaluation, supposition, intention, computation, reckoning. The word comes from the Latin *calculus*, a small pebble used for counting (hence the medical usage of the word *calcul* in French to mean a stone, as in kidney stone). The definition of the word in the *Dictionnaire de l'Académie Française* of 1762 (fourth edition) includes an idiomatic expression: "On dit que l'erreur de calcul ne se couvre point, pour dire, qu'on peut toujours revenir contre l'erreur de calcul." (It is said that an error in calculation does not demand defensive action; one can always rectify an error of calculation). The saying is repeated in the fifth and sixth editions of the dictionary (1798 and 1835). A proverb too is included in all three editions, "Faire un mauvais calcul," which means to misunderstand something or to be under an illusion. Is Jesus laboring under an illusion when he makes his "calculation of probabilities"? Baudelaire suggests that he may be—indeed fears that he may be, in which case it is an error of calculation that cannot be rectified.[38]

Baudelaire uses the Gospel of Luke's version of the Sermon on the Mount:—"Blessed are you who are hungry now, for you will be filled"; 6:21). In Matthew, however, we read: "Blessed are those who hunger and thirst for righteousness, for they will be filled" (5:6). Justice will reign after death—that, after all, is part of the *good news* Jesus proclaims and embodies. Baudelaire concentrates on hunger; he brings the abstract down to earth, which is what the Gospel of Luke does as well. (Luke does not say, for example, "Blessed are the poor in spirit," as Matthew does; he says, "Blessed are you who are poor.") Baudelaire is not talking about hungering (or thirsting) for righteousness; he is talking about being hungry. So too, "La chambre double" brings him down to earth, where the air smells bad and the furniture is "stupid" (*sot*). From a place that is timeless and expansive, which moves the poet to cry "Ô béatitude!" we fall back into "Memories, Regrets, Spasms, Fears, Anguishes, Nightmares, Angers, and Neuroses." The capitalization of all these nouns of despair (influenced, perhaps, by Poe's Germanic tendency in this regard?), coupled with the plural in each case, serve to emphasize the ghastly prison that is daily life; its crushing ubiquity. The moment of "beatitude," that moment of happiness that echoes the original Greek meaning of the term in the Gospels, is dispelled with the return of Time. The only beatitude then becomes the hope that someone wiser will allow the "good news" to be less than terrifying, while Time measures itself out for the slave who is damned as if life were a prelude to the eternal damnation of hell. Hell is something

38. "All that is beautiful and noble," writes Baudelaire in "Éloge du maquillage," "is the result of reason and calculation" (*calcul; OC* 2:715).

that Baudelaire believes in too easily, while eternal reward in heaven, as preached by Jesus, is particularly unlikely for him. Indeed, as we have seen, he even suspects Jesus of a calculated assumption. The Savior himself seems less than certain that, as his own beatitudes preach, the poor, the hungry, those who weep, who are hated—the people with whom our poet clearly identifies—will enter the kingdom of heaven.

Conversely, as the more pragmatic Gospel of Luke would have it, woe to the rich, for they have already received their consolation (Luke 6:24). Those who "are full now" will be hungry, those who laugh now will "mourn and weep," and so on. In other words, we have a symmetry here of debts and payments ("forgive us our debts as we also have forgiven our debtors," reads the Lord's Prayer, in Matthew 6:12). Luke (6:38) has Jesus tell his listeners, "The measure you give will be the measure you get back." If you already have your "reward," according to Jesus, your future in the afterlife does not look good. And vice versa. Much of the language of Jesus has to do with credit. You get no credit, in either sense of the word, if you merely return another's favor: "If you do good to those who do good to you, what credit is that to you? For even sinners do the same" (Luke 6:33). Jesus speaks not only of credit but also of lending and the consequences of debt: "Lend, expecting nothing in return" (Luke 6:35); "Give to everyone who begs from you, and do not refuse anyone who wants to borrow from you" (Matthew 5:42); "If anyone takes away your goods, do not ask for them again" (Luke 6:30). If an "accuser" puts you in prison, warns Jesus, "you will never get out until you have paid the last penny" (Matthew 5:26).

Most of the Sermon on the Mount is based, then, on an economy of "suffer now and be rewarded later"; give, lend, pay your debts, and look for no reward in this life. Baudelaire, who felt he had little reward in the here and now, is torn between contempt for the promises of Jesus, and genuine (if fearful) hope. What, to repeat, if the calculation is wrong? The epiphany of happiness in "La chambre double"—Ô béatitude!—hypostasizes precisely the meaning of the Greek sense of *evangel*—good news. Supreme blessedness is Baudelaire's in the first room. But Baudelaire performs a radical departure from the beatitudes of Jesus because, for the poet, misery in the world is at times cured by leaving that world through reverie, through entrance into a realm that seems far more real than the real, since it allows for freedom from debt, credit, and calculation. Jesus, in other words, is another person from Porlock—brutally returning the poet to the second, shabby room, with the promise of *good news*, news that causes an "inexplicable fear in everyone." Baudelaire's real kingdom is also not of this world, but nor is it a life after death. The poet's fear of death is obvious; but his desire for a place "anywhere out of this world" is a demand for a parallel realm where the concerns of money and hardship, time and debt, do not exist. The first room is that place. The two realms are discrete, and unlike Jesus's postulation of the consequences of this world in the next, they remain noncontiguous, independent, and of a different essence altogether. That is why, conceptually at least, one cannot read "La chambre double" as the experience of a shabby room by a person under the influence of drugs. The two rooms are emphatically not one and the same.

The vision is double in that the poet sees the two places at the same time; but they do not meet or touch. As with the two Bénédictas, the second room serves only to make the absence of the first all the more painful. And if there are resonances between the two (both rooms have furniture, curtains, windows, a bed, and so on) again it is only for the purpose of expressing the huge gap (conceptually, physically, philosophically, emotionally) that separates them. It is an insistent, non-Platonic position, grounded in despairing of a good life after death. There will either be the void, the poem suggests, or the hell the poet so frequently feels he deserves. In the meantime, the paradisal first room and the hellish second one serve to demonstrate the poet's traumatic approach to daily life: it can only be a hell, and if there is an afterlife at all, it will be another hell. Jesus's system of equilibrium, "the measure you give will be the measure you get back" (Luke 6:38), is an economy of exchange; Baudelaire's system is one of denial, escapism, and flight. As there is no connection between the two rooms, so there is no possibility of grace—except for the unexpected (and, like Freud's unconscious, unresponsive to the voluntary) appearance of the first room. And there is death, says the poem, which allows for escape from this world. The first room, like the first Bénédicta, like the *passante*, may never be seen again. But the poet's expression is not only this loss; it is also an insistence on the reality of the realm only he can see. In this sense, bizarrely enough, he is like Jesus. Baudelaire assures his reader of another kingdom that is more real than the world of daily life. The difference, to repeat, is that he believes you cannot "get credit" in this world for the next. Indeed, in the first room, since there is no time, there is also no afterward. There can be no money economy in the first room, not only because it is blissfully void of such concerns, but also because there is no exchange possible with the second room, and no time for parsing out the deadlines of debt or the menace of a *huissier*.

REVERSIBILITY

The indirect presence of Jesus in the poem, and the good news he brings, return us to reversibility. That notion, it will be recalled, participates in a money economy: you pay for original sin with suffering; you can ransom your sin with sacrifice (which Maistre, let us remember, understood as the spilling of blood). The righteous one, Maistre had noted, suffers voluntarily, and thus "satisfies" not only for himself but for the guilty one "by way of reversibility." Maistre's interpretation of reversibility is literal and harsh, as we have seen; but it is the one followed by Baudelaire. Jesus is the prime example of reversibility: the Redeemer is he who allows his blood to be spilled in order to save mankind. The mercantile aspect of this economy, as we noted in the first chapter of this study, was not lost on the church. The point is, however, that given the sinful nature of man, a life of suffering is somewhat to be expected in a theological (Catholic) context. Jesus, however, with his *good news*, does not convince Baudelaire, who rails against the notion of suffering for the sake of being rewarded later. Jesus bargains too, in other words: he makes a "calculation." The beatitudes in Luke's Gospel, with their emphasis on the "now," give the concomitant promise of the "after." But Baudelaire wants neither now nor after—he wants timelessness. And this desire is precisely tied to money economy—because, given that time is money (in the high capitalism of Baudelaire's day), the only realm that allows freedom from the concerns of money must be, by definition, a timeless one. Baudelaire sees no liberation from such financial suffering and bondage in the contract with Jesus (this presumably despite the latter's anger with the money changers in the temple).

It is curious that Maistre elsewhere condemns all forms of the mercantile. Romanticism, as Pichois notes, makes a firm distinction between the grocer and the poet.[39] In the preface to his *Histoires extraordinaires*, Maistre says of John Locke, "How he smells of a store!" (*Quelle odeur de magasin! OC* 1:1509). Baudelaire gleefully takes up such contempt for the mercantile. "Commerce in its essence," he writes in *Mon cœur mis à nu*, "is *satanic*." And he adds, "Commerce is the loaned-returned; it is a loan with the tacit agreement: *Give me more than I give you.*" The merchant

---

39. Significantly in this context, Novalis's *Heinrich von Ofterdingen*, which takes place in the Middle Ages, idealizes that time as one in which the merchant and the poet understand each other. When a young Heinrich leaves home, he travels in a carriage with two merchants who "recognize" his inherent poetic disposition. Like many of the German romantics, Novalis idealizes the Middle Ages as a time of unity, including that of the poetic and commercial.

is "utterly polluted"; commerce is "vile"; it is natural to man "because it is one of the forms of egotism, the lowest and the most vile" (OC 1:703–4). There follows the remark about Jesus's calculation of probabilities concerning the hungry and their hope of being sated in the future. Despite Baudelaire's religious impulses, Jesus is clearly placed within the mercantile economy. Is Baudelaire perhaps thinking that Jesus, in assuaging the suffering with the promise of "after," may himself be asking for more than he will give? Or at least more than Baudelaire thinks is fair. But as usual, it is more complicated than that and certainly more ambiguous. Indeed, Baudelaire is explicit that praying as a means of bargaining with God, or of trying to get what you want, is a form of usury. Some people, like usurers or assassins, may pray, "Lord, make my next transaction a success!" But "the prayer of such low-lifes," comments Baudelaire in a rare moment of self-satisfaction, "does not spoil the honor and the pleasure of my own" (OC 1:705).

A similar prayer is uttered by the narrator of the prose poem "Le joueur généreux," who meets and makes friends with the devil (Le spleen de Paris XXIX, OC 1:325–28). Even more to the point, perhaps, is the prose poem "La corde," based on a real (and infamous) event told to the poet by Manet.[40] A poor boy who had posed for the painter (Manet's name is not given in the story) and lived with him was given to stealing sweets and liquor from the painter's home. One day, Manet angrily threatened to send this otherwise charming boy back to his parents. When Manet, who had gone out briefly, returned home, he discovered (to his horror, of course) that the boy had hanged himself. There follows a gruesome description of the body and of the painter's difficulty in extracting the cord from the dead boy's neck. But the painter's real horror was not ultimately the death of "my little man, the mischievous companion of my life" (OC 1:329). Rather—and this is how Baudelaire's narrator describes the painter's exposition to the story—the painter is concerned with the "strange feeling" one has when an illusion disappears. In this case, the illusion is that of maternal love as a necessary given. "It is as difficult to imagine a mother without maternal love as a light without heat," says the painter to the narrator (328). But for the painter, the story demonstrates that maternal love is not ubiquitous. Indeed, the boy's mother, upon coming to see her son's body, asks the painter to give her what is left of the fatal cord. Assuming that the poor

40. See Pichois's note on this prose poem (OC 1:1339). The boy was Alexandre, the model for many of Manet's paintings, who hanged himself in one of the painter's studios between 1859 and 1860..

woman wants some sort of keepsake of her son, even if a macabre one, the painter complies. The following day however, he receives many letters from his neighbors, each asking for a piece of the same cord. The painter abruptly realizes why the mother wanted the cord: "And then, suddenly, a light went on in my brain, and I understood why the mother was so keen to snatch the string away from me and by what commerce she intended to console herself" (331). The mother intended to sell pieces of the cord because, as one variation for the poem puts it, "one meter of cord from a hanged man, at 100 francs per decimeter, altogether, each paying according to his means, makes a thousand francs; a real, efficacious relief for that poor mother" (1339).

The story, grisly as it is, becomes all the more so because the painter feels little if any guilt. Indeed, he feels only the need to get back to work after the event, "more rapidly than usual, to gradually chase away that little cadaver that haunted the folds of my mind, and whose phantom was tiring me with its big, staring eyes" (331). Most of the painter's response, as we have noted, is to the mother's cold "calculation." The latter word is not used in "La corde," but it is certainly implied. The mother's "commerce" of consolation is money. The narrator does not comment on any of this; he is satisfied, it seems, to tell the story in the painter's words. But the implication is there: poverty creates monsters. The boy's parents were "poor people," and the painter offered to house and feed the boy with little hard work in exchange. But let us note that the painter's assumption—that the mother cannot have loved her child if she sought to make money from the cord—stems from the perspective of a life of physical comforts, such as the painter's. Was the woman desperate, thinking of how to feed her other children, and not just being coldly calculating? Did the boy kill himself out of fear of returning to poverty? Clearly, he was stealing sweets and liquor to indulge needs he had never been in a position to satisfy before. Again, the narrator remains silent.

The entire story is framed in quotation marks, with the exception of "my friend was telling me," at the outset of the story (OC 1:328). What is clear, however, is that the hungry are not blessed. And while the story alludes to the sinful nature of man—his natural inclination toward evil—the painter does not come off very well himself. The poor boy is like the painter's favorite pet; his death is an unhappy image to be erased from the painter's mind. In the painter's fairly rapid dismissal of the suicide, and in his supercilious (and pedantic) discourse on the illusion of maternal love, Marie Antoinette's famous phrase "Let them eat cake" is somehow not far behind. Those who have money do not understand the desperation of those who do not; and those who have never known hunger cannot imagine the wretchedness of those constantly in want of the simplest necessities. "La corde" shows not only that maternal love is not necessarily ubiquitous; it also shows how the evil inherent in man, combined with poverty, leads quite naturally to greed. In this time of capitalistic expansion, not only the merchants are greedy, the painter seems to be saying; the poor, too, scramble for money, regardless, as here, of tragic circumstances. And yet the poor, we might say, cannot afford the elegant indifference of the dandy, or the philosophical musings of the painter. While the poem's general narrator, to whom the story is told, is essentially silent, there is an implied narration that suggests that the story is more desperate, and even more tragic, than the complacent painter imagines.

WHICH ROOM IS COUNTERFEIT?

We recall that Baudelaire suggests in his journal that every person has two simultaneous postulations, one toward God, the other toward Satan, and that these two movements are opposed—the first going up and the second down. The movements are unsurprising, of course, given the usual geographic understanding of heaven and hell. Nevertheless, it is worth noting that this up-and-down notion is also used by Freud in his description of the topographical and, later, tripartite mind. Starobinski has written brilliantly on this topography, and how it relates to the classical texts on the underworld.[41] Baudelaire's own notion of up and down suggests concepts analogous to the conscious mind (going toward God is "a desire for a promotion," like a kind of self-betterment, or superego) and the unconscious (toward Satan is an "animality, the joy of descending," conversations with animals and women—not far from Freud, it must be said, on the feminization and primitivization of the unconscious). But "La chambre double" does not enact those two movements. There is no joy in the descent toward hell—nor is there, in the poem, any real descent at all, unless, like many critics, one is determined to see here the "coming down" from a dream or drug-induced state.

"La chambre double" is closer to another of Baudelaire's famous remarks: "Even as a small child," he writes, also in *Mon cœur mis à nu*, "I felt two contradictory feelings in my heart: the horror of life and the ecstasy of life" (*OC* 1:703). This is the obvious condition, he adds, of "a

---

41. See Jean Starobinski, "Acheronta Movebo," in *The Trial(s) of Psychoanalysis*, ed. Françoise Meltzer (Chicago: University of Chicago Press, 1988).

lazy, nervous person." What better description than this of "La chambre double"? The first room allows for indolence; the soul takes a "bath of laziness in it, perfumed by regret and desire." The second room brings the poet back to his nervous concerns of daily life: time brings with it, as we have seen, "Memories, Regrets, Spasms," and so forth. Unlike the (lowercase) "regrets" of the first room, the "Regrets" of the second are stabs of disproportion and anguish. The indolence of the first room rocks like a lullaby, with regret as a companion of thought, and warmth throughout. The nervousness caused by the second room pummels the poet into consciousness. A cold chimney adds to the chill, while Regret returns the poet to ennui, the other side of the coin of *paressse*. The two rooms are precisely "the horror of life and the ecstasy of life," not in that order. The ecstasy of life comprises a certain amount of wealth: nice furniture, fine curtains, warmth, peace of mind, general opulence. The second room is one of misery. If the first room succeeds in erasing all financial worries, the second, with the return of such concerns, erases poetic vision.

But, like the two Bénédictas, which is the real one? The first room *resembles*, but is not, a reverie. The second room is a nightmare, but all too real as well. Both, in other words, have to do with altered states, and both have to do with comfort or the lack of it, and therefore with money or the lack of it.[42] Are we to suppose that one room is a counterfeit version of the other? Which one? In Baudelaire's prose poem "La fausse monnaie," the narrator watches a friend purposely give a beggar a counterfeit coin. Derrida, in his examination of the story, concerns himself with the notion of the gift, and with "the economy of the story (*récit*) and the story of economy."[43] He is interested in the tobacco that both men are buying when the story opens, and in the way in which drugs help Baudelaire to escape time. All of this is to the point for Derrida's purposes (the gift, giving and given time).

But this is not the poem's real focus, which has rather to do with evil and the awareness of doing evil. "There is no sweeter pleasure," says the friend, "than to surprise a man by giving him more than he hopes for." The narrator realizes that his friend "wanted both to be charitable and to make a good deal; to win 40 *sols* and God's heart; to gain paradise eco-

42. Pichois notes that André Gide was much influenced by "La corde," and by "Le joueur généreux." The devil, writes Gide, can be affirmed by our negation of him. See the entry of January 2, 1921, in Gide's *Journal des faux-monnayeurs* (Paris: Gallimard, 1927), 29–31. Pichois adds that the end of the novel *Les faux-monnayeurs* can be summarized by: "God is nothing but the devil's counterfeit" (*OC* 1:1338).

43. Jacques Derrida, *Donner le temps, 1, La fausse monnaie* (Paris: Galilée, 1991), 133.

nomically; finally, to get for free the certificate of a charitable man."
Money circulates; even counterfeit money. Indeed, whoever is caught
with the false coin risks arrest, writes Baudelaire's narrator: "Couldn't
it [the coin] multiply into real coins? Couldn't it also send him [the beg-
gar] to prison? An innkeeper, or a baker, for example, might have him
arrested as a counterfeiter or as a propagator of fake money" (*OC* 1:324).
It is never excusable to be unkind (*méchant*), says the narrator, "but there
is some merit in knowing that one is. And the most irreparable of vices
is to do evil from stupidity" (ibid.). What the narrator cannot forgive his
friend, he says, is "the ineptitude of his calculation [*calcul*]." There is that
word again.

The friend's calculation is that he will win points from God for entering heaven, make a poor man happy with an unexpected apparent act
of generosity, and save himself "real" money all at the same time. The
calculation is inept because presumably God sees through such bartering;
the poor man will be unhappily surprised and perhaps arrested. Evil has
been done by way of stupidity—perhaps, for Baudelaire, the greatest sin of
all. Like Jesus, the friend is making a "calculation of probabilities." And
while for Baudelaire the question of evil is not related to Jesus, in both
cases the poor are the objects and possible victims of probability theory.
Much like the narrator of "Assommons les pauvres!" who is infuriated by
do-gooders and their writings about the poor, the narrator of "La fausse
monnaie" has no patience with theories about poverty and calculations,
or how to get into heaven while economizing on the backs of the poverty-
stricken. Similarly, Baudelaire has little tolerance for letting the hungry
remain so in the name of some future satiation. Of the poor man in "La
fausse monnaie," the narrator says, "I know of nothing more disturbing
than the mute eloquence of those supplicating eyes, which contain at the
same time, for the sensitive man who can read in them, so much humility,
so much reproach" (323). They are like "that depth of complicated emotion
in the tearful eyes of a dog that is being whipped" (ibid.).[44]

Obviously, in "Assommons les pauvres!," in "La fausse monnaie," in
"Les yeux des pauvres," in the writings on the dandy, and in many other
texts, Baudelaire distances himself from the poor, frequently putting himself in the position of the bourgeois or the indifferent dandy and viewing

---

44. This passage is reminiscent of the eyes of the poor family in "Les yeux des pauvres."
Not all the poor have such pitiful eyes, however. In "Les sept vieillards," for example, a poor
man's gaze is described in poisonous (and anti-Semitic) terms: "One would have thought his
pupil soaked / In venom; his gaze sharpened the winter chill, / And his beard with long hair,
straight as a sword / Projected itself outward, like that of Judas" (*OC* 1:88).

them with a mixture of pity and contempt. In "La chambre double," however, Baudelaire himself is one of the poor; his tawdry surroundings belie his identification with the aristocracy. The two rooms may on one level be mirror images of each other because they are symmetrically opposed. But, as with a mirror, the two rooms do not touch, though each elicits the vision of the other. There is no tangible exchange between the rooms; no sensory contiguity. Baudelaire's vision here is like that of his own narrator in the poem "Les sept vieillards": "Exasperated, like a drunkard who sees double . . ., wounded by the mystery and the absurdity" (OC 1:88). He sees both rooms at the same time; they are both real, even if he wants to believe that only the first room is worth living for. There is no exchange between the two except, as I have repeated, that each reminds the poet of the necessary impossibility of the other. They cancel each other out, but as always in Baudelaire's double vision, they remain nonetheless.

Money, on the other hand, circulates; transaction is exchange and bartering. But Baudelaire's notions of the flow of commerce do not function for him in the money economy any more than there can be trade between the ideal and daily life. When he has money, he spends it. When he has no money, he rants against his fate. And he is constantly given to self-delusion. In July of 1861, for example, he writes to his mother that he will not tell her about his "literary dreams" because the letter would be too long. But of his "dreams of money"

> I will speak even less, because it would be even longer. What combinations moved around on paper! What ingenious manners of living, of paying my debts, my expenses, your 23,000 francs, and even of making a fortune! What dreams! And yet; life is running with a despairing rapidity. In these dreams of money, I even already find a symptom of old age.

Time, and the obsession with time, continue to be connected to money. Such relative self-awareness, however, is short-lived. In the next sentence, he writes with misplaced optimism:

> All of this will be resolved and debated between us. I think that two or three months after I have settled in, I will begin to give you money (almost all of it) with the goal of making you my cashier. But how much there will be needed! I already promised you this; I persist. But you will need the courage to hear a lot of details and a lot of daydreams."
> (Corr. 2:182–83).

His mother must have responded to this lengthy and worrisome letter with concern, because in the next letter he writes to her, two days later, he tries to reassure her: "I will certainly no longer try to write to you with details. It is too lengthy and I am not always understood. When I am with you, I will explain to you my *financial system*" (184). Baudelaire's underlining seems to give his "financial system" some sort of credibility and gravitas. No one was fooled—including his mother or, for that matter, Baudelaire himself. Money, too, functions in parallel universes for him: needing money, and spending it. The two do not associate with one another, any more than do the two rooms. Money for Baudelaire does not circulate; it does not engage an economy of trade and exchange. Rather, money for our poet is a system of desperate want and equally desperate spending. There is no trade or cyclical system here; spending and wanting are two separate economies of waste. This is his "financial system"—another means of seeing double.

Part of Baudelaire's obsession with clock time is, of course, the fear of mortality. As I noted earlier, Balzac's *peau de chagrin*, the shagreen, is in one sense quite close to Baudelaire. For the Balzac story literalizes the consequences of expenditure: each wish makes the shagreen shrink, and its disappearance suggests the end not only of wishes granted but of life as well. Money for Baudelaire is like an allegory of losing time to live; spending money is perhaps too close to using up one's time. This may be why Baudelaire remains willfully blind to the depletion of his assets when he spends, just as he tries to remain ignorant of the time passing even as he rails against its slowness. We will be looking more closely at time in Baudelaire in the next chapter. For now, however, my emphasis is on how the time-is-money equation results for Baudelaire in a panic-stricken flight from daily life. He does not want to see the results of expenditure— whether of money or time. The first room is *"spiritual"* (underlined by the poet) because it protects him from the effects of spending, and thus from time as well as money: "No! there are no more minutes, no more seconds! Time has disappeared; it is Eternity that reigns, an eternity of delights!" The constant exclamation points seem to be the poet's means of convincing himself of his own declaration: time has disappeared; he has attained immortality and bliss. Yes! the exclamation marks seem to be shouting, it's true! But of course as with any *recusatio*, there is too much protesting. The opposite, the horror of time, quickly asserts itself as the second room appears.

"My thesis," writes Adorno in *On Notes to Literature*, "is that the lyric work is always the subjective expression of a social antagonism."[45] There is certainly no lack of social antagonism in Baudelaire, as we have seen in "Assommons les pauvres!" or "A une passante," for example. But Baudelaire studies have too often been divided into two camps: the historical, material-culture camp on the one hand, and the more philosophical, hermeneutic camp on the other. "La chambre double" is one of many examples demonstrating that neither camp will suffice. The poem is clearly about social questions and problems, poverty being the most salient. But in the poem's creation of two worlds, and the fear of debt and mortality, "La chambre double" is also about theology—Baudelaire's variant of it. If, as I have been arguing, there is no exchange in Baudelaire's "financial system" and monetary concepts, and if there is equally no contiguity between the worlds of the two rooms and no circulation between them either, there is one area with respect to which the exchange, bartering, and trade that is money economy does exist for Baudelaire, and that is the Last Judgment.

Baudelaire has nothing but contempt for those who would try to buy their way into heaven. The man in "La fausse monnaie," it will be recalled, wants to win 40 *sols* and "gain paradise economically." To gain paradise economically means to spend less than it seems—to have your cake and eat it too. The man also wants to appear charitable (for free) and win God's heart with (fake) alms. Note, however, that even as Baudelaire disdains such hypocrisy, he does not question the consequences of expenditure in this (Christian) case: if you do the right thing, you may well enter heaven (assuming there is a heaven, which in Baudelaire is open to question even as it is presumed—another double vision). In other words, religion is the only domain where the gift (charity) circulates; where expenditure has consequences; where paying out does not result in dissipation and depletion but, rather, in good marks that may lead to heaven. And this is true for Baudelaire even when people are hypocrites, like the man in "La fausse monnaie," and even if it turns out that there is no heaven, only hell—a frequent Baudelairean perspective. In this precise area of the Christian's contract with God, Baudelaire does understand circulation between realms, the consequences of expenditure, the hoarding of assets, the accumulation of credit for the future, trade, bartering, and exchange. Even when it is all done for the wrong reasons—like the "low-life" who prays, "Lord, make my next transaction a success!"—there is still the matter of the Last Judg-

45. Theodor Adorno, *On Notes to Literature*, ed. Rolf Tiedemann, trans. Shierry Weber Nicholsen, p.45.

ment, a sort of final bookkeeping that cannot be evaded. It is a matter that never leaves the Baudelaire corpus.

Take, for example, the poem "La rançon" (1851). Man, the poem tells us allegorically, has to pay his ransom with two fields that are full of porous rocks. He must plow this volcanic soil "with the iron of reason." (We are already in trouble, and beginning to think we are in some proto-Kafka tale.) For man to obtain the smallest rose from these fields, he must water them constantly with "tears salted by his gray brow." The two fields are "Art" and "Love." Man must labor thus "To make the judge favorable, / When the terrible day of / Stern justice will appear." Indeed, man will have to show barns full of harvest, and flowers "Whose shapes and colors / Will win the votes of the Angels" (OC 1:173). It will clearly be impossible to get enough votes for entering heaven. And if Jesus does not laugh, Satan certainly does: "Recognize Satan by his triumphant laugh," writes Baudelaire in a later poem, "L'imprévu" (1863?). Jesus's comment about a camel getting through the eye of a needle more easily than a rich man can enter the gates of heaven is taken up by Satan more bluntly in this poem. Satan asks the dying man who is going to hell whether he thinks "it is natural to receive two prizes: to go to heaven and to be rich" (OC 1:172). But as far as Baudelaire is concerned, the chances are very slim for either, including the former even if one is poor. Indeed, "La corde," despite its ambiguity toward the boy's mother, shows if nothing else that the poor are not blessed and that few of them, if any, will enter the kingdom of heaven. The fields of "Art and Love" are too hard to plow, and the ransom is too high.

In the autobiographical poem "La voix" (1861), Baudelaire writes that even when he was a baby, "two voices spoke to me." One, insidious but firm, tells him, "The Earth is a cake full of sweetness; / I can (and your pleasure will then be without end!) / Give you an appetite of equal size." The other voice says, "Come! Oh come travel in dreams, / Beyond the possible, beyond the known!" The poet chooses the second voice, and claims that his "wound and fate" date from that time. In "La voix" there are not only two voices; there are also, as in "La chambre double," two worlds, as if the dual audial mirrored the dual visual, despite the singular of the titles in both cases (la chambre, la voix). The poet is explicit about seeing two realities at the same time: "Behind the décors / Of immense existence, to the blackest of abysses, / I distinctly see remarkable worlds." In an image reminiscent of "L'albatros," he adds that "victim of my ecstatic clairvoyance, / I drag along serpents that bite at my shoes." The reminder of Satan remains, yet in one line of the poem he declares that, like the prophets,

"I love the desert and the sea so dearly." The poem closes with another albatross-like image: "I very often take facts for lies, / and with my eyes on heaven, I fall into holes." The "Voice" consoles him: "Keep your dreams; / Sages don't have any as beautiful as those of the insane" (OC 1:170). With his eyes on heaven and his feet in holes, he projects once again the final image from "Laquelle est la vraie?"

THE OTHER SIDE OF THE COIN

Certainly Baudelaire's schizophrenic vision, his refusal to adapt to the money economy, his insistence that both rooms, both worlds, are there, irreparably (to use one of his favorite words) clashing and canceling each other out, can be attributed to his own psychological state. His attempts to force his mother to show love are constantly clothed in supplications (and/ or demands) for money. His behavior that can only be seen as a refusal to "understand" expenditure and its consequences, along with his constant debt and recourse to the ever severe but patient Ancelle, are no doubt attempts to remain childlike and thus attended to—that, at least, is the hope. Along with such psychological symptoms, we need to add Baudelaire's obsession with mortality, Satan, hell, the Last Judgment, and the ever present original sin. These are concepts that give Baudelaire no difficulty in understanding the infamous reversibility, as well as circulation, pay back, debt, credit, and assets. But yet another element needs to be added to the list: what Emile Durkheim, in his study on suicide, calls a disturbance in the collective order.[46] Baudelaire is as much the victim of his time, as we have noted throughout this study, as he is of his own demons (literally, at times). The destruction of the old Paris and the building of the new actualize the two worlds, and double vision, to which he is prey.

And money, it must be said, is as unstable as Paris itself in nineteenth-century France; for money too, is under construction during the first half of the century. The law of 7–17 germinal had given the country a new and simplified money system, the franc. But it took an inordinately long time to produce the new money, and the money of the ancien régime (écus and livres) was finally withdrawn only in 1829. Spang tells us:

46. Emile Durkheim, *Suicide: A Study in Sociology*, trans. George Simpson and John A. Spaulding (New York and London: The Free Press, 1951), 246. For a good examination of Durkheim on suicide, see S. Romi Muhkerjee, "On Violence as the Negativity of the Durkheimian: Between Anomie, Effervescence, and Sacrifice," in *Durkheim and Violence*, ed. S. Romi Mukherjee (London: Blackwell, 2010), 10–17.

Coins issued under Louis XV and Louis XVI remained legal tender as
did those produced under the Republic and Empire. These regimes obviously all had different iconographies, but they also had distinct monetary theories (about the appropriate silver-to-gold ratio, for instance)
and, crucially, different measurements. This meant that, for over fifty
years, confrontation between a decimalized (base-10) monetary *system*
and duodecimal (base-12) *money* was a way of life. ("Taking the Old
Regime Out of Circulation," ms. 12)

Moreover, as Spang points out, old coins frequently were needed to make
up small differences with the new ones; the different systems did not cor-
relate. The law of 1845 was intended to demonetize (the older currency)
and to produce perfected small change. But with the Banque de France is-
suing a five-hundred-franc bill as its smallest note, only the wealthy could
afford state-issued paper. Spang adds that such money was not fungible
in practice but that, rather, physical money-objects marked social distinction much more than they facilitated its erasure (ms. 15). The less well-off,
in other words, carried heavy copper coins (frequently made from melted-
down church bells) of various provenances, while the wealthy had bills of
larger value, or gold and silver of less bulk and weight. A bulging pocket of
heavy change could paradoxically indicate small means.

This situation gives a different emphasis to the opening of "La fausse
monnaie." In the first paragraph of the prose poem, the narrator and his
friend have just left the tobacconist; the narrator notices his friend making "a careful triage of his change." It is an impressively organized system: "he slipped little gold coins into the left pocket of his vest; into the
right, little silver coins; into the left pocket of his pants, a pile of big *sols*,
and finally, into the right, a silver two-franc coin that he had examined
particularly" (*OC* 1:323). The latter is the counterfeit coin. Given the different currencies that circulated, it is no wonder that counterfeiting was
ubiquitous. In any case, the friend's triage also shows the varying forms
of money: the gold coins of the ancien régime; silver that may have been
Napoleonic; old copper coins probably dating from the first Republic, and
the fairly new franc.

The poem is from 1864, but another version of this story can be found
at the end of "L'école païenne"(1852). There, a more idealistic Baudelaire
writes that he has heard of a man who received a counterfeit coin and said,
"I will keep it for a poor man." This man too, like the friend in "La fausse
monnaie," enjoyed "stealing from the poor man and profiting at the same
time from the benefits of a charitable reputation." These things are not

puerilities, writes the narrator. "What the mouth gets used to saying, the heart gets used to believing" (*OC* 2:49). Literature, he concludes, "must bathe its strengths in a better atmosphere." But "La fausse monnaie" is concerned less with the heart's hardening and more (once again) with evil and its inevitability. What the later poem adds, however, is also the proliferation of currencies and coins in Baudelaire's Paris. These different coinages, with their disparate values and inscriptions (various kings, Napoleon, the Republic, and the counterfeit coin), reinforce the noncontiguous worlds of Baudelaire's experience, just as the coins themselves are put into the friend's various pockets, each kind safely removed from the others. The confused money system also gives the poet an excuse for remaining steadfast in his incomprehension of money. No wonder, one might say, that he had his own "financial system"! "Laquelle est la vraie?" is as much a question about the coins in Baudelaire's Paris as it is about the two Bénédictas, or the two rooms. The instability of money in France well into the 1850s, the differing values of each currency, make the question of counterfeit much greater and more complicated than merely a given fake coin.

All of this adds to the unstable environment that is Paris for Baudelaire. "La fausse monnaie" is part of *Le spleen de Paris*," which is dedicated to the poet's friend Arsène Houssaye. In his dedication, Baudelaire says that with these prose poems, he was dreaming, along with all other poets of the day, of "the miracle of a poetic prose; musical, with neither rhythm nor rhyme; supple and uneven enough to adapt itself to the lyrical movements of the soul, to the undulations of reverie, to the jolts of consciousness" (*OC* 1:276).[47] Once again, there are the two planes, or worlds: the soft undulations of the reverie and the joltings of consciousness; or the elegant dandy and the poet with the jerky gait; or the first room of somnambulant peace and the sudden pounding, like a blow to the stomach, on the door of the second room. Both the undulation and the jolting serve to make the prose poem genre—of which "La chambre double" is like a manifesto—and the concretization of the necessary and simultaneous presence of incompatible realms. The ideal of the prose poem, writes Baudelaire in the same dedication, is born mainly "of the frequentation of huge cities, of the crossing of their innumerable connections" (ibid.). The city is this crossing of connections that continue in their trajectory, like the *passante*. The city is a series of counterfeit realms; but the ideal realm

47. Derrida sees "La fausse monnaie" as Poe's "Purloined Letter." Like the letter, "La fausse monnaie" for Derrida is a return to the point of departure, a closing of the circle, which, at the same time, forbids precisely such a closing through an expropriation or an "exappropriation" that obstructs circulation. *Donner le temps*, 191.

is also a false one in the sense that the poet knows, even as he rails to the contrary, that the other, cruel world is always looming. "Do you love gold?" asks the narrator of "L'étranger," also in *Le spleen de Paris*. "I hate it as you hate God," answers the stranger (*OC* 1:277). "So what do you love then, extraordinary stranger?" asks the narrator. "I love the clouds," is the answer, "the clouds that pass . . . over there . . . over there . . . the marvelous clouds." The world of the ideal is that of the three suspension points, the punctuation straining to represent the flight of reverie and its undulations with the clouds. "La soupe et les nuages" bears the same message.

Worlds do not, any more than money, circulate or exchange with one another in Baudelaire. They intersect at times, and provide memories of each other; but movement ends there. Baudelaire's is not an economy of bartering or trade. His vision is double because neither eye is sublated, synthesized, or compromised by, the other. The poet does not understand money; this we have seen. But he also does not understand the varying values that circulate around him: give to the poor, hate the poor; buy things, hate those who buy things; work to be successful, hate those who work to be useful; believe in the progress of art, hate the notion of social progress; believe only in hell and Satan, pray to God every night. And so on. These are contradictions, as countless critics have noted. But we cannot stop (and have not stopped) here. These are double visions that torment the poet—not only because they are antinomies, and thus cancel each other out, but also because he can never decide if he is in the first room, having a nightmare about the second, or in the second room, dreaming of the first. The city that engulfs him, with its endless changes and destabilizing economies, is the echo of Baudelaire's personal dilemma of desire: what, ultimately, to want, and for whom or for what purpose? My point here is not to rehearse Benjamin's seminal depiction of modernity or, even less, to psychoanalyze Baudelaire. Rather, it is to emphasize that Baudelaire has no capacity to *understand* what he sees, and is thus caught inside twin perspectives.

Money is integral to this duality. And if, as I am arguing, Baudelaire does not understand what he sees, it is probably because he is more honest than most in the fairly chaotic times in which he lives. Within the ruins of the past and the rubble of the future, as in "Le Cygne," Baudelaire cannot cease obsessing about both, can give neither up. There is, in this sense, no present for him: it is all memory or the anxiety of anticipation. Benjamin is brilliant in his depiction of Baudelaire as the poet of modernity, the one who writes the city. But Baudelaire himself sees the old world and the hints of the new; what he does not see is a cohesive image of the present that would allow him to describe modernity, let alone reside in it clear-sightedly. He does not describe so much as record the dead past that still shimmers around him, and the increasingly obvious future that awaits him. With both of these visions constantly before him, his strabismus inhibits clarity of vision. His melancholia is a mourning for a past he will not relinquish, but also a fear of a future that he sees as toxic. Both are curiously experienced as memory: memory of the lost past, of course; but also memory of an image of a void—the future he has conjured up and constantly invokes.

Memory brings us to time—which is money. And time is the next problem to consider.

Appendix

La chambre double

Une chambre qui ressemble à une rêverie, un chambre véritablement *spirituelle*, où l'atmosphère stagnante est légèrement teintée de rose et de bleu.

L'âme y prend un bain de paresse, aromatisé par le regret et le désir.— C'est quelque chose de crépusculaire, de bleuâtre et de rosâtre; un rêve de volupté pendant une éclipse.

Les meubles ont des formes allongées, prostrées, alanguies. Les meubles ont l'air de rêver; on les dirait doués d'une vie somnambulique, comme le végétal et le minéral. Les étoffes parlent une langue muette, comme les fleurs, comme les ciels, comme les soleils couchants.

Sur les murs nulle abomination artistique. Relativement au rêve pur, à l'impression non analysée, l'art défini, l'art positif est un blasphème. Ici, tout a la suffisante clarté et la délicieuse obscurité de l'harmonie.

Une senteur infinitésimale du choix le plus exquis, à laquelle se mêle une très légère humidité, nage dans cette atmosphère, où l'esprit sommeillant est bercé par des sensations de serre chaude.

La mousseline pleut abondamment devant les fenêtres et devant le lit; elle s'épanche en cascades neigeuses. Sur ce lit est couchée l'Idole, la souveraine des rêves. Mais comment est-elle ici? Qui l'a amenée? quel pouvoir magique l'a installée sur ce trône de rêverie et de volupté? Qu'importe? la voilà! je la reconnais.

Voilà bien ces yeux dont la flamme traverse le crépuscule; ces subtiles et terribles *mirettes*, que je reconnais à leur effrayante malice! Elles attirent, elles subjuguent, elles dévorent le regard de l'imprudent qui les contemple. Je les ai souvent étudiées, ces étoiles noires qui commandent la curiosité et l'admiration.

À quel démon bienveillant dois-je d'être ainsi entouré de mystère, de silence, de paix et de parfums? Ô béatitude! ce que nous nommons géné-ralement la vie, même dans son expansion la plus heureuse, n'a rien de commun avec cette vie suprême dont j'ai maintenant connaissance et que je savoure minute par minute, seconde par seconde!

Non! il n'est plus de minutes, il n'est plus de secondes! Le temps a dis-paru; c'est l'Éternité qui règne, une éternité de délices!

Mais un coup terrible, lourd, a retenti à la porte, et, comme dans les rêves infernaux, il m'a semblé que je recevais un coup de pioche dans l'estomac.

Et puis un Spectre est entré. C'est un huissier qui vient me torturer au nom de la loi; une infâme concubine qui vient crier misère et ajouter les trivialités de sa vie aux douleurs de la mienne; ou bien le saute-ruisseau d'un directeur de journal qui réclame la suite du manuscrit.

La chambre paradisiaque, l'idole, la souveraine des rêves, la *Sylphide*, comme disait le grand René, toute cette magie a disparu au coup brutal frappé par le Spectre.

Horreur! je me souviens! je me souviens! Oui! ce taudis, ce séjour de l'éternel ennui, est bien le mien. Voici les meubles sots, poudreux, écornés; la cheminée sans flamme et sans braise, souillée de crachats; les tristes fenêtres où la pluie a tracé des sillons dans la poussière; les manuscrits, ra-turés ou incomplets; l'almanach où le crayon a marqué les dates sinistres!

Et ce parfum d'un autre monde, dont je m'enivrais avec une sensibilité perfectionnée, hélas! il est remplacé par une fétide odeur de tabac mêlée à je ne sais quelle nauséabonde moisissure. On respire ici maintenant le ranci de la désolation.

Dans ce monde étroit, mais si plein de dégoût, un seul objet connu me sourit: la fiole de laudanum; une vieille et terrible amie; comme toutes les amies, hélas! féconde en caresses et en traîtrises.

Oh! oui! le Temps a reparu; le Temps règne en souverain maintenant; et avec le hideux vieillard est revenu tout son démoniaque cortège de Sou-venirs, de Regrets, de Spasmes, de Peurs, d'Angoisses, de Cauchemars, de Colères et de Névroses.

Je vous assure que les secondes maintenant sont fortement et solennel-lement accentuées, et chacune en jaillissant de la pendule dit:—"Je suis la Vie, l'insupportable, l'implacable Vie!"

Il n'y a qu'une Seconde dans la vie humaine qui ait mission d'annoncer une bonne nouvelle, la *bonne nouvelle* qui cause à chacun une inexplicable peur.

Oui! le Temps règne; il a repris sa brutale dictature. Et il me pousse, comme si j'étais un bœuf, avec son double aiguillon.— "Et hue donc! bourrique! Sue donc, esclave! Vis donc, damné!"

CHAPTER FOUR

Time (Harmonie du soir)

But he [man] also wonders about himself, that he cannot learn to forget, but hangs on the past: however far or fast he runs, that chain runs with him. It is a matter for wonder: the moment that is here and gone, that was nothing before and nothing after, returns like a specter to trouble the quiet of a later moment. A leaf is continually dropping out of the volume of time and fluttering away—and suddenly it flutters back into the man's lap. Then he says, "I remember . . . ," and envies the beast that forgets at once and sees every moment really die, sink into night and mist, extinguished forever.
—Nietzsche, *The Use and Abuse of History*

The past, while keeping the phantom's sting, will once again take up the light and movement of life, and make itself present.
—Baudelaire, "Le peintre de la vie moderne"

GOD, GRAVES, AND SCHOLARS

Baudelaire's grave in the Montparnasse cemetery is notoriously difficult to find, partly because the cemetery's map is less than helpful. But the more obvious reason is that the grave is small and closely surrounded by many others. Moreover, the name on the unassuming tombstone, in large letters, is not Baudelaire but Aupick. There follow ten lines describing the general's numerous honors and titles. Closer to the bottom of the tombstone is the name Caroline Archenbaut Defayes (the widow Aupick), Baudelaire's mother. Her name is followed by seven lines describing her various nomenclatures and kinships. Between these two Aupicks, visually sandwiched in, appears the name Charles Baudelaire. He gets two lines. It is worth reproducing the odd visual result:

JACQUES **AUPICK**
GÉNÉRAL DE DIVISION, SÉNATEUR,
ANCIEN AMBASSADEUR
À CONSTANTINOPLE ET À MADRID.
MEMBRE DU CONSEIL GÉNÉRAL
DU DÉPt DU NORD. GRAND OFFICIER
DE L'ORDRE IMPÉRIAL DE LA LÉGION
D'HONNEUR. DÉCORÉ DE PLUSIEURS
ORDRES ÉTRANGERS.
DÉCÉDÉ LE 27 AVRIL 1857
À L'ÂGE DE 68 ANS

CHARLES **BAUDELAIRE**
SON BEAU FILS. DÉCÉDÉ À PARIS
À L'ÂGE DE 46 ANS, LE 31 AOÛT 1867

CAROLINE **ARCHENBAUT DEFAYES**
VEUVE EN PREMIÈRES NOCES DE
Mr JOSEPH FRANÇOIS **BAUDELAIRE**
EN SECONDES NOCES
DE Mr LE GÉNÉRAL **AUPICK**
ET MÈRE DE CHARLES **BAUDELAIRE**
DÉCÉDÉE À HONFLEUR (CALVADOS)
LE 16 AOÛT 1871 ÂGÉE DE 77 ANS
PRIEZ POUR EUX

According to the logic of the tombstone, Baudelaire's two accomplishments were that he was the general's stepson and that, as such, he died. Madame Aupick's life is described (unsurprisingly for a woman in the period) by her marital history and by the fact that she was Baudelaire's mother—the latter statement suggesting that, at her death four years after that of her son, his reputation had increased to the extent that such a remark was worth incising into the stone. Whereas the general is identified not by marital or filial kinship but by his professional achievements, Baudelaire is relegated to the feminized position of parentage. The general looms over him on the tombstone, much as he did in life. Baudelaire is, very simply, "his stepson."

There was sufficient outrage (among the literati) at this paltry grave for the poet that in 1892 a committee was formed to raise money for a proper monument to Baudelaire's memory. The initiator of the project was Léon Duchamp, director of the journal *La plume*. The committee comprised an impressive list of forty-two names, including Mallarmé and Leconte de Lisle. The *querelle de la statue* that ensued is thoroughly documented.[1] The projected monument was to be a *monument funéraire*—to be erected not in a public place but in the cemetery at Montparnasse where Baudelaire was buried. But the committee also suggested the Jardin du Luxembourg, a venue that Rodin, who had agreed to produce the work, wanted as well. The sculptor's other choice was the Trocadéro. Ten years of controversy followed, with Rodin increasingly frustrated by the lack of funding. The committee ended up deciding to do both: a bust of the poet, which would at some future point be placed in the Jardin du Luxembourg (a project that was finally realized some fifty years later, in 1941, and not by Rodin but by the artist Pierre Fix-Masseau), and a cenotaph in the Montparnasse cemetery. The committee was fortunate, under the circumstances, in having a young, unknown sculptor propose that his (already accomplished) work be used for the cemetery.

José de Charmoy was only twenty-two years old when he offered his statue to the committee. Obsessed with the poet's writings, the sculptor had been working on a statue with no apparent regard for its ultimate fate. The committee, unable to raise sufficient funds for Rodin, gratefully accepted the monument, which today sits against one of the walls of the Montparnasse cemetery, far from the actual grave of the poet (thus far from that of his mother and stepfather). Charmoy's cenotaph, which is frequently confused with the grave, is quite arresting. It depicts Baudelaire lying down, wrapped in cloth like an Egyptian mummy. A skeletal vampire or bat extends its wings just above him. Over the whole is a "Thinker,"

---

1. Ferdinand Brunetière, the literary critic for the *Revue des deux mondes*, particularly disliked Baudelaire. As early as 1887, he published a thoroughly negative article in the *Revue*, and then again in 1889, calling the poet's work "charlatanism." Brunetière argued that Baudelaire was immoral and tasteless. He professed to have no interest in the poet's private life, and accused him of "having willfully corrupted the very notion of art." See *La querelle de la statue de Baudelaire: août-décembre 1892*, ed. A. Guyaux (Paris: Presses Universitaires-Sorbonne, 2007), 11–12. Mallarmé, usually quite passive, was so outraged by the *querelle* and by Brunetière in particular, that he managed to get several foreign poets to contribute, including Swinburne. Brunetière's attacks ultimately inspired the next generation to a strong pro-Baudelaire sentiment (*La querelle*, 632).

a figure that has been variously described as a dreamer, the genius of evil, an enigmatic demon, or Baudelaire himself, contemplating his own dead body.

There is something oddly (and depressingly) appropriate about all of this—Baudelaire buried in a relatively obscure grave, under a tombstone privileging a name not his own, and described as the stepson of a man he detested. His identity is displaced, as if his worst anxieties about his persona (for want of a better term) were etched onto the stone like a nightmare come true—he can barely be discerned between the general's various accomplishments and his mother's marriages. One thinks of Keats's bitter insistence on having a single line inscribed on his tombstone: "Here lies One Whose Name was writ in Water." The monument to Baudelaire, meanwhile, striking though it is, is like an empty tomb—the poet lies elsewhere. The cenotaph, both in its depiction of the two odd gazes (that of the prone, dead poet and that of the "Thinker" with his malicious stare), and in its status as empty tomb, seems to intensify the sense that the poet is metonymically elided, deported, endlessly displaced, like so many Lacanian signifiers.

The two sites in the Montparnasse cemetery, therefore, seem equally dislocated from the poet, deterritorializing his very identity—both literary and corporeal. While the actual grave crushes him between the two major, if highly problematic figures in his life—his hated stepfather and his adored (and at times greatly resented) mother—the cenotaph iconizes his physical body as bound and constrained in death as he felt himself to be in life. If one imagines the "Thinker," who leans pensively (if creepily) above the mummified Baudelaire, to be Baudelaire himself contemplating his own corpse, the uncanniness is increased. Baudelaire, in such a reading, is doubled as a straitjacketed body contemplated evilly by his own, other self. Such a splitting off of the self, which the French call *dédoublement*, is as if a concretization of the double vision we have been considering: the dead Baudelaire, eyes closed, inwardly considering his paralysis in death, and the evil demon that suggests another Baudelaire looking with a certain satisfaction at the mortality and immobility that always haunted him. The bound Baudelaire is like the wounded man in his poem "La cloche fêlée," who lies "forgotten / On the shores of a lake of blood . . . dying, without moving, with immense effort (*OC* 1:72).

The mummified (and motionless) Baudelaire and the one who contemplates him from the perspective of a certain distance are not only a type of iconized double vision. They are also like the two kinds of time Baudelaire continually invokes: now time and what Bergson calls *la durée*.

The "Thinker" has the perspective and horizon of indivisible time, while the mummified and inward-gazing Baudelaire is the victim of his own, mortal time: the now of death has arrived and is materially emblematized as mummification. One has the impression that if the prone Baudelaire opened his eyes, they would look straight into those of the demon, and both figures would vanish in a flash of lightening.[2] For the confrontation of two different spaces of time could only produce a sort of black hole of consciousness.

For Baudelaire, like Pascal, has two infinites, though they are very different from those of the philosopher.[3] Baudelaire's two infinites are articulated in his article on the essence of laughter. There he writes that man possesses an "infinite grandeur" and "an infinite misery." It is the "perpetual shock" of these two infinites that creates laughter. The man who has fallen does not laugh at his own fall unless he is a philosopher—that is, adds Baudelaire eerily, as if describing his future cenotaph, "a man who has acquired, by habit, the strength rapidly to double himself [*se dédoubler*], and to view, like a disinterested spectator, the phenomena of his ego [*moi*]" (*OC* 2:532). Charmoy may well have had this passage in mind when he sculpted his monument to the poet.

Charmoy's intentions aside, it is the reading of Baudelaire's texts that inspires such considerations in viewing the cenotaph. The present for Baudelaire can only be experienced as the fleeing of time (and thus the loss of the past) or as the menace of the future (and thus the inevitable void). In other words, the present cannot *be* at all, since it produces either regret or foreboding, or both—indeed, the present seems to exist solely for the purpose of such contemplation. In "L'horloge," for example, the clock speaks in the present and the future. "*Remember!*" it says (in English), its "finger" wagging menacingly, and thus invokes a bleak future: "The vibrating

2. Alfred d'Aulnay, an acquaintance of Baudelaire's who went to view the body as it lay in the Duval nursing home (rue du Dôme) claimed that the poet's eyes had not been closed: "When they lifted the sheet that covered his face, I saw his great questioning eyes turned toward me. He had kept in death, as in illness, that same strange, searching look, the look of a man who lives in a world of fantasy, and is constantly pursued by a vision." The comment is from "La mort de Baudelaire," an article by d'Aulnay that appeared in *Le Figaro* four days after the poet's death (September 3, 1867). Most Baudelaire biographers discount this story, including Joanna Richardson, who regards the d'Aulnay account as "increasingly suspect and bewildering." Richardson, *Baudelaire* (New York: St. Martin's Press, 1994), 564 n. 8. Nevertheless, the idea of Baudelaire as burdened by a "strange, searching look" in life as well as death, and constantly "pursued by a vision," is oddly close to Charmoy's cenotaph and the sculptor's own vision of Baudelaire.

3. Another passage also speaks of two "forms of eternity"—reward and punishment, which Baudelaire aligns with the moral world (*OC* 1:403).

Pains in your heart full of fear / Will soon plant themselves as in a target"
(*OC* 1:81).[4] The term "vibrating" (*vibrantes*) also appears in the first line
of "Harmonie du soir" and is central to that poem as well as to others, as
Georges Poulet has shown. Poulet reads vibration in Baudelaire as inspir-
ing "an immediate happiness, a feeling of physical ecstasy."[5] The feeling
does not last, needless to say.

Poulet also articulates the lack of "in-between-ness" in Baudelairean
time, but a bit differently from what I see as the Januslike aspect of a present that looks forward and backward at the same time. "It is as if," writes
Poulet, "sensations had the ability to stretch their vibrations, not only in
the direction of the future, but of the past. Or, more precisely, as if the
present were both the point of departure of a movement opened out toward the future, and the point of arrival of a different and yet identical
movement" (403). I would change only one phrase here. The present in
Baudelaire is indeed an ominous point of departure toward the future (and
the void that it promises); but rather than being the "point of arrival," the
present is simply the constant recognition of the loss of the past. Vibration
is a double move of this kind (as are the two hands of the clock), which is
why the present is not clearly in focus here; it is moving in two directions
at once, backward and forward. The present, then, is like the digit zero
in Baudelaire: a placeholder that allows past and future sequences to be
delineated. Indeed, like zero, the present in Baudelaire is not identical to
itself; it serves to make past and future discernible. "*Remember*," says the
poem, "that Time is an avid player / Who wins without cheating, every
time! It is the law." Even as Time says "*Remember*," thus pushing the narrator toward the past, even as repenting itself (another move to the past) is
"the last inn," the hour will come when "everything will say to you: Die,
old coward! It is too late!" The resonances of "L'horloge" with "La chambre double" are clear. That poem too ends with Time reigning supreme,
having "taken back its brutal dictatorship." And that poem too ends with
imperatives, it will be recalled: "Go ahead and live, damned one!" Finally,
that poem too is filled with exclamation marks as if to underline the in-

4. Shortly after writing "L'horloge," Baudelaire writes to Jules Barbey d'Aurevilly citing
parts of the poem, including "Remember, Esto memor! *My metal throat speaks all languages.*"
Baudelaire asks d'Aurevilly to write a favorable review of his work: "When I desire something,
I am like a clock.—I have the feeling that my tick-tock speaks all languages" (*Corr.* 2:61).
Interesting that Baudelaire humorously refers to this poem, which, as we shall be considering later, is anything but funny. One may assume that the poet, somewhat embarrassed to be
asking for a favor, hides behind an irony that serves as well to "remember" his verses to the
critic.

5. Georges Poulet, *Les métamorphoses du cercle* (Paris: Plon, 1961), 397.

evitability of man's plight. As Poulet points out, the present exists only to be evaporated: "Vaporous Pleasure will flee toward the horizon," we read in the first stanza of "L'horloge." Every instant serves only "to devour another one of your pieces of delight." For the void, writes the poet, is "always thirsty."

"Harmonie du soir," the poem that will be the fulcrum of this chapter, begins with the announcement of *two* (or more) times: "Voici venir les temps . . ." Normally, one would imagine that the line would read: "Here comes the time when, vibrating on its stalk, every flower evaporates like a censer." But "time" is in the plural, adding a certain vertigo, a loss of balance, to the already vertiginous poem. The plural of time adds to the quivering of the stalks (as does the preponderance of *v*'s in the poem), as if the vibrations themselves created a blurring of vision, a doubling of time, and a greater profusion of flowers. "Here" is a deixis, but in this case, it modifies the abstract notion of times ("here come the times"). As such, "here" is at least a doubled referential; it is thus falsely deictic. And yet a double "here" demonstrates precisely the double vision that is Baudelaire's. Moreover, the plural of times make the (false) deictic "here" all the more confusing. The apparent immediacy or demonstrative aspect of "here" is quickly fogged over by the repetitions and dizzying swirling that the poem achieves. We have, then, two different kinds of time—not the future and the past, but another aspect of time's doubled valences, two constant times: eternal, liberating time on the one hand, and crushing, eked-out time—the time of endless minutes striking their endless hours—on the other. "Harmonie du soir" is like a textual preparation for the Charmoy cenotaph. The sculpture suggests at once the immediacy of the demon's gaze, looking down with cruel satisfaction at the mummified corpse of the poet, and the poet himself, contemplating a way of enduring the slow passage of time by directing his splenetic gaze inward. So "Harmonie du soir" suggests immediate time and a more continual time: the "voici" of the flowers, as well as memory and the ever-looming void: "le néant vaste et noir."

But these two times do not quite map onto Bergson's scientific (clock) time and *durée*. It is true that, as Levinas points out, Bergson's *durée* is experienced "by a descent into the self." Every instant is there, he continues; "nothing is definitive because each instant remakes the past."[6] The mummified Baudelaire statue is then like an iconic metaphor for such an inward-turned gaze. But the "Thinker" is not clock time; rather, he looms

6. Emmanuel Levinas, *Dieu, la mort et le temps* (Paris: Grasset, 1993), 65.

like the memory of evil and like a monumentalized, self-satisfied triumph of mortality. The combination of these two cenotaphic figures is a kind of ontological *mise en abyme*: the bodiless monument hypostatizes the void (*le gouffre*) that haunted Baudelaire. In the poem "Le goût du néant," in a line that is brought to memory by Charmoy's Baudelaire-as-mummy, we read: "And Time engulfs me minute by minute, / Like an immense snow [engulfing] a stiff corpse" (*OC* 1:76).

I noted earlier that Baudelaire has his two infinites, like Pascal. Another affinity they share has to do with the *gouffre*. In the first line of the sonnet of the same name, Baudelaire writes, "Pascal had his void [*gouffre*], moving with him" (*OC* 1:142). Indeed, as Pichois points out, Sainte-Beuve had written about the philosopher's terrors, noting that Pascal was apparently haunted by the void, constantly seeing it on his left side.[7] He always had a chair placed to his left to "reassure him"—hence, one imagines, a void "moving with him." Baudelaire shares such anxiety, but his void is not limited to the left. Indeed, he sees it everywhere: "Alas! Everything is abyss," he writes in "Le gouffre."[8] The sonnet sees the void in all directions: "Above, below, everywhere, the depth, the river bank, / The silence, the hideous and captivating space." In a prose poem, "La solitude," Baudelaire echoes Pascal's famous remark about man's inability to stay at rest in a room: "'Almost all of our miseries come from the fact that we did not know how to stay in our room,' says another sage, Pascal, I think" (*OC* 1:314). He thinks correctly: "I have discovered," wrote Pascal famously, "that all of the unhappiness of man comes from one thing, which is that he does not know how to be at rest, in a room."[9] The answer, according to Pascal, is diversion, which allows man some respite. Without it, writes the philosopher in terms that sound a great deal like our poet, ennui results, confronting man with his "nothingness [*néant*], his abandonment, his insufficiency, his dependence, his impotence, his void [*vide*]." Ennui provokes "blackness, sadness, chagrin, spleen, despair" (*Pensées*, 108). Baudelaire, in other words, is not alone in being the philosopher of en-

7. Baudelaire's generation was quite taken with Pascal. Sainte-Beuve's *Port Royal* was published from 1840 to 1859 in three volumes; Victor Cousin's *Discours sur les passions de l'amour* appeared the following year; and in 1844, A. P. Faugère produced his (slightly inaccurate) Princeps edition of Pascal's work.

8. Much has been written on Baudelaire's fear of the void, most prominently by Benjamin Fondane, *Baudelaire et l'expérience du gouffre* (Paris: Seghers, 1947). On Baudelaire and Pascal, see in particular Jean Pommier, *Dans les chemins de Baudelaire* (Paris: Corti, 1945). See also Maurice Chapelan, "Baudelaire et Pascal," in *Revue de France* 1 (November 1933).

9. *Pensées de Pascal*, ed. Ch.-M. des Granges (Paris: Garnier, 1964), 109.

nui, spleen, and the fear of the abyss. "Ah! Never to leave Numbers and
Beings," ends "Le gouffre," in a line that has puzzled scholars. And yet
it is as if clock time, weighty and homogenous though it may be with its
(crushing) units of minutes and hours, is preferable to sleep, which the
poet dreads "as one fears the great hole / Full of vague horror, going who
knows where; / I see only infinity from all the windows" (OC 1:143). The
cenotaph, empty of a body, with the statue of a prone Baudelaire wrapped
in the winding sheet—as if death had always paralyzed him with the mere
thought of its shrouding—stands like a monument to the poet's unceasing
fear of the void.

Critics have noted that the word *gouffre* appears fourteen times in
Les fleurs du mal alone. But the word is everywhere. At times Baudelaire
seems to suggest that art can trump the fear of the void. In "Une mort
héroïque," a prose poem about a great actor named Fancioulle, the narrator
contemplates the performance:

> Francioulle proved to me, in a decisive, irrefutable manner, that the
> intoxication of Art is more likely than any other to veil the terror of
> the void [*gouffre*]; that the genius can act at the edge of the tomb with a
> joy that prevents him from seeing the tomb, lost, as he is, in a paradise
> that excludes all notions of tomb or destruction. (OC 1:321)

If Poe is obsessed with the living dead (and particularly with the cata-
leptic, those taken for dead and buried alive), Baudelaire certainly seems
preoccupied with the grave. We have seen this before, in "Laquelle est la
vraie," among other works. But what is fascinating in this passage is that
it is a resounding *recusatio*: that is, though the capacity of art is to veil
the void and thus to "exclude all notions" of the tomb, the language here
does the opposite—it foregrounds, even as it declares, the tomb as hidden,
forgotten, excluded. The passage does this by repeating the word "tomb"
(*tombe*) three times in one phrase (a phrase, one might add, that is preceded by one ending in *gouffre*). Like a child repeating an obscenity by
insisting that it is a word that must never be said, this passage bludgeons
us with the tomb while assuring us that genius can overcome all thoughts
of it. Art, in other words, is helpless before the void. Instead of an antidote
to thoughts of mortality, art becomes a memento mori (*Remember! Souviens toi!*)—a reminder of mortality, the terrors of the void (*les terreurs
du gouffre*). The veil that art throws over the void, in other words, merely
emphasizes it.

The same logic applies to a monument. Its purpose, ostensibly, is to remind the living of a past greatness; to overcome time's erosion of the memory by erecting an imposing structure that will not permit oblivion. The same can be said of a text—it too can serve as a monument, or a tombstone of sorts with the "engravings" of other writers to commemorate their dead colleague. Indeed, there was such a volume in honor of Baudelaire. In 1895, *Le tombeau de Charles Baudelaire* was published by La Plume whose director, Léon Deschamps, had formed the committee to raise funds for a statue of Baudelaire. Twenty-nine poets contributed to the volume, headed by Mallarmé, with his poem "Hommage" (which appears under the title "Le tombeau de Charles Baudelaire" in Mallarmé's *Œuvres complètes*). The poem is not, by most accounts, Mallarmé's finest poetic hour, but that is another matter.[10] The book, which boasts a frontispiece by Félicien Rops, serves not only to honor the dead poet but to mark his death in a manner more seemly than the unfortunate grave, as though awaiting the monument that in 1895 the committee still hoped would be by Rodin.[11] Baudelaire's financial distress, and his anxiety about his recognition, seem to have followed him to the grave.

Thus, *Le tombeau de Charles Baudelaire* serves as a textual monument to the poet: it reminds the reader of the poet's importance (if nothing else, by virtue of the twenty-nine well-known poets who contributed to the volume), and refutes, by its very existence, any attempt to relegate Baudelaire to obscurity. A kind of posthumous festschrift, the book echoes in textual form the *statuomanie* that gripped France in the latter part of the nineteenth century.[12] The Revolution had instituted new rituals and a new culture for commemorating the dead, but Haussmann, and the new republic that followed Napoleon III, produced their own memorial edifices. In 1885, to take the most obvious example, the Panthéon was conse-

10. For a reading of Mallarmé's poem and its links to Baudelaire, see, e.g., D. J. Mossop, "Stéphane Mallarmé: 'Le Tombeau de Charles Baudelaire,'" *French Studies* 30, no. 3 (1976): 287–300.

11. Rodin produced the bronze *Je suis belle, ô mortels, comme un rêve de pierre* in honor of the Baudelaire poem in 1882, and *Portrait fictif de Baudelaire* in 1898, a bronze head. Both works are now in the Musée Rodin in Paris, as is the sketch for the first work, entitled *Homme soulevant une femme dans ses bras*.

12. The word *statuomanie* is used as the title to some comments by a writer with the pseudonym "Antony W." in 1892: "On signale une attaque de la maladie des statues chez les admirateurs de Baudelaire" (Guyaux, *La querelle*, 137). The same writer also assures his readers in the same year that Rodin will be making a bust and not a statue of the poet, "et ce buste sera placé non sur une place publique, mais sur le tombeau de l'auteur des *Fleurs du mal*" (204). An anonymous writer vents: "When will we finally have done with *statuomanie*?" (71).

crated to the great men of France: "Aux Grands Hommes, La Patrie Recon-
naissante."[13] Commemoration serves to console and to remind; the book
in honor of Baudelaire does both, and simultaneously acts as a retaliation
to the likes of Brunetière, who, for reasons having to do with his own re-
nown, was continually writing against a Baudelaire statue.[14]

The rites of memory produced as monuments or as words on tomb-
stones do not, however, seem to have been notions that consoled our poet
during his lifetime. The narrator of "Le mort joyeux" wants to "sleep in
forgetting, like a shark in the wave." The next line proclaims, "I hate tes-
taments and I hate graves; / Rather than imploring one tear of the world, /
Alive, I prefer to invite the crows / To bleed all the parts of my foul car-
cass" (OC 1:70). We should not take this at face value: Baudelaire's narrator
here is tormenting himself with fear (and anger). He is a "joyful dead man"
in sarcasm and irony, since he wonders "if there is still some torment / For
this old body without a soul and dead among the dead." And, as scholars
are quick to remind us, Baudelaire's "La servante au grand cœur" offers a
compassionate view of the dead's forgotten graves. The servant (the famous
Mariette of the poet's childhood) lies under "a humble plot of grass." We
should bring her flowers, continues the poem, "The dead, the poor dead,
have great pains." When the winds of October blow around their marble,
the dead "must find the living quite ungrateful." The living sleep "warm
in their sheets," whereas the dead feel the years flow by, their graves forgotten: "neither friends nor family / Replace the tatters that hang on their
railings" (OC 1:100). The dead are "devoured by black thoughts, with no
bed companions, with no good talks." It is worth noting, however, that
if the living are ungrateful (in their warm and shared beds) because they
take no notice of the graves and neglect to tend them, the dead themselves
are unforgotten: Mariette lives in the poet's mind, the tattered wreaths on
her neglected grave notwithstanding.

13. The Revolutionaries had already written this *éloge* on the statue of the Renommée,
but the incision on the façade of the Panthéon was to be more permanent. For a history of the
culture of remembrance preceding the nineteenth century, see Joseph Clarke, *Commemorating the Dead in Revolutionary France: Revolution and Remembrance 1788–1799* (Cambridge:
Cambridge University Press, 2007). See also Michael Riffaterre on Chateaubriand's obsession
with "monument vocabulary," in *Text Production* (New York: Columbia University Press,
1983), 124–56.

14. Brunetière was jockeying for entrance into the (conservative) Académie Française, and
wrote about the statue in a manner of which he imagined his jury of *immortels* would approve. For the full story, see Antoine Compagnon, *Connaissez-vous Brunetière? Enquête sur
un antidreyfusard et ses amis* (Paris: Seuil, 1997). See also Brunetière's articles in Guyaux, *La
querelle*.

The grave in Baudelaire is more often than not metonymic of the void or, as here, the cold bed of the dead. It is not, however, a space that can successfully commemorate the departed; nor, with its various funerary architectures, does it suspend time by its insistence on reminding the living of "great men" of the past. Time in Baudelaire is deaf and blind to the funerary efforts of the living, and never suspended or slowed by any reminder of the past (though such reminders can help somewhat in repressing the fearful future). One owes a certain respect to the dead (they deserve flowers, for example);[15] but no monument can serve, for Baudelaire, to mitigate the horrors of the void or to conjure up hopes for a glorious immortality among men. Immortality, if it exists for the poet, is emphatically not to be found in the mortal sphere. And convention (funerary or otherwise) in any case is hardly something Baudelaire could endorse. As Nietzsche puts it in the text from which the epigraph to this chapter is drawn, the fiercest battle "is fought round the demand for greatness to be eternal. Every other living thing cries no. 'Away with the monuments,' is the watchword."[16] The fear of death in Baudelaire is in no way appeased by the prospect of a monument or the marble of a grave; and the fear of the void is not placated by architecture. Time, to repeat, is a problem unsolved and untamed.

IN MEMORY OF THE PRESENT

Reading gives a book the sudden existence that a statue "seems" to receive from the chisel alone: an isolation that shields it from the gaze of a beholder, a haughty distance, a vulnerable chastity that dismisses both the sculptor and the gaze that seeks to shape it further.
—Maurice Blanchot, *L'espace littéraire*

I noted in the section "God, Graves, and Scholars" that for Baudelaire the present could not *be*, except to serve as a place from which to experience

15. Baudelaire's real father, interestingly enough, was buried in a temporary grave in the Montparnasse cemetery, where his son would also lie. Madame Aupick did not continue to pay for the grave, and it is not known where the remains of François Baudelaire have been put (perhaps in an ossuary of the cemetery, suggests Pichois; *OC* 1:1038). Several projects for prose poems seem to allude to this "oversight" and, precisely, lack of respect, e.g., "Le père qui attend toujours" (*OC* 1:369, 589). Though such titles are inconclusive, it is clear that Madame Aupick's nonchalant attitude toward her first husband's grave cannot have pleased their son. As Pichois puts it, her bizarre indifference was certainly not that of Andromache in the swan poem.

16. Friedrich Nietzsche, *The Use and Abuse of History* (Indianapolis: Bobbs-Merrill, 1957), 13.

the past (regret) and the future (apprehension). And yet in the first part of "Le peintre de la vie moderne" we read: "The pleasure we glean from the representation of the present comes not only from the beauty with which it can be clothed, but also from its essential quality of presentness" (*OC* 2:684). Indeed, *le présent* does exist for Baudelaire when it is represented, as he describes it, as that-which-is-present. In other words, it is not the present at all, but rather its (a posteriori) depiction. Paul de Man insists on presence in Baudelaire, and does so a bit too smoothly. De Man cites the same passage as above but translates "sa qualité essentielle de présent" as "the present-ness of the present."[17] While this is a loose but not incorrect translation, de Man does want to force the present-ness, as he puts it, of the present in Baudelaire.[18] In the same essay, pages later, Baudelaire writes: "Woe to him who studies something other than pure art, logic, general method in antiquity! By plunging into that too deeply, he loses the memory of the present; he abdicates the value and privileges furnished by circumstance" (*OC* 2:696). But it is possible (and perhaps easier) to profess a belief in the present when you are talking about producing modern art and describing the taste of the epoch. Such a perspective has to do with the chronology of style, but not with the sense of time—unless time means parsing out what is "in" at the moment from what is old-fashioned or what belongs to the ancients. The "memory of the present," as Baudelaire puts it, is not now-time but, rather, *comme son nom l'indique*, the illustration of the recent present remembered. De Man then shifts his argument: he admits that there is an ambivalence in Baudelaire—the present is coupled, he notes, with terms such as *représentation, mémoire*, or even *temps,*

---

17. Paul de Man, *Blindness and Insight: Essays in the Rhetoric of Contemporary Criticism* (New York: Oxford University Press, 1971), 156.

18. See Terdiman's reading of the same passage in Baudelaire. Terdiman interprets it as "essentializing the presentness of the present." His reading is thus not unlike de Man's, initially. But Terdiman then juxtaposes it with the swan poem, arguing that there, "rather than absolutizing the present, [Baudelaire] radically empties it." Richard Terdiman, *Modernity and the Past*, 133. My argument, however, is that the present is always empty for Baudelaire, regardless of the texts that attempt to experience it, or to give the present some sort of ground from which to be conscious of itself. So, too, history and the social are also always in Baudelaire, despite critical attempts to deemphasize them. The two strains—abstract notions on the one hand, and the historical-social on the other, have too often been segregated by Baudelaire critics, as I have noted more than once. Jean Starobinski makes the same point when he writes, in his analysis of the swan poem "It has been right to assert that 'The Swan' also has a socio-political aspect. It would be wrong to reduce it to that." *La mélancolie au miroir* (Paris: Julliard, 1989), 65. My point is that these two aspects—the psychic and the socio-political—must be borne in mind in all of Baudelaire, not just any given poem.

all opening perspectives of distance and difference "within the apparent uniqueness of the instant" (157).

For de Man, Baudelaire's modernity, like Nietzsche's, "is a forgetting or a suppression of anteriority." The past is so threatening for Baudelaire (as for any writer of literature if we are to follow de Man) that "it has to be forgotten." The present for Baudelaire is thus "severed from all other temporal dimensions, the weight of the past as well as the concern with a future, with a sense of totality and completeness that could not be achieved if a more extended awareness of time were not already involved" (ibid.). But what is a more extended awareness of time in this case? It turns out that we are talking about literary language, which is a movement "that does not take place as an actual sequence in time" (163). Modernity for de Man is the desire to break out of literature "toward the reality of the moment," and, at the same time, literature folds back on itself and "engenders the repetition and the continuation of literature" (162). Such a movement, to repeat, does not take place as an actual sequence in time for de Man. Literature is thus not an event but rather "a metaphor making a sequence out of what occurs in fact as a synchronic juxtaposition" (163). So when Baudelaire speaks of the representation of the present, or the memory of the present, his language, in de Man's view, names at the same time "the flight, the turning point, and the return." Such a narrative can only be metaphorical, de Man argues, because "history is not fiction." We can extend this point of view beyond literature, he concludes, by confirming "that the bases for historical knowledge are not empirical facts but written texts, even if these texts masquerade in the guise of wars or revolutions" (165).

De Man's chapter "Literary History and Literary Modernity" is of use for us here because it presupposes a totalizing metaphoricity of the text; one that insists upon the fictivity and thus ahistoricity of literature. The avoidance/absence of the present in Baudelaire—which I do not dispute— serves, for de Man, to put literature in a saturated gloss of metaphoricity, in which texts "masquerade in the guise of wars or revolutions." Such a view not only erases the clashes of different, very clear time spans in Baudelaire; it is a view that also domesticates the crisis of being-in-the-world that Baudelaire inscribes on most of his pages. Granted, literature, like art, is representation, and as such is not a present moment for the writer. But the searing ontological and social moments that Baudelaire incises onto his pages cannot be amalgamated as "literature" without wiping out the Baudelairean experience. Indeed, one can read many of Baudelaire's poems as an insistence on the intensity of the moment, or *Erlebnis*; as a rejection of the more process-oriented and judgment-cognitive *Erfahrung*. Certain poems of Baudelaire might be called prereflective: "A une passante", for example, is the attempt to force the representation of the moment's intensity into the very fabric of poetic expression. Other works, particularly the prose poems, are based on *Erfahrung*—they are diachronic, narratives that are more process-oriented and didactic, like "Assommons les pauvres!" The prose poems are closer to recollection in, if not tranquillity, at least a reshuffled hindsight.[19] What is so gripping about poems such as "A une passante" is that they refuse all distance from the event that would allow for processing. But there is no obvious artificiality in such a move, unlike the famous writing-to-the moment of an eighteenth-century epistolary novel. In Richardson's *Pamela*, for example, the heroine writes even as a given character walks through the door. Her repeated "He's here!" serves only to increase the comical aspect of writing *now*. But the lightening that illuminates the *passante*'s eyes for a fraction of a second is Baudelaire's production of the flash of the present. Flash moments of recognition, whether biographical or poetic, are one way that Baudelaire gets fleetingly to experience the present. (Another, as we have seen, is the moment of grace, the disintegration of which the poem narrates.)

We might say, then, that Baudelaire in his poems of the moment, of lived experience (*Erlebnis*), ignores literature-as-representation and tries, rather, to render the moment qua moment. If Benjamin wanted the synthesis of both immediacy and reflection, if his notion of aura is partly a search for the intensity of the moment and a recognition of its loss, Baudelaire has not given up on transmitting the instant—even if it is one that is already receding into memory.[20] The flash of lightening in "A une passante," for example, is an attempt at conveying an epiphany. Time in his poetry must be understood as a lived horror, metaphors included. The verse poem "L'horloge," it will be remembered, makes the point. The "vibrant pains" of which the clock speaks, anthropomorphized and personified as they may be, do not lessen the poem's depiction of an ominous given: it is too

19. And many of the prose poems are also doubles of the ones in verse, thus highlighting the difference between, and possibilities of, narrative and the immediacy of a moment.

20. It is worth remembering here that Benjamin, under the influence of Brecht, sometimes welcomes the disappearance of the aura. In other words, its erosion is not only lamented in Benjamin. The canonized, auratic work of art, for example, remains, in its sacrosanct status, for the privileged. This is part of the point of Benjamin's essay "The Work of Art in the Age of Mechanical Reproduction": what happens, he asks, when the artwork is extracted, in modernity, from its "uniqueness and permanence," given reproducibility and the universal equality of things?

late; that is the epiphany, the lived intensity. The prose poem of the same title, on the other hand, is a narrative.

The prose "L'horloge" begins with the "fact" that the Chinese can tell time by looking into a cat's eye. The narrator, however, sees eternity in his own cat's eyes: "I always distinctly see the hour, always the same one; a vast, solemn hour, immense as space, with no divisions into minutes or seconds—an immobile hour, unmarked on clocks, and yet light as a sigh, rapid as a glance" (*OC* 1:299–300). We are back, it would seem, in the paradisal first room of "La chambre double," where time also disappears in an eternal bliss, the moment of grace mentioned earlier.[21] If someone were to disturb him, continues the narrator of the prose "L'horloge," to ask what can possibly be seen in the cat's eyes, if he really sees the time there, the narrator would reply, "Yes, I see the time, it is Eternity o'clock! [*il est l'Eternité!*]." The poem ends with a flourish that portrays the entire piece as a poetic and gallant pirouette: "This is, is it not, Madame, a truly worthy madrigal, and as grandiloquent as you are yourself? In truth, I had such pleasure in embroidering this pretentious gallantry that I will ask nothing of you in exchange" (300). The final lines seem to be an *envoi*, dedicating the poem, as in the ballad tradition, to the poet's ladylove—this along with a reference to the Renaissance part song, the madrigal. And yet the *envoi* is actually for the poet himself, who congratulates himself on his own conceit, taking such pleasure in it that, unlike the Troubadour convention, he is satisfied with his own text sent, as it were, to himself.[22] One thinks of the poet Rostand, for example, a generation younger than Baudelaire, who ends one of his poems with the words "A la fin de l'envoi, je touche" (At the end of the *envoi*, I touch). The poem, in other words, will have granted him favors from his ladylove. The narrator of the prose "L'horloge," however, has charmed himself with his own verbal "embroidery." The *envoi* closes in the past (he had pleasure producing the prose

21. "La Beauté" makes the same point. Beauty, who is the narrator, as it were, says: "My eyes, my wide eyes of eternal lights" (*OC* 1:21).

22. The bawdy poetry of William IX frequently ends in equally lascivious *envois*. "Farai un vers de dreit nien" (I will make a verse about plain nothing) ends, for example: "I have written the verse, I don't know about whom, / and I'll send it to the one / who'll send it to somebody else / toward Poitiers, / because of that box, I would like/to have the other key." A more typical (and less crude) *envoi* is, for example, that of Jaufré Rudel from "Quan lo rius de la Fontana" (When the rills of the fountain): "Without the scroll of a parchment / I transfer this verse, singing / in plain romance language, to Ugo Bru, by way of Filhol." The troubadour Arnaut Daniel almost always puts his own name into his *envois*. For example, the poem "Autet et bas entre'ls prim fuelhs" (High and low between the young leaves) ends: "Arnaut loves and doesn't say much, / since love stops my tongue / so that no wild boasts can possess it."

poem) and the future (he will ask nothing in return). The present, if present there be, is lost somewhere in the poet's gaze into his cat's eyes, in that place where for him there is no time. But as with the first room in "La chambre double," a man from Porlock emerges to ask the poet what he is looking at, what time it is, and thus to break the spell of the vision of eternity. The immediacy of the verse "L'horloge," and the narrative structure of the prose version, provide one example among many of Baudelaire's attempt to produce on the one hand the event of a moment in all its intensity (Erlebnis) and, on the other, to construct a little moral tale, if a twisted one (Erfahrung). The two German terms, though far from being his own, help to articulate the way in which Baudelaire experiences time.[23]

For de Man, any articulated time in Baudelaire engages "an interdependence between past and future that prevents any present from coming into being" (161). Let us reject this view and say that the present for Baudelaire acts as a place from which to see the past on the one hand and the future on the other—not as interdependent but as endlessly, irrevocably noncontiguous. I said earlier that the present for Baudelaire is like the digit zero: it gives significance to the preceding and the following digits, but is not identical to itself. The present does not disappear as if engulfed in a combined past and future, whiting out the difference in times as well as in the moment. Rather, the moment in Baudelaire is the position from which the past and the future irrevocably reassert themselves (separately but equally); the present is the place that allows for this realization; and that place is the lived moment, the Erlebnis that Baudelaire sometimes forces. "La chambre double" can be seen as the most obvious example of such an event (a term I am using contra de Man): the present can allow for a moment of grace, which is quickly destroyed by the return to another reality, another present, which is remembered before it is even attained ("I remember! I remember," cries the poet in "La chambre double"). The present in Baudelaire is the moment when time has the time to show its horror: "Die, old coward! It is too late!" But it is also the place from which memory will allow escape, like the metaphor of the skirt in the prose "Crépuscule du soir." "The transparent and dark gauze," writes the poet, allows occasional glimpses of "the muted splendors of a brilliant skirt, as when the delicious past pierces through the blackness of the present" (OC 1:312).

23. For a reading of these two terms, their history in philosophy, and their implications, see Martin Jay, *Songs of Experience: Modern American and European Variations on a Universal Theme* (Berkeley: University of California Press, 2005). Benjamin too uses *Erfahrung*, and likens modes of experience to Proust's *mémoire volontaire* and *involuntaire*. See, e.g., *The Writer of Modern Life*, 196–205.

The paradisal state, once lost, is remembered as well—as forever unattainable, like the *passante* and the possibilities she so painfully suggests. Metaphoricity is not ubiquitous, nor does it merely analogize in Baudelaire; it records within an anamnesis that allows for no return to another lost present. In "La vie antérieure" the poet writes: "For a long time I lived under vast porticos / . . . That is where I lived." But even there, paradise remembered is stained by memory: naked slaves freshen the narrator's brow with palm leaves, their only care being "to deepen / The painful secret that made me languish" (*OC* 1:17–18). The "painful secret" is an event from another world; an event that has left its mark in recollection. If the eternal is the absence of time, as in "La chambre double" or in the eyes of a cat, the apparent paradise here is debarred from the eternal by the memory of a past as lost as the remembrance of the swaying palm leaves marks an already endless, earlier *antérieur*.

Baudelaire uses rhetorical tropes in all of his texts—whether verse or prose—but his relation to literature is one that does not challenge the power of representation (his art criticism makes the point). He does not, in other words, question the ability of literature or language to give expression. Those theorists of the twentieth century, such as de Man, Blanchot, Deleuze, and others, who follow upon the crisis of literature as articulated by Mallarmé, for example, are concerned with literature turning back on itself, with a writing that resists its own effectuation, as Christophe Bident puts it.[24] Baudelaire is not in the same mental schemata. He cannot be elided with the crisis of language that describes Mallarmé and his heirs—Bataille, Breton, Artaud, Kafka, even Valéry (to name a few). To write, Blanchot says in *L'espace littéraire*, is to make use of language in which "the image, the allusion to a figure, becomes allusion to that which is without figure and, from a form sketched on absence, becomes an unformed presence of that absence, an opaque and empty opening onto what there is when there is no longer a world, when there is not yet a world."[25] To write, for Blanchot, is "to deliver oneself to the risk of the absence of time, where the eternal recommencement reigns" (ibid.). This is a sentence that can only be uttered, I would venture, after Nietzsche, after Mallarmé, and after Freud. And we can add another after: after the *Frühromantiker*, and the theories of Friedrich Schlegel in particular, the retrospective read-

24. Christophe Bident, *Reconnaissances: Antelme, Blanchot, Deleuze* (Paris: Calmann-Lévy, 2003), 120.

25. Maurice Blanchot, *L'espace littéraire* (Paris: Gallimard, 1955), 27. On this point see Timothée Schellenberg, "L'informe et le retour: De l'écriture de Blanchot à la pensée nomade de Deleuze" (PhD diss., University of Chicago, 2010).

ing of which are provided by the likes of Nietzsche, Mallarmé, and Freud, once these, in turn, have been read.[26]

Baudelaire's crisis is not with language; it is with time and mortality (not that these preclude the first), the horrors of which language is fit to recount. Language is still there to articulate; it does not yet turn on itself to question its own being, its own impossibility. It is in this sense that Baudelaire might be said to herald, but not to embody, the modernity that follows and that too often sees him as its architect. The point is of significance because Baudelaire's texts—whether fictional, epistolary, or in journal form—make straightforward linguistic choices, even if the content is less than comfortable. Language conveys for Baudelaire, and we must take him at face value in his syntax and grammar, even if we sometimes strain to follow him in his mental and social landscapes. "Une charogne," for example—concerning a corpse lying on the road—is a poem difficult to read and hard to take. It is like a gruesome version of Ronsard's "Mignonne, allons voir si la rose," in which the poet argues *carpe diem* to get his lover's attentions: like the rose, she too will bloom for a short time only to fade. The sadistic narrator of "Une charogne" tells his mistress ("Oh queen of graces," says the poet, using the common Baudelairean tactic of jolting juxtaposition) that she will be like the corpse; she too will be "this horrible infection," kissed by vermin and covered with mold, a heap of bones (*OC* 1:31–32).

We are not merely confronting a simile here, or a series of metaphors. Language in Baudelaire may provide a myriad of tropes, but all is not metaphor. All trope, all metaphor, is a poetics that is permitted largely (among other things) by the luxury of a life without want. A poetics of metaphor alone, in other words, presupposes the possibility of long reflection, of thinking, of being able to contemplate and remain in the abstract. If we agree (with Derrida, for example) that the paradox of metaphor is such that its discourse cannot exist outside of a metaphorically produced network, then we must put Baudelaire outside of such an economy. "The theory of metaphor," says Ricoeur, "returns in a circular manner to the metaphor of theory, which determines the truth of being in terms of presence."[27] Baudelaire records the social unrest, inequity, and misery not only of himself but of those around him. He writes the city; he does not merely tran-

---

26. The most obvious example being Philippe Lacoue-Labarthe, Jean-Luc Nancy and Anne-Marie Lang's *L'absolu littéraire: Théorie de la littérature du romantisme allemand* (Paris: Seuil, 1978).

27. Paul Ricoeur, *The Rule of Metaphor: Multi-Disciplinary Studies of the Creation of Meaning in Language*, trans. Robert Czerny (Toronto: University of Toronto Press, 1977), 287.

scribe it as a trope. In other words, because Baudelaire's texts assume the tool of language, they also speak, as we have remarked throughout this study, of history, poverty, and social turmoil as much as they do of the poet's personal ghosts and horrors. It is a mistake to read Baudelaire's words as a literature that questions its own existence, as a language that doubts its own ability to convey.

Baudelaire conveys. His works may be cries *de profundis*, but they describe (often sadistically for the reader, or pathetically, or euphorically) his vision, his gaze on time within the city as much as within the poet's psyche. It is a modernity that tells the story of its own crisis, but it is not conscious of itself as thereby laying the cornerstone of modernity. That was to come with Mallarmé, whom I mention, not in the spirit of some sort of great-man-of-history complex, but rather as a metaphysics, an ontology of the act and possibility of writing that could only follow Baudelaire. Baudelaire's texts prepare, even if they do not articulate, the way toward a language suspicious of itself, and condemned to expressing that suspicion by the very means of its distrust. The confusion of double vision lies herein as well: Baudelaire does not grasp that language is itself to become the site of suspicion, and yet everything that he writes points toward the crisis of language that follows him. It is perhaps for this reason that we sense a straining in his writings, as if his right hand were not quite sure of what his left intended.[28]

"In describing literature from the standpoint of the concept of modernity," writes de Man,

> as the steady fluctuation of an entity away from and toward its own mode of being, we have constantly stressed that this movement does not take place as an actual sequence in time; to represent it as such is merely a metaphor making a sequence out of what occurs in fact as a synchronic juxtaposition. The sequential, diachronic structure of the process stems from the nature of literary language as an entity, not as an event. (*Blindness and Insight*, 163)

But Baudelaire, I repeat, is not in the same orbit as Mallarmé or even Nietzsche. For Baudelaire, literature is precisely an event, and this on two fronts: the act of writing as that which mutes the terror of the present's

28. A metaphor also used by Maurice Blanchot—the hand that writes and the interrupting hand, which is the one that is in charge: "Mastery is always the fact of the other hand, the one that does not write, capable of intervening at the necessary moment. . . . Mastery thus consists in the power to stop writing." *L'espace littéraire*, 15.

gaze (both forward and backward) through *divertissement*, and the enormous weight of time that is lightened—though barely—through the production of poetic metaphors of specificity that, in their very invention,
attempt to domesticate what can never be overcome: time. If the abyss for
Nietzsche is a philosophical principle, for Baudelaire it is the grave. And
the grave is not a metaphor; it is the looming reality of oblivion, or the
equally terrifying possibility of eternal damnation.

Metaphor itself, dual like almost everything in Baudelaire, remains
rooted in the real even as it hovers in the heights of the abstract. The
poem "L'albatros" is a case in point.[29] It is an extended simile, with metaphors abounding. Like the albatross ("prince des nuées"), the poet soars
in the skies, but his wings are obstacles on the ground, preventing him
from moving ("Ses ailes de géant l'empêchent de marcher"). Clumsy on
earth, the poet is nonetheless entrenched there; he cannot spend all of his
time flying (a position reminiscent, as previously noted, of "Laquelle est la
vraie?"). So too Baudelaire's poetry articulates various metaphysical crises
and anguish, as we have seen, as well as dicta concerning aesthetics ("Je
suis belle, ô mortels," says Beauty in the poem of the same name, "comme
un rêve de pierre"). But whether by the metaphor's vehicle or tenor, Baudelaire always returns to the ground—unhappily, fitfully, anxiety-ridden,
but nonetheless in the world. And this not only because materiality intensifies the poem (one thinks again of "Une charogne," among other works),
but also because the world is indeed too much with Baudelaire, as his depictions of the city and its figures attest. Metaphor in Baudelaire is not a
device to amalgamate future and past; nor is it an attempt to blur borders
between social ills and abstract thought. After all, a major section of *Les
fleurs du mal*, which appears first in the collection, is entitled "Spleen et
Idéal"; the two terms and concepts remain unjoined, discrete, even as each
serves to display the absence of the other and thus to make a return to the
other inevitable.

For Baudelaire, language is only too capable (one thinks of Maistre's
muscular prose, which our poet so admired) of reminding the poet and his
readers of what lies ahead, what was behind, and the city that provides, in
its very being, the reality of both. This is not Friedrich Schlegel's call for
a *Literatur der Literatur*, or for a *Philosophie der Philosophie*—Baudelaire
is not in the lineage of the *Frühromantiker*, whom Mallarmé was soon to

29. The poem, an early one from "Spleen et Idéal" in the *Fleurs du mal*, was no doubt
composed when Baudelaire was on his (neither desired nor completed) sea voyage to India in
1841. The albatross is a bird of the southern oceans. Baudelaire apparently saw albatrosses at
Reunion Island (see Pichois, *OC* 1:835).

emulate in his fashion. Nor is history a metaphor in Baudelaire; the revolution of 1848, the poverty that surrounds him and gradually engulfs him as well, the social classes and marginalized types that he sees (whores, corpses, the poor, the homeless, beggars, lesbians, and so on), the city itself in its strange transformations—these may be described in metaphors but only to better impart their reality, to depict their presence in a present that all too quickly erodes into memory. So, too, time is no trope for him; it is a way of remembering not only what is lost but what cannot be imagined as anything but a crushing weight, and what will irrevocably be. Baudelaire cannot be relegated to "only" metaphor, or to "only" the textual guardian of the modern, industrial and capitalist city. His writing attests to literature as being-in-the-world, all too much. His metaphors are transmissions of dual but nonetheless actual realities, versed or prosed into concrete and doubled visions, the dual focus of which renders the times he so sadly recognizes as his own.

ANGELS DOING TIME

> We—all of us—have come along either too early or too late. We'll have done the most difficult and the least glamorous job: making the transition . . . The future torments us and the past holds us back. That's why the present escapes us.
> —Gustave Flaubert to Louis Bouilhet, December 19, 1850

In *Fusées*, one of his journals, Baudelaire imagines the future and decides that there is none for mankind: "The world will end," he writes. The only reason for which the world might manage to continue, he adds, is that it already exists (*OC* 1:665). He does not mean that France will turn into one of those "chaotic republics" in South America, nor that we will return to a primitive state, searching our pastures "rifle in hand" in the ruins of our civilization. We don't have enough energy for that anyway. Why? Because "the mechanical will have Americanized us to such a degree, progress will so fully have atrophied the entire spiritual part within us," that we will "die by that we had thought we could live by" (666). We will be destroyed, however, not by universal ruin or universal progress (which are the same thing, he tells us, with different names), but rather by "the abasement of the heart."

"We" in this apocalyptic passage, sometime means mankind, sometimes the French, sometimes modern man (in the West; one notes in these passages Baudelaire's easy colonialist and xenophobic tendencies).

But "You" (*tu*, the familiar form) is emphatically the bourgeois here, who will see his wife vigilantly and lovingly protect her beloved safe (*coffre-fort*), and become "nothing more than the perfect ideal of a kept woman." His daughter, while still in her crib, will be dreaming about how much she will be worth at her marriage. His son will leave home at the age of twelve, not to do heroic deeds, but "to found a business" that will be in competition with his father's (ibid.). The bourgeois's love of money will incur the wrath of God, and modern (read: European) life, like Sodom and Gomorrah, will be destroyed. It is the bourgeois class, in other words, that will destroy "us"; and this not due to wickedness per se (as with the Cities of the Plain), but rather to worshiping money at the expense of the heart. Thanks to the "progress of these times," says Baudelaire to the bourgeois, "all that will be left of your entrails will be the viscera" (667).[30] The earlier equation of ruin and progress becomes clear. Multivalent though the word "progress" is in Baudelaire (as we have seen, it can be good when it has to do with improving the lot of the poor; it is almost always bad when it refers to life in the modern city)—here it is clear that progress means ruin. Indeed, Baudelaire closes with this idea. Often feeling within himself "the ridicule of a prophet," he laments:

> lost in this vile world, elbowed by the crowds, I am like an exhausted man whose eye sees behind him, through the deep years, only disillusionment and bitterness; and in front of him, only a storm which contains nothing new, neither teaching nor pain. (667)

At first glance, this passage bears a notable resemblance to Benjamin's famous description of Paul Klee's *Angelus Novus*. To begin with, the notion of progress is, as in Baudelaire, connected with a catastrophic time and a storm. "But a storm is blowing from Paradise," writes Benjamin of the Klee painting, such that it is impossible for the angel to fold his wings. "This storm," concludes Benjamin, "is what we call progress."[31] The Klee angel becomes the angel of history for Benjamin; an angel that, like Bau-

---

30. Let us not forget the brief period when Baudelaire imagines the bourgeoisie to be educable in art; they are the majority in intelligence as well as number, he writes. And they have founded great museums. This optimistic view is both brief and anomalous for Baudelaire. "Aux bourgeois," preface to *Salon de 1846* (*OC* 2:415–17). Nevertheless, Baudelaire recognizes the bourgeois respect for art, which is an attitude he does not believe is shared by the masses. See "Respect aux arts et à l'industrie," in *Le salut public* (*OC* 2:1032).

31. Walter Benjamin, "Theses on the Philosophy of History," IX, in *Illuminations*, ed. Hannah Arendt, trans. Harry Zohn (New York: Schocken, 1969), 257–58.

delaire's "exhausted man," sees a storm that serves no purpose. Both the exhausted man and the angel of history view the past in calamitous terms. Baudelaire's exhausted man sees the past behind him, with "only disillusionment and bitterness"; while Benjamin's angel of history sees the past as "one single catastrophe which keeps piling wreckage upon wreckage and hurls it in front of his feet."[32]

It is worth taking a closer look at Benjamin's text here. The angel of history's face is turned toward the past: "His eyes are staring, his mouth is open, his wings are spread." The past, that "single catastrophe" that the angel sees piling up at his feet, makes him want "to stay, awaken the dead, and make whole what has been smashed" (257). But he cannot help in this way, because of the storm blowing from paradise. (We can assume Benjamin's interpretation here as partly inspired by Klee's interest in Rilke's angels, those strange creatures that are neither divine nor mortal.) In any case, the storm is so violent that the angel can no longer fold his wings, and is irresistibly propelled "into the future to which his back is turned, while the pile of debris before him grows skyward," presumably blocking his vision (258). Helpless, horrified, and forced to stare at the accumulation of a cataclysmic past, the angel of history cannot see the future into which he is being violently projected. He is condemned to passivity. This passage and its view of time obviously result from the reality of fascism in 1940, shortly before Benjamin was to commit suicide. "The tradition of the oppressed," writes Benjamin in the previous section, "teaches us that the 'state of emergency' in which we live is not the exception but the rule. We must attain to a conception of history that is in keeping with this insight" (257). This, we might say, is his angel of history's insight. Historical materialists know that "whoever has emerged victorious participates to this day in the triumphal procession in which the present rulers step over those who are lying prostrate" (256). History (and the writing thereof) belongs to the victors, and while the angel cannot see where such a tragic practice will lead, he appears distraught by the assumption that it will be more of the same.

32. Benjamin's paragraph on the Klee painting is preceded by a stanza from "Gruss vom Angelus," a poem by Gershom Scholem that Scholem had given to Benjamin for his birthday in 1920. The poem, writes Scholem, is "about the Klee picture which I had had a chance to view for so long." In the same year, Benjamin had met Rainer Maria Rilke, the poet whose *Duino Elegies* had greatly influenced Klee's angel series (which lasted a good twenty-five years). See Gershom Scholem, *Walter Benjamin: The Story of a Friendship* (New York: New York Review of Books Classics, 2003), 125. Benjamin, it should be added, willed the painting to Scholem, who kept it on his wall in Jerusalem until his death.

Robert Alter sees in Benjamin's angel the modernists whose faces are "turned toward the backward vista of tradition, while the winds of history inexorably blow them forward away from the Eden of origins."[33] But another reading (which does not necessarily preclude the first) might be that the storm blowing from paradise, the Fall itself, dooms man to persist in his continuum of horrors as the ages accumulate. If Benjamin, like Baudelaire, was obsessed with the banishment from the Garden, as Alter argues (115), we might say that Alter's positive read of the past as tradition is for Benjamin subverted by the hand of God that forecloses any redemption. There is indeed a "tension between past and future in Benjamin's thinking" (ibid.). Alter reads this as an "iconography of tradition that defines the disasters of secular modernity—the erosion of experience, the decay of wisdom, the loss of redemptive vision" (115–16). An angel, in other words, without a halo, condemned to seeing the raw atrocity that is the modern; and a time without aura, banishing history from all salvation. Perhaps this vision of the angel bereft of a halo explains Benjamin's fascination with two passages in the Baudelaire corpus in which a narrator relates the loss of a halo.[34] "Redemption," writes Benjamin, as if continuing his thoughts on the angel, "depends on the tiny fissure in the continuous catastrophe" (*The Writer of Modern Life*, 161).

And now the Baudelaire passage. The fact that *Fusées* is from a previous century, which in France (and not only in France) knew endless revolutions and changes in governments, has little to do with the horrors that Benjamin feared and indeed saw materialize in his own time. Baudelaire's protagonist is grounded, not in an aerial view of mankind, but in the city, down on the street, knee-deep in a vile world. Elbowed by the crowds, he is a man exhausted by the bedlam of the urban, industrialized culture that surrounds him. The past lies behind him (whereas the angel of history has the past accumulating at his feet), and the future before him (again, Benjamin's angel has the future, into which he is hurtling, at his back).

Keep in mind that the exhausted man sees behind as well as before him—he has an eye, as it were, in the back of his head. What better image to encapsulate double vision? The past for him is not a wreckage but, rather, the result of spleen, or acedia: only disillusionment and bitterness can be seen "through the deep years." The future is a storm brewed not by paradise but (one imagines) by the promise of progress that breeds nothing

---

33. Robert Alter, *Necessary Angels: Tradition and Modernity in Kafka, Benjamin and Scholem* (Cambridge, MA: Harvard University Press, 1991), 67.

34. See "Perte d'auréole," ("Loss of a Halo") in *Spleen de Paris* (*OC* 1:352) and in *Fusées* (*OC* 1:659).

new (neither teaching nor pain)—exactly the opposite of what progress is meant to guarantee. The exhausted man, in other words, is caught between melancholia and chaos, between past and future, neither of which is desirable. The world is vile because it cannot provide succor. The exhausted man lives in a place from which two polarities of time are visible, one worse than the other. That place is the present. It is this in-between-ness, this *entre* of which Derrida and others have made so much, that marks out the place (as opposed to the time) of the present in Baudelaire. The *entre* is also like a hybrid, manifesting itself in many other ways: the woman in "L'invitation au voyage" who is both child and sister as well as lover; the city in the same poem, which serves as the link between East and West but belongs to neither; the thyrsus, which, as Georges Poulet has shown, embodies both the straight and the curved line, and the arabesque, which does the same; the Creole woman who haunts the poetry (Jeanne Duval the obvious model). There are so many more, but they do not display or provide a synthesis of opposites, or a *synthèse disjonctive* as Deleuze puts it. Rather, they provide an in-between-ness that allows for the survey of what we might call a disjunctive coupling—what is behind and what is in front, what is past and what is future, the time before and the time ahead. The present for Baudelaire is not a time but, to repeat, the place or position from which to see the double extensions of time. The present, the place of zero, is the opposite of anamorphosis: for Baudelaire, what could appear as normal is always deformed by twin visions that leave the poet without a breathing space, in-between the two augmented sequences that press in on him.

The modern city is one place inhabited by the present that allows for such a doubled vision in Baudelaire. If there is, for him, a *coincidentia oppositorum*, it is in this space of non-time in the present. There may be forgetting, for him—in the act of writing, for example—but this is not the present, since there is then no consciousness of time. There may be spleen—the sense that time is moving crushingly slowly, weighting the poet down. But this is not the present either, since time engulfs the poet, it will be recalled, "minute by minute, / Like an immense snow [engulfing] a stiff corpse," forcing the poet to ask the avalanche to take him, too, in its fall. He can be conscious only of time itself, not of the present. There may be a sense of the eternal, but that is a place, as we have seen, from which time is absent. There may be memory or fantasy, but these are possible precisely from a place where "now" can only mean, as for the exhausted man, the ability to look at the past and the future with equal melancholia. The present in Baudelaire is a place of anamnesis—the

remembering of an anterior life, the recollection of a present that served
only to provide the memory.

Baudelaire's exhausted man is witnessing not only the erosion of what
Benjamin was to call aura but, at least as forcefully, the disintegration of
the subject as it had been understood before the confusion of the modern
city worked its own erosion in what we now call the modern era. It is no
coincidence that Benjamin is concerned with an angel—itself a hybrid of
sorts (neither male nor female, divine but engaged in the terrestrial) who
looks with horror (mouth gaping, eyes wide) at the deeds of humans as a
whole, as a race. For Benjamin, the angel's frightened gaze has to do with
what mankind is wreaking on itself with the advent of fascism and the
echoes of other atrocities of the past. The angel sees, in other words, history. But Baudelaire's exhausted man sees his own past, its disillusionment and bitterness, and his own future, which seems to promise nothing
but more of the same until he is swallowed by *le gouffre*. From exhaustion
in Baudelaire's man, to horror in Benjamin's angel, we can trace a moment
of difference between Benjamin as theorist of modernity, and Baudelaire as
poet. Caught in the maelstrom that is modernity, Baudelaire can only see
from a double viewpoint that not only prevents an overview, panoramic
discernment, or perspective, but puts him into a solipsism that sees in
historical events, and in capitalist culture, more fodder for his conviction
that progress will eventually atrophy "the spiritual part." Such atrophy
Benjamin will take as a given; indeed, he will articulate its implications,
writing of the lack of aura in the commodity, the mass production that is
the new Paris, the political hegemonies that oppress and destroy, even the
possibilities that such events might allow.

Baudelaire, on the other hand, is trying to come to terms with what
has happened, what is happening. If the world continues to exist, he muses
in the passage of *Fusées* that we have been considering, would it be an existence worthy of the dictionary of history (665)? Politics of any kind will
be of no avail in Baudelaire's dark view of the future: "The time will come
when humanity, like a vengeful ogre, will snatch the last pieces from
those who think they have legitimately inherited from revolutions." Indeed, universal ruin will not come from the failure of political institutions
(that failure being a given), but rather, as we have seen, from the debasement of the heart (*OC* 1:666). Politics for Baudelaire is a material reality,
but it often serves in his work as a metaphor for such a debasement of the
heart: his swan, his Andromache, his exiled figures long for their native
habitats; their unfamiliar contexts (the modern city, foreign shores) are ve-

hicles to the loss of another time—one of happiness, of known and natural surroundings. As the poet himself puts it, quite lucidly, "In certain, almost supernatural states of the soul, the depth of life reveals itself totally in the spectacle, ordinary as it may be, that one has before one's gaze. The latter becomes the symbol of the former" (OC 1:659). This may be as close as Baudelaire comes to experiencing the present: it is a place; but one from which the depth of life can at times be seen in ordinary scenes.

Benjamin comes from an era in which nostalgia has lost both its purpose and the luxury necessary for its indulgence. If anything, poetry and the poetic serve for him as vehicles to the disaster of human events. So Benjamin himself resembles the angel of history in that he can see things (in horror) from something like an aerial perspective; he sees accumulation, not depth. Baudelaire's man is exhausted, not horrified. He sees his own life, not "history." Trapped in the city streets, he is not bothered by the loss of his halo; but it does not occur to him that there are no more halos, even if only as ironic symbols of the poet. That realization will be Benjamin's to make concerning the writer of modern life. Benjamin's aura is not Baudelaire's lost auréole; his aura is, among other things, the loss of the patina on the objects of everyday life; the articulation of that loss. Baudelaire feels and writes the abrasion that is everyday life in the city—no question. But he can still tell the story of the loss of his poet's halo as a bad joke. The loss for him, above and beyond all else, is time—the desperation to forget it in some sort of imagined eternity (the cat's eyes, the first chambre), and the equal despair of ever regaining a moment that has, as Benjamin puts it, flashed out in a moment that is always already past.

For Nietzsche, writes Paul de Man, humans act by "ruthless forgetting," unburdened by "all previous experience." Such forgetting, de Man concludes, "captures the authentic spirit of modernity" (Blindness and Insight, 147). Nietzsche describes the man who acts as lacking a conscience, such that "he forgets everything in order to be able to do something." This man who forgets is reminiscent of Pascal's notion of divertissement. But although Nietzsche is here portraying a man who contemplates both past and future, this figure is neither Baudelaire's exhausted man nor Benjamin's angel of history. Nietzsche's man who forgets "is unfair toward what lies behind and knows only one right, the right of what is now coming into being as the result of his own action."[35] And so, de Man tells us,

35. The passage is from Nietzsche's "Vom Nutzen und Nachteil der Historie für das Leben," in Unzeitgemässe Betrachtrung II, ed. Karl Schlechta, in Werke (Munich, 1954), 1:215.

Modernity exists in the form of a desire to wipe out whatever came earlier, in the hope of reaching at last a point that could be called a true present, a point of origin that marks a new departure. This combined interplay of deliberate forgetting with an action that is also a new origin reaches the full power of the idea of modernity. (148)

Nothing could be more different from Baudelaire's exhausted man, who is weighted down by the past and unable to imagine anything new in the future. De Man sees Rimbaud and Artaud as examples of Nietzsche's ruthless forgetter—figures who follow Baudelaire by a generation or two, and who write after the crisis that Baudelaire records. One might argue that the man Nietzsche describes is a fine example of the bourgeois so loathed by Baudelaire, and that it is de Man (and certainly not Nietzsche) who identifies this "forgetter" with some of the great poets who follow in Baudelaire's footsteps. And for Baudelaire too, as we have noted, the act of writing allows for the repression of time. But if modernity means forgetting the past and looking forward to new origins in the future, de Man's modernity cannot include Baudelaire. Benjamin, Artaud's close contemporary (Artaud was four years younger), views modernity as obsessed by time and also by history. Benjamin sees in Baudelaire a consciousness of modernity—a view that we have resisted throughout this study—but he reads him compellingly in relation to the past that overwhelmed him, and a future that was alarming.

De Man, significantly enough, mentions Benjamin in only three passages in *Blindness and Insight*—once in reference to allegory; a second time to mention how sixteenth-century literature and Baudelaire are brought in proximity in Benjamin's work; and a third time to mention Hölderlin's poetry. History, in other words, does not appear in de Man where Benjamin's readings are concerned. I am not trying to rehearse de Man's murky relation to the events of the Second World War; I am only pointing out that "modernity" in Baudelaire pertains to a generation of writers and artists that he initially saw as full of promise ("The Painter of Modern Life," for example), and ended up characterizing, with himself the example, as exhausted by the splenetic demands of memory and the apprehension of an incomprehensible and bleak future. If Baudelaire writes of a subjectivity at risk, Benjamin turns to the terrifying perspective of the angel of history. Benjamin's reading is, of course, as much dictated by the times as are Baudelaire's writings by his own. But by defining modernity as the wiping out of what came earlier combined with the search for a "true present" and a point of origin that "marks a new departure," de

Man is participating in the very forgetting and optimism that he presents as modernity itself. He is the one who forgets that Nietzsche is railing against a life that consists in a cheerful avoidance of time and memory. Rimbaud and Artaud, it should be added, are not themselves guilty of such forgetting; their articulation of new beginnings is based on a poetics of rejection (of the past) and recognition of the absurdity of life. Their idea of the new is an attempt to build on a willful repression of the past precisely because the past cannot, paradoxically, be forgotten.

Benjamin believed that Baudelaire's poetry was marked by the disintegration of the aura (*The Writer of Modern Life*, 205). Baudelaire, I have been arguing, was in a time of transition such that his double vision produced a scene too close for him to see what was happening historically. Baudelaire describes the erosion of the subject; he does not attach it to modernity as Benjamin does. By the time Benjamin writes, the two perspectives of the past and future have combined into twin horrors. What the angel of history understands is that the atrocities committed by mankind in the past can only be repeated endlessly in the future. The angel does not have to see behind him to know this; his vision is not double but single because it is prophetic.

In 1919, Freud was to struggle with the depressing barbarism of human action in his essay on the disillusionment caused by the First World War. In "Thoughts for the Times on War and Death," he observed that "civilized nations know and understand one another so little that one can turn against the other with hate and loathing" (*SE* 14:279). Is repetition compulsion to be applied even to historical atrocity? Can mankind ever stop going to war? Our hopes for a civilized mankind were based on illusion, argues Freud: "In reality our fellow-citizens have not sunk so low as we feared, because they had never risen so high as we believed" (285).[36]

Benjamin's angel knows that repetition is the horror of reality—it stands like an icon for the thought of Nietzsche and of Freud. But Baudelaire is still crushed by two times in the space I have called the present, and is thus burdened with seeing behind him as well as in front. Modernity, we might say, was to come with the fusion of those times; but it is a fusion that Baudelaire neither understands nor sees. It is Benjamin's angel who sees it, and who—with hindsight—marks modernity as a repetition compulsion inevitable and inextricable from both poetry and history. His-

---

36. The primitive mind is imperishable, adds Freud, and can return at any moment, while the more "civilized" aspects of the mind can be easily lost forever, since they are like so many band-aids, superficially covering up the constant, which is the primitive.

tory is in Baudelaire as much as is his own poetic project, but his eyes do not see, nor even comprehend, what Benjamin so brilliantly articulates for him.

HARMONICS: THE POEM

"Repose," writes Bachelard, "is a happy vibration."[37] So "Harmonie du soir" would seem to assume, at least initially. Bachelard, who draws his notion of time from, among other things, vibration as understood in physics, ties vibration to harmony: "Without harmony, without a well-ordered dialectic, without rhythm, life and thought cannot be stable and secure" (ibid.). Certainly the poem begins with such a pleasant promise: flowers are evaporating and swaying on their stalks; sounds and perfumes turn in the evening air like a waltz. The waltz is languorous, and we do not worry yet that it is melancholic. "Things vibrate," writes Georges Poulet, "thought vibrates."[38] Such profusion, he continues, inspires "an immediate happiness, a sentiment of physical ecstasy" (398). And yet, as Poulet himself notes, this is a world whose existence cannot last. Of course, happiness never lasts, particularly in Baudelaire, even when it is fleetingly present—which is rare, as we have seen. What is this poem doing then, and how does it reveal something central to us about Baudelaire's notion of time?

Earlier in this chapter I remarked that the poem performs a false deixis: "Here come the times" is confusing because there is more than one time. Where, then, is "here"? Much of Baudelaire's poetry is about "there"— "Anywhere out of the world," for example, or "C'est là que j'ai vécu" in "La vie antérieure," or the famous "Là tout n'est qu'ordre et beauté" from "L'invitation au voyage." Or, even more explicit, from "Anywhere out of the world": "It seems to me that I will always feel good there where I am not" (là où je ne suis pas; OC 1:356).[39] The poet seems always to be attempting an escape from the here and now, so this poem with its "here" and its emphasis on "the times" is particularly intriguing. Baudelaire's double vision, I have argued, articulates two kinds of time: the eternal (which turns out to be timeless for the poet), and the splenetic, the time that besets him with its divisions into minutes and seconds. The first time is one of happiness or at least the lack of anxiety; the second is only anxiety along

---

37. *The Dialectic of Duration*, 21.

38. Georges Poulet, *Les métamorphoses du cercle* (Paris: Plon, 1961), 397.

39. A sentence that was to resonate with Lacan, one imagines.

with boredom. At first glance, "Harmonie du soir" seems to be, like the first paradisal room in "La chambre double," a moment of grace—one of those moments suggesting eternity, where everything stops to make room for the contemplation of beauty: "Here come the times where, vibrating on its stalk / Every flower evaporates like a censer; / Sounds and perfumes turn in the evening air; / melancholy waltz and languorous vertigo!" Once again—apart from the word "melancholy," a cliché of what we might call romantic sentimentality with its dash of *Weltschmertz*—the poem seems quite benevolent in its perspective. Even the title, "Evening Harmony," is auspicious. But the poem is one where the form itself of the verse belies any moment of bliss and suggests the double vision we have been considering.[40]

"Harmonie du soir" is a *pantoum*, a Malay or Sumatran verse form, properly consisting of repeated lines with interlaced (abab) refrains, each appearing only twice. The second and fourth lines of each stanza are repeated as the first and third of the following stanza; and the final line of the poem is traditionally a repetition of the first. Quatrains should be either octosyllabic or decasyllabic, and the number of stanzas is unlimited. The form is considered "exotic" by romantic poets such as Gautier or Leconte de Lisle—mainly because of its origin. The *pantoum*, moreover, is like an "exotic" dance: two steps back, three forward. The French rhetorician Morier remarks that the form suggests consciously repetitive caresses. "Originally an erotic poem," he adds, the *pantoum* by its structure "could happily depict all types of throbbing return: the whispers of seduction, voices of temptation, the question that conscience asks and asks again, the desires that people Don Juan's agony."[41] The *pantoum* is limited, however, given to neither "great lyricism nor the epic," writes Morier, because its repetitions make it obsessional. On the other hand, it is good for satire (836).

But Baudelaire has given us a false *pantoum* "without warning us," as Morier rather curiously puts it. Indeed, there are many ways in which our poet bends the form. First of all, Baudelaire chooses alexandrines, not octo- or decasyllabic lines. Second, the entire poem includes only two

---

40. "Harmonie du soir" is one of nine poems written to Mme Sabatier, the woman Baudelaire called an angel and for whom he had platonic and idealized sentiments (unlike his feelings for Jeanne Duval). The bizarre relationship has been thoroughly documented by biographers. See, e.g., Pichois, *OC* 1:906.

41. Henri Morier, *Dictionnaire de poétique et de rhétorique* (Paris: Presses Universitaires de France, 1961), 835. See also the 4th edition (1989), which has an expanded article on the *pantoum*.

rhymes, which are enclosed rather than alternating (abba instead of abab). Moreover, the last line of the poem does not repeat the first, and there are only four stanzas. As critics have noted, the poem's limit of two rhymes gives the reader a sense of claustrophobia—the repetition is necessarily constant. The fact that the rhymes are enclosed adds to the sense of confinement. Movement in the poem is similarly limited: the circling stems of the flowers, the languorous waltz, the sounds and perfumes turning in the evening air, the trembling notes of the violin, the sky likened to an altar for the sacrament, the setting sun coagulating in its own blood. Everything is trembling or vibrating, but nothing is going anywhere; things are turning in a circle. Even the wailing violin (its vibrato suggested, amplifying the vibratory images and the alliteration of the "v" sound, in itself a vibration) is limited to the shaking fingers on the instrument's fingerboard.[42]

As Morier notes, "Harmonie du soir" reveals "a dizzying style" (un style de tournoyant; Dictionnaire, 836). Morier describes the poem as having movements that bear no relation to each other, such that the reader's attention is fatigued, not knowing where to alight. Instead of having the regular pantoum's dancelike motion—two steps back and three forward—Baudelaire's poem simply piles image upon image, metaphor upon metaphor, producing a distinct feeling of vertigo.[43] Movement, in the sense that a different image—a human one—is introduced, is made with the appearance, in the second line of the third stanza, of "a tender heart that hates the vast and black abyss." This is like a conceptual step backward, as if the tender heart were withdrawing in horror from the approaching night. The fourth stanza tells us that this tender heart gathers all that remains of the "luminous past." The last line opens a different vista (since it is new in the poem) and, at the same time, closes the poem's thought: "Your memory shines in me like a monstrance." The soft evening light

---

42. Although the conductor Roger Norrington is convinced that vibrato on violins appeared in France only as of the early 1920s, most musicologists believe that it was prevalent in the nineteenth century to accommodate the "bigger sound" of romantic music. In any case, Baudelaire's use of the verb frémir (to vibrate or quiver) suggests that he was thinking of vibrato; but he may only have been referring to the instrument's quavering melodic tone. Mutatis mutandis with respect to my argument here, but see Norrington, "Bad Vibrations," The Guardian, March 1, 2003. Norrington calls for an end to vibrato, which he says taints orchestral sound, and he demands a return to "pure tone."

43. Pichois notes that "Le balcon," an early poem (1850), has a pantoum-like effect because the stanzas themselves are enclosed: the first line of each stanza is repeated in the last of the same stanza. But the effect is less claustrophobic than in "Harmonie du soir"—in part because there are more rhymes and fewer repetitions.

and the sinking red sun, both fading, are in contrast to the shining light of memory. The last line, moreover, unlike the rest of the poem, contains the only pronouns and thus the only clearly personal aspects of the poem: *ton souvenir* (your memory) and *en moi* (in me) now replace the impersonal "an afflicted heart" and "a tender heart."

The ecclesial terms, though only three, are pervasive given their placement and repetition. Moreover, these terms denote receptacles used in the celebration of the Mass. The *encensoir* contains burning incense; the *reposoir* is the altar on which the materials for the Eucharist are placed; the *ostensoir* (monstrance) is the vessel for the veneration of the Host. The emphasis, then, is on transformation, as with the Eucharist. But despite the religious terms, the context is sentimental and sensuous rather than sacramental: the flowers evaporate into incense, sounds and perfumes turn in the air like so many waltzes, the violin is like a heart that is afflicted, the sky becomes a vast altar, the red sunset is blood. Or, put another way: there is a mystery here but it is not that of the Eucharist, though the images echo it. All that is sensorially or visually discernible is abstracted into the repetition of a trembling nonmateriality. The last line, "Your memory shines inside me like a monstrance," is not only the sole personal note; it is also the place where the poem suggests memory as the mystery of transformation. The memory does not tremble or turn, unlike the other images: it gleams steadily. There is, then, a transubstantiation of sorts: the various aspects of the world (sounds, perfumes, flowers, the sky, the sun) are Hosts that allow for the monstrance of memory. The poem suggests a "Do this in remembrance of me," though the religious form will belie the poem's context.

Note, however, that it is not "you" who shines in the poet, but "your memory"; we are at least twice removed from the source (the person remembered, and then the memory itself that shines). In a way, this poem is what "A une passante" also foresees: your memory will shine in me; I will remember the memory of you. If the Eucharist is the mystery of the transformation of bread and wine into the body and blood of Christ, here the transformation is the luminous appearance of memory out of the evening's waning light. The present, for Baudelaire, is here the accumulation of senses that together form the receptacle for memory. Once again, the present is not a time; it is rather a place from which to view, to bring back or conjure up, a lost other.

Appropriately enough, the poem is almost entirely written in the present tense. The only exception is the *passé composé*, "the sun has drowned" (*le soleil s'est noyé*); but with *est*, the present of the auxiliary verb *être* (to be), the past participle *noyé* functions as an adjective and serves to preserve the present tense that motivates the poem. Here we have, then, *Erfahrung* (the entire description of things that form the first fifteen lines of the poem) transmuted into *Erlebnis*—a moment of intensity and strength—in the last line. The present has served to produce the *Erlebnis*, but it is a moment that allows for the resurgence of memory. The present here serves as a kind of open sesame into the past. Unlike Proust's involuntary recollection, it is the willed memory in "Harmonie du soir" that creates a privileged moment. What a younger Baudelaire proclaims in "Le balcon" seems still to have some truth: "I know," he writes there, "the art of evoking happy minutes" (*OC* 1:37). They are, however, minutes that have already been, even if the moment that allows for their evocation can in itself become privileged by virtue of having unlocked the past.

This, I think, is how we should read a passage in *Fusées* in which Baudelaire also writes of privileged moments of existence, "in which time and duration [*l'étendue*] are more profound, and the feeling of existence immensely augmented" (*OC* 1:658). For him, these more often than not are moments having to do with a present that has produced the evocation of memory. Such a *sorcellerie évocatoire*, as Baudelaire puts it in the same passage from *Fusées*, is the precise phrase he famously chooses to describe the poetic gifts of Théophile Gautier, in the 1859 article of the same name. In the Gautier article, Baudelaire describes the older poet's art in terms that sound, initially, very much like "Harmonie du soir" as well as with Baudelaire's own "Correspondance." Gautier, writes Baudelaire, combines an immense intellect "of universal *correspondence* and symbolism." He knows how to "define the mysterious attitude that objects of creation hold before the gaze of man." There is something "*sacred*" in the process of word and verb. To know how to use language (through the *sorcellerie évocatoire*) allows for color to speak "like a deep and vibrating voice; for monuments to rise up and jut out on the depth of space . . . ; perfume provokes the corresponding thought and memory" (*OC* 2:117–18).

What Baudelaire describes in Gautier is the ability to intensify space (and thus existence) by using "objects of creation" to achieve a kind of synesthesia of the poetic sacred. Clearly, much of this is how the young Baudelaire understands the role and urgency of poetry. Vibration is to be noted here (Gautier's "deep and vibrating voice"); it occurs too in the passage we have been considering in *Fusées*, where it is also a phenomenon related to space: the supernatural (*le surnaturel*) is "intensity, sonority, limpidity, vibrativity, profoundness, and repercussions in space and in time" (*OC* 1:658). Baudelaire invents the neologism *vibrativité* to keep the assonance in the catalog of nouns. But "vibrativity" is also a special warning, foreshadowing of a privileged moment to come, much like exposition for an epiphany caused by the tea-and-madeleine episode in Proust. In "Combray," the narrator tells us, he feels a certain affinity with the Celtic belief that the soul of those we have lost are trapped "in some inferior being, in an animal, in a plant, in some inanimate object." They are lost to us, continues Marcel, until the day when we happen to pass by the tree or to possess the object in which they are imprisoned. Our recognition of the lost souls releases them from their prison. Their liberation is presaged by a type of "vibrativity": the souls "start and tremble . . . ; liberated by us, they have vanquished death and come back to live with us."[44] Trembling and vibrating portend in both Baudelaire and Proust a change of dimensions; the recapturing of a lost time and those who inhabited it. But note how much more optimistic Proust can be. His involuntary memory allows for a return to the past, to its veritable recovery—all of Combray will rise up out of the narrator's cup of tea. But in Baudelaire, there is no liberation of what is lost; there is, on the contrary, an act of will that keeps the past glowing, but as memory.

If the voluntary memory allows for privileged moments in Baudelaire, it is only, to repeat, to keep alive a memory that is always recognized as forever lost. No recognition of the past will allow for the "liberation" of what is lost. It is true that for Baudelaire, the voluntary memory does succeed in willing images of the past: "I know the art of evoking happy minutes" is the young Baudelaire's confident declaration. But "Your memory shines in me like a monstrance" is the more mature poet's acknowledgment of a different ability. The effort to retain a remembered image by an act of will remains, as before; but now there is also the capacity to see in the fading light of the present-as-place the unchanging luminosity of memory itself as that which both gives back the vision of a vanished past and simultaneously keeps it within the confines of that which cannot be recaptured. Existence is "augmented," more profound, perhaps because when the dimension of the past opens up as an icon of memory to be contemplated, the present-as-place is deepened by the added dimension, vibrating between two places.

Poulet, it will be recalled, observes that in Baudelaire it is as if the present were both the point of departure of a movement opened out toward the future, and the point of arrival of a different and yet identical

44. Marcel Proust, *Du côté de chez Swann*, vol. 1 of *A la recherché du temps perdu*, ed. Jean-Yves Tadié (Paris: Gallimard, edition de la Pléiade, 1987), 43–44.

movement coming from the past. For Poulet, sensations are what allow for moving into the past and for eliciting an image of the future through their vibratory diffusion. He too sees the present in Baudelaire as a place. But it is important to note for Poulet the sensory is what motivates the movement that transports Baudelaire forward and backward in time. The present allows for the "point of departure" toward the future, and a "point of arrival" for that which comes from the past. The present for Poulet might be compared to a train station, with trains going in two different directions. But these trains, as we will see later, converge for Poulet into a huge space of undifferentiated time.

Baudelaire, however, is more visual than that, and his time zones are not contiguous; they do not bleed into each other. Just as the two rooms of "La chambre double" were noncontiguous in their mental spaces, so the past and the future do not meet—nor does the present serve to facilitate their motion. On the contrary, there is a temporal parataxis in Baudelaire that serves to make the break between past and future clear. The last line of "Harmonie du soir" performs such a parataxis. Two of the four lines in the fourth stanza (one and three) are repetitions, *pantoum* style, tying them to the rest of the poem. The second line introduces the past, since the "tender heart that hates vast and black nothingness" (line one in the stanza) gathers all vestiges of the "luminous past." "Vestiges" prepares the reader for the fact that the past is left as only a trace (and returns the reader to the assonant *vertige*), but the luminosity already contrasts with the dying light of the evening. The past, in other words, possesses a light that the setting sun cannot match. The last line is a tour de force that not only fails to repeat the first line of the poem (unlike the classical *pantoum*, as we have noted) but produces a dimension completely unlike the rest. The personal pronouns, as we have said, add a different timbre entirely, and so the line itself reads like a mental shock: "Your memory shines in me like a monstrance." The register, tone, and image do not partake of the melancholy waltz and fading light informing the rest of the poem. The parataxis is visual, aided by the etymology of *ostensoir*. From the Latin *ostensus*, the word means to show (the Host) in a transparent or otherwise open receptacle. Thus the memory of the beloved (a woman we may assume) shines like that which is meant to be venerated and is prepared for transformation. The monstrance is thus the real deixis of the poem; it is the "here" (*voici*) that is far more immediate than the surrounding landscape of the present; far more luminous than the darkening light enclosing the rest of the poem.

But what do I mean by parataxis in Baudelaire? Auerbach reads the

Song of Roland as a series of friezes unconnected by conjunctional bonds. Such parataxis, argues Auerbach, can only be comprehended by the reader/ listener of the epic tale when the gaps are filled by (in this case) medieval ideology—in other words, the feudal order. For example, the scene of the dying Roland throwing down his glove is nonsensical if the reader/listener of the *Roland* does not know feudal tradition and hierarchy. As he lies mortally wounded, Roland throws down his glove to show vassalage to God; God is his liege. Parataxis in medieval stories—or in much of the Hebrew scriptures and the New Testament—produces a series of pictures, or framed textual moments, that are understood by context and cultural ideologies and are thus connected *après coup*, if almost instantaneously, by the informed reader.[45] Baudelaire's paratactic imaging is less narrativ- ised than visual. In other words, the gaps between the images are not filled so much as they are reverberated through contrast. The last line of "Har- monie du soir" echoes much of the rest of the poem with its reference to light; but the fading light of the first fifteen lines is at variance with the sudden, yet steady shining of the monstrance in the poet's memory. There is no attempt to connect the two, except to underline that the memory possesses a light that the paltry light of day (to echo Novalis's *Hymns to the Night*) can never achieve. The shock of the last line, then, is not only that it introduces a new idea but that the image is not in the same register as the rest of the poem. Everything about the earlier lines, about the im- ages and sensations of the present, is vertiginous and unreal by compari- son to the shining memory of the last line.

Indeed, we might say that Baudelaire's notion of time is, as Hegel puts it, a picture-thought.[46] The past can produce luminous images through an act of will; the future looms as an unknown series of imaged possibili- ties. The present, what Hegel calls "the side of *immediacy* and *existence*" (*Phenomenology*, 478) is for Baudelaire a place that pales in contrast to the intensity of memory or the terrible anxiety provoked by imagining the future (bankruptcy, death, loneliness, his mother's health, and his own, and above all, as here, "vast and black nothingness"). All of the sensory as- pects of the present (flowers, sunsets, the sky and so on) serve in "Harmo- nie du soir" to trigger the image of the past that, in turn, functions (with its shining light) to repress the blackness of night that must inevitably fol-

45. Auerbach, let it not be forgotten, ties much of the difficulty in parataxis to Christi- anity and to what he calls the figural. See Erich Auerbach, *Mimesis: The Representation of Reality in Western Literature*, trans. Willard R. Trask (Princeton: Princeton University Press, 1968), 73 ff.

46. But for different reasons. See *The Phenomenology of Spirit*, e.g., 478.

low the sun coagulating in its own blood. One has the impression, at the
end of this poem, that the image in the memory, the monstrance, serves as
a lantern in the night for the poet, protecting him from the abyss of what
must come. The gathering of all vestiges of the luminous past then, produces the "lantern." It is in this sense that the poem achieves the transformation that a monstrance promises. Indeed, the suspension dots leading
to the last line serve not only to create a pause in preparation for the final
image; they also gather all of the energy produced by the rest of the poem
to break away from what has preceded.

The present is that place where such a transformation is performed;
it is the gathering of sensory perception for the paradoxical purpose of rejecting the present in order to bring forth memory as an inner light, thus
combating the hated darkness. The economy of transubstantiation, and
even the theological logic of Communion, are put into action. The amo-
rous tenor of the last image seems falsely secular. The vision is double
because the sensory productions of the present produce the luminous image of the past.

But, to repeat, these are pictures more than movement. The picture of
the past, when the voluntary memory is successful, is a privileged moment
that is retained in the mind ("O you whom I could have loved, O you who
knew it!") The picture of the future, when the mind cannot extinguish
it, is an abyss (a nothingness that is vast and black). These are paratactic
images, which no ideology can serve to connect; indeed, the picture of the
past strains to veil the image of the future, even as the present works to
evoke both.

Memory in Baudelaire is largely voluntary—evoked by the poet's will.
"La chevelure" manifests the poet's voluntary evocation of memory.[47] But
even when memory is involuntary for Baudelaire, as it is in Proust, it is
transported into a present that is intoxicated with the past, and therefore—
for Baudelaire—blessedly less vivid. In the poem "Le parfum," for example,
we read that the scent of incense creates a "Profound charm, magical, by
which the restored past intoxicates us in the present" (*Charme profound,
magique, dont nous grise / Dans le présent le passé restauré; OC* 1:39). In
other words, the restored past goes to the poet's head, such that the present
is necessarily blurred by the dominance of memory. "Harmonie du soir"

---

47. The line that is particularly a propos in this context, as Pichois and others have
noted, is "Je la veux agiter dans l'air comme un mouchoir" (I want to wave it in the air like a
handkerchief)—the poet thus forcing his reverie by shaking his mistress's hair. "Agiter" is a
kind of vibration too, as in "Harmonie;" shaking or vibration serving to preface the return of
memory.

is like a dilated version of "Le parfum"; as we have seen, "Harmonie" is the gathering of all the sensory impressions of the present, such that the image in the last line can suddenly appear as that which, by virtue of its steady light, blinds the poet to all surroundings. And yet the surroundings are what foster the move to the past.

We might consider a line in Novalis's *Hymnen an die Nacht* a more narrativized example of something similar. After contemplating his unhappiness over the death of his beloved, the poet breaks away from the here-and-now: "Und mit einemmale riss das Band der Geburt."[48] (And in a single moment, the tie to birth is torn). But if Novalis describes such a break, "Harmonie du soir" performs it. The last line is the break away from now-time; the icon of memory erases everything else, even though the everything else has triggered the memory. It is the present in this poem that fades in the light of the past. The poem performs a double vision because both fields of vision remain; but they remain in an ocular economy in which the function of the present is to withdraw into the background once it has accomplished its task of producing the past. Thus the last line of "Harmonie" is an afterimage, much as we noted in "A une passante." As in "Passante," the poet's sensory environment (the present) produces an image that remains in the eye. But the flash of lightening that produces the image in "Passante" becomes, in "Harmonie," the evocation of an event already past. The light shines rather than flashes in "Harmonie," suggesting that here the image has already been sealed in the memory so that, once conjured up again, its steady light can endure against the dreaded night that is the future.

Time in Baudelaire tends to be space—or rather, spaces. Since time is spatialized, Poulet notes, "all of lived experience appears spatialized as well and, consequently, as identical to space" (*Métamorphoses*, 407). Poulet's reading argues that, in Baudelaire, existence has "neither a completed past, nor a future in suspension, since everything is simultaneously present in the length of its course." In the Baudelairean experience, he adds, "lived duration (*durée*) and lived space are exact analogs of each other" (ibid.). As Poulet would have it, everything in Baudelaire converges into a space of the present which is one and the same as a vast, homogeneous expanse of time. We have seen, however, that the present for Baudelaire is indeed a space from which the parallel (but not identical) spaces of the

48. Novalis, *Werke und Briefe* (Munich: Winkler, 1968), 55. We might note here that for Novalis, the torn thread, or cord, of birth includes a tear away from the light as well: "des Lichtes Fessel."

past and future are able to appear. Time in Baudelaire is precisely not the collapse of everything into one eternity of space. There are two times in Baudelaire: the past, which can serve as an antidote to the present, and the future, which poisons the present. What the poetry can do, then, is to transform the present into that space from which the future is averted and the past reanimated. Thus the present is the place in which a double vision not only is made possible but is demanded. It is for this reason that the first line of the poem insists upon *times*—"Here come the times" (*voici venir les temps*). The fading light, dusk, is the present from which both the terror of the future and the (frequently) consoling memory of the past will be elicited. Both will be seen at once. Even if the future is that time that must be repressed and indeed blinded in the light of the past, both are seen simultaneously from that place called the present, where the sensations eliciting them both are produced.

Harmony means concord, but also the simultaneous sounding of several notes. That is what the present offers here—the sounding of two visions: the combination of what is feared in the future and what is remembered (lovingly, in this case) from the past. That is how one can read the title "Harmonie du soir." The present is like the instrument that allows these two temporal chords; the poet loses sight of neither. Far from being a vast space of spread-out time, Baudelaire's vision of the temporal is rigorously dual, with the present producing the vision of what lies ahead, and the image of what is remembered as eternally left behind. "Je suis autrefois" says the clock in "L'horloge" ("I am times past"). This statement is like a temporal equivalent of Rimbaud's famous cleavage of subjectivity: "Je EST un autre." Though the clock is a "sinister god, frightening, impassive," tormenting the poet with its *"Souviens-toi"* (remember), and with the fact that it is always already too late, there is a way in which the clock is itself the poet's doubled vision of time.

The clock performs the two visions of time we have been arguing are Baudelaire's: on the one hand, the clock is a constant reminder of the past as lost (*"Remember!"*), of a life that the clock has pumped (*pompé*) out of the poet. Three hundred and sixty times an hour, the second hand whispers *souviens-toi*! Time here drags along as in the Spleen poems, heavy-handed and crushing: "I have more memories," writes the poet in one of the Spleen poems, "than if I were a thousand years old." Or again, "Nothing equals in length the limping days . . . ; ennui, fruit of a gloomy lack of curiosity, takes on immortal proportions" (*OC* 1:73). The seconds drag on in an endless present, yes—but it is a present that accumulates into a heavy past with memories that the poet is always too late in recovering.

The present itself, it will be noted, is as if timeless in these instances, because it does not seem to move, or moves only in agonizingly slow motion.
Eternity, as Baudelaire states more than once, is timeless. Ironically, that
very eternity for which he always yearns is also the place of spleen: timeless because seemingly unending.

On the other hand (as in "Harmonie"), time in "L'horloge" also rushes
inexorably to its obvious end: "The day wanes; night augments" Time is
speeding to the abyss here, echoing the *néant* of "Harmonie": "The abyss
is always thirsty; the water-clock is emptying." The abyss, unquenchable,
is as if drinking the hours of the clock. The last hour will soon strike,
and everything will say "It is too late!" (*OC* 1:81). As with the poet, the
clock has no present: by the time it whispers its seconds, they are already
past. And once time has passed, it is too late and the abyss looms. "Je suis
autrefois" is a statement that Baudelaire himself could make with respect
to time: I am past times because I cannot let go of my memories; I am past
times because I am hurtling toward the abyss, and will soon be no more.
I speak as one who is already dead; my text itself is being written as I die,
is being read as from beyond the grave. Like the Heauton Timorumenos,
or self-tormentor, the poet torments himself with his own obsession: the
loss of time (the past is too fleeting, gone; death comes too quickly), and
his incapacity to live in the present (there is no time there, only endless
seconds). The two hands of the clock seem to actualize such movements:
the cruelly slow and the terrifyingly rapid.

AND TIME AND THE WORLD ARE EVER IN FLIGHT

It would be easy to remain within the abstract here—to speak more of
Bergson, Heidegger, or Kant on time. Or to enter some sort of psychoanalytic reverie: the paradisal time the child Baudelaire had with his mother,
between her two husbands, which makes the past into something that
must always be cherished, and the future something that must always be
feared. But Baudelaire is one of those curious writers who—more specifically and overtly than most—was formed both by his own neurotic temperament (Proust's love of his mother, to take but one example, has nothing on Baudelaire's twisted relation with his own) and by the depraved
times in which he lived. Indeed, this poet is a bellwether of his age. His is a
discourse of crisis, one that describes the absence of a code for comprehension, an inability to see how one event necessarily, or even possibly, follows logically from another. It is a crisis that comes with modernity—the
modern industrial city, the changing face of Paris, the upheaval in social

classes, the aftershocks of the revolution, the rise of a bourgeoisie grounded
in murder and committed to *bienséance* (as if decorum could disguise the
bourgeoisie's guilt with respect to the urban working class), the still fresh
memory of the guillotining of the king and his aristocratic retinue, the
rise of poverty in the city. How, in this crisis, to present a coherent narrative that makes sense, that is sequential? It is not merely a question of
learning, within the sea of sensory stimulation that is the modern city,
to see differently, to blot out overstimulation. It is also a question of rid-
ing out, surviving, the turning point that is the modern world—of leaving
behind the world that was, without feeling either conventional in one's
nostalgia, or undefined in the fairly incomprehensible future that seeks to
understand itself as the present.

   "Je suis autrefois" is also Baudelaire's struggle with a time and a Paris
that he feels are no longer his. The dandy does not merely observe; nor does
he merely stand apart, aloof and indifferent in his ironic stance. He is out
of step with the times—a pose he willfully chooses, perhaps to hide his
own discomfort, his own sense of not belonging to the here and now. "The
old Paris no longer exists," writes the poet in "Le Cygne"; and he adds there
that "the form of a city / Changes more, alas! than the heart of a mortal"
(*OC* 1:85). It is not only a question of nostalgia for a lost city. (True, the city
Baudelaire describes, in its rubbles of the past and its ruins from which
its future will rise, is not one he recognizes, any more than do the various
exiles who people the swan poem.) It is also that for Baudelaire the city
enacts a visual parataxis, so to speak; that is, a series of disconnected moments that the ideology of the culture presumably connects. One can assume that the culture of capitalism could impose its ideology to fill in the
blanks, to put in the missing links. But for Baudelaire as well as for much
of the underclass he describes, the code is missing for comprehension—
there is no coherent narrative to explain the upheaval and chaos of the
city, its new social classes, its new money system, its inaccessible (for the
poor) and yet apparently indispensable (for the bourgeoisie) commodities.
It is no surprise that in such a situation, Baudelaire's is a discourse of crisis; one that does not comprehend much of what it describes but records
an unraveling of the old social codes, and the production of new cultural
networks that are as obscure as they are ubiquitous. Baudelaire's memory
is as if under erasure by a triumphant capitalist present; it is a present that
creates a cultural and visual pandemonium and, in so doing, destroys the
sequential narrative that most of Baudelaire's contemporaries understood
as history. Only the culture of making money could see in the ruins of old
Paris a superstructure that would cohere in the city of the future. Those

with power, in other words, saw the future as the expansion of that power, and the past as well worth leaving behind.

For the bourgeoisie, the present is but a demonstration of that power. Indeed, it has often been remarked that modernity is precisely a desire to eliminate the past, an attempt to create its own origin. It may be the case, as Paul de Man believes, that in cutting itself off from the past, modernity "has at the same time severed itself from the present" (*Blindness and Insight*, 149); de Man then cites Nietzsche on the impossibility of escaping history (150). But it all depends on one's definition of modernity. If we are talking about Baudelaire, then his crisis, as I have been demonstrating, consists in being unable to experience the present. He rejects the new order—and rejects it cognitively as well as psychologically. Baudelaire's crisis is the rejection of modernity in the sense of the new at the expense of memory. He may talk of *le moderne* and be enraptured by the productions of contemporary art and literature; but he emphatically neither wants nor acknowledges the erasure of the past. Indeed, as the past is increasingly wiped out around him, Baudelaire becomes obsessed with memory, even as he grows ever more fearful of a death that, in its annihilation of consciousness, closely parallels the eradication of history that the new Paris professes to accomplish. The discourse of crisis in Baudelaire is the refusal of a present that, in its mercantile triumphalism, erects codes that the poet rejects and an ideology that he chooses to see as incomprehensible. The new anthropology of time, as established by the bourgeoisie, is one on which the poet instinctively turns his back. His *horloge* will not be theirs. Baudelaire's experience of time, in its avoidance of the now, alternates between the past and the future—both, let it be noted, outside of clock time. It is an alternation that I have presented as another kind of double vision; and it is an alternation that creates a vibration between two times. "Here come the times" is the recognition of a space that prepares the sighting of such a dual perspective.

Appendix

Harmonie du soir

Voici venir les temps où, vibrant sur sa tige
Chaque fleur s'évapore ainsi qu'un encensoir;
Les sons et les parfums tournent dans l'air du soir;
Valse mélancolique et langoureux vertige!

Chaque fleur s'évapore ainsi qu'un encensoir;
Le violon frémit comme un cœur qu'on afflige;
Valse mélancolique et langoureux vertige!
Le ciel est triste et beau comme un grand reposoir.

Le violon frémit comme un cœur qu'on afflige,
Un cœur tendre, qui hait le néant vaste et noir!
Le ciel est triste et beau comme un grand reposoir;
Le soleil s'est noyé dans son sang qui se fige.

Un cœur tendre, qui hait le néant vaste et noir,
Du passé lumineux recueille tout vestige!
Le soleil s'est noyé dans son sang qui se fige . . .
Ton souvenir en moi luit comme un ostensoir!

CONCLUSION

This double vision, this inability to see now-time because of the weight of what lies behind and what looms ahead, is a perspective that would largely be resolved with (ironically, one might say) time. It is resolved, that is, when modernity becomes habitus and when daily life grows isomorphic with the life of the city (thus Mallarmé, for example, largely mentions the city only indirectly, even when he returns to Paris). Baudelaire's time is one of transition, as we know: from the ancien régime to a capitalist and industrialist culture; from well-defined social classes to an amalgam in which the bourgeoisie, in all of its triumphant manifestations, is emphatically evident; from a medieval Paris to a city of wide boulevards and commercial spaces that leak into the private; from an art that prides itself on the focused figural to one that gradually forces blotches of color and form to seep, blurringly, into patches of perspective; from republics, monarchies, and empires to republics again—all marked by revolution, coups d'état and abdications; from home and small businesses to department stores and the commodification and glorification of material objects. As Hobsbawm has noted, the world of the 1840s was "out of balance": there were too many changes in the economic, technical, and social spheres. Baudelaire's entire generation suffered these upheavals, and if he had the poetic genius to record such transformations, he was no less overwhelmed by them than his contemporaries. That generation never recovered, much as the generation of 1968 never quite recovered from the events that were called "the Movement."

Such ambivalence and confusion can be seen in the textual accounts of the revolution of 1848. Michelet, for example, worries that he does not have the voice to be heard by the people, since his only language is that of "cultivated minds." In writing his history of 1789, Michelet worries about

243

popular culture and its literature, whose readers are the ones he wants to reach. But his language is of the high style, and he fears he is doomed to an elite and restricted readership. His gaze is thus fixed on two revolutions: the one he narrates and the one he witnesses. He writes, as one critic puts it, like a snake run over by a cart; by means of an effort both great and painful. The poet Lamartine, meanwhile, has his own stylistic problems. His history of '48 opens with a strange apology: "the slightly literary and slightly epic form of this narrative," he bashfully acknowledges, "in which I refer to myself in the third person," is the result of trying to write history "in the rather solemn manner of antiquity, in the Greek or Roman world. It is a lapidary and impersonal style, which is the only appropriate one, in my opinion, for the real epics of nations." But he begins to feel uncomfortable: "When I realized my error," he continues, "half of the first volume had been edited, and it was too late to retrace my steps. I continued in the same style, even while I had changed my perspective." An apology follows: "It is an error of composition, not of expediency [*convenance*]. I beg the reader's forgiveness."[1] It is no longer appropriate, Lamartine realizes, to write in the classical style. The order and hierarchy that such a style presupposes are now defunct. New methods of addressing the reader—more intimately, or perhaps conversely, not at all—must be found. Lamartine's gradual discomfort with a style he had always used before with ease is a mark of the times: not only did the center no longer hold; no one quite knew where the center lay.

Marie d'Agoult, who wrote under the pseudonym Daniel Stern, has similar problems of composition. In her *History of the Revolution of 1848* she dares hope "that a book in which the author disappears entirely in order to let the facts speak for themselves will be all the more useful in propagating truths that I consider useful."[2] Eighteen years later, Flaubert will be writing to George Sand (both safely on their estates) in a similar vein that a novelist *"has no right to express his opinion* on anything whatever." He chokes on some of the things he feels, but he "swallow[s] them rather than spitting them out. Indeed, what is the point of saying them?"[3] Sand, who writes about the heart with a vengeance, is horrified: "To put nothing in your writing that comes from the heart? I do not understand that at all; I mean, not at all" (ibid.). Flaubert answers, "I didn't express

1. Alphonse de Lamartine, *Histoire de la Révolution de 1848* (Paris: Garnier, 1859), ii.

2. Daniel Stern, *Histoire de la Révolution de 1848* (Paris: Charpentier, 1862), v.

3. On December 5, 1866. Flaubert, *Correspondance*, 1:575.

myself properly." He adds, "All I meant is that one's personality should not be brought into play" (578–79) They never speak of the disagreement again; but the differences in their manners of narrating speak for themselves.

The confusion concerning how to write, what tense to use, and to what extent to be present, as narrator, in one's writing, are questions that have been raised and brilliantly analyzed by Roland Barthes in *Le degré zéro de l'écriture*, as I mentioned in chapter 1. After 1848, declares Barthes, in France it is no longer possible to assume the preterit, or *passé simple*, when writing a novel. Balzac, according to this logic, was the last to sit comfortably and start writing. Flaubert is the first of the "modern" writers—uncomfortable, if consistent, in his use of the blander and less temporally focused *imparfait* and in his willed disappearance, as narrator, from his own texts. But the problem persists in the writing of history as well as fiction. The examples just given—Michelet, Lamartine, Daniel Stern, Flaubert, and George Sand—show the extent to which writers had difficulty in finding their narrative voice after the events of 1848. And this was true whether the text was a novel or a history, whether the events were recounted or just as assiduously avoided (Sand, for example). How do you write about a crisis that has changed the very perception of your relation to history, and thus to time itself? One writer who remained unperturbed in his prose, if not in his political views, was Tocqueville. His *Souvenirs*, which relate the '48 revolution, are, on the level of prose, a masterful and sure-footed narrative—autobiographical (Tocqueville is very much present), magisterial (he knows the "smell" of revolution), pedagogic (after the June debacle, he writes "The people have just demonstrated that they are unworthy of living in liberty"). This is a man who is at home in narrating history, clear on what should be done, worried about the political future of France, but unworried in his tenses depicting the crisis. And yet even the *Souvenirs* begin with Tocqueville's complaining about "the confused traits that form the indecisive physiognomy of my time."[4] Moreover, he reminds the reader that the instigators of the 1830 revolution are the same as those for 1848; for there is only one revolution, "of which our fathers saw the beginning and, it seems, we will not see the end" (13). This is part of what we need to keep in mind with respect to the generation that saw 1848: many of them believed that the revolution was to continue, unabated, during the whole of their lifetimes. With respect to Tocqueville's generation, and to Baudelaire's, this was an accurate prophecy. Though neither would live to

4. Alexis de Tocqueville, *Souvenirs* (Paris: Gallimard, 1964), 12.

see the revolution of 1870 (the Commune), they both inhabited an era of continuous political chaos.

The trauma of 1848 was in part the realization that the ancien régime was really gone, and gone forever. As the politician of the time, Garnier-Pagès, put it, a monarchy is omnipotent, solid, founded on the presumption of a long dynasty. Adjectives proliferate in Garnier-Pagès's description of the apparent unshakability of the monarchy. Then, with a long dash that mirrors the rupture from the old order, he writes: "——All of a sudden, this monarchy of such splendor, so richly constituted, so well protected by its means, crumbles and disappears."[5] Garnier-Pagès, who favors the past perfect tense, uses the present here as if to underline the suddenness of the change. He then describes the upheaval of 1789: "dazzling as lightening, striking by surprise, and breaking the throne after having overturned it" (ibid.). By comparison with the "real" revolution of 1789, the revolution 1848 seemed staged and farcical, as Marx was to put it. After the euphoria of 1848 (which Baudelaire later calls ridiculous), the generation that fought on the barricades suffered a permanent complex; unlike their fathers and grandfathers, they had failed to upend the status quo—the bourgeoisie continued to reign, and reign supreme. The generation of '48 is one of rupture or, at least, tends to see itself as such. It represents itself as coming of age with a consciousness of division: division of class, political activism, writing, history, language and style, time, and representation itself. The vocabulary of rupture is rampant in their texts, at many levels, with the repetition that trauma necessarily imposes.

We should note, moreover, that Louis-Napoleon's physiognomy was just as "indecisive," to return to Tocqueville, as Louis-Philippe's had been, and as was the era itself. The "Bourgeois King" was ousted in '48 only to make room, a few years later, for "the nephew," as Marx called the man who became Napoleon III. But both men—the king and the emperor—are described as nondescript businessmen with no particular intelligence or ardor. As the politician Louis Blanc puts it in his own history of the events,[6] Louis-Philippe had an "utter inability to comprehend all that was chivalrous and elevated in the genius of France." Similarly, Blanc said baldly to Louis-Napoleon himself, "Under the sway of your uncle, despotism was at least wrapped up in the purple mantle of military glory."

5. Louis-Antoine Garnier-Pagès, *Histoire de la Révolution de 1848* (Paris: Pagnerre, 1866), 11.

6. Louis Blanc, *1848: Historical Revelations* (London: Bradbury and Evans, 1858), 498.

Nothing purple remained, not even intellect. Blanc was later to say of the Emperor Napoleon III that he mistook "the power of the sword for that of the mind" (ibid.).

The era, then, is a peculiar combination of constant political earthquakes, utter boredom, and the commercialization of the spirit. This combination of fear and ennui is not, it will be noted, very far from the alternating states of mind that describe our poet. If I have given this brief rendition of the times, it is to highlight the fact that (as seen throughout this study) Baudelaire is in many ways the natural child of his epoch. But he takes a willed (and disdainful) distance from that epoch, dismissing it as a brief foray into "intoxication." It was a drunken state based on "the taste of vengeance," which is the *natural* taste of destruction" (OC 1:679). He does, however, mention his "fury" at the fake Napoleon's coup d'état: "Another Bonaparte! How shameful." These are notes to himself in *Mon cœur mis à nu*—scribblings apparently intended to have been essays but never completed. Again on the failed revolution he jots down: "1848 was amusing only because everyone turned it into utopias like castles in Spain. 1848 was charming only because of the very excess of its ridiculousness" (680). He tries to convince himself, as well as an eventual reader, that politics are a waste of time; the status quo will prevail even as the regimes change. But as we have seen, and as many critics have observed, Baudelaire could never give up entirely on politics. Part of his political stance is not forgetting. It is a praxis central to Baudelaire, not only because memory can provide some hope, but also because the memory of the past is a rejection of the present and of its self-satisfied bourgeois ethics of utilitarianism. "To be a useful man," declares Baudelaire, "has always struck me as something quite hideous" (679).

As mentioned at the outset of this study, Georges Bataille, in disagreement with Sartre, believes that the poet's denial of the Good is basically a denial of the future. It follows that for Baudelaire the unsatisfactory is "agonizingly attractive," and the refusal to work is validated by the maintenance of what Bataille and Sartre both see as the transcendence of obligation. But it will be recalled that Bataille then parts company with Sartre: this is not an individual error in Baudelaire, and Sartre's mistake is to think it is. It is not only individual necessity that is expressed in *Les fleurs du mal*, adds Bataille; the poems are also the result of "a *material* tension imposed, periodically, from without" (*La littérature du mal*, 43). This is a point of view that the present study has assumed. We might say that Baudelaire's obsession with original sin, his turn to Maistre, is a perverse way of returning a sacred aspect—even if an irrevocably sinful one—to the practice of being, or what Georg Simmel calls "the technique of life."[7]

Baudelaire's genius is that he puts the reader into the same mael-strom as himself: history constantly interrupts the "pure" text; just as the text itself can cover over external events. Baudelaire, in other words (one thinks again of the long lists of contradictory polarities we have been considering), forces the same conceptual discordance upon his reader: he puts together divergent, opposing notions in order to blast the bourgeoisie out of its continuum, to use a phrase from Benjamin. The chaotic events surrounding Baudelaire can never be discounted or placed in some sort of atmospheric background: they must remain central, foundational, to his writings.

But contradiction, as I have been arguing from the beginning of this book, is insufficient ammunition to "get at" Baudelaire. Nor is the provo-cation that marks his verse, a provocation in which he constantly reveled. What I have been calling his double vision is the result, not of some clarity of thought born of a coherent perspective on the chaos of early modernity, but rather of the overlaying of disparate realities that remain, opposingly, in the poet's gaze. As we have seen, because so much of his poetry grows out of contradiction and antinomies, Baudelaire scholars have too fre-quently assumed that he knew what he was seeing and recording; that he was drawing the contours of modernity (or *le moderne*) in terms of diamet-ric contrasts as he encountered them. But for Baudelaire, the past has not yet caught up with the present—indeed, must not do so, even as it cannot. It is perhaps for this reason that Baudelaire, unlike the other writers to whom I have just referred, has no difficulty in finding his narrative pitch. He writes in more than one voice (the confident art critic, for example, as against the lyricist, and again as against the self-pitying letter writer), and he sees in more than one perspective. But intellectually, if not chronologi-cally, he keeps himself anterior to the rupture that is incited by the events of 1848. There is no question concerning language in Baudelaire, as I have stressed: language for him conveys. Mallarmé will be able to internalize some of the Baudelaire tropes and motifs; but, unlike his predecessor, Mal-larmé is able to stand back and aestheticize the modernity that Baudelaire could only record. Baudelairean motifs were to reappear in Mallarmé, but self-consciously, positing the incapacity of language to represent, and with

7. Georg Simmel, "The Metropolis and Mental Life," in *The Sociology of Georg Simmel*, trans. and ed. Kurt H. Wolff (Glencoe, IL: Free Press, 1950), 409.

a critical distance from the modern and a resignation to its empire that Baudelaire neither achieved nor, finally, wanted.

In the period during which Baudelaire is writing, there are so many changes in daily life that he frequently does not fully understand what he is seeing, even as he records the varying versions of life that his splintered gaze encounters. His double vision is the result of an incomprehensible world to Baudelaire; a world that would later (with Baudelaire as chief spokesman after the fact) become the hallmark of modernity, and the trigger for modernism. But for Baudelaire, such a double vision makes for a shattered, if at times exquisite, vision. Progress was generally to be resisted, both because it was the *cri de guerre* of the society that had triumphed and that he loathed, and because progress meant moving toward the future, which he saw as menacing on every level imaginable. Writing, then, had to oppose all resolution, and contradictions had to be maintained; language itself, however, had not yet become the source of impotence and blank pages. Seeing double for Baudelaire is less a matter of choice than it is the accurate rendition of his psychological as well as historical being-in-the-world.

Baudelaire's crisis stems from the concatenation of incommensurables that are mutually exclusive but remain side by side nonetheless. He does not have the distance from modernity that would allow for the conscious stances too often attributed to him. He is a brilliant critic, as we have seen, and probably the greatest poet of the nineteenth century. He is one of the inventors of the term "modern." But the upheaval of '48, combined with all of the other aspects of the new style of life in modernity, deny him a unity of vision. It is this lack of ontic concordance with its attendant absence of temporal coherence that Baudelaire records with such force. The recording is grounded in a vision that inscribes itself, as if despite its author, as irremediably—at times tragically and also masterfully—doubled.

INDEX